SUPRANATIONALISM IN THE NEW WORLD ORDER

Supranationalism in the New World Order

Global Processes Reviewed

Paul Close
Senior Lecturer in European Policy
Policy Research Institute
Leeds Metropolitan University

and

Emiko Ohki-Close

First published 1999 by
MACMILLAN PRESS LTD
Houndmills, Basingstoke, Hampshire RG21 6XS
and London
Companies and representatives
throughout the world

ISBN 0–333–63756–9

A catalogue record for this book is available from the British Library.

This book is printed on paper suitable for recycling and made from fully managed and sustained forest sources.

10 9 8 7 6 5 4 3 2 1
08 07 06 05 04 03 02 01 00 99

Printed and bound in Great Britain by
Antony Rowe Ltd, Chippenham, Wiltshire

To Amber Kimi Eleanor

Contents

Preface

Forty years [ago, on] 25 March 1957, the six original members of the Common Market signed the Treaty of Rome and changed the world – as much for Great Britain, who stayed out, as for Germany, France, Italy and Benelux who joined [. . .]. It was nostalgia that kept Britain out of the partnership from the very start [. . .]. Then as now, the problem was sovereignty [. . .]. Sceptics feared that the continentals were determined to create a European super-state and that any agreement to do more than promote free trade would eventually lead to federalism. They were right to predict that outcome, but wrong to allow its prospects to stand in the way of all the Union had to offer. The inevitability of political union was obvious from the day in 1950 when France and Germany decided to form the Coal and Steel Community [. . .]. The notion of federalism would have to be accepted from the start [. . .]. The text of the draft Coal and Steel Treaty was explicit: *By pooling of basic production and the establishment of a new high authority whose decisions will be mandatory on France and Germany and the countries which join them, this proposal will lay the foundation for the European federation which is indispensable to the cause of peace.* Britain's fear was that a continental alliance would reduce the United Kingdom's status in the world. That is exactly what a continental alliance – with Britain *outside* the inner circle – has done [. . .]. On March 25, 1957, when the Treaty of Rome was signed, hardly one influential British voice advocated membership of 'a common European market free from all tariff barriers' – the minimalist description of what Europe would soon become [. . .]. In 1951 and 1957 [Britain] stayed out because we were frightened by the prospect of political union. In 1971, we went in, and advocates of membership pretended that the prospect [of political union] did not exist [. . .]. [But, it] is impossible for a group of nations to agree radical and irreversible changes to their economic and social organisation without reducing the sovereignty of the individual countries. The compensation is an increase in power and influence (as well as prosperity) for the group as a whole [. . .]. [When] Britain accepted a 'common external tariff' and the negotiation of trade agreements by the European Commission – by any standards [it meant] dilutions of national sovereignty [. . .]. Fear of more integration is the principal reason for the unpopularity of Europe, yet integration has immense advantages. We have failed even to examine the benefits because we have chosen to pretend that political union is a slander put about by Europhobes. [It] is [not] possible for Britain to participate within a single currency without taking it another step along the road to a federal state. Monetary union is essential to the prosperity of the whole continent [. . .]. But it [. . .] does involve the sacrifice of rights and responsibilities which were once the prerogative of the Westminster Parliament [. . .]. Three cheers for political union. On the 40th anniversary of the Treaty of Rome, we ought to accept European Union for what it is and argue the benefits of One Europe.

(Roy Hattersley, 'Euro visionaries', *The Guardian*, 25 March 1997)

Here, Roy Hattersley, former Deputy Leader of the Labour Party in Britain, is celebrating the fortieth anniversary of the signing of the Treaty of Rome, which created the European Economic Community (EEC) and led to the European Union (EU), by enthusiastically declaring his commitment to the process of European integration and the goal of European political union, and even federation. As if to commemorate the same anniversary, the early months of 1997 also saw, first, the EU's 1996–7 Intergovernmental Conference (IGC) completing its review of the Treaty on European Union (which was signed by the European Council in Maastricht on 7 February 1992 and finally came into force on 1 November 1993) with the aim of drawing up a new treaty to put before the European Council's Amsterdam meeting in June; second, a General Election campaign in the United Kingdom in which the UK's relationship with the EU assumed a high profile; and third, the completion of this book, the first of two resulting from our *Supranationalism in the New World Order* project.

Roy Hattersley's article touches on several of the threads running through our project overall and this book in particular, including that of the relationship between the progress of the EU, on the one hand, and the character of the global system, global processes and global change, on the other. At the same time, however, his terminology is not always ours. For instance, assuming we have correctly grasped what he means by 'European super-state', we would use instead 'European supra-state'. This is an example of similar-sounding expressions with perhaps considerably different connotations (on a related example, see our Chapter 6, note 14). Furthermore, whereas the focus of Hattersley's article is Europe, the topic of our project is the prospects for more widespread *supranationalism* and supranational political formations – an imminent possibility being, in our view, a global system largely dominated by such formations and the relationships between them. The *Supranationalism in the New World Order* (SNWO) project evolved out of the research and writing which led to *Citizenship, Europe and Change* (Close, 1995). That project was about the consequences of the progress of the European Union and the emergence of *European supra-citizenship* for the everyday lives, relationships and experiences of the people of Europe. *Citizenship, Europe and Change* addresses the way these consequences are crucially mediated by social and systemic inequalities, most

Preface

notably those associated with social class, age–generation, race–ethnicity and
sex–gender. An analytical framework is presented according to which European social formations, processes and developments are decisively shaped
within a hierarchical pattern of political communities and conflicts, and in a
connected fashion are driven by fundamental societal contradictions. Both
the attention paid to conceptual and theoretical questions, on the one hand,
and the critical examination of the impact of economic and social policy, on
the other, were motivated by a commitment to European integration and
supra-citizenship in so far as these things benefit the people of Europe,
especially the relatively disadvantaged and socially excluded.

The SNWO project has its roots in the *Citizenship, Europe and Change*
(CEC) study, while having moved on. The driving concern of the SNWO
project is the character, practical ramifications and theoretical implications
of the advent, growth and spread of supranational economic and political
organisations (or regimes) within the global system.[1] The SNWO project
entails a comparison of supranational trends, prospects and consequences
between global regions in general, but between two regions in particular,
selected in view of their economic-cum-political global prominence: (i)
western Europe and (ii) the Asia Pacific region. The EU is the most organisationally advanced supranational regional regime (SRR), a status within
the global system which the European Commission along with EU Member
States appear keen to preserve, as reflected in the reports, proposals and
machinations marking the build-up to the EU's IGC which got underway at
the end of March 1996.[2]

But, it appears that the Asia Pacific region has embarked on the task of
producing its own SRRs, as signalled by the creation of, for instance, the
North American Free Trade Agreement/Area (NAFTA), the Asia Pacific
Economic Co-operation forum (APEC) and the Association of South East
Asian Nations (ASEAN), as well as (perhaps most significantly) the proposed East Asian Economic Caucus (EAEC). Numerous commentators,
writers and politicians have begun to portray ASEAN as the next-most
advanced (organisationally speaking) regional regime, and some as the successor-in-waiting to the EU as the most advanced.[3] There is a widely held
view that ASEAN will become, in a similar way to the EU, both institutionally deeper and regionally more inclusive, even to the point of embracing
Japan, Australia and New Zealand (albeit by way of its re-emergence as the
EAEC). Such developments could then be interpreted as reflecting the
intense competition and rivalry among the various regional regmines,
SRRs and other prominent global players, including most notably (an
expanded or a *Greater*) China.

The SNWO project is concerned with the relationship between (a) the
continuing ascendency of ASEAN (or its successor) among other Asia
Pacific regional regimes (otherwise often labelled 'economic blocs' or

'trading blocs') and SRRs, and (b) the EU, its Member States and people; and, in this regard, with the consequences of the way that Pacific Asia's continuing economic surge[4] is being accompanied by a distinctive 'home grown' approach to such matters as citizenship, labour standards and human rights. The question arises of how far the rivalry between the EU and Pacific Asia will bring pressure on the EU, its institutions and Member States to reassess and re-work their own social programmes, policies and laws relating to, for instance, the rights, protection and opportunities of paid employees and of women, and more specifically will encourage the EU to adopt an approach to these matters which is closer to Pacific Asia approaches. The question arises of how far the developing 'new world' economic and political order will result in the EU and its Member States pursuing a less progressive – even a regressive – approach to economic and social programmes, policies and legislation. Indeed, a serious debate over the possibility of Europe 'emulating' the 'Asian tigers' is well under way.[5]

The SNWO project is an exploration of the practical ramifications of the emergence, spread and consolidation of economic blocs, regional regimes and SRRs for a set of issues ranging from *international relations, patterns and processes* to *personal relations, opportunities and experiences*. The project is facilitated by a focal empirical investigation and comparison of two cases: Britain within the EU and Japan within the Asia Pacific and, more narrowly, within the Pacific Asia geo-political arena. The project draws on the *Citizenship, Europe and Change* study, while proceeding to explore fresh sources of information and ideas of relevance to the cutting-edge of global social change and, connectedly, of scholarly discourses and debates.

SNWO's issues include (a) the links between supranational developments and the process of globalisation, especially since the end of the Cold War and so the advent of the New World Order (NWO); (b) the implications of supranationalism (as a 'doctrine') for global economic, political and military patterns, arrangements and trends; (c) the part played by supranationalism in global cultural and *civilisational* divisions, rivalries and clashes; (d) the impact of supranationalism on such items as the nation-state, nation-state sovereignty, the state, nationalism, 'localism(s)', and 'tribalism(s)'; (e) supranationalism's consequences for citizenship, human rights and 'supra-citizenship' (see Close, 1995); (f) supranationalism's influence on people's everyday lives, experiences and opportunities, both within and beyond the regimes and regions directly involved; (g) the relationship between supranationalism and sex–gender systems;[6] (h) the implications for scholarly discourses and debates, and analytical, interpretative and theoretical tools, concepts and procedures; and (i) the lessons and messages for economic and policy concerns, programmes and alternatives.

Supranationalism in the New World Order: Global Processes Reviewed presents a framework which, it is hoped, makes a contribution to the means for pursuing these issues and tasks in a more fruitful fashion.

Acknowledgements

We are grateful for the help given to us during the writing of this book by Annabelle Buckley, Helen Burns, Mike Campbell, Andrea Davis, Sarah Holden, Jean Richardson, David Chandler, Derek Grant, Barbara Gregory, Sadao Ohki, Rieka Ohki, Chikako Ohki, Mayumi Takegoshi, Anna Takegoshi, Gwen Wallace and Edward Wallace. We also wish to thank the following for their generous support: the British Academy; the Canon Foundation of Europe; the Daiwa Anglo-Japanese Foundation; and the Japan Society for the Promotion of Science (JSPS).

Introduction

The relatively sudden and unanticipated end of the Cold War that chilled Europe for over forty years appears to be turning into an ever more complicated peace. Moreover, one of the seemingly most liberal and peaceful of the former 'societies of actually existing socialism', Yugoslavia, has subsequently provided the setting for an increasingly complicated war, the first 'hot' war since 1945 in Europe [see Meštrović, 1994]. One possible implication [...] is the emergence of a 'new world order', but not quite the order American President George Bush seemed to have in mind when he articulated his 1990 vision of a post-Cold War world. The idea and implied possibility of an orderly world is a familiar feature of modernity as an accomplished form of social life, a form of life bound up with the growth of Enlightenment. However, it is clear that the emerging 'new order' is paralleled by manifestations of extensive and intensive forms of disorder. Not for the first time the promise of modernity to cultivate orderliness in the world simultaneously precipitates an awareness of forms of disorder, not so much as symptoms of failure, incompletion or lack of realisation, but rather as necessarily corollaries of the pursuit of order itself. The idea of order as a task, as a practice, as a condition to be reflected upon, preserved and nurtured is intrinsic to modernity. The modern quest for order constitutes 'the least possible among the impossible and the least disposable among the indispensable; indeed [it is] the archetype for all other tasks, [the] one that renders all other tasks mere metaphors of itself' [Bauman, 1991a, p. 4]. Order and disorder are inextricably connected, they are simultaneously constituted and spiral in a double-helix like fashion around the axis of modernity. Hence the perpetual preoccupation with the elimination or reduction of forms of disorder through the engineering and management of orderliness in modern forms of life. A preoccupation which is regenerated and reconstituted through the realisation that ordering interventions seem to promote other disorders, to precipitate effects or 'unintended consequences' of disorder.   (Smart, 1993, pp. 40–2)

Here, Barrie Smart is touching on some of the guiding issues and main themes of *Supranationalism in the New World Order*, our research and writing project which continues beyond this particular publication. Our project is about the post-Cold War *new world order*; about the simultaneous presence and pursuit of *orderliness*, on the one hand, and the pervasive, practical and political 'problem' of *disorderliness*,[1] on the other, within Europe and *the world* – and so, within the *global system* (Axford, 1995); about the *management of orderliness* – or, that is, about the interventions, means and mechanisms employed in the process of *managing disorderliness* in the *pursuit of orderliness*; and about not just the simultaneous, and perhaps contradictory, pursuit of global order(liness) in the face of constant (constantly regenerated) global disorder(liness), but also the simultaneous, and non-contradictory, presence and use within pertinent discourses and debates, studies and analyses, interpretations and theories of two alternative notions of 'order' – one of which is reflected in the phrase *new world order*, the other of which is reflected in the distinction drawn between *orderliness* and *disorderliness*.

For us, order(liness) and disorder(liness) are contradictory, but inherent and inevitable, features of the New World Order (NWO), where the latter refers to a particular distribution of power (economic, political, military, perhaps cultural) and an associated configuration of *players* (nation-states, for example) within the post-Cold War global system; just as they are, likewise, inherent and inevitable features of any manifestation and phase of *world order* – of any global distribution of power and its associated, or correlated, configuration of global players (not just nation-states), of the past, present and future.

A similar view of the post-Cold War NWO *and* disorder(liness) to that presented by Barrie Smart is to be found in Barrie Axford's more recent *The Global System: economics, politics and culture* (1995). Axford questions whether 'the end of the Cold War' has brought the 'end of History' (Fukuyama, 1992) – 'the triumph of the West' (*ibid.*, p. 21)[2]:

> Despite Francis Fukuyama's (1992) sanguine predictions on the triumph of the West and of Western liberal democracy as a global institution, there is continued doubt about the ideological cast of the global system, and about its orderliness. In part this is because while 'global' ideological conflict seems to have faded with the end of the Cold War, new demons in the shape of fundamentalist mullahs, or warlords and drug barons straight out of the script of *Mad Max*, have come to challenge the 'peace dividends' purchased so dearly. Aside from the threats of inter-ethnic and religious conflict, a world in which 'traditional weapons' can be carried in public places, and children are frisked for drugs at entrances to schools, leaves very little room for equanimity about the future.
>
> (Axford, 1995, p. 180)

Perhaps a case which illustrates Axford's post-Cold War *disorderly* scenario is that of Cuba's recent transition and experience[3]:

> Cuba's harvest of the fruits of capitalism, such as foreign investment and taxation, has been accompanied by some less welcome by-products. Only a few years ago, the island state's media portrayed such crimes as prostitution, corruption and drug-trafficking as the exclusive preserve of capitalist

societies, especially that of Cuba's political arch enemy, the US. But cut loose from the defunct Soviet bloc, Cuba has increasingly opened up to the outside world and its rulers are starting to confront these problems on their own doorstep. (Fletcher, 5 April 1997)

The particular symptoms and sources of post-Cold War disorderliness aside, however, order(liness) is otherwise challenged, threatened and undermined within the NWO phase of history as it is within any phase, and moreover as it is universally (throughout the global system) within any phase, by virtue of a general, inherent and fundamental feature of social life, processes and developments. Thus, Axford concludes his book by referring again to 'Francis Fukuyama's (1992) insistence on an end to the long march of History and the triumph of modernity', and commenting:

> However, even Fukuyama is willing to allow the possibility that the 'last man' [see note 2] may slough off his historical role, start again and – whisper it – reinvent himself. So the idea with which this book began, that of seeing the world as a single place, must now acknowledge that the singularity of the global system is continuously subject to the interpretative practices of agents in the making and remaking of the conditions of their existence – and that *systemness* implies no more, but significantly, no less than this. (Axford, 1995, p. 219)

In other words, while on the one hand, 'any litany of recent events does reveal dramatic changes and a growing disorder, notably in the period since the mid 1980s [and, especially since] the end of the Cold War [and the accompanying] new uncertainties' (*ibid.*, pp. 3–4); on the other hand, 'the "disorder" widely spoken of as characteristic of these "new times" [...] is itself a systemic phenomenon and should not be confused with burgeoning chaos but be seen as a property of dynamic systems and of the transformative capacities of agency' (*ibid.*, p. 4) – of people either individually or collectively acting and interacting as conscious and subjective, meaningful and purposeful agents (see Archer, 1989; Craib, 1992b; Giddens, 1990 (1991); Giddens, 1993a) of change, order(liness) and disorder(liness).[4]

Axford summarises his 'idea of global systemness':

> [It] refers to the reproduction and transformation of a system through the conscious and the routine practices of agents. In a globalized world these practices are conducted increasingly without constraint of time or space and may lead to either the reproduction or the transformation of that system [...]. The component elements of the gobal system – individuals, voluntary groups, localities, regions, ethnic groups, nation-states, and all kinds of transnational actors – will be construed as socially constructed features of a global 'reality', which becomes meaningful for them through practice. Thus, and here Friedman (1993) is right, the 'order' in the global

system should be seen [...] as a negotiated and contingent condition arising from the articulation of local structures and subjects with more encompassing global ones. The growing number and complexity of these conditions intimate the possibility of a systemic *disorder* as much as they confer a functional order, since the connections constitute new sites for potential conflict and new opportunities for structuration, including the possibility of individual and systemic transformation. The processes of globalization not only make it more difficult for societal and individual systems to effect closure but [...] also open new imaginaries, 'new practices and new institutions' (Friedman, 1993).   (Axford, 1995, pp. 5–7)

At various points in his book, Axford mentions one relatively *new practice or institution, component element* or *agent*, of the global system; one which he may have in mind when, in the above passage, he refers to 'transnational actors'; and which in *a globalised world* – where, following Axford, 'the term "globalization" refers to those processes which are serving to "compress" the world in David Harvey's (1989) sense, and thus help fashion a single global space' (*ibid.*, pp. 4–5; see also pp. 23–32) – is assuming, at least for us, an increasingly important part as a global player in the process of *managing disorderliness* in the *pursuit of orderliness* (of 'global order' [*ibid.*, p. 29]) within the new world order, a process which (in our lexicon) can be otherwise referred to as 'global governance' (see *ibid.*, p. 31).

Axford introduces this new type of global player as follows:

[When] state socialism seemed a permanent fact of life [in] 1986, the member states of the then European Community put in place a rather prosaic measure called the Single European Act [SEA], trying to relaunch the Community on a voyage it should have completed more than a decade earlier [through the completion of a single internal market]. By 1995 it was [...] not entirely fanciful to depict the completion of the internal market in Europe and the [coming into force on 1 November 1995 of the] Maastricht Treaty on European Union [TEU] as harbingers of a new, fully institutionalized regional polity, with some of the attributes and core functions of stateness transferred to a supranational level [...]. But in our more confused reality a number of different futures remain possible for Europe [...].
(Axford, 1995, p. 4)

By inference, the road to European union by way of the SEA and the TEU, and thereby towards a fully institutionalised regional polity of the supranational, or of the *supra-state* (as opposed to the nation-state) kind, based on 'the "surrendering" or "pooling" of key areas of [nation-state] sovereignty (Wendt, 1994)' (Axford, 1995, p. 41), can be understood in terms of the character, conditions and *imperatives* (see Laffan, 1996, p. 1), of the encompassing Cold War global system; or, in other words, of the 'bi-polar' *old world order* (see Axford, 1995, Chapter 7). In the more confused reality of the post-Cold War NWO, the prospects for further European regional political union are uncertain. None the less, Axford appears to favour the conclusion that the trend begun during the Cold War will continue, *vis-à-vis* both the particular example of the EU itself and the more general, widespread and universal consolidation and proliferation of *institutionalised regional polities*. It would seem that, for Axford, post-Cold War reality, conditions and imperatives may favour both further European political union and the evolution of similar transnational – indeed, supranational – actors or players within the global system.

With the European Union in mind, Axford argues:

> the state-centric view of political realism has been eroded by the rapid growth of genuinely transnational phenomena of an economic kind [...].
> In the political realm too there are challenges to the realist orthodoxy, [including from] the extent to which the European Union may be creating a qualitatively new sort of political space not tied to territory and built upon mutual cooperation (Agnew, 1994; Hix, 1994; Wendt, 1994).
>
> (Axford, 1995, pp. 37–8)

At the same time, however, while the European Union is a novel political space, this does not mean that it will remain unique. Although the 'surrendering' or 'pooling' of nation-state sovereignty can be 'seen most obviously in the history of the European Union, [it] would apply presumably to many situations in which cooperative behaviour produces outcomes that are more preferred or less costly than individual, self-interested action (Stein, 1990)' (Axford, 1995, p. 41). Thus, what Axford refers to as 'international regimes' may appear 'as pragmatic [co-operative] responses to [economic] insecurity' and 'as institutional [political] anchors in a turbulent world' (Axford, 1995, p. 41):

> the concept of 'international regimes' [is] borrowed from international economics but [...] for [present] purposes refers to arrangements covering rules, norms, principles and decision-making procedures (Keohane and Nye, 1988). Regimes are institutionalized systems of cooperation in a particular issue-area, and they may or may not be elaborated in organizational form. Activity is regime-governed to the extent that the behaviour of actors conforms to the rules laid down by, or the expectations implicit in, the regime, even though these may not be binding in a strictly legal sense.
>
> (Axford, 1995, p. 41)[5]

The history of the European Union is indicative of how international regimes which may start out being largely co-operative *economic* responses to the competitive character of the global (economic, market-capitalist) system, may then proceed, or progress, to Member States pooling more of their nation-state sovereignty, and so to becoming increasingly supranational in their institutional make-up, and becoming more and more co-operative *political* responses, especially in reaction to the turbulent (political) character of the NWO global system.

Signs of the current or imminent spread of SRRs beyond Europe and throughout the NWO global system can be read into the following report:

> Stilling their suspicions of US economic and cultural dominance [...] the 33 countries of North and South America agreed [at the beginning of December 1994] to establish a Free Trade Area of the Americas. They [...] decided [...] to complete negotiations by 2005. President Clinton, whose strategy is to place the US at the heart of the vast new trading blocs of the global economy, hailed the FTAA [on 11 December 1994] as a historic step that will create the world's largest market. The US had to overcome its own doubts [...] as the price of dominating the new economic order for the two continents. But the unity on display [...] in Miami disguised a monstrous disparity in size and in economic prospects, far sharper than the fast-track, slow-track divisions in Europe. The North American Free Trade Agreement [NAFTA] states – the United States, Canada, Mexico and soon Chile – are the dominant and most developed partners with about 40 per cent of the population of the two continents and more than 80 per cent of their wealth. Argentina and Brazil [are members of] a secondary weaker grouping, the Mercosur group, with which the EU is to open trade co-operation talks [...]. A series of regional trade groupings like Nafta [sic], Mercosur, the Andean Pact, the central American Common Market and Caricom, the Caribbean community, are in place, pursuing their own separate agreements with Japan, the Apec-Asia Pacific group [presumably, the Asia Pacific Economic Co-operation forum (APEC)], and the EU.   (Walker, 12 December 1994)

Three weeks after Martin Walker's article trumpeting the plan for the Free Trade Area of the Americas (FTAA) under the heading 'Americas to establish largest free trade bloc', despite the 'monstrous economic disparities' among its prospective members, John Palmer reported that from 'midnight tonight, the European Union will become the world's richest supra-national commercial and political grouping, with the accession of Austria, Finland and Sweden' (Palmer, 31 December 1994), a development which may be seen as adding weight to the warning issued by Eduardo Frei, the president of Chile, of an 'evident multiplicity of treaties, both bilateral and multilateral [which] threatens to create a real Tower of Babel for trade' (quoted in Walker, 12 December 1994). The connotation – the danger – being that the FTAA represents a proliferation of trading blocs, following in the wake of the EU, which could feed confusion (Room, 1992, p. 43) and insecurity into the global economy, and thereby turbulence (to recall another of Axford's terms) into the global system, the response being – following Axford – more and deeper co-operative political responses in the direction of supranational regional regimes.

Elaborately organised international regimes of the kind blazoned by the European Union, and so of the kind that can be distinguished as supranational (political, institutional) regional regimes (SRRs), may increasingly appear as a pragmatic, self-interested response to the reality, conditions and imperatives of the turbulent post-Cold War NWO. It is in this regard that Axford refers to how the 'problem of world order, or the lack of it', has informed a strand of 'the institutionalist reworking of the traditional [or *realist*] model of international relations' (Axford, 1995, p. 41; see also pp. 35–9). Faced with this problem:

> Some institutionalists [. . .] have chosen to [see] hegemonic power [. . .] as a source of stability and, *contra* realism, as a vehicle for the promotion of cooperation in the form of international regimes. The position of the United States as a global hegemon has prompted much of this debate, along with the consequences for international cooperation which follows from its putative decline as a 'manager' of the world order (Gilpin, 1987) or as a relatively benign facilitator of interstate cooperative behaviour (Keohane, 1984). (*ibid.*, pp. 41–2)

In a manner consistent with a perspective on the progress of SRRs since the advent of the NWO which pays particular attention to the role assumed by this particular type of global player in world order management, Brigid Laffan prefaces her volume on *Constitution-Building in the European Union* (1996) as follows:

> The intergovernmental conference (IGC) which opened in Turin on 29 March 1996 is the fourth such conference since 1985 [. . .]. The European Union is engaged in an intense process of constitution-building and Treaty revision. The agenda of constitution-building has changed significantly. The Single Act was about market integration, and was designed to enable Europe to respond to competitive market pressures from the USA and Asia. The Treaty on European Union envisaged further economic integration but this time coupled with a concern for political union because of German unification and the collapse of communism in the former Soviet bloc. The 1996 intergovernmental conference takes up the unfinished business of the TEU and looks forward to the enlargement of the Union to include many more states. (Laffan, 1996, p. v)[6]

While, guided by Axford, the road to European union in the form of a fully institutionalised regional polity of the supranational, or of the supra-state kind can be understood in terms of the 'imperatives' (Laffan, 1996, p. 1) of the Cold War 'bi-polar' old world order (Axford, 1995, Chapter 7), in the 'more confused reality' (*ibid.*, p. 4) of the post-Cold War NWO, further European regional political union has been enticed, and furthermore has been achieved through the Maastricht Treaty on European Union (which finally came into force on 1 November 1993); and has been further pursued through the 1996–7 IGC.

As reported by John Palmer:

> The prospects for the adoption of a new European Union treaty at [the June 1997] Amsterdam summit have been boosted by signals that Paris, Bonn and the British Labour Party are ready to compromise. The Dutch presidency of the EU hailed as a breakthrough a declaration by the shadow foreign secretary, Robin Cook, that an incoming Labour government expects to conclude a new treaty in the weeks between the general election and the summit on June 16 and 17. [Some] major issues remain to be resolved. The British government – with Labour backing – is strongly resisting proposals by France and Germany to bring the West European Union (WEU), the defence arm of the EU, directly under the control of EU heads of government. The Foreign Secretary, Malcolm Rifkind, said this week that the integration of the WEU and the EU posed a threat to the unity and effectiveness of Nato [the North Atlantic Treaty Organisation]. Britain accepts that the two bodies must work more closely, but wants a 'Chinese Wall' to separate EU foreign policy and WEU responsibility for military action. However, even John Major's government now agrees that EU common foreign and security policy should be strengthened, with the transfer of responsibility for new foreign and security policy proposals from national capitals to Brussels. The German government now accepts that all major decisions on security policy will still be taken by unanimity, leaving majority voting for the implementation of detail.
>
> (Palmer, 15 March 1997)

A few weeks later, John Palmer summed up the IGC's 'progress towards a new EU treaty' by telling us that (i) there will be 'a modest extension of majority voting' and that it 'will become the rule for those policies covered by EU law to be decided on a majority vote'; but (ii) the 'latest draft treaty texts [. . .] confirm that the key decisions on tax, foreign policy and defence will remain with national governments'. Accordingly, the Amsterdam *treaty* 'will fall well short of the comprehensive political union sought by Chancellor Helmut Kohl [of Germany] and others' (Palmer, 4 April 1997).

None the less, the steps taken will still be progressive ones, albeit modestly so, when judged in terms of what counts as political union. There have been no signs that the 1996–7 IGC, or any of the various machinations concerning the future course of the European Union, will actually result in regression away from political union. This is not to ignore the bevy of politicians who have prescribed, and the notable pundits who have gone further than Axford and confidently predicted, political regression. There is neither any solid evidence nor any convincing theory which suggests that what is already occurring or what will be occurring in the foreseeable future is a process of EU political unravelling and unpacking, deconstruction and 'post-modernisation' as prophesied by Stjepan Meštrović (1994, p. vii), for instance.

Meštrović declares in his *The Balkanization of the West*:

> way back in 1989, as the so-called Velvet Revolution or the fall of communism had just [begun, not] for an instant did I believe the widespread views promulgated by American opinion-makers that communism would be transformed easily and swiftly into American-style democracy and free-market institutions. Instead, I told my friends, colleagues, and audiences that a brutal war would emerge in the former Yugoslavia; that it would be a prelude to a much larger and bloodier unravelling of the former Soviet Union; and that Balkanization would eventually engulf the Western world as well. Ridicule emerged as the most dominant reaction from my listeners. Why was I such a pessimist? What was wrong with me?
>
> (Meštrović, 1994, p. vii)

So, what does Meštrović mean by 'Balkanization'? He tells us: 'Consider the definition of Balkanization as the breaking up of a unit into increasingly smaller units that are hostile to each other' (*ibid.*, p. ix). It is in this sense that 'the West is slowly succumbing to Balkanization' (*ibid.*, p. ix), and thereby to *postmodernisation*:

> my argument falls into the broad discourse called postmodernism, which concerns itself with the end of the Enlightenment project, and which can no longer be ignored. Indeed, the disciples of the Enlightenment who make up the corps of American opinion-makers have projected the most fantastic apocalyptic fears onto this Balkan War ([. . .] despite themselves): it is supposed to signal the end of Europe, the UN, NATO, the New World Order, civilization [. . .]. It is also alleged to symbolize the return of [. . .] the Crusades, and the extermination of Islam.   (*ibid.*, p. viii)[7]

Although Meštrović's notion of 'postmodernism' may be simplistic and crude, something of a distortion and somewhat misleading,[8] it nevertheless bears some resemblance to other representations, including Axford's in his discussion of 'the distinctions between tradition and modernity, and between modern and postmodern' (Axford, 1995, p. 12). In this context, Axford refers to Francis Fukuyama's (1992) version of 'universal history' (Axford, 1995, p. 14) as 'a directional theory of history', according to which:

> the march of history displays not smooth but punctuated evolution so that, although the denouement is the triumph of liberal democracy and the

market society, progress towards it remains contingent and crab-like. Of course, for Fukuyama, the 'end of History' is only postponed by the breakout of little local and historical difficulties, by moments of arrested modernization [...].   (Axford, 1995, p. 14)

Axford then proceeds to 'point up the contrast between' this kind of theory 'of large-scale, long-term social change' and that kind which asserts 'the impossibility of order and [instead which posits] the triumph of chaos or disorder in these "new times"' (*ibid.*, p. 14):

Clearly it is not difficult to attach this description to many of the features of contemporary life, and therein lies its appeal. Zygmunt Bauman, thinking of the disorder seen in the wrack of south-eastern Europe, envisages a falling off into a new kind of chaos, visible in the 'unanticipated flourishing of ethnic loyalties [...] and the continuous redrawing of boundaries in contemporary cultures' (1990, pp. 167–8). Indeed, it is the prospect of increased contingency, greater risk and threats to secure identities that supports the claims of those who see a new kind of social order[9] in prospect, called *postmodern conditions* or sometimes just *postmodernity* (see Harvey, 1989; Giddens, 1990; [Giddens, 1991a]; Smart, 1993).
                                                         (Axford, 1995, p. 14).[10]

This new kind of social order is characterised by 'the disorder exacerbated by "voracious" modernity' (*ibid.*, p. 15). In an attempt to clarify the conceptual and historical differences to which he is drawing attention, Axford sums up by telling us:

modernity is said to be distinguishable from traditional cultures by virtue of the predominance of reflexivity or self-monitoring, and from the notionally postmodern by the excess of flux, contingency and complexity which characterizes the latter.   (*ibid.*, p. 15)

In other words, putative postmodernity is distinguishable from modernity primarily by an *excess* of what distinguishes modernity from 'traditional cultures' – hence, postmodernity (in so far as it is distinctive) hinges on *voracious* (greedy, ravenous) displays of what basically characterises and defines modernity:

The idea of reflexivity, or 'self-monitoring' in the sense that Giddens (1993) suggests, is central to the concept of modernity as this has developed in much Western social theory. Giddens says that reflexivity is 'that quality of human action that subjects social practices to constant examination and reformation in the light of incoming information about these practices, thus constitutively altering their character' (1990, p. 38). He uses the extent and intensity of reflexive practices to distinguish traditional from modern cultures (Giddens, 1985; 1990; 1993) [...]. In modern social orders [see note 9], reflexivity consists of an 'interminable interrogation' of institutions and social practices by rational subjects (Castoriades, 1987). The word is not given but made, and made through the choices of actors engaged in a reflexive monitoring of all areas of life [...]. Now whether the notionally 'postmodern' also represents a break with modernity, or just a further intensification of contingency with even greater scope for individual reflexivity, remains a matter of much debate. (Axford, 1995, pp. 11–12)

Whether or not the notion of 'postmodern' is epistemologically and sociologically, methodologically and analytically warranted and useful – given the possibility that the purported postmodern social order (postmodern social configurations, conditions and contingencies) is merely a continuation of the modern social order – the crux is 'the disordered feel of the contemporary world' (*ibid.*, p. 12; see Lash, 1993, pp. 3–4). If nothing else, at least this *feel* is *real*; is a symptom of the exaggerated and perhaps excessive presence of the central and defining features of modernity, and in particular of self-reflexivity; and may account for those observers (such as Meštrović) who have been prompted to declare a sense of qualitative *dis*continuity.

Axford suggests:

The flavour of these debates is conveyed in Ulrich Beck's attempt to distinguish between *simple* modernity and the idea of *second* modernity, through the use of the concept of the *risk society* [Beck, 1992a; Beck, 1992b; Beck *et al.*, 1994]. (Axford, 1995, p. 16)

Axford adds that in risk society:

the scope for contingency [...] increases vastly, almost to the point that the reflexivity characteristic of simple modernity founders altogether and modernity becomes a more plural, fluid and altogether more unmanageable *postmodernity*. But Beck does not reason in this way. (*ibid.*, p. 17)

In contrast, we can impute that Meštrović does 'reason in this way' given that, he claims, his 'argument falls into the broad discourse called postmodernism' (Meštrović, 1994, p. viii), which he interprets as 'rebellion against the grand narratives of the Enlightenment' (*ibid.*, p. 3), and accordingly as 'anti-modernism' (*ibid.*, p. 1; see note 7). Meštrović regards 'communism, socialism, and capitalism [as] modernist doctrines'; and asserts that 'all three doctrines are collapsing as part of a postmodern rebellion against modernity' (*ibid.*, pp. 4–5). Meštrović gives a prominent place in the 'postmodern rebellion', it would seem, to 'Islamic cultural movements, nationalism [and] fundamentalism' (*ibid.*, p. 5) – these being at the forefront of the various 'anti-rational phenomena' that now 'affect the USA and Western Europe' (*ibid.*, p. 5), and indeed are gathering to inflict a disintegrative impact on the *West*:

The conclusion that capitalism is next in line for demolition strikes terror in the hearts of so-called Westerners, even if it flows logically from the premise that all narratives spun from the Enlightenment are in serious jeopardy in the postmodern era. Yet evidence abounds to support this hypothesis, even if it is disturbing and therefore rarely admitted openly [Kennedy, 1992; Lukacs, 1992; Paepke, 1992]. For example, following the end of the Cold War, capitalist, socialist and formerly communist nations have focused on Islamic fundamentalism as a threat, sometimes even as a common enemy. Akbar Ahmed (1992) as well as Gellner (1992) have depicted Islamic culture as the opposite of modernity. In a sense, contemporary Islam constitutes a genuinely postmodern phenomenon in that it rebels at Western, modern cultures.   (Meštrović, 1994, p. 5)

But, Meštrović goes on to say, the 'important point is this':

the war that began in the former Yugoslavia in 1991 [...] came to be perceived eventually as the model for most postcommunist development. As I shall demonstrate [...], this Balkan War was depicted in the media as having divided the West in a way the formerly communist Soviet Union never did, and to have put an end to the dream of a united Europe, a New World Order,[11] and American leadership in world affairs.

(Meštrović, 1994, pp. 31–2)

Certainly, the 'theme of America in crisis and of hegemonic decline is canvassed widely' (Axford, 1995, p. 183; see *ibid.*, pp. 183–94). However, what about Meštrović's radical assertion about 'the symbolic and moral implications of the [...] Balkan War on Western nations' (Meštrović, 1995, p. 107): that because of the Balkan War, 'America lost its prestige in foreign affairs', and the 'EC and UN lost their credibility' (*ibid.*, p. 107)? What about Meštrović's claims that as 'of 1993, Western opinion-makers write with cynicism when they address the topics of Europe, America's role in the post-Cold War world, NATO, the UN [...] and other topics, symbols and phenomena that pertain to Western culture and societies'?; that this reflects how the 'Balkan War [has] resulted in the Balkanization of the West'?; and 'that the Balkanization of the West will also continue unabated' (*ibid.*, p. 131)? In our view, it is not obvious, (empirically) evident or (theoretically) expected that:

Nowadays, large Empires [sic], trading blocs, and other huge national chunks are disintegrating into ever smaller units, from the Balkans proper to California, which is threatening to break up into three chunks. The fruits of modernist, [...] global culture co-exist in an unhappy balance with anti-global, provincial, particularistic social forces.

(Meštrović, 1994, p. 135)

Meštrović is convinced that, *on balance*, the provincial and anti-global, the anti-modernist (or postmodernist) and anti-trading bloc, and the disintegrating *social forces* he has in mind will be – and indeed are already being – successful (cf. Dobbs-Higginson, 1994). He claims in his Conclusions to have presented evidence to 'make some concrete predictions' (*ibid.*, p. 176):

> I predict that the process of Balkanization in the former Yugoslavia has not yet run its course and will probably cause still more fragmentation and violence; that Balkanization will spread to the former Soviet Union and that Russia will take on the role of Serbia relative to the other, former Soviet republics; and finally that a form of Balkanization will tear apart [...] both East and West. The conflict between Islam and the West predicted by Ahmed (1992) will probably come to pass, but it will not replace the Cold War in the sense of a unified Islamic world against a unified Western world. Rather, the existing divisions within both Islamic and Christian nations [...] will probably worsen. Western Balkanization threatens not only the existence of the UN, NATO, the EC and a number of other globalizing organizations. It also threatens race relations, the relations between the sexes, and the very fabric of liberal institutions built on the remnants of the Enlightenment tradition. So Balkanization is a genuinely postmodern phenomenon, if one understands postmodernism to be a rebellion against the grand narratives of the Enlightenment.
>
> (Meštrović, 1994, p. 176)

Meštrović finally tells us:

> The current crisis in former Yugolsavia is a microcosm not only of the fate of much of the postcommunist world, but of Europe and the rest of the world as well [...]. The Disneyworld dream of a united Europe is slowly but steadily unravelling as Britain, France, Germany and the other EC states bicker on issues ranging from a common currency, open borders, and especially – Bosnia-Herzegovina. Balkanization is affecting the West, not just the Balkans; the large trading blocs desired by the West are becoming smaller; metaphorical wars are waged by the West against Japan and other nations in the economic sphere and against drugs, violence, and other fictions within their own borders [...].   (*ibid.*, p. 192)

Apart from the degree of terminological uncertainty and confusion surrounding what is meant by 'the East' here (see note 7), and the glaring absence of space given in his book as a whole to Japan and East Asia (Pacific Asia; the Orient) and their relationships with the West (the Occident), Meštrović provides no evidence that trading blocs are becoming smaller, whether these be ones in 'the West' or ones in 'the East'. For us, this is not surprising because, if anything, it is evident that, on the contrary, trading blocs are spreading, both in the sense of proliferating in number and in the sense of expanding to embrace further members. Moreover, it is clear that trading blocs are not just spreading, but also are, if anything, tending to deepen. The European Union in particular, but not exclusively, is becoming more deeply integrated institutionally and politically (as illustrated in later chapters).

The evidence in this regard is then consistent with certain strands of pertinent theorising, strands to which both we and Meštrović have paid attention. Against Meštrović's strident assertions about the demolition, destruction and fragmentation of capitalism and capitalist edifices – notably trading blocs, principally the European Union – on the grounds both of 'evidence' and of 'logic' (*ibid.*, p. 5), in our view the trends are palpably in the opposite direction, spurred on by what Meštrović identifies as postmodernism or what Ulrich Beck distinguishes as risk society.

As Axford (1995) reports, guided by Anthony Giddens, the extent and intensity of reflexive practices distinguish traditional from modern cultures (Giddens, 1985; 1990; 1993). Modernity entails a reflexive monitoring of all areas of life; and the notionally 'postmodern' may merely represent a further intensification of contingency with even greater scope for individual reflexivity (Axford, 1995, pp. 11–12). The resulting 'disordered feel of the contemporary world' (*ibid.*, p. 12) is, following Axford:

> likely to be experienced as dislocating, and may produce uncertainty and loss of identity. The order[liness] associated with traditional [social] forms of life gives way to the disorderliness of modern conditions [...]. So modernity is at least unsettling for individuals and groups having to confront its momentum, and at worst it is totally destructive of whole ways of life. The destruction of order[liness] and a growing sense of personal anxiety [lend appeal] in the West [to] invitations to bury individuality in the collective idyll and embrace communitarianism [...].
>
> (Axford, 1995, p. 13)

If so, then the appeal of collective and communitarian, or co-operative, responses and attempted resolutions can only be enhanced by, following Zygmunt Bauman (1990), the exacerbated disorder (Axford, 1995, p. 15) and the prospect of increased contingency, greater risk and threats to secure identities which distinguishes the so-called postmodern condition (*ibid.*, p. 14); or by the excess of contingency and of reflexivity or self-monitoring of what Ulrich Beck prefers to label 'risk society' (*ibid.*, p. 16).

As summarised by Axford:

> a world in which everything is contingent summons up the prospect of greater autonomy for agents, but also may erode their sense of 'ontological security', where this refers to a 'sense of continuity and order in events' (Giddens, 1991a, p. 243). Thus the burden of most discussions of

modernity is that it tends to produce ambivalence rather than wholeness of identity, in some cases leading to a perpetual state of anomie and anxiety. Possible resolutions to ambivalence may involve a search for more secure identities, for example those based on faith or tradition [. . .]. So the question of how people come to terms with or are 'dismembered' by the experience of modernity is of central importance when discussing the notional crisis of modernity [i.e. *notional postmodernity*].

(Axford, 1995, pp. 15–16)

Remaining with the theme of 'possible resolutions' to the ambivalence, uncertainty, insecurity, anxiety, contingency and disorderliness of risk society in *Citizenship, Europe and Change* (Close, 1995), it is argued:

In *risk society*, the quantitative and qualitative increase in personal risks reflects the extent to which the individual is required to make ever-more and never-ending individualised decisions about managing self, image and identity. The decisions entail risks [. . .]. We can speculate on the implications of Beck's *risk society* [. . .] for citizenship. In attempting to reflexively manage and secure self, image and identity, the highly *individualised* individual will be presented with, and will look to, non-traditional, 'secondary' sources, such as *citizenship*. The individual will look to the state, and thereby to the defence, extension and expansion of citizenship rights [. . .].

(Close, 1995, pp. 183–4)

This is not to suggest that the individual will necessarily succeed in finding what he or she seeks through his or her chosen (re)solutions:

Within the late-twentieth-century society portrayed by Giddens, Beck and Bauman, perhaps precisely because consumption has become *critical* to identity formation, individuals will seek, demand and defend citizenship rights both as a way of variously expressing and furthering their individuality and as a way, at the same time, of dealing with the identity problems, risks and anxieties which the process of individualisation has brought, and for which consumption and the consumption market by themselves fail to provide the answer. (*ibid.*, p. 186)

In *risk society* the process of selecting solutions to the problem, challenge or threat of disorderliness at not only the individual level, but also at any level of all social formations, is problematic – is uncertain, risky, and itself a prospective source of disorder.

Here, we can recall how at the beginning of this chapter we outlined Barrie Smart's (1993) thesis that order(liness) and disorder(liness) are inextricably linked. They are simultaneously constituted, and they spiral in a double-helix like fashion around the axis of modernity. For Smart, this accounts for a perpetual preoccupation with the elimination or reduction of disorderliness through the management of orderliness 'in modern forms of life' (*ibid.*, p. 42) – a preoccupation which reflects how 'ordering interventions seem to promote other disorders, to precipitate effects or "unintended consequences" of disorder' (Smart, 1993, pp. 40–2).

In our view, the preoccupation with (as we prefer to put it) managing disorderliness in the pursuit of orderliness within the global system – or, that is, with *global governance* – has lent itself to the search for collective and communitarian (Axford, 1995, p. 13), or co-operative, solutions on a grand scale – indeed, on a *supranational* scale. This is not to suggest that the nation-states and supranational organisations involved will be wholly successful – on the contrary. In a contradictory manner, supposed supranational solutions may to some extent feed *disorderliness*. But, if such writers as Axford, Bauman, Beck and Smart are to be believed, disorderliness is in any case an inherent and inevitable, or far from wholly manageable, quality of *risk society*. For us, it could be that, under the prevailing circumstances, supranational regional regimes (SRRs) represent the best available (albeit partial and somewhat contradictory) solution – that is, the most effective *realist* response – to the problem, challenge and imperative of the confluence of those sources of disorderliness which specifically afflict the post-Cold War global system. If so, then this would account for what appears to be the increasing appeal of *supranationalism in the new world order*.

1 The New World Order and Supranationalism

Only half of all Ukranian schoolchildren questioned identified Josef Stalin as the iron-fisted man who led the Soviet Union for three decades, pollsters said. Of 200 children aged nine to 14, polled in Khemlnitsky, 31 said he was an executioner; 13 said they had never heard of him. Dozens gave other professions. And 11 said he was a pop star.

(The Guardian, 7 September 1996)[1]

Methodological questions aside, these survey results can be interpreted as a sign of the times, as a small part of a huge swathe of evidence of the new times which had been suddenly, surprisingly and even shockingly (Ambrose, 1993, p. 352) sprung upon the world towards the close of the twentieth century. These findings are symptomatic of how the world had become a remarkably different place from what it had been before, and in particular from what it had been during the previous four or five decades: of how the world system[2] or global system[3] had undergone a swift, sweeping and fundamental transformation initiated by a set of events in 1989.

The character of the transformation lends itself to the claim that what occurred warrants being called a *revolution.* There is a widely held view that the inter-locking train of events which began in 1989 – coincidentally, the bicentennial year of 'the great French Revolution' (Tilly, 1993, p. 1) – qualify as revolutionary. For instance, Charles Tilly, in assessing what he refers to as 'European events of 1989' (*ibid.,* p. 4), argues that if by 'revolution' is meant 'any abrupt, wide-reaching, popular change in a country's rulers, [then] most Eastern European countries experienced revolutions in that year' (*ibid,* p. 4).[4] Tilly expands:

> [i]n 1989 [...] the people of Eastern Europe [...] made their own revolutions [notwithstanding the way in which] their dominant state, the Soviet Union, helped them unwittingly [...]. What is more, demands for independence or autonomy gathered strength in regions of Yugoslavia, Czechoslovakia and the Soviet Union itself. The Soviet Union began an unravelling that undid it entirely by 1991. The Soviet Union's changed position also precipitated major shifts of power outside Europe: in Mongolia, Ethiopia, Somalia and elsewhere. A number of African states that the Cold War had hardened into tyrannies began to melt toward democracy or anarchy. (*ibid.,* pp. 2–4)

In the light of these and other incidents – such as in China, South Africa and Central America (Ambrose, 1993, p. 352) – another eminent historian,

Stephen Ambrose, similarly but more embracingly refers to 'the world revolution of 1989' (*ibid.*, p. 353). Prompted by Ambrose's perspective, however,
just as it is appropriate to regard the revolution as stretching well beyond
Eastern Europe, so for us it is appropriate to regard the transformation as
continuing beyond 1989; as covering several years: minimally, the three years
spanning 1989 to 1991.[5] Over this revolutionary period, the global system
which emerged and became established was considerably different from that
which had prevailed during the Cold War era. The difference is such that the
post-Cold War global system has attracted the (somewhat contoversial)
description 'new world order', a phrase commonly attributed in the first
instance to George Bush, the president of the USA from 1989 until 1992.
Thus, as summarised by Barrie Axford[6]:

The idea of a new world order, bruited [. . .] by American President George
Bush during the build up to the Gulf conflict in September 1990, stems
from the ending to the Cold War and from changes in the cognate areas of
'bipolarity' and nuclear proliferation (Wagner, 1993). 'Bipolarity' refers to
the particular distribution of power in the global system after the Second
World War, in which many states were members of two hostile coalitions
(blocs), each dominated by a superpower. It also refers to the nuclear
hegemony exercised by these superpowers (Wagner, 1993) [. . .]. As a global
institution the impact of bipolarity[7] was short-lived but intense: indeed it is
not too fanciful to suggest that, for forty years or so of superpower
domination of world politics, history was frozen if not stopped (Joffe,
1993). During the Cold War an international system which [previously]
had been structured by the realist strategies of nation-states in shifting and
unstable alliances[8] was transformed into a politics of ideological blocs
dominated by two superpowers that were champions of quite different
world views [. . .]. The 'old' world order was constituted by the stable
condition of bipolarity known as the Cold War, when antagonisms
between the superpowers and their cohorts consisted of an 'imaginary
war' along the main frontiers which divided the hegemons in Europe and
turned bloody only at the margins, in Asia and Africa [. . .]. The putative
new world order (NWO) which [from the point of view of George Bush
among others] looked set to replace [the old world order] consists [. . .] of a
number of related elements. First, the voluntary withdrawal of the Soviet
Union from its 'historical' world role [would leave] it still intact and
militarily capable, but benign as a player with global pretensions. As a
result, the United States would be the only real superpower. Second, the
prospects for lasting peace and prosperity in the NWO would be enhanced
by revitalized bodies like the United Nations [. . .]. Third, [a] globally
sanctioned *pax Americana* would have a geo-economic dimension,
carrying market liberalism to former state-socialist economies through

multilateral institutions like the European Bank for Reconstruction and Development (EBRD), the IMF [International Monetary Fund] and the OECD [Organisation for Economic Co-operation and Development]. Overall the flow of world trade would continue to be liberalized through GATT [the General Agreement on Tariffs and Trade through which the World Trade Organisation was established on 1 January 1995] and through the growing interconnectedness and interdependence of the world economy.   (Axford, 1995, pp. 180–2)

The old world order of the Cold War era hinged on a bipolar division of political-cum-military power within the global system between two rival hegemons, the United States and the Soviet Union, backed by their respective camps or coteries. During the period 1989–91, a revolutionary transformation of the global system occurred, centred on the 'implosion of the Soviet empire [which] unbalanced world politics' (*ibid.*, p. 182). The bursting inwards of the Soviet empire entailed the collapse of the Eastern bloc and, perhaps most dramatically, 'the dissolution of the Soviet Union' itself (*ibid.*, p. 182),[9] the result being a New World Order (NWO) which putatively (following Axford) is distinguished by a distribution of political-cum-military power within which there is only one superpower – only one global hegemon – the USA. None of the constituent parts of the Soviet Union (the Union of Soviet Socialist Republics) emerged from the dissolution process as a successor superpower. In particular, the dominant republic of the former USSR, the Russian Federation, was left not only weakened politically, militarily and economically, but also with its own geo-political cracks, divisions and challenges, perhaps most notoriously within the Caucasus (or Bolshoy Kavkaz) region.[10]

Despite the immediate and major difficulties, disruption and damage of the revolutionary period during which the Cold War old world order was turned into the post-Cold-War NWO, by the mid-1990s there were signs to be seen of the 're-birth',[11] and certainly of the re-growth, of Eastern Europe,[12] including of the Russian Federation. Of huge significance and practical importance, was evidence of a favourable swing in the economies of central and eastern Europe: economies which were now firmly (largely, but by no means fully) entrenched along market-capitalist lines. Thus, while the 'institutional transformation following the 1989 upheavals was attended by a sharp reduction in economic output in Eastern Europe' (Lane and Ersson, 1996, p. 32),[13] by the end of 1996, there was a solidly based assumption that '[c]apitalist Russia [was] set for [economic] growth' (Brummer, 1996). As reported by Alex Brummer:

When the countries of the former Soviet Union and Eastern Europe – including Russia – finally emerge from the transition to capitalism they could achieve growth levels on a par with much of the rest of the developing world, according to the International Monetary Fund. A new analysis [...] suggests that once reforms are in place the countries concerned have the potential for long-term growth rates of between four and five per cent per annum – far higher than that being achieved by their counterparts in the European Union. Inevitably, the closest focus [...] is on Russia [...]. This year the IMF is forecasting that output will be only marginally down, by 0.6 per cent, against the 4 per cent decline in 1995 and the calamitous 15 per cent reduction in output in 1994. However, given that the reform process continues, the IMF believes 1997 will see Russia return to growth. The IMF staff hold up Poland as the best example of what can be achieved with a growth rate this year of 5.5 per cent, following two previous years of robust expansion. This means that Poland is now growing at levels above those seen when it was a centrally planned [socialist] economy[14] [...]. [I]n the IMF's view, the laggards in the former Soviet empire could begin to catch up with those like Poland and the Czech republic which have been powering ahead as free market economies.   (*ibid.*)

This prognosis for the former Soviet empire conforms with the evidence and argument presented by Jan-Erik Lane and Svante Ersson, according to whom during the 1990s 'the economies of Europe differ in terms of total [aggregate] output, mainly along the West–East division', but what 'limits the implications in the differences in wealth is that economic growth tends to be higher in the less affluent countries [of Eastern Europe] than in the more affluent ones of Western Europe [...], [something] which is conducive to economic [wealth, affluence] convergence' (Lane and Ersson, 1996, p. 197); and something, therefore, which is consistent with the 'convergence model of economic growth' (*ibid.*, p. 32; cf. Davis and Scase, 1985, especially pp. 5–10).

Lane and Ersson explain that the 'convergence model of economic growth implies that more affluent regions will grow at a less rapid pace than the less affluent regions (Barro, 1991; Barro and Sala-i-Martin, 1992)', so that 'economic development may bring about convergence in affluence among countries or regions within a country, if they interact with each other on a regular basis' (Lane and Ersson, 1996, p. 32). That is, what Lane and Ersson then refer to as 'economic growth theory' carries 'the implication that the levels of affluence should in the long run be equalized between regions and countries, given the free movement of capital and labour between them' (*ibid.*, p. 32). While Lane and Ersson claim that 'the conditions for economic convergence [were] not fulfilled [...] when Western Europe adhered to one kind of economic system and Eastern Europe to another economic regime with little interaction between the two', since 1989 there has been a 'trend towards convergence on economic institutions and [a] pick up in trade between Western and Eastern Europe' (*ibid.*, p. 32).

What Lane and Ersson appear to be doing is reverting to – some might say regressing to – the *convergence thesis*, as originally formulated during the 1950s, 1960s and 1970s under the stewardship of such writers as Galbraith (1967), Kerr *et al.* (1960) and Lipset (1960), but since dismissed by, for instance, Howard Davis and Richard Scase (1985):

> The determining effects of modern technology were [...] strongly empha-sised during the immediate post-war decades when the position of a number of Eastern European regimes became consolidated. During this period, it was often argued that the effects of industrialism were such that two processes would ultimately occur. First, it would bring about the destruction of totalitarianism. Secondly, it would bring about a conver-gence of state socialist and Western capitalist countries [...]. According to such arguments [...], the totalitarian regimes of Eastern Europe were seen as nothing more than temporary features of the European landscape: with the ever increasing impact of the industrialisation process, they would inevitably become more 'open' and 'democratic', taking on the features of [...] modern [Western market capitalist, liberal democratic] industrial countries. Two decades later, such claims seem absurd.
>
> (Davis and Scase, 1985, p. 5)

Within a few years of Davis and Scase's scathing attack on the conver-gence thesis, however, the Eastern bloc alternative to western market capit-alism and liberal democracy began to collapse, and soon more or less disappeared (at least in Eastern Europe). On the other hand, for some writers, this development still does not necessarily validate the convergence thesis. As summarised by Axford:

> The convergence theories of the 1960s and 1970s predicted that pretty nearly all societies were moving towards the same point, though at variable speeds. When applied to the 'convergence' of East and West, this implied that the two 'sides' were moving towards some hybrid model of industrialized society. The collapse of state socialism has led some theorists, Fukuyama [1992] included, to suggest that what was presented as convergence was only ever a one-way flow (Offe, 1991) and that, because of this, modernization theory [with its pivotal assumption about the globalisation of 'the great themes of Western modernity', including 'market capitalism' (Axford, 1995, pp. 1–2)] has been vindicated in the face of attacks both of those [...] who believed that modernization theory was a Western prejudice [...] and those designated Marxists, who saw it as an ideological front for an exploi-tative system of global capitalism secured under American dominance (Fukuyama, 1991, p. 660). (Axford, 1995, pp. 45–6)

For Fukuyama (1991; 1992), the one-way flow from west to east has meant an 'end to History' in the sense of 'the triumph of global liberalism and global liberal democracy, because there are no longer any serious alternatives to these features of the Western cultural account' (Axford, 1995, p. 45; see also Fukuyama, 1995).

The issue of the intricacies of the meaning of 'convergence' aside, however, for Lane and Ersson, the institutional convergence (around the principles, practices and processes of market-capitalism), in the wake of the post-1989 'institutional transformation' of eastern Europe (1996, p. 32), combined with the connected boost in economic – trade, goods, services, capital, investment, labour – interaction, movement and transfers across the western–eastern boundary, accounts for the evidence which suggests that '[w]hat is taking place in the [. . .] 1990s' is a 'convergence in affluence' (*ibid.*, p. 32) between the west and the east.

For Lane and Ersson, there are differences 'in economic affluence' between eastern European countries (which 'are poor, by European standards') and, especially, European Union members (each of which is either 'affluent' or 'very affluent') (*ibid.*, p. 45); but, at the same time, economic convergence is taking place in conjunction with an underlying process of '[e]conomic integration in Europe' (*ibid.*, p. 45), proceeding as this is 'along two lines, one concern[ing] economic institutions and the other relat[ing] to trade' (*ibid.*, p. 45). With regard to trade:

> there is the ever-growing reciprocity between the economies of Europe as manifested by the explosion in intra-regional and between-region trade in goods and services as well as in the mobility of labour. The internationalization of the country economies of all European states with a sharp increase in trade between almost all the countries of the European continent is a profound process enhancing convergence.
>
> (Lane and Ersson, 1996, p. 45)

In the case of 'economic institutions', Lane and Ersson mention 'the integration of financial markets in Europe, including their extension to cover East European countries' (*ibid.*, p. 45). At the same time, both this ('institutional') aspect and the 'trade' aspect of the integration process can be attributed to further, explanatory developments:

> Today there are institutional processes resulting in [. . .] common institutions and the harmonization of regulations for economic activity. They are driven by the [European Union] on the one hand, and by the profound system transitions taking place in the former Communist countries on the other hand. The introduction and implementation of the institutions of the market economy in Eastern Europe has met with varying success in different countries. In Estonia,[15] Poland, the Czech Republic and Hungary the so-called capitalist institutions safeguarding extensive private property rights, allocating capital to joint stock companies by means of stock

exchanges and providing for currency convertability are in place. In Bulgaria, Romania and Lithuania several of the large enterprises remain state companies and collective ownership of land is still a reality. [Lane and Ersson] predict that [nevertheless] the European economies will grow more alike on macroeconomic aggregates as these two major integrative forces work themselves out in full scale.[16] Thus, [there will be] more economic convergence around the year 2000. The process of increasing similarities between the European economies includes not only total output but also unemployment, inflation and deficit spending and state debts.

(Lane and Ersson, 1996, p. 45)

For Lane and Ersson, the two basic developments which have been driving the process of pan-European economic and institutional integration and convergence are, first, the revolutionary transformation of the Eastern bloc which has resulted in, what has been distinguished as, a New World Order centred on the (economic) principles, practices and processes of market capitalism; and second, (economic) integration in western Europe through the progress of the European Union, organised as the EU largely is around the principles, practices and processes, requirements and results of market capitalism. For us, this argument raises a number of questions, including: what is the relationship between these two underlying developments?; is either of these developments dominant?; are there any additional developments which are either driving Europe in the same convergent direction or, alternatively, hindering convergence?; is there an even more basic, determining development underway (as perhaps indicated in the accounts of globalisation provided and assessed by such writers as Amin, 1996; Axford, 1995; Mann, 1997; Robertson, 1992; Waters, 1995; and Woodiwiss, 1996)?

Lane and Ersson suggest that there are 'forces that work against convergence', namely (what they refer to as) 'historical legacies', such as 'ethnic and religious cleavages' (1996, p. 11), but they do not go very far towards clearly and categorically answering our other questions. After mentioning that '[b]asically, "convergence" stands for increasing similarities' (*ibid.*, p. 7), and noting that '[o]ne may find convergence ideas in the major schools of sociology such as Marxism and modernization theory',[17] Lane and Ersson tell us that their 'enquiry into European countries is basically about the thin concept of convergence', which means being 'first and foremost interested in measuring the extent of similarities between the countries in Europe with regard to a few subsystems or social sectors, as things now stand after the demolition of the Iron Curtain in 1989' (*ibid.*, p. 9). Beyond this, they claim to 'make no assumption about an inner logic of convergence which would drive societies towards a common end state' (*ibid.*, p. 9).[18] They point out that '[s]ocial system convergence [...] could concern any kind of social system such as a society, or a subsystem like the polity or the economy' (*ibid.*, p. 11). The 'subsystems or social sectors' to which the 'convergence theme is relevant' include: 'the socio-economic one', the issue being the 'extent [of] the [economic; affluence] catch-up development in the former Communist states' (*ibid.*, p. 1); 'the political', whereby the 'system transition involves not only the insertion of western economic institutions but also western political institutions in the form of democracy'; and 'the cultural', whereby 'political attitudes and social belief-systems [are becoming] more similar between the countries of Europe' (*ibid.*, p. 1).

Lane and Ersson's main focus is on 'European politics' (*ibid.*, p. xii); on convergence in this sector, their aim being 'to analyse the politics of [. . .] European countries from [the] angle [of] convergence' (*ibid.*, p. 1); as well as on the 'macro conditions [which] have brought increasing similarities in the politics of European states' (*ibid.*, p. xi), such as those 'economic conditions [entailing] growing trade and economic integration' (*ibid.*, p. xi).

Indeed, in their 'approach to European politics' (*ibid.*, p. 9), while recognising 'the autonomy of politics' (*ibid.*, p. 11), Lane and Ersson 'emphasize the implications of economic integration in Europe'. They acknowledge that in 'their emphasis on economic structure' (*ibid.*, p. 14), factors and forces (*ibid.*, p. 11), they 'have borrowed from' the 'two main convergence models' (*ibid.*, p. 14): 'Marxist analysis and the modernization approach'. Both of these 'convergence approaches' (*ibid.*, p. 14) are 'economistic, underlining economic change as the main causal mechanism' (*ibid.*, p. 14). Lane and Ersson elaborate as follows:

> Among the conditions that promote convergence in politics [are] socio-economic forces. [At the same time, however, convergence is] driven not only by unintended development trends in the economy and the social structure but also by the conscious adoption of similar legal institutions. The EU integration process with its emphasis on harmonization of legal institutions plays a major role here. (*ibid.*, p. 11)

In other words, for Lane and Ersson, it 'is impossible not to include and underline the convergence implications of the making of the European Union' (*ibid.*, p. xi). While '[c]onvergence may be either intended or unintended, recognized or unrecognized, explicit or implicit, manifest or latent' (*ibid.*, p. 13), it is possible to hypothesise that 'convergence is driven [largely] by latent forces, meaning that socio-economic development matters more than institutional integration' (*ibid.*, p. 13). The 'contrary hypothesis' (*ibid.*, p. 13) is that 'explicit and intended convergence has been of [greater] importance', and accordingly in the case of European convergence this perspective draws attention to the 'considerable part [played by] the explicit and intended efforts at political convergence [which] have been channelled through the EU framework in the post-Second World War period' (*ibid.*, p. 13).

The manner in which the 'intended efforts at political convergence which have been channelled through the EU' is helping drive the convergence process throughout Europe, and in particular between the west and the east, is inferred by Lane and Ersson in arguing:

> When the EU is looking east reflecting on the possibility of permitting new states to enter its institutions, then it seems as if there is a two-step procedure involved: the first possible enlargement covering a few core Eastern states such as those that have association status today – Poland, Hungary and the Czech and Slovak Republics, Romania and Bulgaria – and the second possible extension including the remaining states. There has been talk about Turkey entering, but this seems [...] unlikely, as Europe does end at the Bosporous, as it were. Looking forward one may expect the EU to invite new member states among the countries that are most similar to its already included members. (*ibid.*, pp. 12–13)[19]

The inference here is that in so far as non-members of the European Union seek to become members, the procedure through which they do – or, perhaps more to the point, through which they are permitted to – become members will entail a process of intentional, deliberate and purposeful convergence, including of the cultural kind; or, that is, a process of EU-required, imposed and managed *assimilation*, whereby the non-members are intentionally *re*-moulded in accordance with an EU-sanctioned (economic, political and cultural) social system, social model or social ideal: with that social system to which the EU currently adheres, or at least aspires. This interpretation of the relationship between the EU and those central and eastern European non-member countries which are seeking membership is given credibility by various other reports and accounts. According to Pascal Fontaine (1995):

> On 22 June 1993 the Copenhagen [summit of the] European Council [made up of the Heads of Government or (in the case of France) of State of the Member States (*ibid.*, p. 9)] adopted the principle whereby associated countries in Central and Eastern Europe that so desire could become members of the European Union: 'Accession will take place as soon as an associated country is able to assume the obligations of membership by satisfying the economic and political conditions required'. These conditions include stable democratic institutions, respect for minorities, the existence of a market economy with the capacity to cope with competitive pressure within the Union and the ability to adhere to the aims of political, economic and monetary union. (Fontaine, 1995, p. 34)

Subsequently, in view of the likelihood of several central and eastern countries soon being able to meet the conditions of entry into the European Union, Adrian Hamilton has asserted '[t]he old order is dying in Europe'

(Hamilton, 1994), but not just because of the EU-required assimilation of the prospective 'members from Eastern Europe'. For Hamilton, if 'the fall of the [Berlin] Wall is to bring any benefit other than a reunified and potentially overpowerful Germany then the newly freed countries of the former Soviet bloc must be locked in', something which will 'necessarily change the Community fundamentally. Wider membership [...] impels constitutional reform to make any kind of reasonable decision making possible' in 'a Community of 20 or more' (*ibid.*).

Apart from the possibility of continuing enlargement *per se* having implications for the EU's decision-making procedures, for Hamilton there is the specific issue of the impact on the Union of 'enlargement eastwards', as distinct from *northwards*. For Hamilton, there is the matter of 'the sheer cost of bringing in new members other than the wealthy Scandinavians' to consider (*ibid.*). This 'cost' theme and its ramifications within the EU has been taken up by other writers, including John Palmer who argues that 'the EU will have to pay a hefty price for accepting the newcomers':

> the east Europeans [will be] determined to get their share of the so-called EU 'cohesion funds'. These are used by Brussels to help close the wealth gap between the rich northern and poorer southern EU countries. If and when all the east Europeans join, even the poorest Mediterranean member states such as Portugal and Greece should end up net contributors to the EU budget. (Palmer, 9 December 1994)

The prospect of the entry of central and eastern European countries leading to a diversion of funds away from what are currently the less affluent parts of the Union has remained a considerable cause for concern within the EU, as indicated by Paola Buonadonna:

> The leaders of Europe's regions fear that they may lose out on funding as the Union looks towards bringing in poorer countries from the former eastern bloc. The pressures of enlargement and the race towards a single currency could leave the regions worse off, according to 200 local and regional government representatives meeting for a conference sponsored by the European Parliament in Brussels. (Buonadonna, 1996)

While such concerns are unlikely by themselves to inhibit the programme of enlargement eastwards, they could add to the impetus behind the pre-enlargement convergence and assimilation process, which although largely EU-driven has been readily and eagerly accepted by several central and eastern European candidates for EU membership. The central and eastern European governments involved may be further inspired by the way in which the EU has been reportedly preparing for their inclusion by seriously considering alterations to its decision-making procedures along the lines anticipated by Adrian Hamilton (2 December 1994). Thus, as reported by John Palmer on the day of the European Council's summit meeting in Essen in December 1994:

> The Essen summit [...] marks the moment when the European Union's opening to central and eastern Europe becomes 'irreversible [...]. In Copenhagen two years ago the EU accepted that, with the end of the cold war [sic], it could not refuse the right of entry to democratic states in eastern Europe. The discussion at Essen will be about the nuts and bolts of making that promise reality. This will involve not only further change in eastern Europe but also a radical transformation of the European Union itself. The best estimate [...] is that negotiations to enlarge the EU – eventually perhaps to 30 member states – could begin in 1997 or 1998, following approval of the reforms of the EU's institutions to be agreed on during the 1996 review of the Maastricht treaty.[20] All the signs are that the EU will emerge from the 1996 conference significantly further down the road to a single currency, to a European defence union, to far stronger powers for the European Parliament and to greater majority voting in the Council of Ministers. None of this worries the six potential east European candidate countries – the Czech Republic, Hungary, Poland, Slovakia, Bulgaria and Romania – nor Slovenia or the three Baltic states who also plan to join the membership queue [and by the middle of 1996 had joined this queue]. They want a more federal-style European Union precisely because they believe it will enable their security to be locked in more closely with the destinies of Europe as a whole [...]. At Essen the talk will be about strategies to prepare the candidates for membership, including the harmonisation of their economic and legal systems with those of the EU. (John Palmer, 9 December 1994)

On the one hand, the central and eastern European candidates for EU membership will be required to harmonise their social systems with that of the EU's social system, facilitated by complying with 'the *acquis communautaire* (general policy framework) which [has] to be accepted as non-negotiable by any new members' (Williams, 1991, p. 44). On the other hand, the EU itself would be required to undergo – and has certainly been flagging its willingness to undergo – a 'radical transformation' in the direction (if Palmer is to be believed) of a more *federal-style* of decision-making, an alteration welcomed by and of encouragement to the in-coming members.

Another way of representing or conceptualising any internal EU progress towards a more federal-style of decision-making is that it is about the evolution and enhancement of the EU's internal *governance*. For us, the term 'governance', guided by the *Concise Oxford Dictionary of Current English* (1990, p. 511), refers to 'the act or manner of governing', the closest synonym for present purposes, it seems to us, being 'management' (although 'administration' also comes to mind).[21] This approach to the meaning of 'governance' seems consistent with that adopted by writers who employ the term in other contexts, and so by for example Robert Monks and Nell Minow (see note 21), who argue:

> in the century to come, as multinational companies create the borderless world of global markets, the focus will be on ensuring that corporate power is compatible with the rights of individuals in a democracy. The challenge is to encourage the creative energy of corporations without imposing unacceptable costs on individuals and society.
>
> (Monks and Minow, 1996, quoted in Dickinson, 1996)

Martin Dickinson reports how for several years Robert Monks 'has been [...] one of the most active leaders of the US corporate governance movement' (Dickinson, 1996), and how (at a conference in Cambridge at the beginning of July 1996) he had portrayed:

> the US corporation as overwhelmingly powerful and accountable to no one. His solution: that long-term institutional investors, particularly pension funds, should become 'corporate monitors' – a party to which management could be held accountable [...]. Despite much talk about stockholder and shareholder power, 'the prevailing governance system in the US boils down to the chief executive acting as a trustee for the public good' [...]. However, he rejects government [i.e., state] interference and says that institutional investors [...] are a 'valid proxy for the population as a whole', and should fill the void. Critics think Monks' description of corporate power is exaggerated and point to the practical problems of implementing his solutions. With the exception of some large pension funds, most institutional fund managers have been reluctant to assume the mantle of corporate governance, since this imposes extra costs on them and risks alienating their corporate clients.   (Dickinson, 1996)

Our notion of 'governance' resembles Monks', although we are employing it for the purpose of studying, analysing and making sense of matters in a somewhat different context: *vis-à-vis political* management, rather than *corporate* management. As such, our usage appears similar to Barrie Axford's, whose assumptions about global governance appear, in turn, to overlap with Monks' about the prevailing governance system in the 'borderless world of global markets' (Dickinson, 1996). Thus, Axford argues that ' "new", less manageable conflicts have broken out in the vacuum caused by the ending of superpower geopolitics', something which raises 'the question of global governance' (Axford, 1995, p. 31). However, for us, an alternative candidate to that of the corporation or the corporate manager for filling the void, or the vacuum, in the prevailing governance system within (in the first instance) Europe by assuming the mantle of governance is the European Union. Indeed, the evidence suggests that the EU is already well advanced in this regard: that the EU is well on the way to playing a – even *the* – major role in pan-European governance; that it is doing so purposefully by way of (i) taking in new members, and (ii) enticing new members and applicants; and that one notable effect is pan-European convergence.

Lane and Ersson examine an aspect of 'governance' in their account of European convergence under, what they see as, the dual impact of the collapse of the Soviet empire and the process of European integration, centred on (and, as far as we are concerned, largely managed by) the European Union. That is, Lane and Ersson devote their concluding chapter to 'party governance' (1996, pp. 196–213), arguing 'that convergence in European politics may be understood in terms of the institutionalization of the basic mechanisms of party governance in the post-industrial society' (*ibid.*, p. 196).[22] Lane and Ersson neither explictly define nor otherwise clearly indicate what they understand in general terms by 'governance'. However, it would seem from their discussion that by 'party governance' they mean something akin to *internal political party management*. Their sense of 'governance' could have been made more clear if they had examined other manifestations, such as that which takes place at the European Union (organisational, institutional, systemic) level or at the pan-European level or, even, at the global level. One question they could have addressed is 'what part do political parties play in the process of European Union governance?'; and another question could have been 'what part, in turn, does the European Union play in the process of pan-European governance, and perhaps thereby in pan-European convergence?'

Lane and Ersson's evidence and discussion concerning trends in, for instance, economic growth, trade, 'affluence' and 'party governance' seem to reflect an overall process of pan-European convergence which is being largely decided, directed and managed by the European Union in favour of an EU-approved, sanctioned and determined economic, political and cultural (albeit somewhat imaginary) model, framework or system. Following Axford, 'in the vacuum caused by the ending of superpower politics', the European Union has stepped into the breach by playing a prominent part, in the first instance, in the process of *European governance*; and, furthermore (by extension), in the process of *global governance*. That is, what Lane and Ersson refer to as 'the evolution of European integration in terms of EC institutions and the enlargement of the EC to cover more and more states in Europe' (Lane and Ersson, 1996, p. 12) is, for us, ensconced in a multi-faceted, dialectical process which also entails pan-European convergence and the EU's growing involvement in pan-European (and thereby, global) governance. As pointed out by Lane and Ersson:

The extent to which convergence takes place in Europe must be influenced [...] by the overall development of the European economy as well as that of the national economies in Europe [...] [But also,] the development of the EU (EC) must be looked into, both in terms of increasing the depth of the collaboration among the already accepted member states and with regard to extending the EU to include all countries in Europe.

(ibid., pp. 13–14)

As the EU evolves by expanding its membership and, it would seem connectedly, by becoming institutionally deeper – more politically integrated and unified – its ability to effectively engage in European governance will be enhanced, perhaps largely as a direct result of these developments; but also partly as a consequence of its growing attraction to, and so influence over, various non-members. The outcome will be both: (a) convergence within and beyond the European Union; and (b), assuming that it is in the interests of the EU to play an ever greater role in European and global governance, an incentive for the EU to proceed even further with its institutional (political) integration, and to embrace more members, or at least hold out the prospect of embracing more members. From the standpoint of non-members, gaining EU membership could become not just more and more appealing, but also an imperative given the EU's multi-stranded trajectory of expansion, institutional deepening and ever-growing capacity to engage in governance (political management, with its economic and cultural ramifications) both within and beyond – even well beyond – its own borders.[23] In a manner which is consistent with the aforementioned dialectical process, this increasing appeal will then feed into the EU's capacity to engage governance.

The argument that European convergence can be understood to a large extent in terms of the EU's objective of and capacity for (through pan-European governance) realising its own interests – which may be primarily economic interests – ties in with what Lane and Ersson pinpoint as the 'two main convergence models', namely 'Marxist analysis and the modernization approach' *(ibid.,* p. 14). As Lane and Ersson mention, each of these two perspectives is 'economistic' in its basic assumptions about the driving forces behind social change. As we have noted, Lane and Ersson 'have borrowed from these two convergence approaches their emphasis on economic structure', factors and forces *(ibid.,* p. 14). Confusingly, however, in answer to the question 'Is convergence in European politics driven by economic or social forces or does it result from the political forces themselves?', Lane and Ersson 'suggest that it is the latter that holds for Europe, one of the chief reasons being the evidence of the autonomy of politics' *(ibid.,* p. 196).

While we are sceptical about any claim, explicit or implicit, that there is convincing 'evidence of the autonomy of politics', and although there is (if anything) evidence that Lane and Ersson have indulged in inconsistent, even contradictory, reasoning about the autonomy of politics, we do accept that the EU's achievements in deliberately promoting pan-European convergence through the mechanism of, and in turn in order to further facilitate, pan-European governance (geo-political management) – notwithstanding the possibility that the EU's primary motive is *economic* – will be mediated by the EU's distinctively *political* (institutional) framework and associated decision-making procedures, responsibilities, competences and powers. The particular extent, speed and direction of pan-European *systemic* – economic, political and cultural – convergence will be crucially mediated by, and so very largely dependent upon, the EU's degree of institutional and constitutionally based (see Borchardt, 1994; Shaw, 1996, especially Chapter 3; Stone, 1994) political power and authority, independence and sovereignty in relation to its Member States and *their* institutions.

For Lane and Ersson it is clear that the European Union (its set of institutions) is acquiring a sizeable degree of political independence in relation to its Member States: its own independent, sovereign political institutions, procedures and powers for engaging in decision-taking, policy-making and various legal activities; and therefore the capacity to engage in geo-political management (legitimately, legally, constitutionally) within its borders, and relatedly further afield. The EU's accumulated sovereignty has implications for the conduct and consequences of political activity at the Member State (nation-state) level, as indicated by Lane and Ersson. For instance, it helps account for evidence suggesting that '[a]lthough West European and East European countries [have] come [along] very different paths of development, the [political] outcomes in the 1990s show many similarities' (Lane and Ersson, 1996, p. 208). For Lane and Ersson, there is a process underway of 'convergence in European politics', judged in terms of 'the basic mechanisms of party governance' (*ibid.*, p. 196). Lane and Ersson argue:

> At the same time as [...] political parties are the main actors in [...] European countries, they are operating in a less and less secure post-industrial society. Increasing electoral volatility, mass media pressure, the welfare state crisis and European integration have changed the environment for political parties [...]. The European game of politics shows more and more similarities despite [any lingering] economic and social differences as well as [...] historical legacies. If this analysis of the mechanisms operating behind party government [sic] has something to say, then we might expect more convergence in European politics.
>
> (*ibid.*, pp. 212–13)[24]

In other words, for Lane and Ersson, what has 'weakened political parties' throughout Europe, and what will continue to weaken them in a convergent manner, is 'European political integration' (*ibid.*, p. 210), manifested as this is in, more specifically, the construction and consolidation of what they label *supranational bodies*. That is:

the relevance of the national [political] arena has been reduced by the emergence of new supranational bodies within the EU. Increasingly, policies are being framed within the EU [supranational] institutions. Thus far, [...] political parties have not been able to come up with a response to the consequences for party government [sic] of European integration. The attempts to strengthen their influence at the top of the new supranational structures have met with only limited success, as the European Parliament where the political parties participate remains weak in relation to the other main EU institutions [...]. In the late 1980s and early 1990s the Commission and the Council of Ministers expanded EU legislation considerably in various directions and many ways. Simultaneously, the EU Court [the European Court of Justice (ECJ)] has increasingly underlined the federal implications of the existence of the bulk of EU law, namely that EU directives and regulations have to be implemented in the member states, even when they contradict [Member State] legislation.   (*ibid.*, p. 210)[25]

Here, Lane and Ersson are touching on such problems as the *democratic deficit* (see Close, 1995, pp. 424–4, 249–52, 260) and such purported solutions as the *principle of subsidiarity* (see Emilou, 1994; Shaw, 1996, Chapter 3; Spicker, 1991; Steiner, 1994; Toth, 1994; Wistrich, 1994) within the European Union. The European Commission clarifies the democratic deficit as follows:

Alongside the Community's instruments of economic policy is a political structure to ensure democratic control. The powers of the EC's institutions have developed over the years as the activities of the Community have expanded and deepened. This is particularly true of the European Parliament. Its rights have been extended with the successive constitutional reforms of the Community.[26] But the expansion of Parliament's powers has not always matched the pace of the transfer of authority from individual countries to the EC. As a result, a 'democratic deficit' has arisen. National parliaments have lost the control over executive power transferred by their governments to the EC, while their right of control has not been fully handed on to the European Parliament.

(European Commission, *Strengthening Democracy in the EC*, 1993, p. 1)

Guided by the European Commission and by Lane and Ersson, the EU as an organisation and set of institutions has been gradually acquiring much of the power and authority (of the 'right of control') previously enjoyed and exercised by its Member States. In conjunction with the territorial (and thereby geo-political) expansion and institutional progress (political integration) of the Union, a greater and greater share of power and authority has been transferred from the nation-state level to the Union level, and more specifically to the Union's *supranational* institutions and decision-making procedures. The Union, through the progress of its supranational institutions, has become increasingly endowed with *legitimate control* over its Member States – over its Member States' institutions, political procedures and practices, electorates and citizens. However, at the same time as being transferred from the nation-state level to the Union level, decision-making authority and control have been spread among the Union's supranational institutions in a markedly skewed manner. In particular, the European Parliament has been left relatively impoverished as far as the (re-)distribution of decision-making authority and control is concerned. The theme of the particular supranational character of the European Union – historically, the first ever supranational organisation – will be pursued in the next chapter.

2 European Supranationalism and the Global System

The European Union's one directly, democratically elected and accountable political institution is relatively under-developed. The European Parliament has not accumulated anything like the degree of decision-making responsibility or competence which balances out that degree which has been relinquished by the equivalent institutions (the parliaments) at the nation-state level, leaving aside the degree relinquished by the full range of political institutions (including the governments and the courts) at the nation-state level. The decision-making powers which have been transferred from the nation-state level, including from the parliaments, to the Union level have been largely *re*-distributed to supranational institutions which are not directly (electorally) accountable at nation-state level. It would seem that the Union, by virtue of the particular way in which it has re-distributed its acquired and accumulated supranational decision-making powers among its institutions, currently participates in the process of governance (geo-political management) in a far more top-down (see Elliott, 3 March 1997; and our Chapter 3) manner than has traditionally been the case among its current Member States. The more the Union progresses as a supranational organisation without altering its managerial style so as to far more closely resemble the approach to governance which has traditionally characterised and distinguished western liberal democracies (see Dunleavy and O'Leary, 1987; Hancock, 1993; Laffan, 1996a; Richardson, 1996), the more the Union's democratic deficit will grow; and the more the Union will be a supranational regime that leaves itself open to the accusation of being a dictatorship:

> John Major yesterday made Brussels' 'dictatorship' over Westminster a central battleground for the next election, after the European Court threw out Britain's objection to the 48-hour Working Time Directive. 'What I object to is working conditions being dictated from Brussels when they should be determined here in this House,' the Prime Minister told the [House of] Commons to loud [Conservative] cheers [...]. Mr Major said that unless the United Kingdom was exempted from the directive, and all further attempts at imposed 'social engineering', he would veto the new European treaty currently being negotiated [in the Intergovernmental Conference] by the 15 member states. (Bevins and Helm, 13 November 1996)

Even though there are Union institutions and procedures through which Member States can exercise vetoes over decision-taking, including crucially over amendments to basic treaties and over agreements on new treaties (and therefore in relation to mechanisms for making major leaps in the EU's supranational progress), the clear message of the British prime minister's response to the European Court of Justice's decision on the 48-hour Working Time Directive (which the British government had contested was a 'social policy' measure – rather than a working conditions 'health and safety' measure – and so, given the provisions of the Treaty on European Union, was inapplicable to Britain) is that the British government, none the less, endorses the *final* decision-making authority of the European Court over the British government and parliament,[1] and their preferences, choices and decisions.

The democratic deficit problem of European Union governance is well recognised at all political levels; is the cause of considerable consternation, not to mention great antagonism, especially in some political circles; has so far eluded any widely accepted solution; and could strike observers as somewhat ironical, even hypocritical, in view of the Union's stringent demands on its eastern neighbours as preconditions for their membership.

Chris Bovis argues:

> Supra-nationalists support the theory of [the] irreversible transfer of powers of Member States to Union Institutions [sic]. Although this theory is verified through the case law of the Court of Justice,[2] practice shows that Member States retain substantial sovereignty, especially in the areas that touch on defence, foreign policy, and even social policy.[3]
>
> (Bovis, 1996, p. 22)[4]

The degree to which and the areas, or domains, within which sovereign powers have been transferred from the Union's Member States to the Union's supranational institutions have been subjected to (sometimes toughly) negotiated and eventually agreed restrictions. But, first of all, the meaning and accuracy of Bovis' claim about Member States retaining 'substantial sovereignty' in certain areas is rendered somewhat problematic by European Court decisions which, while purportedly relating to areas within which it can legitimately make decisions, none the less relate *in practice* to what can be readily interpreted as social policy matters. This aside, Bovis alludes to the way that 'substantial sovereignty' has been transferred from the nation-state level to the supranational level. For Bovis, this development is consistent with what he refers to as the *theory of the irreversible transfer of powers*. Be that as it may, in the first instance, it is certainly consistent with the preferences, prescriptions and policies of those Europeans whose purpose has been the progressive, substantial and *irreversible* transfer of sovereignty to the Union's supranational institutions; and who are referred to by Bovis as 'supranationalists', but who are otherwise labelled 'integrationists' or 'federalists'.[5] Thus, in the wake of the European Court's 48-Hour Working

Time Directive decision, 'mainstream Tories [fell] into line behind an election-eering campaign against what will be presented as creeping federalism [by] the Foreign Office' (White *et al.*, 13 November 1996).

Backing for Bovis' suggestion that the theory of the irreversible transfer of sovereign powers is, as he puts it, 'verified' in the case law of the European Court of Justice comes from Stephen Weatherill (1996), according to whom:

> European Community law is enforced at two levels. This phenomenon is commonly known as the principle of 'dual vigilance'. The first level of enforcement is at the 'supranational' level, whereby the European Com-mission supervises the observance of EC law and if necessary initiates proceedings in the event of default. This may lead to decisions made by the European Court of Justice in Luxembourg which record violations of Community law. The second level of enforcement is at national level, based on the direct effect of Community law. 'Direct effect' means that Community law may be enforced at national level before national courts and tribunals in proceedings initiated by private individuals [...]. Under the second limb of dual vigilance, a national court is expected to apply the substantive rules of Community law buttressed by the key constitutional principles of supremacy[6] and direct effect.[7] It must uphold rights derived from Community law, if necessary refusing to apply conflicting national law. EC law creates individual rights enforceable within the national system against public and private bodies. EC law has major constitutional implications and it demands active support from national courts and tribunals.				(Weatherill, 1996, pp. 233–4)

Essentially, to quote the European Court of Justice in its summing up of a pivotal case brought before it in 1963, 'the Community constitutes a new legal order of international law for the benefit of which the states have limited their sovereign rights' (*ibid.*, p. 234 footnote 4)[8] by way of, for instance, the Community's EEC Treaty of 1957 among other basic treaties. These treaties (including the 1992 Maastricht Treaty on European Union) on which what is now the European Union is founded have entailed transfers of sovereignty to the Union's supranational institutions from the Member States in accordance with 'the key constitutional principles of supremacy and direct effect. [A national court] must uphold rights derived from Com-munity law, if necessary refusing to apply conflicting national law. EC law creates individual rights enforceable within the national systems against public and private bodies' (*ibid.*, pp. 233–4).[9] The 'major constitutional implications' (*ibid.*, p. 234) of the Union's founding or 'constitutive treaties' (Shaw, 1993, p. 151) are that the Union's constitution, laws, institutions and decision-making procedures are *supreme* (hence the term 'supranational') *vis-à-vis* – or are superior to and take precedence over – Member State constitu-tions (written or not), laws, institutions and decision-making procedures.[10]

Klaus-Dieter Borchardt suggests that, in the course of carrying out its functions, the European Court of Justice 'acts as a constitutional court' (Borchardt, 1994, p. 27). But, for us, there is an alternative way of representing and categorising the Court in the light of the supranational sovereign powers of the European Union, the European Court's role in sharing in, supervising and safeguarding these powers, the 'supremacy of Community law' (Shaw, 1993, p. 151), and so the 'supremacy of the Community legal order' (*ibid.*, p. 105). In a sense, the European Court of Justice is a *supreme court*; and moreover, in this role displays similarities to Germany's Supreme Court (see, for instance, Gow *et al.*, 24 February 1997) and the USA's Supreme Court (as distinct from, say, the UK's Supreme Court, composed of the Court of Appeal and the High Court). The USA's Supreme Court, for instance, is the 'highest [. . .] judicial tribunal' (*Hutchinson Softback Encyclopedia*, 1991, p. 796) – notwithstanding the fact that the USA (like Germany) has a federal system of government, enshrined in a federal constitution, or of governance (of geo-political management) and operates as a single, unified nation-state (see Gillespie, 1996, who addresses the question: 'Is the United States a model for Europe?').

As Josephine Shaw puts it, 'the evolving Community legal order has established itself as a superior legal order operating within, but nonetheless independent of the national legal systems' (1993, p. 151), hence the 'supremacy of Community law' (*ibid.*, p. 151), the 'supremacy of the Community legal order' (*ibid.*, p. 105), and the supremacy of 'the Court of Justice' in its task of making 'the Community legal order fully and uniformly effective throughout the Member States' (*ibid.*, p. 151; see also, Shaw, 1996). Shaw explains:

> Nowhere in the constitutive Treaties is it stated that Community law takes precedence over national law, although such a position can be derived from the [EEC Treaty]. Nonetheless, the supremacy of Community law has not seriously been challenged since the early 1960s. Possible bases for supremacy [include accepting that it] is inherent in the ideal of creating a new 'federal-type' legal order which lies at the heart of the project of economic integration in Europe, which has always had as its objective a 'union of peoples' (see the Preamble to the Treaty of Rome establishing the EEC).[11] The process of integration would be much less effective if Member States were able to hinder the attainment of Community goals by denying the superiority of Community norms.   (Shaw, 1993, p. 164)

Informed by the Court of Justice's 1964 judgement – 'in Case 6/64 Costa v. ENEL' (*ibid.*, p. 156) – that the 'transfer by the States from their domestic legal systems to the Community legal system of the rights and obligations arising under the [EEC] Treaty carries with it a permanent [irreversible] limitation of their sovereign rights', Shaw comes to the conclusion that the 'sovereignty of all the Member States is limited, or perhaps better "pooled" or "shared" by accession to the Community' (*ibid.*, p. 156). In the particular case of 'the sovereignty of the UK as a nation state' (*ibid.*, p. 156), Shaw argues that, therefore, 'the UK has acceded to a political entity within which absolute Parliamentary sovereignty is no longer tenable, [and] must be regarded as abrogated, with legislative and judicial sovereignty passing to the European Community, within its sphere of competence' (*ibid.*, p. 157).

Likewise, while Klaus-Dieter Borchardt suggests that, on the one hand, the 'situation must not be regarded as one in which the Community legal order' has been 'superimposed on' the 'legal order of the Member States' (Borchardt, 1994, p. 56), he notes that, on the other hand, none the less 'Community law constitutes a legal order that is self-sufficient in relation to the legal orders of the Member States' (*ibid.*, p. 56); that 'Community law, which was enacted in accordance with the powers laid down in the Treaties, has priority [primacy] over any conflicting law of the Member States' (*ibid.*, p. 61); that 'through the establishment of the Community, the Member States have limited their legislative sovereignty and in so doing have created a self-sufficient body of law that is binding on them and on their nationals' (*ibid.*, p. 55) – a body of law which can be applied directly to Member State nationals; can be used to by-pass or override Member State institutions, constitutions and laws, courts and legal procedures, governments and parliaments, parliamentary preferences, choices and decisions.

A convincing illustration of the primacy of Community law is provided by the case, already mentioned, of 'the European Union's Working Time Directive' (Atkinson, 8 September 1996; Atkinson, 5 January 1997; Bevins and Helm, 13 November 1996; McSmith, 17 November 1996; Milne, 13 November 1996; Moorman, 19 October 1996; Taylor, 23 November 1996; White *et al.*, 13 November 1996), especially given the decision that had been taken by the UK government led by prime minister John Major to reject the inclusion of the Social Chapter in the 1992 Maastricht Treaty on European Union. The proposed (by the European Commission) Social Chapter of the Maastricht Treaty aimed 'to set minimum conditions for workers across Europe' through the adoption of 'a range of measures such as a right for workers to have a say in the running of their companies, additional job-creation schemes, equal opportunities for men and women, increased spending on training and improvements in health and safety at work' (Elliott, 18 May 1993). More specifically, the inclusion of the Social Chapter in the Treaty would have meant that the 'working week – excluding overtime – [would have been] no more than 48 hours' (*ibid.*). More precisely, the Social Chapter would have meant that many (but by no means all) paid employees would have had the right (through negotiations with their employers) to a maximum (averaged) working week of forty-eight hours; it did not mean that employees would not be allowed by law to work more than (an average of) forty-eight hours per week. But, the UK government's 'opposition, not only to the 48-hour week [measure] but to many other parts of the Chapter' (*ibid.*), 'on the grounds that it would impose onerous conditions on business and push up costs' (*ibid.*; see also Atkinson, 5 January 1997; and McSmith, 17 November 1996), meant that it had to be omitted from the final Treaty, its provisions thereby being 'relegated to a protocol of the treaty' (Elliot, 18 May 1993). The result was that the final Treaty included a 'Protocol on social policy', entailing an annex in the form of an 'Agreement on social policy concluded between the Member States of the European Community with the exception of the United Kingdom of Great Britain and Northern Ireland' ('Protocol on social policy', *The Treaty on European Union*, 1992), according to which:

> The Community and the Member States shall have as their objectives the promotion of employment, improved living and working conditions, proper social protection, dialogue between management and labour, the development of human resources with a view to lasting high employment and the combating of exclusion. (*ibid.*, Article 1)

The Social Chapter could not be included as part of the main text of the Treaty on European Union because it was not unanimously approved by all the Member State governments at the Maastricht summit meeting of the European Council in December 1991 – because, in other words, it was vetoed by the UK government. However, this did not prevent the European Commission from subsequently proposing and securing approval for a legal requirement on all Member States, including the UK, to implement 'the 48-hour work week' (Atkinson, 8 September 1996):

> Before the end of the month, the European Court of Justice in Luxembourg is due to deliver a judgment expected to reject the UK's challenge to the European Union's Working Time Directive. The British work the longest hours in Europe – 43.4 hours a week compared with an EU average of 40.3, according to the commission [sic]. Defeat will oblige the UK for the first time to introduce laws providing for a maximum 48-hour work week and stipulating minimum amounts of rest periods and holidays.[12] The directive, introduced under Article 118A of the [EEC] Treaty of Rome, was adopted [within the Council of Ministers in accordance with the majority voting procedure (Moorman, 19 October 1996)] in November 1993 [and so within a few days of the Maastricht Treaty finally coming into force] as a health and safety measure [even though] the UK abstained from the vote. The European Commission argues that the directive is a way of ensuring minimum standards in the workplace and protecting workers from unscrupulous employers [...]. But the [United Kingdom] government is contesting the directive on the basis that it relates to

employment rights rather than health and safety.[13] [The UK government] claims Brussels is trying to sneak in the Social Chapter of the Maastricht Treaty, from which the UK has an opt-out clause, through the back door [...]. The Government [...] genuinely fears the directive could be the thin end of the wedge of damaging social legislation. But [...] it is rare for the court [sic] to disagree with its Advocate General, which ruled against the UK earlier this year.[14] According to reports, the [UK government's] European policy committee flirted with the idea of defying the judgement but changed its mind after civil servants pointed out that to do so would mean blatantly disregarding European law, and the risk of heavy fines. [Consequently, the] Government will abide by the law.

(Atkinson, 8 September 1996)

As Jane Moorman then mentions, if 'the enforceability of the directive is upheld, the Government will have very little time in which to rush through regulations – to give it force – and so avoid sanctions' (Moorman, 19 October 1996). That is, 'unless it wants to risk infringement proceedings by the EC, [the United Kingdom] will have to enforce the Working Time Directive by its final implementation date of November 23 1996' (*ibid.*).

As we have noted, on 12 November 1996, as 'expected, the European Court of Justice upheld the directive, providing for holidays, maximum working hours and rest periods under health and safety legislation, which [the British government] says interprets the scope of the Treaty of Rome far more broadly than agreed by Britain' (White *et al.*, 13 November 1996; see also Milne, 13 November 1996). Consequently:

Almost as soon as the court's decision was delivered, Sir Stephen Wall, Britain's ambassador to the European Union, tabled proposals for [an] opt-out [from the directive] at a meeting of the inter-governmental conference (IGC), which is up-dating the Maastricht Treaty. Sir Stephen also demanded that the new treaty should re-write the health and safety powers currently governed by majority voting [within the Council of the European Union, the formal title adopted by the Council of Ministers, 'the main decision-making institution' within the EC/EU (Fontaine, 1995, p. 9), shortly after the Maastricht Treaty came into force on 1 November 1993] to allow a national veto. The demands for a new working hours 'opt-out', to extend the existing social chapter opt-out, and for a veto of further health and safety measures, is unlikely to be agreed by the other member states in their IGC talks [...]. Ian Lang, President of the Board of Trade, told the [House of] Commons: 'This House should not seek to disobey the law. We obey the law until we can secure a change in it, and we are determined to secure that change in the law through lawful means.' Mr Lang said earlier that the Government expected to take two to three months to consult business and industry about the implementation of the new law, which would then be speedily introduced, in a matter of weeks, by Statutory Instrument. (Bevins and Helm, 13 November 1996)

Despite the UK government's opposition to and action against the enforcement of the 48-hour Working Time Directive, it would obey the decision of the European Court on the matter; would obey European law (as interpreted by the Court); and would follow European institutional procedures in an attempt to secure a change in the law, or at least an 'opt-out' from the law, as well as an alteration of the procedures themselves. Emphatically, the UK government would *not* disobey European Community laws and institutional (and in particular Court) decisions, and would *not* in any way act unlawfully or unconstitutionally; it would accept the Union's *dictates*. This means that, in the particular case of the Working Time Directive, the UK government had less than two weeks following the European Court's decision before the legislation was due to come into force, the date fixed for its enforcement being 23 November 1996.

Just as it is rare for the European Court of Justice to reject an advocate general's preliminary judgements in cases brought before it on the validity of rules and procedures, so it is rare for Member State governments not to comply with the Court's final judgements. As reported by Terence Daintith:

What [Brussels] bureaucrats [...] have, in profusion, are rules: rules for us and for our governments, in the shape of laws to govern our activities [...]. Yet having neither armies nor police, the Brussels legislators have little or no capacity to enforce their laws themselves; for this they rely on the resources of the States which are members of the European Community. It is remarkable how rarely, over nearly half a century of the life of the European Community institutions, those resources have been explicitly withheld. Notwithstanding the frequency with which each and every Member State has been at odds with Community policy, and hence in disagreement with the content of Community law, on one subject or another, the proclamation of a refusal to comply with that law, or to co-operate in making it effective in the Member State's own territory, has been a rare event; and it has been all but unknown for it to extend over a broad range of legal regulation, as opposed to the specific law on which there is disagreement.[15] The rarity of express refusal of compliance or co-operation [is consistent with] the expectation of Member State enforcement [of] European Community [...] laws, [which] in the majority of areas of [EC] competence [...] are designed to function indirectly. [This means that] the Community [...] relies on the Member States, not simply to provide enforcement tools like criminal [...] process [...], but also to see to the transposition of the Community rules into the national legal system.

(Daintith, 1995b, pp. 3–4)

The rarity with which EU members resort to such strategies as refusing to comply with, implement or enforce Community rules, even when they have contrary policy preferences,[16] is manifested in some perhaps unexpected details:

> Britain ranks among the top five European Union countries for putting into place laws on social policy, according to a league table to be published by the European Commission today [28 January 1997]. The UK, along with Sweden, Germany and Denmark, has translated 96 per cent of 50 EU directives covering labour law, equality and health and safety issues into national law. Only Finland has done better with a 100 per cent record. EU officials said Britain's record was surprising, given the UK's strong opposition to social legislation from Brussels. The UK has an opt-out from the EU social chapter [sic] and recently sought to have the EU's working time directive struck down by the European Court of Justice.
>
> (Southey, 28 January 1997)

The uncommon cases of EU members refusing to enforce Community rules, especially following Court judgements confirming their validity, seems to reflect a commitment on the part of the Member States in general to the founding treaty provisions and obligations according to which they are required to defer to the Community's institutions, decisions and demands, which in practice often or in the end means the European Court of Justice's decisions and demands.[17] This is not to ignore the influence of the threat of punitive, or coercive, sanctions being imposed upon miscreant Member States. Coercive sanctions are available:

> In order to sanction those Member States that do not implement rulings of the European Court of Justice, the European Commission will ask the same Court to impose periodic penalty payments, while the infringement continues. As for the infringements that would attract the severest penalties, the Commission has put at the top of its list violations of the principle of non-discrimination between EU citizens, along with attacks on the EU's four freedoms: the free movement of people, goods, services and capital [...]. This, in substance, is how the Commission intends to implement Article 171 of the EC Treaty, as modified by the Treaty of Maastricht, according to its decision of 5 June [1996].
>
> (European Commission, 'Criteria for future sanctions', 1996).[18]

The EU's four freedoms are those of the single internal market: 'the single market rests on the pillars of the four fundamental freedoms – the free movement of goods, persons, services and capital' (Borchardt, 1995, p. 34), the single market programme having been incorporated into the EEC Treaty with the entry into force on 1 July 1987 of the Single European Act (*ibid.*, p. 32). This Act:

added a new Article 8a to the EEC Treaty (now Article 7a of the EC Treaty [following the coming into force of the Treaty on European Union on 1 November 1993]) reading as follows: 'the Community shall adopt measures with the aim of progressively establishing the internal market over a period expiring on 31 December 1992 [...] [comprising] an area without frontiers in which the free movement of goods, persons, services and capital is ensured.   (*ibid.*, p. 32)

By May 1996, a report on the progress which had been made towards the full implementation of the single internal market, entailing an inventory of the 'transposition' of the Community laws designed to ensure the four freedoms, was published:

> More than three years after the opening of the single market, as many as 173 national measures are still missing. These are measures which should have been taken by the EU Member States implementing the 221 European 'laws' provided for in the 1985 White Paper on the single market. As of 15 May [1996] the Fifteen [Member States] had transposed 92.6%, on average, of these measures into national law, according to the Commission's latest report of the implementation of the single market. The transposition rate ranged from Denmark's 99.5% to Austria's 80.4%. In the case of all 1378 of the European directives which are relevant to the single market – they include the 221 'laws' mentioned earlier – the average rate of transposition stands at 89.7%, with a maximum of 96.6% for Denmark and a minimum of 77.4% for Finland.
>
> (European Commission, 'The internal market in practice: still some way to go', June 1996)

Of course, Austria and Finland, along with Sweden, were in the last wave of new EU members, an event which took place on 1 January 1995. This aside, there is no evidence to suggest that the delay in transposing all of the 1378 directives of relevance to the single internal market into nation-state law is due to anything apart from procedural and other practical impediments or simple indolence or a mixture of both; that the delay is due to defiance or deliberate obstruction. This is not to say that there is no evidence of Member States using deliberate delaying tactics in implementing Community law:

> British bosses do not believe the 48-hour working week will destroy jobs. So says a survey by the Institute of Directors, which has campaigned against the legislation. The poll [...] undermines the Government's claim that giving employees the right to refuse excessive hours will put them out of a job [...]. The legislation, which technically came into force on 23 November [1996], gives employees the right to a minimum three weeks' paid holiday, a 48-hour week, maximum night shifts of eight hours, a maximum working day of 13 hours and a maximum working week of six

days. The Government is engaged in a three-month consultation exercise with industry on putting the directive into practice. This effectively delays the implementation until after the [general, parliamentary] election [expected for May 1997].   (Atkinson, 5 January 1997)

The UK government's delay in implementing the directive does not mean that it is not enforceable. In this regard, we can recall Stephen Weatherill's point that '[u]nder the second limb of dual vigilance, a national court is expected to apply the substantive rules of Community law buttressed by the key constitutional principles of supremacy and direct effect' (Weatherill, 1996, pp. 233–4). Accordingly, as reported by Robert Taylor, 'Britain's public sector employers face the threat of legal action if they have not implemented the terms of the European Union's working time directive that came into force today in all EU member states' (Taylor, 23 November 1996). The UK government's delay is just that: a *delay*. It will without doubt eventually, albeit very reluctantly (at least in the case of a Conservative government), fully implement the directive.

For present purposes, the significance of the European Court of Justice's final decision in the case of the EC's Working Time Directive lies not so much in the content of the directive and its consequences for paid employment conditions and experiences, as in its *political* implications as reflected in the UK government's response. If a Court judgement about a rule or law (a treaty provision, a regulation, a directive, or whatever[19]) goes against a Member State's policy preferences and prevailing domestic legal framework, that Member State is required none the less, by virtue of its treaty obligations, to comply with the judgement, to implement and enforce the rule, to alter its legal framework accordingly, and thereby to signal its acceptance of and deference to the authority of the Court.

In exercising its authority, the Court portrays itself as, and is generally accepted as, representing and operating on behalf of the Union as a whole – of the Union as a *unified* collection and *cohesive* system of 'actors' (Borchardt, 1995, pp. 23–30): its Member States and its framework of supranational institutions; and, connectedly, as acting in support of the Union's decision-making procedures (mechanisms, methods); the Union's constitution and body of treaties and rules; and the Union's aims or objectives (*ibid.*, pp. 23–7):

the principal aims [are] to preserve and strengthen peace, to achieve economic integration [. . .] through the creation of a single internal market, to work towards political union and, last but not least, to strengthen and promote social cohesion in the Union.   (Borchardt, 1995, p. 23)

In spite of the purported finality of Borchardt's list of principal aims, there is room for at least one further, related aim. What Borchardt could have included is the objective of enhancing the EU's profile, presence and power as a *global player* (see, for instance, Borchardt, 1995, pp. 74–8; Emilou and O'Keefe, 1996; the European Commission's *Europe in a Changing World*; the European Commission's *The European Union and World Trade*, 1995; Nør-gaard, 1993; and Waites, 1995). With this particular goal in mind, Borchardt points out:

> The European Union is the largest single trading bloc in the world and as such plays a leading role alongside the United States and Japan on the world stage, with interests in practically every corner of the globe. More than 100 countries have diplomatic missions to the EU in Brussels, while the Community itself has representative offices throughout the world and at all major organizations. This is partly a reflection of Europe's respon-sibilities for peace, freedom and prosperity in the world, but it also reflects a very basic need in view of Europe's economic dependency on a wide variety of imports [and exports]. (Borchardt, 1995, p. 74)

In 1993, the EU Twelve accounted for 20 per cent of global exports, with the USA accounting for 16.3 per cent and Japan 8.2 per cent. The seven Euro-pean Free Trade Area (EFTA) countries at that time (Austria, Finland, Iceland, Liechtenstein, Norway, Sweden and Switzerland) accounted for 7.4 per cent of global exports. Also in 1993, the EU Twelve accounted for 19.2 per cent of global imports, the USA for 20.4 per cent, Japan 12.7 per cent, and the EFTA group of countries for 6.6 per cent. Herein lies the European Commission's claim that the EU is 'the world's largest trade grouping, accounting on its own for just over one fifth of total global trade in goods. More than either of its main competitors – the United States and Japan' (European Commission, *The European Union and World Trade* p. 5).

The dependency of the EU on world trade is important in helping to understand why '[p]romoting free trade has been one of the chief aims of the European Union [. . .]. [I]t has created the world's most important mar-ket, boosting [internal] trade between its members [see European Commis-sion, 'An 11% rise in internal trade', *Frontier-Free Europe* 1995] and is heavily dependent on international commerce – more so than the United States – for its economic livelihood. [Connectedly, the] EU has been a central member of the General Agreement on Tariffs and Trade (GATT) established in 1947 to supervise global trade rules and [has] played a key role in the various negotiations to reduce trade barriers from the 1960s onwards' (Euro-pean Commission, *The European Union and World Trade*, 1995, p. 4). The last round of GATT negotiations, the Uruguay Round, was launched in 1986 and resulted in an agreement which was finally endorsed 'by all the governments concerned in Marrakesh in April 1994' (*ibid.*, pp. 5–7). The Uruguay Round agreement was intended to 'substantially liberalize interna-tional trade and [it] gave birth to a new, and stronger supervisory body, the

World Trade Organization (WTO)' (*ibid.*, p. 4). Within GATT, and now the WTO, 'the individual Member States are contracting parties', but 'major agreements are signed by the Union in its own right' (Fontaine, 1995, p. 36). Pascal Fontaine argues that it was 'because the Union presented a united front' within the Uruguay Round of GATT negotiations 'that it was so effective in defending the viewpoints of each of its Member States' (*ibid.*, p. 37). Hence the Union's aim of enhancing its collective and united profile and presence as 'an economic and trading power', and moreover as a 'political power' (*ibid.*, p. 37) on the world stage (Borchardt, 1995, p. 47) – or, that is, within the *global system* (Axford, 1995).

Consistent with the same aim and strategy, the 'Union enjoys observer status at the United Nations', and (by the time Pascal Fontaine was writing in December 1994) had 'signed some 50 UN conventions and agreements in its own right' (Fontaine, 1995, p. 38). In November 1990, both the Community and its Member States jointly signed the Transatlantic Declaration with the United States (*ibid.*, p. 36; see also Peterson, 1996), and as Fontaine reported in 1995:

> The Union has concluded framework cooperation agreements with Argentina, Brazil, Mexico, Uruguay and the Andean Pact countries (Bolivia, Columbia, Ecuador, Peru and Venezuela) with the [intention] of supporting regional economic integration. Similar agreements were concluded with the Association of South-East Asian Nations in 1980 and the Gulf Cooperation Council in 1988.   (Fontaine, 1995, p. 39)

Of course, as we have already noted, since the EC signed its framework cooperation agreement with the Andean Pact – true to the EC's professed intention of supporting regional economic integration – the Pact has been re-formed as the *Andean Community*. On 10 March 1996, the presidents of the Andean Pact countries (Bolivia, Colombia, Ecuador, Peru and Venezuela) founded the Andean Community, declaring that 'they had sought inspiration from the example of the European Union' (European Commission, *Frontier-Free Europe*, April 1996, p. 3): the 'new Community, which replaces the Andean Pact, will include a presidential council, a permanent secretariat and a parliament, whose members are elected through universal suffrage. This set up clearly recalls the structure of the 15-nation European Union' (*ibid.*).

Apart from the Andean Community exemplifying the march of regional economic integration in the Americas, there is for instance the Central American Common Market (Dresner, 1994, p. 215) which when established in 1960 was, 'Latin America's first attempt to form a free trade area' (Buckley, 1994, p. 18); and there is the more successful Mercosur, created on 1 January 1992 by Argentina, Brazil, Paraguay and Uruguay (Dyer, 28 December 1996), and forging an agreement in December 1996 'to integrate

Bolivia gradually [. . .]. The agreement [being] similar to that already reached with Chile' (*Financial Times*, 16 December 1996).

As we have also already noted, the European Community's 1980 co-operation agreement with ASEAN was followed by regular meetings between the two organisations, including that in February 1997 which led Nicholas Cumming-Bruce to proclaim 'East–West dialogue enters a new era' (Cumming-Bruce, 14 February 1997). The developing relationship between the EU and ASEAN is underscored by, and indeed may be largely driven and motivated by, the changing economic relationship between the two organisations, as reflected in the evidence on trade flows:

> the dynamics of EU-Asian trade is [illustrated] by the EU's trade with ASEAN. Imports from ASEAN rose by some 80% over the five years from 1990 to 1994. The change in composition of these imports was equally striking. Manufactures, including not only textiles and clothing, but also electronic products, accounted for 80% of the total in 1994 (as compared to 70% in 1990). But EU exports have shown a similar dynamism, rising by 73% between 1990 and 1994. The EU's exports to ASEAN are roughly equal in value to its exports to the 19 Latin American countries. Over half the EU's exports consist of machinery, telecommunications and transport equipment. But the EU is also helping to meet the growing demand for quality consumer products from ASEAN's expanding middle class.
>
> (European Commission, *Frontier-Free Europe* (supplement), April 1996)

Finally, at this juncture on the matter of the European Union's goal and strategy of enhancing its profile and presence both as an *economic and trading power* and as a *political power* (Fontaine, 1995, p. 37) within the global system, it is pertinent to note how since the signing of the Transatlantic Declaration in 1990, the United States, Canada and Mexico have constructed the North American Free Trade Agreement (NAFTA). Since January 1994, NAFTA has been the basis of a 'trade pact' which, judged in terms of population and GDP, matches the EU's size; and which may eventually be transformed into the far more extensive Free Trade Area of the Americas (FTAA), as proposed by US President Clinton, the first step in this direction being that attempted in 1994–5 when the US government 'sought to link NAFTA with Mercosur' (Peterson, 1996, p. 188).

Perhaps the emergence of the Andean Community, the progress of Mercosur, the creation of NAFTA, the prospect of an FTAA and the development of other (integrated) economic or trade pacts, blocs or organisations, as well as of inter-bloc ties (such as those between the EU and the Andean Community; the EU and ASEAN; NAFTA and Mercosur; and NAFTA and ASEAN within the Asia Pacific Economic Co-operation [APEC] forum) confirm Peterson's claim:

As political structures are adjusted to reflect increasing economic inter-dependence, the emergence of protectionist or even mercantilist trade blocs could become a defining feature of the international order [...]. Part of the problem is that the saliency of the Cold War military alliances, which usually discouraged inward-looking or mercantilist trade policies, has declined. Defence commitments in Asia and Europe traditionally provided the US with substantial leverage in negotiations with the EU and Japan on trade and monetary issues. This leverage diminished as the Soviet threat receded. Meanwhile new tensions emerged on the industrial and economic side of military alliances.   (Peterson, 1996, pp. 186–7)

Here, apart from the economic tensions, clashes and conflicts which emerged as 'major US–Japanese trade disputes of the mid-1990s' (*ibid.*, p. 187), what comes to mind is the 'anti-Cuba law dispute' (de Jonquières, 21 February 1997; see also de Jonquières and Dunne, 21 February 1997) of 1996–7:

the US–EU dispute over the Helms–Burton anti-Cuba law [that threatens to] plunge the World Trade Organisation into an institutional crisis and embitter transatlantic relations was averted yesterday [20 February 1997] by an 11th-hour diplomatic finesse in Washington. The US move aims to buy time to resolve the starkest conflict between national sovereignty [in particular, the USA's] and multilateral rules since the WTO was estab-lished two years ago [...]. The EU complained last year that Helms–Burton violated multilateral rules and asked the WTO to establish a disputes panel to rule on the case. But the US says Helms–Burton is an issue of foreign, not trade, policy. Washington insists that the law is justified by Article XXI of the WTO treaty, which says a member may take any action 'it considers necessary for its national security interests'.
                    (de Jonquières, 21 February 1997)

The Helms–Burton law (introduced in March 1996) 'threatens penalties against foreign companies judged to be "trafficking" in expropriated proper-ties in Cuba formerly owned by US nationals or Cubans who are now US citizens' (Fletcher, 27 December 1996).

But, what is of particular significance for present purposes is that the dispute was between the United States and the EU. The EU acted on behalf of its Member States, their companies and their interests; the EU being represented by its institutions and institutional personnel, in particular by the European Commission and the EU trade commissioner, Sir Leon Brit-tan:

Sir Leon Brittan, the European trade commissioner, described the US's Helms–Burton legislation as unacceptable, unjustified and unproductive [...]. The dispute is due to go before a conciliation panel at the World

Trade Organisation in Geneva tomorrow [20 February 1997] if agreement between the two parties cannot be reached. (Bates, 19 February 1997)

In response:

President Clinton has promised to continue waiving the law's main provisions every six months, provided the EU keeps pressure on Cuba to promote democracy. Sir Leon says the US must provide stronger safeguards against the application of Helms–Burton and of the D'Amato Act, which penalises foreign investors in the energy industries of Libya and Iran. (de Jonquières and Dunne, 21 February 1997)

At the eleventh hour, as reported by de Jonquières:

Faced with [the] deadline [of 21 February 1997] for naming two WTO panel members, the US fudged. It said it would not invoke the national security defence at this stage, but would not participate in the panel hearings either [. . .]. [T]rade diplomats in Geneva are hoping that an amicable US–EU settlement will mean that the issue does not need to be put to the test [of a WTO panel]. (de Jonquières, 21 February 1997)

Again, however, what is of particular significance for present purposes is not so much the eventual outcome of the dispute between the United States and the EU over the Helms–Burton Act, as the role and authority assumed by, and indeed accorded to, the EU and its institutions in relation both to the outside world and to the EU's Member States; in the task of trying to achieve the aims (realise the objectives; satisfy the interests) of the EU, its Member States, its Member States' companies, and so on. In the case of external (as well as internal) trade matters and disputes, the EU and its institutions have acquired considerable authority (legitimate power or competence) as an internal–external intermediary or interlocutor; or, what Eileen Denza refers to as 'an international legal personality':

The entry into force of the [Agreement establishing the World Trade Organisation on 15 April 1994 provides] the European Communities [with] an important step forward in its struggle to win full acceptance as an international legal personality and so to achieve what the European Court of Justice has described as 'the requirement of unity in the international representation of the Community'. (Denza, 1996, p. 3)

Of course, having acquired its own role, authority and legal personality within the global system is one thing, but what the particular powers or competences of the EU and its institutions are as an internal–external interlocutor is another. The matter is complex (as is often the case with legally related issues), and has begun to attract legal scrutiny, analysis and disagreement (see, for instance, Chalmers, 1996; Denza, 1996; Elles, 1996; Emilou,

1996; Emilou and O'Keefe, 1996). For our purposes, however, it is convenient and sufficient to be able to quote Baroness Diana Elles:

> The express powers granted to the Community under Articles 113 and 238 [of the EEC Treaty] have been influenced and extended through the case law of the ECJ [European Court of Justice]. It has been held that every internal power implies a power on the international plane, the Treaty establishing the principle of parallelism. The international commitment must, however, be necessary for the attainment of a specific object. Whether an international commitment is necessary is for the Council to decide and where there is an unresovolved conflict between the Council and the Commission, resort may be had for the opinion of the ECJ under Article 228 (6).   (Elles, 1996, p. 23)

Guided by the 'principle of parallelism', given that the Community and its institutions are responsible for internal trade matters, then they are responsible for external trade matters. What the Uruguay Round GATT Agreement did was, in effect, to extend this principle into the global system, at least as far as trade and the World Trade Organisation are concerned. Following Diana Elles, the principle is rooted in a combination of the founding treaties of the Communities and ECJ case law; and if a dispute should arise over the application of the principle, then the problem is taken to the ECJ for adjudication – for a resolution.

Klaus-Dieter Borchardt sums up by telling us that the 'function of the Court of Justice is to ensure that in the interpretation and application of the Treaties and of the instruments enacted under them the law is observed', explaining that a 'system [organisation, or whatever] will only endure if its rules are supervised by an independent authority', a consideration which accounts for 'the establishment of a Community Court of Justice as soon as the ECSC [European Coal and Steel Community] was created' under the 1951 Treaty of Paris (Borchardt, 1994, p. 27).[20]

At the same time, however, the installation of the European Court of Justice as 'an independent authority', boosted by its confirmation as such both from within the EU and from outside (from the WTO, for example), may be viewed as contributing not only to the endurance of the organisation against the threat posed by internal clashes, but also (in a manner which complies with the ECJ's view of the benefits of 'unity' [Denza, 1996, p. 2]) to the profile, presence and power of the Union within the global system – in spite of, and perhaps to some extent because of, the latter's vicissitudes, exemplified by the recent revolutionary transformation of the global system from that era characterised by the bipolar old world order to that distinguished by the post-Cold War new world order.

3 The Supranational Regional Regime and Governance

The idea of the European Court of Justice operating as an 'independent authority', albeit on behalf of (and in *concert with*, to use Charles de Gaulle's phrase – see Nelsen and Stubb, 1994, Chapter 5) the supranational EC/EU system as a whole, brings us back to the notion of 'sovereignty' which Klaus-Dieter Borchardt (1994; 1995) and Josephine Shaw (1993; 1996) seem to have in mind. Their notion is similar to that to be gleaned from various other, less legally focused but still highly pertinent, writings, including those by Clive Archer and Fiona Butler (1992); Jamie Shea (1993); Neill Nugent (1991); and Monica den Boer (1994). Archer and Butler argue:

> To understand the European Community, one must comprehend the position of the sovereign state in Europe. The sovereign state is [...] a European invention and its genesis can be dated back to the fourteenth century [Strayer, 1970, p. 57] with the touchstone of 'constitutional self-containment' [Manning, 1962, p. 166] having been well established by a number of states in Europe by the Peace of Westphalia in 1648. If it is true that 'sovereignty [...] consists of being constitutionally apart, of not being contained, however loosely, within a wider constitutional scheme' [James, 1986, p. 24], then [the] Peace of Westphalia, which ended the Thirty Years War, established [...] that there existed sovereign states in Europe that could not be contained within the Holy Roman Empire [...]. It 'paved the way for a system of states to replace a hierarchical system under the leadership of the Pope and the Hapsburg family complex [...]' [Holsti, 1991, p. 26]. (Archer and Butler, 1992, pp. 1–2)

For Archer and Butler (following James, 1986), nation-states are constitutional, or more precisely constitutionally discrete, geo-political entities, the emergence and persistence of which distils down to the concomitant emergence and resilience of nation-state sovereignty, something which in turn is rooted in their (in nation-states') constitutional independence from any encompassing constitutional schemes. These schemes include imperial ones, exemplified by the Holy Roman empire of Charlemagne and his successors, and the German empire (962–1806) (Upsall, 1991a, p. 518), a constitutional scheme which was 'formally abrogated' on 6 August 1806, by Francis I of Austria – that is, Francis II of the Holy Roman empire (*ibid.*, p. 421) – 'at

French insistence', following 'Prussia's defeat at the hands of Napoleon at the Battle of Jena in 1806' (Perry, 1976, p. 3). Other examples of constitutional schemes of an imperial kind include the empire of Napoleon, whose Berlin Decree of 1806 initiated the so-called 'Continental System' (Grun, 1991, p. 376); and the Soviet empire, the formal end of which was signalled on 5 September 1991 when the Congress of the People's Deputies voted itself out of existence (Upsall, 1991b, p. 679; see also Ambrose, 1993, Chapters 16 and 17).[1]

Our argument is that in Europe, the cradle of the nation-state, most nation-states have embarked on a process of redistributing their 'independent authority' or sovereignty – as gained relatively recently by establishing their 'constitutional self-containment' (Manning, 1962, p. 16) – to a 'wider constitutional scheme' (James, 1986, p. 24). In Europe, nation-states are engaged in redistributing their sovereignty to a (in a constitutional and institutional sense) supranational scheme or system of governance, in the shape of the European Community and Union, which then resembles both federal systems of governance (as exemplified within the EU by Austria, Belgium and Germany) and imperial constitutional schemes of governance, as illustrated by the Holy Roman empire. Just as Europe invented the nation-state as a constitutionally discrete and sovereign geo-political entity, so several hundred years later Europe has invented the supranational system of governance based on a constitutional scheme which encompasses – and an accompanying set of institutions which share in, not to say siphon off, the sovereignty of – its member nation-states. Just as Europe led the way with the nation-state, it appears to be doing so with the supranational system of governance: with the supranational constitutional regime (see Borchardt, 1994; Alec Stone, 1994; and Shaw, 1996, Chapter 3).

For us, there is the strong possibility, in the light of supporting evidence, that supranational constitutional regimes (SCRs), like nation-states, will spread – will grow in terms of their number, their geo-political size and their economic and political importance – within the global system, especially following and to a not inconsiderable extent because of the end of the Cold War and therefore the advent of the new world order. Moreover, just as historical evidence indicates that imperial constitutional schemes exercised governance in ways which was not strictly confined within their own (constitutionally and otherwise drawn) geo-political boundaries, so post-Cold War evidence indicates that supranational systems of governance will participate in the process and problem of external governance, and indeed of *global governance* within the NWO. There is an external dimension to the supranational system of governance, which means that the internal governance of SCRs and the problem and process of external-global governance will sustain a mutually dependent, dialectical relationship (see Weigall and Stirk's 1992 discussion of a new pan-European order).

Brigid Laffan prefaces her *Constitution-building in the European Union* collection of essays (1996a) by telling us:

> The aim of this volume is to assess the major issues confronting the European Union during the process of constitution-building which is set to continue with the convening of the intergovernmental conference (IGC) in March 1996. The focus of [this] study is on the three major imperatives that challenge governance in the European Union: legitimacy, effectiveness and diversity.   (Laffan, 1996, p. 1)

What Laffan does here is to identify three *internal* challenges to – imperatives that feed the problem and enliven the process of – European Union governance. But, for us, accompanying, impinging on and threading through these three is a further imperative, one representing an external challenge. Governance in, of and by the European Union is challenged and shaped and re-shaped by the conditions of the external or encompassing global system (and so by the global distribution of power, for instance) within which the EU as an SCR operates along with – variously in alliance with, in competition with, in conflict with, and so on – other global players, including emerging or embryonic SCRs as well as nation-states (see Axford, 1995, Chapters 4 and 5).

Allan Johnson defines a nation-state as:

> a nation governed by a state whose authority coincides with the boundaries of the nation. Until the nineteenth century, the world was not organized in terms of nation-states, but consisted instead of a diverse collection of ethnic groupings with relatively fluid political boundaries instead of the relatively rigid geographical boundaries and administrative control associated with the modern state. This was primarily because there were few if any states powerful enough to administer and control nations. In contrast, the world today is largely organized as nation-states.
>   (Johnson, 1995, p. 188)

This account begs a number of questions, including: what is meant by 'nation'?; what is the relationship between 'nations' and 'ethnic groupings'?; what would be the implications of defining 'nation' as an (example and type of) 'ethnic grouping'? (see Gellner, 1983, 1994; Hedetoft, 1994; Zetterholm, 1994a, 1994b); if nation-states represent a correspondence or congruence between 'nations' (national boundaries) and 'state' (administrative) boundaries, where (sociologically) does that leave the widespread (administrative, governance) 'problem' of what are otherwise perceived as national diversity, nationalism(s) and nationalist challenges – to recall Laffan's list of imperatives that challenge governance – within and across nation-state boundaries?; how many Catalans or Basques, not to mention Estonians, Latvians and

Lithuanians, would concur with Johnson's account of the relationship between nation-state, nation and state? (See Beazley, 1992; Fernández-Armesto, 1994; Goddard, *et al.*, 1994; Gowland *et al.*, 1995; MacClancy, 1993; Macdonald, 1993; O'Brien, 1993; and Shelley and Winck, 1995.)

Lizanne Dowds and Ken Young (1966) make the important point that there is a 'distinction between *nation* and *state*', before claiming:

> These separate words have commonly been used as interchangeable abbreviations for a much more specific entity – the *nation-state*. The hyphenated term was coined specifically to describe the case of a territorial-political unit (the state) whose borders coincided with the territorial distribution of a national group (the nation). Such nation-states are less common than is often imagined (Connor, 1978). And Britain is not among them.
>
> (Dowds and Young, 1996, p. 153)

Dowds and Young, although adopting a similar notion of 'nation-state' to Johnson, come to the opposite conclusion to Johnson, for whom 'the world today is largely organised as nation-states' (Johnson, 1995, p. 188).[2]

Like Dowds and Young, we recognise distinctions between 'nation', 'state' and 'nation-state', but along the more conventional lines from which Dowds and Young distance themselves. We regard nation-states as geo-political entities;[3] as geographically, or territorally, bounded but politically constituted and constructed, shaped and sustained social formations; as constructed by, through and around 'states'. Following Patrick Dunleavy and Brendan O'Leary (1987), the 'state is a recognizably separate institution or set of institutions, so differentiated from the rest of society as to create identifiable public and private spheres' (Dunleavy and O'Leary, 1987, p. 2). Moreover, it is that set of institutions which 'is sovereign, or the supreme power, within its territory, and by definition the ultimate authority for all law' (*ibid.*, p. 2). Here, Dunleavy and O'Leary are defining 'the state' in a similar manner to Max Weber (1978, 1958), as indicated by Allan Johnson:

> As defined by Max Weber, the state is the social institution [or set of social institutions] that holds a monopoly over the use of force. In this sense, the state is defined by its authority to generate and apply collective power. As with all [sets of] social institutions, the state is organized around a set of social functions, including maintaining law, order, and stability, resolving various kinds of disputes through the legal system, providing common defense, and looking out for the welfare of the population in ways that are beyond the means of the individual [...]. From a conflict perspective, however, the state also operates in the interest of various dominant groups, such as economic classes [...].
>
> (Johnson, 1995, p. 275; see also Dunleavy and O'Leary, 1987, pp. 1–4; Giddens, 1985, pp. 15–29; Giddens, 1993, Chapter 10; and Close, 1992b)

In practice, the geo-political territorial boundaries defended by states do not necessarily coincide in a neat and tidy way with what may be defined, distinguished and discerned as 'nations'. Guided by such writers as Ernest Gellner (see Gellner 1983, especially Chapter 1; see also David Gowland *et al.*, 1995, especially Chapter 13; and Benedict Anderson, 1983), for us nations are 'ethnic groupings'. A 'nation' is a type of 'ethnic grouping': it is an 'imagined community' (Anderson, 1983; see also Gowland *et al.*, 1995, p. 270) rooted in ethnic identity and thereby in ethnicity, where (following Allan Johnson) ethnicity 'is a concept referring to a shared culture and way of life, especially as reflected in language' (Johnson, 1995, p. 99).

In practice, the relationship between *nation-states* and *nations* is highly complex, and connectedly characteristically displays tensions, conflicts and flux (see Hobsbawm, 1990). The character of the relationship between nation-states and nations is then crucial in accounting for the everyday, often coercive, activities of states aimed at defending (perhaps extending) their respective geo-political boundaries; as well as, connectedly, at maintaining internal social order, stability and cohesion (see Cohen, 1968, Chapter 2; Scott, 1995, Chapter 2). But, in addition, the same factors very much help to account for the way nation-state boundaries sometimes change, collapse, disappear, and so on. In this regard we can recall Charles de Gaulle's assertion (made in the context of his rejection of the doctrine, as he referred to it of European *supranationalism*) that, in Europe, 'arbitrary centralization [has] always provoked an upsurge of violent nationalism by way of a reaction' (de Gaulle, 1994, p. 32; see also Gellner, 1983, 1994). In Europe, as elsewhere, arbitrary centralisation and associated arbitrary geo-politically bounded nation-states constructed by, through and around *states* have a rich history of invoking violent nationalism(s) aimed at reconstructing nation-states so that they more closely correspond with nations: 'nationalism is a theory of political legitimacy, which requires that ethnic boundaries should not cut across political ones' (Gellner, 1983, p. 1), and vice versa.

Supranationalism is a political doctrine (de Gaulle, 1994, p. 30) or ideology (see Thompson, 1994) and movement in favour of the submission of (a particular, selected set of) nation-states and nations to the legitimacy, authority and sovereignty of a supranational constitutional regime (SCR). Supranationalism and nationalism(s) are not necessarily, at least wholly, oppositional and mutually exclusive. Supranationalism is about reconstructing geo-political boundaries beyond and at the expense of nation-state and 'national-ethnic' borders, while none the less doing so in a manner which corresponds with a certain, chosen range of such borders. The boundaries of an SCR may well be diligently constructed around a highly selective and exclusive set of nation-states or nations or both; and may be carefully constructed to ensure that they do not stray beyond certain, acceptable *ethnic limits* – hence, for instance, the European Union's Turkey issue and problem (see Fernández-Armesto, 1994; Goddard *et al.*, 1994; Gowland *et al.*, 1995; Macdonald, 1993; Mandel, 1994; Shelley and Winck, 1995; Traynor and Nutall, 7 March 1997; Wilson and van der Dussen, 1995). The notion of 'Fortress Europe' when applied to the European Union draws attention not just to the EU's economic protectionism (see Emilou and O'Keefe, 1996; Harrison, 1995; Harrop, 1992), but also to its political-security protectionism and its national-ethnic protectionism (see Mandel, 1994; Close, 1995).

Even if Allan Johnson's realist claim (see Miall, 1993, Chapter 2; Nelsen and Stubb, 1994, Part 3) that 'the world today is still largely organized as – is largely governed or managed by, through and on behalf of – nation-states' is valid, there is an alternative (a competitor) looming on the horizon. This alternative displays features which hark back to before the European invention of the nation-state, and as such seems to have played a part in inspiring Kevin Wilson and Jan van der Dussen's argument that something resembling a *neo-medieval* Europe is evident:

> On the matter of the dispersal of power and authority there are some striking parallels between the emerging Europe and the Europe of the Middle Ages. The medieval system consisted of a complex patchwork of overlapping authorities [. . .]. The rights of government were territorial but they did not entail much exclusion [. . .] and therefore the result was the [. . .] patchwork of overlapping rights of government that were superimposed on each other such that each was incomplete [. . .]. In looking at Europe today there are some strong reminders of the criss-crossing authority relations that typified medieval social and political organization. In some respects the EC is moving towards a super-state [sic], yet [. . . at] the same time, sub-state [sic] processes are of increasing importance [. . .]. Issues in Europe, even quite important ones, are decided at different levels. From 1993, money, tariffs, border controls, move to the increasingly European (EC) level; [. . .] while law-making is spread across the EC, national [nation-state] and Länder [*sub*-nation-state] levels [. . .]. The principle of [nation-state] sovereignty, exclusivity and territoriality is giving way to a pattern of overlapping authorities reminiscent of the medieval system.   (Wilson and van der Dussen, 1995, p. 193)

While what is emerging in Europe is similar to the social systems or formations that existed in the medieval period, and so before the invention of the modern nation-state, in our view the particular, distinctive and novel features of what is currently emerging owe much to the prior, intervening, existence of the nation-state and nation-state sovereignty, in that it has evolved through nation-states 'pooling their sovereignty under a supranational community' (Borchardt 1995, p. 27; see also Borchardt, 1994, p. 10). What is emerging, in other words, is what we have labelled a *supranational constitutional regime* (SCR).

We have suggested that SCRs, or supranational systems of governance, resemble *both* federal systems of governance (or federal nation-states), as indeed Wilson and van der Dussen's account of the parallels between the emerging Europe and the Europe of the Middle Ages appears to confirm (see also Wilson and van der Dussen, 1995, pp. 205–8), *and* imperial constitutional schemes of governance, as illustrated by the Holy Roman empire. At the same time, however, on the issue of the most appropriate way of categorising the supranational systems of governance, Klaus-Dieter Borchardt, with reference to the European Community, argues:

The points of resemblence between the Community order and the national order of a State [sic] do not [...] suffice to confer on the Community the legal character of a (federal) State [cf. Gillespie, 1996, pp. 144–52; Marquand, 1994; and Shaw, 1996, Chapter 3]. Sovereign powers have been conferred on the Community institutions only in [...] limited spheres [...], and those institutions have not been given any power to increase their competence merely by their own decisions. Thus, the Community lacks both the universal jurisdication characteristic of a State and the powers to create new fields of competence. Even if the Community is not yet a State, it is certainly more developed than an organization set up under traditional international law. Its only essential point of similarity with traditional international organizations is the fact that it, too, was created by treaties taking effect under international law. But these treaties are at the same time the foundation documents establishing independent Communities endowed with their own sovereign rights and competence. The Member States have pooled certain parts of their own legislative powers in favour of the Communities and have placed them in the hands of Community institutions [...]. The Community is thus a new form of relationship between States, something between a State in a traditional sense and an international organization. The concept of 'supranationality' has become accepted among lawyers as a means of describing their legal nature. This is intended to indicate that the Community is an association endowed with independent authority, with its own sovereign rights and a legal order independent of the Member States to which both the Member States and their citizens are subject in matters for which the Community is competent.   (Borchardt, 1994, p. 10)

Whether or not the European Community, or its set of supranational institutions, not only resembles a '(federal) state', but also qualifies categorically as 'a state' (whether federal or otherwise) obviously depends on the definition of 'state'. Borchardt does not make clear what he means by 'state' in general, nor connectedly what he takes to be the conceptual relationships between 'state', 'nation' and 'nation state'. The closest he comes to clarifying his concept of 'state' is when he infers that it is something which has unlimited (universal) 'jurisdication', or sovereign powers or competence(s), including the particular sovereign power to 'increase its competence by its own decisions' (*ibid.*, p. 10), by its own volition. By implication, the universal jurisdiction, sovereignty, power and competence attached to supranational associations exemplified by the European Community is territorially, or geo-politically, circumscribed. As we have previously noted, this feature of 'the state' is explicitly included by Patrick Dunleavy and Brendan O'Leary in their definition of the term. For Dunleavy and O'Leary, the state is 'the sovereign, or the supreme power, and so the ultimate authority for all law, within its territory' (Dunleavy and O'Leary, 1987, p. 2) – the 'it' being 'a recognisably separate set of institutions' (*ibid.*, p. 2).

In our view, the EC/EU *does* have a recognisably separate set of institutions through which it exercises (a degree of) sovereignty, or supreme power, within its territory – within the geo-political boundaries enclosing its Member States. On these grounds, for us, the Community does have the 'legal character of a (federal) State [sic]' (Borchardt, 1994, p. 10; cf., Gillespie, 1996; Marquand, 1994; and Shaw, 1996); does participate in 'the state' within the European Union, even though it does so in 'limited spheres' of competence; does participate in 'the state' at the supranational level as distinct from the Member State level, where there are further (lower level) sets of (nation-state) institutions sharing in (the 'pooled' sovereignty of) 'the state' within the Union as an overall social formation and system. The participation of institutions at the nation-state or Member State level in 'the state' within the EU is purportedly facilitated by the principle of 'subsidiarity' (see Emilou, 1994; Shaw, 1996, Chapter 3; Spicker, 1991; Steiner, 1994; Toth, 1994; Wistrich, 1994), according to which 'the Community will only take action when its objectives cannot be sufficiently achieved by member states acting separately and when it is considered that these objectives could be better achieved by the Community' (Wistrich, 1994, p. 10). The presence of the principle of subsidiarity, notably in the Treaty on European Union, simply adds weight in our view to the conclusion that the Community *does* participate in 'the state' within the EU, and moreover does so at a distinct (upper, supreme) Community level.

Guided by Archer and Butler (1992) rather than by Johnson, historically, nation-state sovereignty emerged towards the end of the medieval period (fifth–fifteenth centuries), and originated more precisely with the decline of the (encompassing) Holy Roman empire. However, while duly acknowledging Archer and Butler's points, there is a distinction to be drawn between the advent and consolidation of the nation-state and of (nation-state) sovereignty as general notions, organising principles and geo-political features, on the one hand, and the presence of particular instances, collections and patterns of (sovereign, constitutionally independent) nation-states, on the other. In this regard, we can note the following observation by Norman

Davies (1996): 'Of the sovereign states on the map of Europe in 1993, four had been formed in the sixteenth century, four in the seventeenth, two in the eighteenth, seven in the nineteenth, and no fewer than 36 in the twentieth' (Davies, 1996 – quoted in Jacques, 13 October 1996; see also Norman Stone, 17 October 1996).

Of the thirty-six European nation-states which, following Davies (see also Almond *et al.*, 1994), have been created during the twentieth century, many have emerged, or re-emerged, as a result of the conclusion of the Cold War and the associated collapse of the Soviet empire. Mark Almond (1994) mentions:

> the sudden appearance in the wake of the collapse of communist rule in both the USSR and Eastern Europe of no less than 22 new countries, the bulk of them within the former Soviet Union itself. Thus, the three Baltic states, Belarus [Byelorussia], the Ukraine, Moldova [Moldavia], Georgia, Azerbaijan and Armenia gained an independence which they had not known since before the Second World War. (Almond *et al.*, 1994, p. 188)

Almond's list of countries invites several comments. First, of course, it includes only nine of the former Soviet Union's fifteen republics, the others being Kazakhstan, Kirghizia (Kyrgyzstan), Russia (the Russian Federation), Tadzhikistan (Tajikstan), Turkmenistan, and Uzbekistan. The second comment is touched on by Almond himself:

> These new states within the former Soviet Union were not destined to live in peace. Break-away movements emerged, threatening to inflict on the region a fatal combination of old hatreds and new destructive power: the Transnistrian Republic [or, that is, the Russian majority in eastern Moldova] declared independence from Moldova; Chechenia declared its independence from Russia; and the Crimea sought to break away from the Ukraine and join Russia; Armenia invaded Azerbaijan. [But, the] fall-out from these sudden events [marking the end of the Cold War and of the Soviet empire] was most extreme [outside the former Soviet Union, and more specifically] in Yugoslavia, which in 1991 simply disintegrated under the long-suppressed rivalries of its ethnic groups. In June that year the republics of Slovenia and Croatia declared their independence, following which Serbian forces attacked them both [...]. In January [1992] further fighting broke out between Serbs, Croats and Muslims in the newly independent Bosnia-Herzegovina [...]. Only Macedonia, which had declared its independence in 1992, remained uneasily free of fighting. In Czechoslovakia, meanwhile, the general election of June 1992 revealed the tensions between Czechs and Slovaks and at the end of that year the country broke into two, the Czech Republic and Slovakia.
> (Almond *et al.*, 1994, p. 188)

Almond goes on to mention several other break-away movements and associated armed clashes and conflicts that erupted after the end of the Cold War and the collapse of the Soviet empire, including ones within the Soviet Union and, even, within Russia:

> a bitter civil war raged in Georgia, as well as fighting against the break-away region of Abkhazia [see Meek, 2 March 1997]; Armenian forces occupied most of Nagorno-Karabakh, claiming it from neigbouring Azer-baijan; separatist movements arose in parts of the Russian Federation itself, from Tartarstan [on the western edge of the Ural Mountains] to Chechenia [. . .].   (*ibid.*, p. 191)

With the strife in Bosnia-Herzegovina, or more inclusively within the Balkans, in particular in mind, Panos Tsakaloyannis (whose focal concern is the consequences for 'pro-EC sentiment in Greece) refers to 'the new European disorder' (Tsakaloyannis, 1996, p. 194). But, in our view, the same phrase is useful in depicting the conditions throughout Eastern Europe – from the Baltic to the Balkans and further east – in the aftermath of the collapse of the Soviet Union and of the bipolar Cold-War old world order (see also Ken Jowitt's *New World Disorder* (1992); and Michael Dobbs-Higginson's *Asia Pacific: its role in the New World disorder* (1993)).

In turn, this development (perhaps especially in view of the way, following Tsakaloyannis, it has been reflected in, for instance, 'Greek attitudes' to European integration) brings to mind a third, connected, point concerning Almond's list of 'new countries' which (re-)emerged with the collapse of the Soviet empire, a point which Almond himself touches on, but only fleetingly at the very end of his account prefaced by the heading 'Western Europe: economic blocs from 1957' (Almond *et al.*, 1994, p. 191):

> The Second World War gave renewed impetus to the idea of preventing future wars by uniting the European states in some form of federal arrangement. In 1957 the European Economic Community was established by the Treaty of Rome to pursue these goals. The Community grew from its original six members (France, Germany, Italy, Belgium, the Netherlands, Luxembourg) with the accession of Denmark, Ireland and the United Kingdom (1973), Greece (1981), and Spain and Portugal (1986) [. . .]. The European Free Trade Association (EFTA), set up in 1959 by Britain as an alternative to the EC, gradually lost members to [the EC/EU]: most of the remaining EFTA countries – Finland, Sweden, Norway and Austria, but not Iceland – were accepted in principle as members of the EU in early 1994.

Given Almond's claim that the Second World War was the impetus behind European unification, even federation (see also Dinan, 1994; Joll, 1990; Nelsen and Stubb, 1994; Therborn, 1995; Urwin, 1992; Weigall and Stirk,

1992; Williams, 1991; Wilson and van der Dussen, 1995), it is worthwhile examining further EFTA and the EU and the relationship between these two organisations. To begin with, as Harry Drost tells us, EFTA was established in 1960 as an intergovernmental organisation,[4] and with economic-related and trade-related objectives:

> The Treaty of Stockholm, signed on 4 January 1960 and in force from 3 May 1960, defines EFTA's objectives as [foremost, the promotion of] a sustained expansion of economic activity, full employment, increased productivity and the rational use of resources, financial stability, and a continuous improvement in living standards [...]. [During 1994] EFTA [had] seven members: Austria, Finland, Iceland, Liechtenstein, Norway, Sweden and Switzerland. The seven founding members were Austria, Denmark, Norway, Portugal, Sweden, Switzerland and the United Kingdom. Iceland joined in 1970. Denmark and the United Kingdom left at the end of 1972 to join the European Community (EC), as did Portugal at the end of 1985. Finland [...] became a [...] member in January 1986. Liechtenstein, which had been an associate member through its customs union with Switzerland, became a full member in May 1991.   (Drost, 1995, p. 198)

In May 1991, it would seem that Liechtenstein joined EFTA in its own right as a full member, rather than merely as an associate member (by virtue of its customs union, established in 1924, with Switzerland – see Drost, 1995, p. 375) specifically in anticipation of the finalisation in October 1991 of the terms for the creation of a European Economic Area (EEA) between EFTA and the European Union (*ibid.*, p. 199), and the subsequent signing in May 1992 of a formal EEA Agreement. Apart from anything else, membership of the EEA – within which 'virtually all restrictions on the movement of people, goods, services and capital' (*ibid.*, p. 199) were to be removed – was viewed, or more to the point had become viewed, as 'an important intermediate step towards full EC membership for those [EFTA] countries [wishing] to join the EC' (Eurostat, 1994, Preface).

Indeed, several EFTA member governments decided to apply for membership of, what was still only, the European Community concurrently with engaging in the process of negotiating, agreeing and creating the EEA. Austria applied to join the Community in June 1989, as did Sweden in July 1991, Finland in March 1992, and Norway in November 1992. Switzerland's government lodged an application to join the EU in May 1992, but this was subsequently suspended following a referendum in December 1992 when voters rejected the EEA Agreement (*ibid.*, pp. 197–9), leaving Switzerland as a member of EFTA but not of the EEA, which by then had been in effect transposed into the *intermediate* – in the sense of the *preparatory* (Eurostat, 1994, Preface) – organisation between non-membership and full membership of the Community. In June 1994, Austria, Finland, Sweden and Norway signed Treaties of Accession to what had now become (since 1 November 1993) the European Union; and subsequently on 1 January 1995, Austria, Finland and Sweden (but not Norway) joined the EU,[5] leaving Iceland, Liechtenstein, Norway and Switzerland as the remaining four members of EFTA. Switzerland, the government of 'which signed the original [EEA Agreement] but did not ratify it, has [acquired] observer status' in the EEA (Drost, 1995, p. 196).[6]

Drost accounts for the timing and the surge of applications from EFTA members to join the Community/Union in terms of the combination of two events. What accelerated the moves by EFTA members 'to seek full EC membership' (*ibid.*, p. 199) was (i) 'the establishment of the EEA – which in effect realized EFTA's original objective', that 'of creating a single market including all the countries of Western Europe'; and (ii) the 'collapse of communist rule in Eastern Europe' (*ibid.*, p. 199). In line with its original, or as Drost puts it 'ultimate' (*ibid.*, p. 199), objective, the 'last restriction on free trade in industrial goods between the two blocs was removed [as long ago as] January 1984' (*ibid.*, p. 199; see also Pedersen, 1992). In April 1984, 'EFTA and the EC agreed on general guidelines for developing the relationship between them, including closer cooperation in transport, agriculture, fisheries, energy, economic and monetary policy, telecommunications, information technology and other fields' (Drost, 1995, p. 199). However, there were restraints on the extent and types of co-operation that could be forged between EFTA and the EU. In particular, '[c]loser political cooperation was not possible because several EFTA members were committed to neutrality' (*ibid.*, p. 199) during the Cold War era (see Joll, 1990, Chapter 15). Drost elaborates:

> The call for the creation of a 'European economic space' was first issued by EFTA leaders at a summit meeting in March 1989, which had been called to discuss the implications of the plans by the then European Community (EC) to establish a single internal market by the end of 1992 [see also Pedersen, 1992]. The EFTA countries would or could not consider full EC membership at this time because they were politically and militarily neutral, but they did desire closer economic cooperation so as not to lose out on the benefits expected from the single market [see also Wallace and Wessels, 1992]. The two organisations began discussions in June 1990 [. . .]. [But, the] collapse of communism in Eastern Europe and the end of the Cold War around this time created a new geo-political situation in Europe, and closer political cooperation with the EC now became possible or attractive for the previously neutral countries [of Austria, Finland, Sweden and Switzerland].   (Drost, 1995, p. 197)

Freed from the constraints of the Cold War era, one manifestation of which had been a firm commitment on the part of several European (among other) governments not to align themselves with either of the two superpowers but instead to remain firmly neutral (see Axford, 1995, pp. 180–1; Joll, 1990, Chapter 15; Keatinge, 1996), the European Economic Area (as signalled in October 1991 when a draft agreement [. . .] was initialled) was suddenly transformed from being a politically acceptable alternative to full membership of the EU into an 'intermediate step towards full EC membership' (Eurostat, 1994, Preface). The EEA became an *interlocutor* – a provisional and preparatory location – both (i) between the EU and another organisation (i.e. EFTA); and connectedly, (ii) between EU membership and EU non-membership. Essentially, the EEA's purpose, or 'function', was amended in response to the implications and ramifications of the abrupt conclusion of the Cold War and collapse of the Soviet empire. It suddenly became politically more acceptable, permissible and even desirable for Cold War neutral countries to align themselves with, what had been within the Cold War bipolar global system, an organisation with both its economic and its political-cum-military feet firmly planted within the US-led, western camp. Apart from anything else, eleven of the twelve Member States of the European Community were members of the North Atlantic Treaty Organisation (NATO), the exception being Ireland. At the end of the Cold War, NATO's sixteen members were Belgium, Canada, Denmark, France, West Germany, Greece, Iceland, Italy, Luxembourg, the Netherlands, Norway, Portugal, Spain, Turkey, the United Kingdom and the United States – although, in '1966 France, acting on a pledge first made by President de Gaulle in 1959, withdrew from the integrated military structure on the grounds that it could not support a defence system that deprived it of sovereignty over its own armed forces' (Drost, 1995, p. 442; see also Urwin, 1992, Chapter 2; and Perry, 1976, Chapter 18):

> France is planning to step up negotiations with the US on reform of Nato, which a new Franco-German defence document hails as the key to European defence [. . .]. [It] appears [. . .] essential that France reaches agreement with the US at [the July 1997] Nato summit meeting on Europeanising the Atlantic alliance. Paris has set this as its price for rejoining the Nato integrated military command it quit in 1966. But Mr Chirac's bid to put Europeans in charge of Nato's regional commands has so far foundered on steadfast US refusal to surrender control of the US Sixth Fleet in the Mediterranean. (Buchan, 27 January 1997)

Similarly, as reported by Drost writing in 1994, Iceland (which has no armed forces) and Spain (which joined NATO in May 1982) 'do not participate in the integrated military command structure' (Drost, 1995, p. 441): the 'Spanish government's rhetoric in the field of defence organization is pragmatic, seeking a formula to participate fully in European security, without formally modifying its mode of integration into NATO' (Barbé, 1996, p. 120). As Drost outlines:

[The] North Atlantic Treaty Organization (NATO) [is an] [i]ntergovernmental organization [...] founded in 1949 as a military and political alliance of Western European countries, the United States and Canada as a counterweight to the Soviet Union and its allies, which formed the Warsaw Pact in 1955. Providing for the collective defence of its member states, it operates an integrated military structure under centralized control and command.

(Drost, 1995, p. 440; see also Archer, 1990; Joll, 1990, Chapter 15; Perry, 1976, Chapters 17–19; Rees, 1993; Waites, 1995, Sections 2 and 3)

Drost adds that, however, following 'the collapse of communism in 1989 and the dissolution of the Warsaw Pact in 1991', NATO now 'sees itself as – and is widely seen as – a key player in the construction of a new pan-European security system. To this end it is strengthening [its] ties with other intergovernmental organizations such as the Conference on Security and Cooperation in Europe (CSCE)' – which in December 1994 became the Organisation for Security and Co-operation in Europe (OSCE) – 'and the Western European Union (WEU), and [is] developing cooperation with its former adversaries' (Drost, 1995, pp. 440–1) in central and eastern Europe. Indeed, NATO has plainly flagged its 'plans to expand the alliance to states in central Europe [...]. The most likely candidates [for membership being] Poland, Hungary and the Czech Republic. Slovenia also appears to be a front runner [...]. Bowing to fierce Russian objections, Nato will not include Estonia, Latvia and Lithuania in the first phase of the enlargement' (Palmer, 14 January 1997). As well as having selected its most favoured countries for admission, by December 1996 NATO had decided on the date of the first phase of enlargement:

Invitations to Central and East European states to join the Nato alliance will be issued at a summit meeting in Madrid on 8–9 July [1997], Nato foreign ministers announced in Brussels yesterday [10 December 1996]. Poland, the Czech Republic and Hungary are the most likely countries to be in the first wave to join Nato on or before its 50th anniversary in April 1999. Slovenia and Romania are also candidates, though the former is the more likely, as it forms a land bridge between Italy and Hungary.

(Bellamy, 11 December 1996)

In anticipation of the 10 December NATO foreign ministers meeting, Lionel Barber assessed the relationship between NATO and the European Union, especially in view their overlapping approaches to 'eastward expansion' (Clark and Freeland, 22 February 1997) following the end of the Cold War:

now that the Cold War is over, the EU and Nato have grasped that their civil and military missions are no longer so far apart. Their enemy is no longer a Soviet tank column racing through the Fulda gap [east of Kassel in what was West Germany]. The enemy is political instability in central and eastern Europe, the territory running from the Baltics to the Balkans where two wars started this century. Nato and the EU have promised to open their doors to the central and [eastern] European countries [...]. The challenge [being] to manage the twin enlargements in a manner which reassures the Russians without handing them a veto or a new sphere of influence [...]. So far, no one has come up with a satisfactory answer, but most recognise that the EU and Nato would be ill-advised to pursue enlargement without taking due account of each other's plans and thinking. Which [explains] the incipient dialogue. The push comes form the US [...]. One driving force in Brussels is [...] the Transatlantic Policy Network (TPN), a Brussels and Washington-based group of politicians, businessmen and academics set up [...] to cement US–EU ties in the post-Cold War era. (Barber, 9 December 1996)

However, the search for the 'satisfactory answer', as Barber puts it, to the issue of (in our terms) pan-European geo-political management, or governance, from the EU side has not been left to the TPN. The EU itself has been approaching the question through the development of its 'common foreign and security policy' (CFSP) in conjunction with its plans for the Western European Union (WEU) (see Hill, 1996; Nørgaard *et al.*, 1993; Rees, 1993; Regelsberger and Wessels, 1996; Krenzler and Schomaker, 1996; van den Broek, 1996). As Borchardt points out, while the European Community 'forms the core of the "European Union" established on 1 November 1993 with the entry into force of the Maastricht Treaty' (Borchardt, 1995, p. 8), there are altogether 'three pillars of the European Union' (*ibid.*, p. 59; see also *ibid.*, p. 207), the other two pillars being 'the common foreign and security policy' (*ibid.*, pp. 60–1) (CFSP) and co-operation in 'justice and home affairs' (*ibid.*, pp. 62–3; see *ibid.*, p. 207) (CJHA). Borchardt clarifies the CFSP (as laid down in the provisions under Title V of the Treaty on European Union) as follows:

In the Treaty on European Union the Heads of State or Government agreed to pursue the gradual development of a common foreign and security policy, centred on [such] goals [as] safeguarding the [...] independence of the European Union; strengthening the security of the Union and its Member States; [...] strengthening international security, in accordance with the principles of [...] the Conference on Security and Cooperation in Europe [...]; [and] developing and consolidating democracy and the rule of law and ensuring respect for human rights and fundamental freedoms [...]. The common security policy relies on the structures of the Western European Union (WEU). The WEU is regarded as an integral part of the European Union's development. Its task is to elaborate and implement decisions and actions of the Union that have defence implications. In a special declaration on the role of the WEU and its relationship with the EU and NATO [Article J.4], the [...] member states of the EU that are also members of the WEU [its founding members] (Belgium, France, Germany, Italy, Luxembourg, the Netherlands, Portugal and the United Kingdom) of 1955; Spain which joined in November 1988; and Greece, which 'joined the WEU officially on 6 April 1995' [(Tsakaloyannis, 1996, p. 203)] agreed a programme of future cooperation. The objective [being] to build up the WEU in stages as the defence component of the EU, and [thereby] to strengthen the European pillar of the Atlantic Alliance [NATO]. (Borchardt, 1995, pp. 60–1)

Whereas the 'the core of the EU, the EC, is a "supranational" organization, i.e. one to which the member states have transferred specified legislative and executive powers and whose decisions are binding on them and their citizens', the 'CFSP and CJHA are forms of intergovernmental cooperation, in which the member states retain full sovereign rights, and hence decision making is by unanimity' (Drost, 1995, p. 207).

Likewise, the Western European Union is an intergovernmental organisation (*ibid.*, p. 635), having been founded in 1955 by the Benelux countries, France, Italy, the United Kingdom and West Germany 'with wide-ranging ambitions' (*ibid.*, p. 635), which were subsequently narrowed when the 'organization was reactivated in 1984 in response to a growing desire among Western European governments to cooperate more closely on defence policy and arms procurement. In recent years', and especially since the end of the Cold War, as Drost summarises, 'the WEU's role has been redefined as a "bridge" between the European Union (EU) and the North Atlantic Treaty Organization (NATO) and an "integral component" of the European integration process' (*ibid.*, pp. 635–6). It is to this end that the Treaty on European Union 'states that "the objective is to build up the WEU as the defence component of the European Union" and "to develop the WEU as a means to strengthen the European pillar of the Atlantic Alliance" [Article J. 4]' (*ibid.*, p. 636).

Although the WEU has fifteen members, only Belgium, France, Germany, Greece (1995), Italy, Luxembourg, the Netherlands, Portugal, Spain (1988) and the United Kingdom are full members; Iceland, Norway and Turkey are associate members, having joined in this capacity in November 1992. Also in November 1992, however, Denmark and Ireland became attached as observer members (*ibid.*, p. 636; see also Heurlin, 1996; and Keatinge, 1996) – although Keatinge reports that the Irish government 'agreed that the Minister of Foreign Affairs would attend WEU meetings on 19 and 30 September [1991] as an observer' during the 'attempt to find a peaceful resolution to the [Yugoslavia] conflict' (Keatinge, 1996, p. 217); and, moreover, in 'May 1994 nine former communist states in Central and Eastern Europe signed

cooperation agreements with the WEU and became "associate partners" '
(Drost, 1995, pp. 636–7).

What would have made it easier for Ireland (the only one of the EU's
twelve Member States prior to the Union's enlargement of 1 January 1995
not to have been a NATO member), a Cold War neutral country – albeit in
something of a qualified manner (see Keatinge, 1996, pp. 208–16) – to
become involved in the WEU was the end of the Cold War and so the
advent of 'a new European order' (*ibid.*, pp. 214–16), and indeed of, in our
terms, the new world order; what would have been encouraging was the
signing in May 1994 of the co-operation agreements with countries of the
former Eastern bloc, mirroring their prospective entry into the European
Union; what would have made it 'pragmatic' was the issue of responding to
and 'coping with [the] disorder' which 'the Twelve' suddenly found on
their doorstep, by virtue of especially 'the Yugoslav civil war' (*ibid.*, p.
217); but what might have made it seem necessary is the EU's development
of a common foreign and security policy (CFSP) in conjunction with its
plans for the Western European Union (WEU) as outlined in the Treaty
on European Union, a treaty to which after all Ireland was a signatory,
notwithstanding what can be interpreted as the treaty's opt-out clause:

> When it came to the final phase of the negotiations [leading to the Treaty
> on European Union], Ireland could balance its general commitment that
> the Common Foreign and Security Policy (CFSP) should include 'all
> questions related to the security of the Union' with the fact that commit-
> ment to defence remained an aspiration, to be returned to at a further
> intergovernmental conference in 1996. Furthermore, although Ireland
> agreed to accede to WEU observer status on a permanent basis following
> ratification of the treaty, the latter's provisions on security, Article J.4,
> includes the somewhat opaque qualification that the policy of the Union
> 'shall not prejudice the specific character of the security and defence policy
> of certain Member States'. (Keatinge, 1996, p. 218)

The issue of further developing the CFSP is firmly on the EU's 1996–7
intergovernmental conference agenda, which got underway in Turin on 29
March 1996 for the purpose of reviewing the Maastricht Treaty on European
Union, as signalled in the *Commission Report for the Reflection Group:
Intergovernmental Conference 1996*).[7] It is possible that through the IGC's
negotiations and final agreement, the CFSP pillar of the Union will be
strengthened by bringing it into the supranational framework which (as we
have noted) the Treaty on European Union established as being, at least so
far, exclusive to the EU's core – to, that is, the (economic) European Community. This would happen if qualified majority voting, the Maastricht
Treaty 'provisions for [which] were explicitly excluded from defence-related

issues' (Keatinge, 1996, p. 218), were to be extended to the CFSP. As explained by Julie Wolf:

> At the moment, qualified majority voting (QMV) applies to laws covering agriculture, health and safety, foreign trade, transport and most environmental matters. It has been used to establish the single market [...]. Under QMV a proposal needs just over 70 per cent of the total votes allocated to EU member states to become law. [The] big countries [judged in terms of population] have more votes than smaller ones [...]. Germany, Belgium, [the] Netherlands, Luxembourg and a number of other member states want to see majority voting extended to foreign policy matters, although opinions vary greatly on the degree to which this should be done [...]. Defence [...] poses a problem for neutral countries such as Ireland, Austria, Sweden and Finland. They do not belong to any military alliance, and might not want to be committed to a common EU policy.   (Wolf, 26 March 1996)

As the planned (summer of 1997, in Amsterdam) completion of the IGC drew near, it was revealed that a strong push towards a supranational CFSP was imminent:

> France and Germany are to press on with their attempts to whittle away the national veto in the European Union by tabling joint proposals [...] on greater majority voting on foreign and security policy in the EU. After talks in Bonn [on 3 March 1997] the German foreign minister [...] and his French counterpart [...] announced they wanted to extend majority voting in [these] policy areas and to embark on 'institutional reform' of the EU to pave the way for negotiations on expansion into eastern Europe [in 1998]. [The] joint proposals [are] to be unveiled [on 10 March 1997] at a meeting of the intergovernmental conference [...]. France and Germany, opposed by Britain, agree that an EU expanded into eastern Europe will be paralysed unless decision-making is streamlined and consensus yields to majority voting.   (Traynor, 4 March 1997)

As indicated on the same day as the meeting of the German and French foreign ministers, the UK supported the eastward expansion of the EU: the 'enlargement of Nato into eastern Europe should be accompanied by an expansion of the European Union to include former Warsaw Pact states, Michael Portillo, the Defence Secretary, said [on 3 March 1997] in Washington' (Walker, 4 March 1997). On the other hand, also on 3 March, back in Europe, the UK's Foreign Secretary, Malcolm Rifkind, 'urged the European Union to [resist] calls for increased majority voting [even though] the prospects for changing minds in Paris and Bonn seem poor' (Black, 4 March 1997; see also Elliott and Milner, 8 March 1997).

Perhaps the UK can look forward to sympathy and support from the traditional neutral countries of Austria, Finland, Ireland and Sweden: the neutral four. Fortunately, each of these Member States is in a position to stand firm and resist any attempt to extend supranational procedures into the CFSP, and moreover to do so even by itself. This is because each of them has a veto over any proposed final treaty resulting from the 1996–7 IGC. That is, all new treaties or treaty amendments are necessarily approved by the European Council (Borchardt, 1995, p. 30; Shaw, 1996, pp. 121–2); and are necessarily approved in this particular forum on the basis of unanimity rather than QMV. As Shaw summarises:

> The most prominent and most powerful form of intergovernmental co-operation within the EU is the European Council. The practice of summit meetings between the leaders of the Member States has long existed. Regular meetings have occurred since 1974, and the European Council was finally formalised in Article 2 of the [Single European Act], now superceded by Article D [of the Treaty on European Union]. This provides that the European Council should meet at least twice a year and that it should be attended not only by the Heads of State or Government, assisted by their Foreign Ministers, but also by the President of the Commission and one other Commissioner. It is given the task of providing the EU with 'the necessary impetus for its development' and of defining 'the general political guidelines thereof' [. . .]. The European Council has remained formally outside the structures of the European Community (i.e. the supranational pillar), not subject to the control of the Court of Justice. Conversely it has no [formal, constitutionally based] legal power to act in pursuance of the Community's objectives or power of decision.
>
> (Shaw, 1996, pp. 121–2)

The European Council is the institutionalised mechanism through which the EU's basic treaties and treaty amendments are finally decided in an inter-governmental, and so unanimous, fashion. No amendment to the Treaty on European Union, including any entailing the development of the CFSP, can go ahead without the approval of all current Member States, including Austria, Finland, Ireland, Sweden and the United Kingdom.

In spite of this, however, there was no guarantee that in any final vote the neutral four would withhold their approval from a treaty designed to extend QMV to CFSP matters and decision-making; to extend, that is, 'decisional supranationalism' (rather than 'normative supranationalism', which 'concerns the authority of the Court of Justice to give binding [. . .] rulings [. . .], and to fashion a legal system in which EC law takes precedence over national law' (Shaw, 1996, pp. 13–14)) to the CFSP pillar; and so to (further) compromise their 'neutrality'.

Keatinge assesses the dilemma facing Ireland and the other 'neutral' Member States during the 1996–7 IGC negotiations over the future development of the CFSP:

Irish politicians can no longer rely solely on the mantra of 'neutrality' to avoid taking positions. Ireland's adaption to the exigencies of the post-Cold war international system is [...] underway. [There is] the possibility that a future negotiation [will] involve Ireland in a common defence policy. The [IGC] in 1996 [is] just such a negotiation, but the content of a 'common defence policy' is not self-evident; it remains to be negotiated. The first preference of an Irish government may well be a minimalist approach, [...] leaving a mutual assistance guarantee – the Rubicon of Irish neutrality – for the ultimate stage of security integration, a 'common defence'. [...] Ireland might find partners in procrastination, now that Austria, Finland and Sweden are member states and in no hurry to abandon the last vestiges of their neutrality. A more threatening security environment, on the other hand, might persuade the latter states, which are potentially more exposed than Ireland to security threats, to undertake alliance commitments; it would also presumably increase incentives to reinforce such commitments by those countries which had long since made them. If Ireland were isolated in the [IGC] in this way, it could prove very difficult to avoid a linkage between security and economic interests [...]. The price of continuing solidarity in the economic sphere might have to be paid by subscribing to mutual assistance guarantees; if so, Ireland would be making the most significant foreign policy change since joining the EC more than twenty years ago [...]. The hallmark of the Irish approach to the future of the CFSP nevertheless remains one of caution and gradualism [...]. The reservations on defence obligations puts Ireland near the minimalist end of the spectrum [...]. Yet the increasing uncertainties associated with the post-Cold War international system represent a very different setting from that prevailing ten years ago, and the traditional basis of Irish foreign policy [...] may be subjected to a more fundamental adaption than at any time since 'Europe' became the focus of Ireland's external relations.   (Keatinge, 1996, pp. 221–3)

Keatinge acknowledges that all of the EU's 'neutral countries', those Member States that still do not belong to either the WEU (Ireland's observer status aside) or NATO, may agree to extending a degree of QMV, and so of supranational decision-making competence, authority and sovereignty, to the CFSP, albeit at the minimalist end of the spectrum. The proposals which emerged from the Bonn meeting between the German and French foreign ministers on 3 March 1997 for placing before the IGC on 10 March can be categorised as 'minimalist':

Both countries were agreed [...] that fundamental strategic decisions on EU foreign and security issues should be taken by consensus in the European Council. Subsequent action to implement the strategic decisions, however, should be subject to qualified majority voting.   (Traynor, 4 March 1997)

The neutral four may be persuaded to go along with this parsimonious encroachment on their sovereignty and neutrality, encouraged by further considerations, including, to paraphrase Keatinge, the difficulty of avoiding the linkage between security and economic interests. The neutral four may come to accept that the price of continuing solidarity in the economic sphere might have to come at the cost of subscribing to mutual security guarantees, or at least by agreeing for the time being to a 'minimalist' extension of QMV and so supranational decision-making and unity into the CFSP. At the same time, this does not necessarily mean that any such acceptance would be reluctantly conceded under duress and due to coercion. Any extension of supranational decision-making to the CFSP could simply reflect a 'realist' assessment (see Miall, 1993, Chapter 2; and Nelsen and Stubb, 1994, Part 3) on the part not just of the neutral four but of the EU's Member States in general that their economic objectives, interests and unity, on the one hand, and their security-cum-political objectives, interests and unity, on the other, are indeed unavoidably linked, interwoven and intimately interdependent. It could simply reflect a realisation that their economic objectives are best pursued by accepting a degree of CFSP supranational decision-making and unity, especially in view of the imperatives (Laffan, 1996) stemming from the *external* conditions in post-Cold War central and eastern Europe: imperatives and conditions which, after all, the Member States in general have no doubt warrant the EU's eastward expansion and intervention – the EU's *eastern* presence, management and governance.

Shortly after the end of the Cold War, the European Commission published its view of *Europe in a Changing World*, and under the heading 'The Community in the new world order' the Commission revealed:

> One fundamental principle lies behind the Community's policies towards the outside: enlightened self-interest. The Community's own economic well-being depends on a liberal, multilateral world economic order as well as on the welfare of its partners, particularly [. . .] its eastern neighbours [. . .].
>
> (European Commission, *Europe in a Changing World*, 1993, p. 6)

But, the Commission laments:

> The unique nature of the Community – more than an intergovernmental organization but less than a sovereign State – makes its international role [. . .] difficult. [I]ts basic constitution, the Treaty of Rome, [has given] the Community wide economic powers but few political ones [. . .]. The special nature of the Community and the way responsibilities on some external issues are shared between it and Member States can cause problems for the Community and its partners [. . .]. Certain areas like defence have hitherto lain outside the competence of the Community altogether. Despite its shortcomings and its limited ability to intervene in some crisis situations

like the war in the former Yugoslavia, [o]utside events and the creation of
new internal structures are pushing the Community to assume the fuller
role in world affairs which is commensurate with its economic weight [...].
                                                                    (*ibid.*, pp. 5–6).

Gradually, in a manner which is consistent with the 'pragmatic position [...]
taken by so-called *neo-functionalists* who [advocate an] incremental and
piecemeal approach to European integration' (Shaw, 1996, p. 12; see also
Nelsen and Stubb, 1994, Parts 2 and 4):

> Over the years, the Community has grown from a commercial and eco-
> nomic power to become a political power as well. EC Member States [...]
> started coordinating their national foreign policies from 1970 onwards
> [and] the Community took [a] big step towards a greater world role with
> the creation in the Maastricht Treaty on European Union of a common
> foreign and security policy (CFSP).
> (European Commission, *Europe in a Changing World*, 1993, p. 4).

This is a sign of how in an incremental fashion, the Community is gaining 'a
political role in keeping with its growing economic importance' within Europe and the global system (*ibid.*, p. 4). Today, the 'Community, along with
the United States and Japan, represents one of the three pillars on which the
global system of pluralist democracy and market economy is built. Solutions
to specific international economic and [...] political problems will depend
[above all on the approaches of these] three' (*ibid.*, p. 4), the Commission
argued. In effect:

> the European Community has become a major actor in world affairs. It
> has been propelled into this position by external and internal factors.
> The collapse of communism in the former Soviet Union and in Central
> and Eastern Europe presents the Community with new responsibilities
> on its own doorstep. The pace of economic and political change in
> other regions of the globe also calls for rapid responses. [A] new
> world order is emerging. But it still has to be defined. Clearly the
> Community is destined to become one of its principal actors. The
> disappearance of one of the two super-powers which controlled the global
> balance of power is leading to a multi-polar world and to new relation-
> ships among nations and regions. Within Europe itself, questions of
> security and immigration are being posed in new ways [see Close, 1995;
> Collinson, 1994; Wrench and Solomos, 1993]. At the same time the
> globalization of the economy is creating a state of interdependence and a
> growing realization that trade problems need to be solved wherever poss-
> ible in multilateral frameworks [such as through the World Trade Organ-
> isation].   (*ibid.*, pp. 4–6)

What is more, there is a growing realisation that economic problems and progress are dependent upon political-cum-security problems and progress, perhaps especially under the conditions, imperatives and exigencies which characterise and distinguish the post-Cold War new world order and highly interdependent global system that, none the less, is largely constructed around, shaped and determined by the three main pillars (centres of global power). In accordance with this:

> As [post-Cold War] East-West *détente* strengthened, the [...] Member States of the Community who belong to the Western European Union (WEU) have used this forum to strengthen their defence cooperation. So as to reinforce their ties in the face of a shift in NATO priorities, the United States and the Community adopted in November 1990 a Declaration on EU–US relations which created, *inter alia*, a new institutional framework for mutual consultation.   (*ibid.*, p. 6)

This event reflects the way in which the demise of the 'confrontational relationship [between] the Warsaw Pact and NATO' has thrown up 'new challenges to which the Community is responding. It is developing a variety of new instruments – a new generation of "Europe" agreements with its eastern neighbours, new types of cooperation with the Republics of the former Soviet Union,' and so on (*ibid.*, p. 6).

The aforementioned statement by the UK's Defence Secretary, Michael Portillo, on 3 March 1997 during his visit to Washington (Walker, 4 March 1997) can readily be interpreted as endorsing the argument that, to paraphrase Lionel Barber (9 December 1996), now that the Cold War is over the EU and NATO have acquired a common enemy – the political instability or 'disorder' (Tsakaloyannis, 1996; Keatinge, 1996) problem and threat posed by central and eastern Europe, the 'territory running from the Baltics to the Balkans'. This sense of an instability or 'disorder' – and so geo-political management (governance) – problem is not confined to a few politicians and political commentators: it is far more widespread. Furthermore, there is a widely held perception that the problem is far from being restricted only to 'Eastern Europe': to those parts of Europe which until the end of the Cold War were contained and restrained within the Soviet empire; that, instead, the problem is *global* in its dimensions and proportions: a problem of *global governance* in a *globalised* NWO.

Thus, Barrie Axford in addressing the issue of 'the geopolitics of the global system', and in this context examining 'the implications of [the post-Cold War] multipolar world for global stability and change' for 'the question of global governance' (Axford, 1995, p. 180), tells us that 'the ending of the Cold War and the demise of the global institution of bipolarity', an 'obvious and momentous shift in world politics' (*ibid.*, p. 180), has lent itself to a 'sense of growing systemic disorder' and 'the idea of a "new world disorder"' (*ibid.*, p. 179; see Jowitt, 1992; Dobbs-Higginson, 1994). This idea has surfaced in the writings of 'those authors who have spoken with almost biblical gravity of the "epochal" changes now in train across the world'. Some writers have identified ' "megatrends" which are transforming the global system', and some who have used 'language [which] is full of apocalyptical imagery' (Axford, 1995, p. 195): the 'themes of disorder, uncertainty and transformation run through these accounts, which differ only on whether the changes are to be feared or celebrated' (*ibid.*, p. 195).

Axford suggests that 'the sheer speed of systemic change [...] in the former Soviet Union', for example, may have created a ' "vacuum of meaning" [...], despite the frantic attempts to reconstruct identities around the marketization of those societies (Stark, 1992; Jowitt, 1992)' (*ibid.*, p. 197; see also Jeffries, 1993). Axford canvasses a degree of caution, however:

> Jowitt talks about the lack of 'form' in such 'genesis environments', where the removal of the dominant institution of the socialist state has both left a legitimation gap and opened up the prospect of a completely new beginning (Offe, 1991). Stark, however, cautions against a tendency to treat all aspects of the situation as new, seeing in the fall of communism not the collapse of a single monolithic identity but the further transformation of scripts, which were already negotiated and ambiguous, by actors accustomed to manage uncertainty through improvising on established routines.
>
> (Axford, 1995, pp. 197–8)

While the expression here renders the message somewhat obscure, the essence of the argument is perhaps reflected in the use of the phrase 'further transformation'; and is perhaps inferred when Axford goes on to suggest that any 'destructive effects of the fall of communism' should be viewed in the context of 'the processes of systemic transformation in general' (*ibid.*, p. 198) – in the context, that is, of more inclusive spatial (geo-political) and temporal (socio-historical) processes. For Axford, the 'dramatic changes and growing disorder, notably in the period since the mid 1980s' (*ibid.*, p. 3), need to be viewed in relation to 'global trends and processes, which are ordered [sic] increasingly without constraint of place or time' (*ibid.*, p. 3); in relation to 'the growing pace and intensity of globalized life' (*ibid.*, p. 4); in relation to 'globalization', which following Robertson (1992), can be interpreted as 'the "processes by which the world is being made into a single place with systemic qualities" ' (*ibid.*, p. 5). Or, that is:

> the term 'globalization' refers to those processes which are serving to compress the world in David Harvey's sense (1989), and thus help fashion a single global space. The richness and diversity of various 'transnational practices' (Sklair, 1991), which are serving to broaden and deepen the

extent of global interconnections between individuals or groups, are seen in many areas of life.   (Axford, 1995, p. 5; see also pp. 25–32)

One area of life in which transnational practices are increasingly evident as an aspect of the overall globalisation process is that covered by the economic sphere of the global system; or, that is, in the *global economy* (see Axford, 1995, Chapter 4; Ohmae, 1990, 1995; Waters, 1995). Significantly within this sphere, there is the spread of transnational corporations (TNCs, as distinct from multinational corporations (MNCs) – see Axford, 1995, Chapter 4; Waters, 1995, Chapters 2 and 4). But for us, another area of life in which transnational practices are on the increase is in the political sphere of the global system. In this sphere, transnational practices assume the form of existing, emerging or embryonic supranational regional regimes (SRRs) – a manifestation of transnational practices which both reflects and, in turn, reinforces the overall globalisation process. Perhaps one way of viewing SRRs is that they are the global political-sphere equivalent to the global economic-sphere TNCs; and perhaps it makes sense to interpret the growth of SRRs as being accountable to some extent in terms of the concurrent growth of TNCs. In this regard it is pertinent to note, as Axford does:

> Truly transnational actors [. . .] are still few and far between, and the ties that bind even the biggest corporations to particular nation-states remain strong. According to Yaio-Su Hu (1992), only a very few companies, like Shell, Unilever, Nestlé, ABB and ICI, can be defined as real transnationals.   (Axford, 1995, p. 97)

Likewise, truly supranational actors are still 'few and far between', the most advanced and even only clear-cut example still being the European Community (within the European Union). However, the paucity of SRRs may well be short-lived, as the proposed extension of supranational decision-making to the CFSP within the EU may be taken to signal.

Axford argues:

> it is possible to conceive of a global system, or rather of relations between [. . .] global scripts, actors and processes and those operating at lower levels of generality, which display features of *systemness* and thus offer a frame of reference that permits us to conceive of the world as a single place. The notion of global 'systemness' is crucial to [. . .] recognizing [. . .] that the disorder fed through global processes produces disorder in localities and among local subjects, [as well as] vice-versa [. . .].   (Axford, 1995, p. 6)

Axford then makes a crucial analytical assumption about 'the processes which are reproducing and transforming the structures of global *systemness*'; about the 'constitution [and presumably re-constitution] of the global system' (*ibid.*, p. 1); and so about the overall process of globalisation. This assumption concerns 'the relationship between globalization and modernity', the assumption being that globalisation can be identified or equated with 'modernization', and more specifically with *Western* modernisation (*ibid.*, p. 23; see Woodiwiss, 1996). Thus, Axford asserts, it 'is quite true that the main institutions of Western modernity – industrialism, capitalism and the nation-state – have become truly global', citing Anthony McGrew's examination of 'A global society?' (1992) in his support (cf., Giddens, 1991a; Woodiwiss, 1996). In other words, the global system and the process of globalisation are 'built around the great themes of Western modernity' (Axford, 1995, p. 1), these themes being: 'the institutional forms of *market capitalism*'; '*industrialism*'; 'the territorial *nation-state*'; 'the *international system of [nation-] states*'; and 'the whole corpus of *cultural and philosophical knowledge* which provides the underpinning of the "Western cultural account" [Meyer *et al.*, 1987, p. 29]' (Axford, 1995, p. 2). Axford otherwise refers to these 'great themes of Western modernity' as the 'axial features of globalization' (*ibid.*, p. 28), while clearly regarding one of these axes as the primary source of and driving force behind the other main features, the general character and the overall trajectory of the modern global system:

> the historical origins of the global system [lie in] mercantilist and then capitalist expansion [...]. During the early phase of capitalist expansion, which in Europe [...] may be traced back to the thirteenth century, aspects of earlier, transnational arrangements and identities were eroded and replaced by the nascent national communities and state-like forms of the modern period (Wallerstein, 1974; Abu-Lughod, 1989, 1991) [...]. The [subsequent] global expansion of capitalist, market-driven economic activity has produced a truly world-wide economy, now expanding directly into the old Soviet empire and established in newly dynamic areas like southern China. To all intents there is a 'borderless world' in financial markets and in foreign direct investment (FDI) [...] (Porter, 1990; Ohmae, 1990). [I]t is clear that these and other broadly economic processes are having a significant impact upon the second institutional component of globalization, namely the nation-state [...]. The nation-states are still seen as the principal actors in [the world political] order, but it must now include a plethora of supra-state and non-state transnational actors and networks of actors. [Moreover, recently, in] the wake of the Cold War, [and so] since the demise of the Soviet Union as a global superpower and the emergence of post-communist regimes within its former sphere of influence [...] 'new', less manageable conflicts have broken out in the vacuum caused by the ending of superpower geopolitics. Signs of a new global military order in a much more fluid, multipolar world are visible [...], but the role of global peacekeepers or brokers of human rights sits uneasily on bodies like the

United Nations (UN) or the European Union (EU) [...]. These issues [are about] global governance [...].   (Axford, 1995, pp. 28–31)

For us, the part played by nation-states in the post-Cold War NWO (*ibid.*, Chapter 7) is increasingly problematic, making the assertion that nation-states are still the principal actors in the global political order more and more questionable (cf. Mann, 1997). In our view, the European Union, as 'a new, fully institutionalized regional polity, with some of the attributes and core functions of stateness transferred to a supranational level' (Axford, 1995, p. 4), is the principal example of a 'plethora' of similar (existing, emerging or embryonic) regional polities, organisations or regimes which are undermining and replacing nation-states within the globalisation process, the global system and the process of global governance (global geo-political management).

The origins of SRRs lie again in Europe; and the main driving force is again 'capitalist, market-driven economic activity' (as Axford puts it). On the other hand, the seat of this driving force is no longer in Europe, nor for that matter in the west: in the Occident as distinct from the Orient. The modern, late-twentieth-century world may be 'a much more fluid, multipolar world' (Axford, 1995, p. 31), but the poles vary in size and strength: economically, politically and militarily; and judged specifically in economic terms, the tallest and sturdiest pole is now in the east: in, that is, East Asia (see Bowles and Maclean, 1996; Dixon, 1991; Dobbs-Higginson, 1994; Megarry, 1995; So and Chiu, 1995; Wilkinson, 1991). This feature of the post-Cold War NWO (distribution of power and associated configuration of global players) is one of the keys to making sense of the course which is being taken by regional regimes wherever they are evolving and in whatever manner they are evolving, including with whatever degree of supranational decision-making and unity they are aquiring. This feature means that the future development of SRRs will be increasingly shaped by that *market-driven economic activity* (Axford, 1995, p. 30) which is conducted within and from East Asia; and, moreover, which is conducted within and from East Asian SRRs, the harbinger of which in this region being the Association of South East Asian Nations (ASEAN) (see Bowles and Maclean, 1996; Close and Ohki-Close, 1996; Dixon, 1991).

Axford touches on this aspect of the NWO:

While modernity has supported a progressive globalization of human affairs (McGrew, 1992, p. 65), this is not to say either that globalizing tendencies or global 'visions' are unique to [western] modernity, or that these processes under modern conditions are homogenizing to the extent of producing a global totality [...]. But I do want to argue that globalization at its current phase is part of the radical transformation of Western modernity, making societal closure all but impossible, most clearly in economic matters, but increasingly in aspects of culture and politics [not to mention security].   (Axford, 1995, p. 24)

Thus, Axford refers to 'the globalizing trends' in terms of which the late-twentieth-century 'putative "transformation" ' of modernity is to be understood' (*ibid.*, p. 179):

> Most interpretations recognize that the transformation of modernity is a global reordering, in which the constitutive power of Western modernity is being reworked and 'dehegemonized', and the locus of economic power in the world is being shifted ever westwards [across the Atlantic; across the Pacific]. The dissolution of the communist version of modernity is sometimes taken as a quickener of the breakup of this global cultural hegemony and not an indication of its vitality (Wallerstein, 1991a, 1991c).   (Axford, 1995, p. 179)

While, on the one hand, the processes and pressures of globalisation and modernisation may be the key to understanding the 'dissolution of the communist version of modernity' and the ensuing local disorder within the former Eastern bloc, in central and eastern Europe and elsewhere; on the other hand, the demise of the Cold War old world order (*ibid.*, pp. 180–3), and so of the 'stable condition of bipolarity' (*ibid.*, p. 181), has infused considerable pace into the same processes, with notable consequences for the NWO distribution of global (economic, political and even military) power and its associated configuration of global players:

> In practical affairs, the major force of Euro-centred modernization has been vitiated in recent years, to the extent that Europe, the European Union in particular, is seen as losing out to the economic power of other trading blocs [for instance]. In one sene, this loss of centrality is the direct result of the successful and rapid modernization of other parts of the globe, of Western modernity globalized, but it is also the outcome of a conscious reversal of the 'power geometry' (Massey, 1991) of Western modernization, whereby the forces of globalization are indigenized, localized and 'played back' on their progenitors [. . .]. As such, the *single* global space turns out to be extraordinarily plural and the *totality* associated with the idea of the spread of modernity is shown to be remarkably fragile. For some social theorists these conditions suggest not modernity but postmodernity, an excess of contingency over order and the end of all grand narratives. Globalization now appears less as the handmaiden of totalizing modernization, and more as the convenor of disorder and global restructuration.
>
> (Axford, 1995, pp. 24–5; see Axford, 1995, Chapters 1, 2, 6 and 8; and Sarup, 1993)

Due to the confluence of the process of globalisation and the end of the Cold War (Meštrović, 1994) – mutually enhancing developments – there has been a perceived upsurge of political volatility, instability and disorder throughout the global system. The attendant geo-political management, or governance, problem appears to have been especially acute, however, in the central and eastern European portions (assuming that these include the trans-Caucus Mountain republics) of the old Soviet empire. The principal themes and points of Axford's account of the overall, long-term and enveloping process of globalisation and linked demise of the Soviet empire – and accompanying dissolution of the communist version of modernity (*ibid.*, p. 179), or cultural account (*ibid.*, p. 2), heralding the 'end of History' (*ibid.*, p. 159; see also *ibid.*, Chapter 6 and pp. 45–6; Fukuyama, 1991, 1992) – in so far as they apply to Europe have been otherwise expressed by Larry Elliott:

> [The] theory [was that the] end of the Cold War would usher in an era of peace, prosperity and cultural renaissance, yoked together by [...] a growing sense of pan-European consciousness. [...] Europe would be suffused with the spirit of a new Enlightenment. Eight years on, the vision of a rational, ordered Europe is still powerful, but its attainment looks further away than it did in 1989. The internecine struggle of the former Yugoslavia, a seemingly endless period of poor economic performance and a cultural cringe in the face of the hegemony of Hollywood, Walt Disney and Macdonald's have seen to that. There are two main reasons. First, it has proved to be hard to impose a top-down blueprint of ever-closer union [see the beginning of our Chapter 2] on post-modern societies which are splintering along cultural, ethnic, regional and national lines. More importantly the extent to which communism and the external threat posed by the Warsaw Pact acted as the glue which had held western Europe together between 1950 and 1989 was underestimated. (Elliott, 3 March 1997)

The view that the attempt to 'impose a top-down blueprint' in favour of an 'ever-closer union' in Europe would (notwithstanding the contribution made by, according to Elliott, the way 'European capitalism has become tighter and meaner in an attempt to emulate the Anglo-Saxon flexibility of the United States and the dynamism of the fast-growing Pacific Rim economies' – see Coffey, 1993; Richardson, 1996; Ugur, 1995; Waites, 1995) help 'undermine the social democratic settlement on which [...] the European Union was built' (Elliott, 3 March 1997; see also Bailey, 1992; Burrows and Mair, 1996; Hantrais, 1995; and Room, 1991) finds echoes in the UK Foreign Secretary's plea in his Paris speech of 3 March 1997 that further 'transfers of power from member states to EU institutions would undermine Europe's democratic legitimacy in the eyes of voters', leading to 'mounting popular alienation from the EU' (Black, 4 March 1997; cf., Lane and Ersson, 1996).

The argument that any top-down attempt to impose an ever-closer union on people who display considerable (and perhaps, in accordance with the process of globalisation, increasing) diversity and heterogeneity along cultural, ethnic, religious and national lines, finds support in the accounts and prognoses of such commentators as Stjepan Meštrović (see also Shelley and Winck's *Aspects of European Cultural Diversity*, 1995; Wilson and van der Dussen's *The History of the Idea of Europe*, 1995; and Zetterholm's *National Cultures and European Integration*, 1994a), as well as of various writers whose focus is on other regions of the global system, such as Endymion Wilkinson:

> In spite of the trend towards regional economic cooperation in other parts of the world, it is unlikely that a tightly organized trading bloc will emerge in the Asia Pacific region in the near future. The region is too large; its political systems, economies and cultures too heterogenous [...]. Like Germany in Europe, Japan is the major agent of peaceful change in its region, but unlike Germany, Japan has no [and is unlikely to have anything like a] European Community 'umbrella' to cover its growing regional influence.
>
> (Wilkinson, 1991, p. 27)

Julie Wolf has touched on the implications for the development of the European Union as a 'supranational regional polity' (Axford, 1995, p. 4), or as a 'supra-state' (*ibid.*, p. 30) – and thereby its role as a 'supra-territorial form of governance' (*ibid.*, pp. 131–2) – of the political volatility, instability and disorder in Eastern and Central Europe. She mentions how, in particular, the 'tragedy of the war in Bosnia showed that the EU was not good at handling a crisis on its doorstep. Many EU countries, and as we have seen the European Commission (*Europe in a Changing World*, 1993) believe that the key obstacle to European cooperation on foreign issues is the unanimity requirement' (Wolf, 26 March 1996).[8]

Wolf underlines and broadens her message by suggesting that 'in an increasingly global political and economic environment, EU countries gain more from "pooling their sovereignty" and acting together [because] the rest of the world pays more attention to a strong and united Europe' (Wolf, 26 March 1996). Wolf is echoing an argument which has been presented by various politicians in support of the 'pooling' of sovereignty:

> Sovereignty; is it enhanced or diminished by being shared? [For] Sir Leon Brittan [...] as one of the senior European commissioners in Brussels [...] Europe has enhanced not diminished Britain's sovereignty if one interprets the word as meaning the power to determine, or at least shape, events in which the country's interests have been deeply involved [...]. Would Britain, he asks, have had the same influence in negotiating with the US

over questions like information technology and, even more recently, financial services, if it spoke alone or alongside its European partners?

(Milner, 5 March 1997)

Similarly, and at about the same time, the Irish Ambassador in London,
Ted Barrington, 'told the *Observer*' that the ' "[Irish] experience of membership [of the EU] is that it enhances [Ireland's] sovereignty in a real sense, if
you define sovereignty as a capacity to [determine] your own destiny, by
being able to take decisions on huge issues, which affect the economic
welfare of the continent" ' (Kemp, 2 February 1997). Leaving aside the
issue of the questionable meaning being attached here to the term 'sovereignty', the pertinent point for present purposes is that, to paraphrase Wolf,
unity means strength, and unity depends upon nation-states 'pooling' their
sovereignty within, what we have labelled, supranational regional regimes.
This is the lesson of the Union's geo-political impotence in the face of the
Yugoslavian *débâcle*.

The advantages to be gained from supranational decision-making and unity
in performing the tasks associated with the CFSP pillar of the EU – those
tasks concerned with external relations and geo-political management and
with security and defence, or (what we will label) 'geo-political protection' –
especially since the advent of the post-Cold War historical era and so under
the conditions of the NWO, could be enough to persuade EU Member States
in general to further pool their sovereignty by extending QMV decision-
making to CFSP matters, and relatedly to become full members of the
Western European Union. As such, the Member States involved would simply
be opting to extend into the external relations, geo-political management and
geo-political protection sphere a development which is already well-advanced
in the economic sphere, that of supranational decision-making and unity. The
outcome would be what we distinguish as *domain spill-over* (on the *neo-
functionalist* notion of 'spill-over', see Shaw, 1996, pp. 12–14); and the
objective, motivation and reasoning could be very largely rooted in assumptions about the means (given the prevailing internal and external imperatives)
for securing and furthering the EU's economic strength, strides and success.

Perhaps Ireland's decision to become attached to the WEU as an 'observer
member' is a sign of further shifts yet to come in the same direction: towards
all EU Member States becoming full members of the WEU, including all
current Member States (in spite of their Cold-War neutral past) and all
future ones. Of course, some of the future EU Member States from central
and eastern Europe are lining up to become NATO members, and so presumably would have no difficulty in joining the WEU – the intended defence
component of the European Union and the means by which the EU plans to
reinforce the European pillar of the Atlantic Alliance (Drost, 1995, p. 636;
Treaty on European Union, Article J. 4).

It is not too fanciful to assume that in the near future all current and additional EU Member States will become WEU members as a matter of course, if only because of the way in which the Treaty on European Union specifies that the objective is to build up the WEU as the defence component of the European Union. The more this objective is realised by being constitutionally enshrined in the EU treaties, the more likely it is that all EU Member States will be automatically required to become WEU members, just as following the 1996–7 IGC (or, if not, the next IGC) they could find themselves constitutionally and legally required to respect any supranational decision-making authority extended to the CFSP pillar of the Union.

Certainly, all new members of the EC/EU are subjected to the *acquis communautaire*, the 'general policy framework [...] which [has] to be accepted as non-negotiable by any new members' (Williams, 1991, p. 44). This applies to Austria, Finland and Sweden when they joined the EU on 1 January 1995. They had to accept all the Maastricht Treaty provisions, objectives and plans regarding the CFSP, the WEU and the Atlantic Alliance, in spite of their Cold War neutrality, a sure sign that the Cold War had come to an end; that the NWO had arrived with its new geo-political management problems; and that, as far as we are concerned, the CFSP pillar of the Union will be eventually embraced by (the doctrine of) supranationalism.

Austria, Finland and Sweden had had prior experience of the principle and practice of the *acquis communautaire* through the creation of the European Economic Area. As summarised by Klaus-Dieter Borchardt:

> Starting from the basis of existing [...] community law (the *acquis communautaire*),[9] the EEA was intended to cover the free movement of goods, persons, services and capital [among other matters]. The EEA Agreement would thus open up the single market to EFTA countries and, with their taking over almost two thirds of Community law, would provide a sound basis for their later accession to the European Union. However, the entry into force of the EEA Agreement was then delayed following its rejection in a referendum in Switzerland [on 6 December 1992] [...]. [F]resh negotiations [meant that] the European Economic Area came into being on 1 January 1994 [...]. Liechtenstein's membership was suspended pending clarification of certain issues connected with its special [*customs union*] relationship with Switzerland. Now that Austria, Finland and Sweden have become members of the Union, a new question mark hangs over the future of the EEA Agreement, which now covers only Norway, Iceland and (from 1 May 1995) Liechtenstein [...].   (Borchardt, 1995, p. 77).[10]

In our view, while the future of the EEA – specifically the EEA – may be problematic, none the less some kind of similar, intermediate 'European economic space' (Drost, 1995, p. 197), or set of spaces, is probably assured.

In so far as the EU continues to accept requests from extra-EU organisations such as EFTA for a degree of integration[11] or requests from individual non-member countries to be considered for full membership,[12] there is a good chance that at least one extra-EU European economic space will be maintained due to its preparatory and protectionist value or 'functions' *vis-à-vis* the interests of the EU. As illustrated by the EEA, a European economic space can be of value to the EU for the purpose of preparing prospective members for membership through, for instance, their induction into the *acquis communautaire*: through ensuring, and indeed monitoring, their assimilation into the EU's economic, political and cultural fabric.

At least one European economic space, similar to the EEA, for occupation by extra-EU organisations seeking a degree of integration with the EU and/ or by non-EU countries seeking full membership of the EU will be maintained in so far as it serves the the EU's 'enlightened self-interest', as the European Commission puts it (European Commission, *Europe in a Changing World*, 1993, p. 6): in so far as it helps the EU realise its economic, political and protectionist objectives. Essentially, the presence and preservation of a particular European economic space which encompasses both the EU and non-EU countries will depend on the degree to which it facilitates the EU's economic objectives, intimately linked as these are to the EU's political objectives and tasks of internal and external (perhaps pan-European) governance.

The construction, character and course of the EEA is indicative of the EU's more general self-interested, realist engagement in extra-EU geo-political management; and is illustrative of the presence, purpose and operation of the EU's differentiated zones of governance, whereby the EU (assisted by the EC's supranational institutions, decision-making and unity) exercises decision-making power, control and authority not just internally, but also externally.[13] In turn, the EU's zones of geo-political management exemplify a more widespread pattern and trend of governance within the overall global system, especially since the end of the Cold War and the advent of the NWO.

We contend that within the NWO (post-Cold War distribution of global power and associated configuration of global players), the European Union is just one of a number, and furthermore of a growing number, of regional organisations or regimes which are assuming increasingly prominent parts in the process of global governance, to some extent by way of *differentiated zones of geo-political management*. The EU may well be the most advanced example of a regional regime, organisationally speaking, by virtue of having the novel EC at its core – the EC being uniquely organised around supranational institutions, decision-making and unity. However, in our view, the EC's uniqueness is unlikely to last for very much longer. The competition (not to mention conflict), the evident competitive advantages of supranational decision-making and unity, and the *realist* tendencies of the players within the NWO global system will combine to encourage regional regimes to become more and more supranational in a manner which is consistent with the *neo-functionalist* approach to and perspective on the development of the European Union.[14]

In our view, the particular case of the EEA is an example of a European economic space through which the European Union – or the Union's core supranational institutions – engages in the process of governance within an extra-EU geo-political arena; through which the Union's supranational institutions engage in geo-political management in relation to various non-member governments: in particular, the non-member governments of those countries (or nation-states)[15] or organisations (such as EFTA) which are seeking integration with or membership of, or even merely closer co-operation with, the EU. The details of the relationship between the EU and EFTA by way of the EEA are indicative of how more generally the EU and its supranational institutions engage in the process of governance beyond its own (constitutional, sovereign) borders; and so of how the EU engages in geo-political management in, for instance, central and eastern European. These details are, therefore, highly instructive.

The main objectives of the EEA are set out in Article 1 of the EEA Agreement, according to which 'the aim of the EEA is "to promote a continuous and balanced strengthening of trade and economic relations between the contracting parties with equal conditions of competition". To attain this objective, the EEA [was meant to] (i) establish a single market based on the freedom of movement of goods, persons, services and capital, and (ii) foster closer cooperation in other fields [. . .]' (Drost, 1995, p. 196).

Essentially, therefore, the EEA Agreement was designed to extend the single internal market programme, together with the enabling provisions of the Single European Act (1986),[16] 'to the entire eighteen nation bloc (albeit with some limitations)' (Harrison, 1995, p. 162). On coming into force on 1 January 1994, the EEA Agreement brought together eighteen countries to create, as reported by David Harrison:

> what has been described by the [European] Commission as the world's biggest integrated market, responsible in itself for more than two-fifths of all world trade. Total EEA GDP is put at $7,501 billion. This can be compared to the total GDP of $6,770 billion for the US, Canada and Mexico which at the same time in 1994 joined together in the North American Free Trade Agreement (NAFTA).   (Harrison, 1995, p. 160)

In addition, to facilitate the task of realising the EEA's objectives, the Agreement 'creates a new institutional system to enforce common rules in this wider market' (*ibid.*, p. 162). To begin with, the 'EFTA countries have set up a body which in some respects mirrors the Commission, known as the

Surveillence Authority'; along with a Court 'to arbitrate on differences within the EFTA area' (*ibid.*, p. 162). That is, the 'Surveillance Authority and the Court are responsible for supervising and enforcing the implementation of the EEA Agreement respectively' (Drost, 1995, p. 198) *within EFTA*. But, furthermore, beyond EFTA, as Drost puts it, the 'EEA has two main joint EU-EFTA bodies to ensure the proper functioning of the single market and to deal with any disputes arising from its implementation' (*ibid.*, p. 196). These bodies are:

> (i) the Council, the senior political body, composed of ministers of the 18 governments and a member of the European Commission [...]; and (ii) the Joint Committee, composed of government representatives and responsible for day-to-day administration and resolving disputes. There are also two consultative committees: (i) the Joint Parliamentary Committee, composed of members of the European Parliament and the national parliaments of the EFTA states; and (ii) the Consultative Committee, composed of representatives of employers' associations and trade unions from the participating countries.   (Drost, 1995, pp. 196–7)

At first sight, the EEA may seem to have been established in accordance with the vision espoused by Jacques Delors, 'the President of the European Commission', in 'a keynote speech to the European Parliament on 17 January 1989' (Borchardt, 1995, p. 76), according to which the EEA would represent ' "a new, more structured partnership [between the EC and EFTA] with common decision-making and administrative institutions" ' (quoted in Borchardt, 1995, p. 77). But, as far as we are concerned, the use of the term 'common' here belies the character and operation of the EEA's administrative institutions and decision-making procedures as these have since emerged in practice. In practice, these institutions and procedures operate in a one-sided, skewed or biased fashion, reflecting the way in which they are largely and *ultimately* controlled by the EU. They are, in effect, used by the EU to engage in extra-EU governance; or, more precisely, are used by the EU's core supranational institutions to engage in such governance.

For the purpose of developing this argument, we can recall how within a few months of the creation of the EEA, several members of EFTA took a major step towards becoming members not just of the EEA, but of the EU; and precisely a year later, three members of EFTA duely became full Member States of the EU. That is, in June 1994, Austria, Finland, Sweden and Norway signed Treaties of Accession to the European Union, and three of these countries then proceeded to become full members of the EU on 1 January 1995. As a result of a referendum held in November 1994, Norway withdrew its application for membership. A retrospective explanation for the referendum result against joining the Union has been presented by Sarah Ryle:

After Saudi Arabia, Norway is the biggest exporter of oil in the world [...]. Little wonder that in November 1994 Norway [...] felt confident enough to reject EU membership by a majority of 52 per cent to 48 per cent. [But] there are other reasons behind the 'no' victory. There was a powerful lobby of fishermen and farmers who feared for their resources and subsidies [...]. And a general dislike of centralisation did not help. But [...] Norway's economy was basically in good shape. The statistics suggest that Norway has not suffered at all from her isolation in Western Europe. Norway is [...] the only country other than Luxembourg that has already achieved all the Maastricht criteria for monetary union [planned for 1999] [...]. Until the next wave of enlargement, the European question is now considered on all sides to be a non-starter. The only problems are with political representation in Europe, to achieve which, through the back door, ministers have worked hard through their Nordic neighbours.

(Ryle, 1996)

While economic factors help account for Norway's 'No' vote – '[s]ince the "No" vote national output has increased by between 3.9 per cent and 5.7 per cent annually' (Ryle, 1996) – 'political' issues were and remain prominent in influencing the Norwegians' negative view of membership of the European Union, as recognised at the time of the referendum:

Prime Minister Gro Harlem Brundtland's campaign to persuade Norwegians to vote 'yes' in tomorrow's referendum on joining the European Union [will be resisted due to] a fusion of present self-interest and emotions rooted in the past. Norway's Euro-sceptic backbone is provided by enthusiasts of the welfare state. Many are women aged between 25 and 50 who either work in education, health and welfare services or are dependent on them. Financed by oil revenues, public sector employment has more than doubled in 20 years [...]. Brussels, [Hallvard] Bakke [leader of the anti-Europeans in Brundlant's own Labour party [sic] [...] calculates joining the EU would cost Norway as much as [...] £2 billion [...] a year. 'We are afraid of losing the welfare state if we join,' is a cry often heard. Were Norway to enter monetary union, Bakke continues, the government would no longer have the power to reduce unemployment by stimulating the economy, an argument popular among a Norwegian Left that [...] despises 'market liberalism'. The struggle for independence [from Sweden], not achieved until 1905, was powered from the countryside. Farmers became the symbol of Norwegian sovereignty and [...] [r]ural and provincial Norway is expected to vote against EU membership by a margin of more than two to one.   (Frankland, 27 November 1994)

Following Ryle and Frankland, the rejection by Norwegian voters of their government's argument in favour of EU membership can be understood in terms of their resistance to Norway forfeiting its independent control over its economy, government revenues, public expenditure and welfare system[17]; to political centralisation in 'Brussels' (a euphemism for the EU's core – or EC – supranational institutions, decision-making procedures and authority); to the anticipated loss of political power to the EU; and so to Norway relinquishing its (nation-state) sovereignty.

But, in a manner which reminds us of Sir Leon Brittan's argument that 'Europe has enhanced not diminished Britain's sovereignty' (Milner, 5 March 1997), and of Ted Barrington's identical claim that 'the Irish experience of membership of the EU is that it enhances Ireland's sovereignty' (Kemp, 2 February 1997), Ryle touches on the point that in rejecting membership of the European Union, Norway has had to suffer the diminution of precisely what it (the majority of its voters) was trying to preserve: its decision-making powers; its control over its own destiny. The Norwegian referendum vote rejecting membership of the Union has meant that the Norwegian government has had to forgo full, direct 'representation' within the Union's political decision-making procedures, something which has brought problems. These problems are signalled by David Harrison:

> the constitutional/legal relationship between [an] individual EFTA country and the EEA is not that of [a] member state of the EU. As the EFTA Secretariat has put it: 'Unlike in the Community there will be no transfer of legislative power from the contracting parties to the EEA institutions' [EFTA Secretariat document on the EEA Agreement (1992)]. [However], through the act of signing the EEA agreement, the individual EFTA countries have committed themselves to incorporating within their national legislations a backlog of some thirty years of Community legislation [...] none of which they [have] had [any] direct control in drawing up. In addition, the degree of influence of EFTA countries over future EU legislation affecting the EEA will be limited. There will be an EEA Joint Committee, comprising the Council of the EU and the Standing Committee of EFTA, which will endeavour to reach a consensus [...] on decisions affecting the overall EEA, but in which the institutions of the EU retain decision-making authority. (Harrison, 1995, p. 163)

The retention by the EU's core, supranational institutions of 'decision-making authority' over the EEA, and thereby control over the EEA's members, was incorporated into the provisions of the EEA Agreement, something which was accepted by all the non-EU members of the EEA, including Norway. Poignantly, this was done by virtue of, in effect, what might have been included in the Agreement but which was not – which was deliberately omitted, purposefully excluded – at the insistence of one particular EU supranational decision-making institution, namely the European Court of Justice (ECJ). The ECJ assumed the role of final, or supreme, arbiter over the provisions of the Agreement, over what could be and could not be included; and in carrying out this role, the ECJ paid particular attention to the EEA's own (or 'common') institutions, to the issue of the decision-making powers of these institutions, and consequently to the issue of the implications of these powers for the core, supranational institutions of the EU and *their* decision-making powers. As summarised by Drost:

> A draft agreement on the European Economic Area (EEA) was initialed in October 1991. [But, the] EC Court of Justice objected to the provision for a joint EC-EFTA court to adjudicate disputes, and the terms were modified to give it [the ECJ] the sole power to interpret EEA laws. The [resulting] agreement was signed in May 1992.   (Drost, 1995, p. 197)

While EFTA could have its own Court with responsibility for 'enforcing the implementation of the EEA Agreement' (*ibid.*, p. 198) specifically within EFTA, the EEA was denied its own 'common', independent court by the EU's core, supranational Court (the ECJ), on the grounds that it (the ECJ) was the 'sole power' – or, the *supreme authority* – within and on behalf of the EC/EU: on matters to do with EC/EU law, even when these relate to the operation of the (joint EC-EFTA) EEA. The ECJ decided that it could not permit its supreme authority in relation to EC/EU law to be diminished to any extent or compromised in any way by the presence of a separate, independent EEA court. Indeed, the ECJ ruled that its supreme authority – its ultimate decision-making powers and control over matters to do with EC/EU law – could not be diminished or compromised by any arrangement, agreement or treaty entered into by the EU with any external body, organisation or whatever else. The upshot is that the ECJ simultaneously confirmed and consolidated its supranational identity and authority in its own particular area of competence, that of EC/EU law; its role as the vehicle of 'normative supranationalism' as distinct from 'decisional supranationalism' within the Union (Weiler, 1981; see Shaw, 1996, pp. 12–13); and its status as an emerging, if not already firmly established, Supreme Court within the EC/EU.

As Jo Shaw points out:

> In the eyes of many, the Opinion which the Court of Justice handed down on the incompatibility of certain institutional aspects of the Agreement on the creation of the European Economic Area (EEA), especially as regards the creation of a court and a separate legal order, represented a high watermark in the evolution and authority of a single and autonomous Community legal order, charactersied by a close link between law and legal prossesses and the inexorable march towards 'integration'. According to Weatherill it marked a 'zenith' in the 'Court's description of the Treaty structure as a Constitution' [Weatherill, 1995, p. 184]. As a result of the

accession of most of the (EFTA) countries originally involved in the EU in January 1995 [. . .], the creation of the EEA lost much of its practical importance; however, as an essay in creating a novel and enhanced form of cooperation between the EU Member States and third countries partially modelled on, but not quite attaining, the level of integration *within* the EU, its legal importance should be underlined.

(Shaw, 1996, p. 95)

There may be lessons to learn from the conclusion that the remaining three EFTA countries (Iceland, Liechtenstein and Norway) 'have less say than EU members in common decision-taking' (Harrison, 1995, p. 164) within the EEA; this being a consideration, Harrison claims, which lay 'behind the decisions of Austria, Finland, Norway and Sweden to apply for full membership of the EU more or less at the same time as negotiating the EEA agreement' (*ibid.*, p. 164). A similar consideration appears also to have played a major and decisive part in the build-up to and outcome of the Swiss referendum held in December 1992 on the question of whether Switzerland should participate in the EEA: 'All the three main parties, employers' associations and trade unions recommended acceptance', but voters 'narrowly rejected (by 50.3% to 49.7%) Swizerland's participation' (Drost, 1995, p. 591).

Those members of EFTA that did join the EEA but have not since joined the EU are in an intermediate location – in what might be otherwise regarded as a state of limbo – as far as decision-making procedures, powers and control are concerned. As long as they remain in the EEA, the non-EU members are subjected to the (supranational) decision-making procedures, control and sovereignty of the EC/EU without being able to fully, directly participate in these procedures. In so far as the EEA survives and Iceland, Liechtenstein and Norway remain EEA members, then these countries (their governments, institutions, voters, and so on) will be required to defer to the EC/EU, and its 'aims, methods and actors' (Borchardt, 1995, pp. 23–30), thereby keeping afloat the issue of whether in rejecting EU membership, Norwegians have lost more control over their country's fate than they would otherwise have done.

The possibility arises that the disjunction, or contradiction, between being subjected to decisions arrived at within the EU and being excluded from directly participating in the EU's decision-making procedures will have the effect of eventually convincing not only the Norwegian government, but also the majority of the Norwegian people about the self-interested, economic and political advantages of becoming an EU Member State, in spite of the downside judged with reference to the transfer of sovereignty to the EC's supranational institutions.

With this prospect in mind, as Harrison points out, at least 'the process of incorporating EU legislation by the EFTA countries will have started', making any future 'formal accession negotiations easier' (Harrison, 1995, p. 165). Or, as Pascal Fontaine puts it, 'the EEA looks increasingly like a transitional arrangement [serving] as an ante-room for countries economically but not yet politically integrated into the Union and other European States seeking closer ties' (Fontaine, 1995, p. 33).[18] The EEA is at least functioning as a preparatory European economic space on behalf of the European Union, as well as mutually on behalf of any remaining EEA members that do eventually join the EU. In the meantime, apart from the EEA also functioning as a protectionist geo-political space on behalf of the Union, the Norwegian government, as Sarah Ryle notes, has to be content with securing as much *indirect* political representation within the EU as it is able to do through its Nordic links with Denmark, Finland and Sweden.[19] Also in the meantime, Gro Harlem Brundtland, 'Norway's hugely popular prime minister [who] tasted bitter defeat [...] when Norway voted [...] in 1994 not to join the European Union' decided to step down: on 23 October 1996, Brundtland 'said that she and her minority Labour Party government would formally resign' on 25 October (Henley, 1996).

4 The Supra-State, Governance and Global Processes

During the run-up to the UK's spring 1997 parliamentary General Election, the contesting political parties variously set out their stalls on a range of issues while, without exception, prominently displaying their views on the UK's part in the process of European integration by way of the progress of the European Union. For instance, John Major, prime minister and leader of the Conservative Party, attempted to 'push the threat to British jobs posed by the EU's social chapter into the forefront of the [...] election campaign with an attack on [the] Labour [Party] for wanting to import a "Trojan Horse" that would supposedly bring industry to its knees' (White, 4 February 1997; see also Palmer and White, 5 February 1997; and Kampfner, 1997). At the same stage in the election campaign, Robin Cook, the Labour Party's shadow Foreign Secretary, fuelled the debate about the UK's participation in the programme of European economic and monetary union (EMU) entailing the introduction of a European single currency, planned for January 1999,[1] by letting it be known that a 'Labour government would take sterling into a European single currency by 2002 if it proved to be "stable"' by then (Parker and Peston, 3 February 1997): 'Echoing comments made by [Hiroshi Okuda, the president of Toyota], the shadow foreign secretary warned that Britain would lose out on inward investment if it stayed outside the single currency in the longer term'.[2] In response to Robin Cook's statement, one journalist commented that the 'stage was set yesterday for a lurid election on the biggest issue of the moment', that of whether 'sterling [should be taken] into a European single currency, the euro' (Young, 4 February 1997). For others more directly involved as partisans in the election campaign, however, there were even bigger issues.

Alongside the stances adopted by the main political parties could be seen the European manifestos of several minor contenders for parliamentary seats,[3] including that of the UK Independence Party (UKIP) which, according to its founder Alan Sked, speaking at his party's election campaign launch at the beginning of February 1997, was 'the UK's only democratic party in favour of complete British withdrawal from the EU':

'The main parties cannot take us out of Europe – the Tories, by word and deed, are an EU party,' [Alan Sked] said [...]. 'Beware of Europe – your pension will be stolen and you will be taxed until there is rioting in the streets,' he cried [...]. Since UKIP was founded in August 1993, he has built it into a party with 16,000 members [...], which will field 185 candidates [...] at the general election.[4] Mr Sked [...] has published widely on the dangers of giving up British sovereignty. UKIP feels that withdrawal from the EU [...] would bring economic prosperity to the UK. 'Our rights to make our own laws, levy our own taxes and set our own priorities – [...] these rights are under unprecedented attack,' Mr [Bill] Jamieson [economics editor of the *Sunday Telegraph* and prospective parliamentary candidate for Putney] told the [audience]. [Mr Jamieson] was careful to distance his organisation from Sir James Goldsmith's Referendum party [sic]. 'We thank you Sir James, for spending £7m putting Europe on the general election map, but you are a protectionist – and we believe in free trade; you are happy to stand on a single-issue, and we have a full manifesto.'   (Halligan, 3 February 1997)

The Referendum Party, led by Sir James Goldsmith, was explicit: the 'Party has been created for one reason only: To obtain a fair referendum on Europe. Once that has been held, the party will dissolve [...]. The public should be allowed to vote on the broad issues of Britain's future in Europe – and not just on the single currency issue of the [...] referendum' which has been paraded by both the Conservative Party and the Labour Party (*News From the Referendum Party*, February 1997, p. 8). Sir James Goldsmith tried to put the Referendum Party's single issue into context:

Some say that the Referendum Party is just a single issue party and cannot compete with the traditional parties which propose full electoral programmes. [However, all] the powers needed to make good on the bulk of the electoral promises of the traditional parties have been or are being abandoned to Brussels [the location of the European Union's European Commission (see Borchardt, 1995, p. 59)]. Therefore, their promises are almost totally empty [...]. The Referendum Party stands for the issue from which all policies inevitably must flow. It is the only issue which counts. Do we want to be an independent nation with our own Parliament or do we want to be a province of Europe run from Brussels?

(Goldsmith, February 1997, p. 3)

Here, Goldsmith was alluding to the Referendum Party's own answer to the question of the part the UK should play in the process of European integration by way of the progress of the European Union, an answer which is clearly spelled out by Goldsmith in his article under the heading 'We are being led blindfold into a federal superstate':

Consider for a moment the qualities that define a sovereign nation such as Britain, and which distinguish it from a mere province of a larger nation or empire. They are the right to pass laws in our own land, the right to run our economy for the benefit of our people, to organise our national security and to control our own borders. Each of these fundamental national rights has either already been abandoned or is now under imminent threat. When our political leaders assure us they will never allow us to be part of a federal European state they are not telling the truth. *They have already signed treaties which have surrendered an indispensable part of our sovereignty. And they did so without explaining the facts to us, indeed by purposely misleading us, and without our consent.* Already laws passed in Westminster [by the UK Parliament] are no longer supreme. As British judges have confirmed, the supreme law of this land is now European law. Already we have signed away our right to run our economy for the benefit of our own people. The Governor of Germany's central bank put it concisely. Referring to economic and monetary union, he says 'it will lead to member nations transferring their sovereignty over financial and wage policies as well as in monetary affairs...' It is an illusion to think, he adds, that states can hold on to their autonomy over taxation policies. *And the governing European political caste has put forward proposals to transfer to Brussels control over our foreign policy, our national security and our frontiers* [...]. The facts are out in the open. Chancellor Kohl's foreign policy spokesman is both clear and honest. He explained that Germany's ruling party wants what he calls 'a country', a federal Europe which will have one Parliament, one Government, one Court of Justice, one currency, into which would be fused 26 existing European nations including our own. He goes further and proclaims that nation states have already lost their sovereignty and that sovereignty, in his words, is no more than 'an empty shell'. It was the Conservative administration which signed away our rights to self-government [presumably when the Conservative government under prime minister Edward Heath signed the UK's Treaty of Accession to the European Community on 22 January 1972 before leading the UK into the Community on 1 January 1973], and which through weakness has given in to, and in fact continues to give in to, the demands of the Eurocrats. The Government's recently adopted 'tough stance' is not credible. They are just posing for the gallery prior to the election. Labour has fully supported the Conservatives' policy of federal integration into the European superstate and voted in favour of the federalist Maastricht Treaty. This has put us on auto-pilot to a federal corporatist Europe dominated by the bureaucrats of Brussels. The [Liberal-Democrats] are also Euro-enthusiasts and quite simply proclaim: 'We are supranationalists.'

(Goldsmith, February 1997, p. 3 – original italics)

In view of how Sir James Goldsmith labelled Liberal-Democrats – who form the third major political party in the United Kingdom behind the

Conservative Party and the Labour Party – as *supranationalists*, it is inter-
esting to note the 1995 *British Social Attitudes* survey's findings on the
typical characteristics of supranationalists in the UK (Jowell *et al.*, 1996),
as summarised by David McKie: they 'score low on the wish to exclude, and
low on national sentiment (the "inclusive" values). They are more likely than
not to be libertarian, well-educated, female, and readers of the *Guardian* or
Independent. They are more likely to back the Labour Party' (McKie, 21
November 1996).

The *British Social Attitudes* survey (BSAS) is carried out under the aus-
pices of Social and Community Planning Research (SCPR), led by Roger
Jowell. The *13th Report* includes a chapter in which, on the basis of their
1995 survey data, the researchers 'explore the dimensions of national identity
among [their] respondents'. The researchers (in particular Lizanne Dowds
and Ken Young) 'construct a typology of national identities and, in the light
of this, consider one of the greatest constitutional challenges facing British
people in the coming years: the re-articulation (or even survival) of national
identities in the face of what many view – some with enthusiasm, others with
dismay – as a relentless drive towards European integration' (Dowds and
Young, 1996, p. 142).

Dowds and Young constructed a typology of national identity according
to how respondents in the 1995 BSAS scored on either of 'two inclusive
aspects of national identity (pride in heritage and culture and in the way the
nation functions)' and on either of 'two exclusive aspects ([...] labelled as
protectionism and xenophobia)' (*ibid.*, p. 148). On the basis of the respondents' scores on the inclusive aspects and the exclusive aspects of national
identity, Dowds and Young categorised their respondents into 'four groups'
(*ibid.*, p. 148). Group 1 were low 'in exclusiveness and low in national
sentiment'; Group 2 were low 'in exclusiveness and high in national sentiment'; Group 3 were high 'in exclusiveness and low in national sentiment';
and Group 4 were high 'in exclusiveness and high in national sentiment'
(*ibid.*, p. 148).

Dowds and Young label Group 2 'the patriots', Group 3 'the belligerents'
and Group 4 'the John Bulls' (*ibid.*, pp. 148–9), and suggest that Group 1
'may be labelled *supra-nationalists*' (*ibid.*, p. 148). Dowds and Young sum-
marise the characteristics associated with the Group 1 type: 'Low in exclusiveness and low in national sentiment, *supra-nationalists* tend to be
unmoved by symbols of nation. Generally respondents who fall into this
category are likely to be libertarian,[5] better educated, younger, female and
rather more likely to read *The Guardian* or *The Independent*.' Supranationalists 'are not attached to their locality' (*ibid.*, p. 148), in the sense of
'"feeling close to" their neighbourhood or their town/city' (*ibid.*, p. 155).
Dowds and Young argue that the four 'national identity categories show that
there are four distinct ways of "being British"', but the first – the suprana-

tionalists – 'are the least distinctively British of the four, and might be reasonably said to have little sense of national identity' (*ibid.*, p. 149).

Dowds and Young propose that the kind of people belonging to the four national identity categories 'might reasonably be expected to react differently to, and perhaps exercise a potent if divergent influence upon, the politics of European integration in the coming years' (*ibid.*, p. 149). In this regard:

> the 1995 figures [indicate that] *[s]upra-nationalists* and *patriots* are quite close in their response to the perceived benefits of European Union membership (58 and 52 per cent respectively think that Britain benefits from membership) and differ sharply from the *belligerents* and the *John Bulls*, whose adverse judgements (22 and 28 per cent) are also similar to one another. A similar position can be seen in responses to the proposition that Britain might leave the European Union.[6] Very different, however, are the patterns of response on other issues. *Supra-nationalists* are alone in their substantial degree of support for a closer relationship with the Union,[7] at least on a generalised level; on the specific benefits (and obligations) of closer links, there is more of a continuum. *Supra-nationalists* are alone too in their remarkably high level of support – a bare majority – for 'uniting fully' with the European Union, a position which just a third of the *patriots* and less than a quarter of the other groups espouse.[8] And while levels of support for a single currency are modest, it is here too that the *supra-nationalists* distinguish themselves. Hardly enthusiastic (with only 28 per cent in favour), nonetheless the proportion giving it their backing is around twice as high as that of the other [...] groups, all united in their deep distrust of such a move. (Dowds and Young, 1996, pp. 150–1)

Dowds and Young speculate:

> in other historical contexts, the views of the *supra-nationalists* and the *John Bulls* could well have lain claim to represent the 'heart of Britain'. The *supra-nationalists* articulate a set of values quite consistent with those of Edmund Burke and other 18th century Parliamentarians in their view of Europe and their acknowledgement of interdependence between Britain and its colonies.[9] The *John Bulls*, on the other hand, could be seen as representing a view that became consolidated in the first decades of the 19th century, in the wake of Britain's victory in the Napoleonic wars, and lasted into the Victorian and Edwardian eras, sustained by the increasing perception of a threat from a unified and powerful Germany.
>
> (*ibid.*, pp. 153–4)

At the end of the twentieth century, Sir James Goldsmith and his Referendum Party as well as Alan Sked and his UK Independence Party seem obvious candidates for the category 'John Bulls' in the sense indicated by Dowds and Young. But doubts about the process of European integration and the progress of the European Union are evidently far from confined to the British or, for that matter, to *older* people. David Short, reporting on a 'survey of the political and moral thoughts of young Europeans aged between 16 and 24' carried out by 'pop music television channel MTV Europe' in eight countries tells us:

> A majority of [younger Europeans] think that European countries are too diverse for a federal Europe to work, and most also object to the power of Brussels [. . .]. More than half (54 per cent) said a united Europe could not work because of national differences and even more (57 per cent) were against the EU deciding how their countries should be run [. . .]. But, as ever, the young are no strangers to contradictory views. They may be against a united Europe, but 76 per cent think 'a more closely integrated Europe' is a good thing and 61 per cent favour a single currency.
>
> (Short, 6 February 1997)[10]

Any contradictory views, or ambivalence, about European integration expressed by younger people, not to mention their older contemporaries, may be interpreted as reflecting even more sharply than the categorical attitudes and identities *vis-à-vis* the same issue (as purportedly revealed through the *British Social Attitudes* survey) the following characterisation of what Dowds and Young refer to as the 'New World Order':

> Beyond the rhetoric of the New World Order lies a wide-spread unease, against a backcloth of failing empires, disintegrating nation-states, and new regional and ethnic claims to loyalty. The sense of identity traditionally derived from the old collectivities no longer claims special attention. And yet that sense of identity, of being 'among one's own', remains a powerful human need. The 1990s could be said to be a decade characterised by a search for a more elemental sense of identity than the years immediately preceding it; moreover, an identity made special by ties of 'blood and belonging' (Ignatieff, 1993). So, at least goes one argument about our current predicament. But there are other, less regressive constructions to be put on this new order. One of these is to regard the nation-state as the quintessential product of modernity and to let it pass away unlamented. The passage into post-modernity is, it has been argued, one into a more transient and contingent world, of flux and paradox, in which a single or firm sense of identity – of who one is – is neither sought nor offered. Instead, *situational* identities are adopted, reflecting a wider range of life-experiences that cut across the concept of 'nationhood'. The prospect is held up of a life of multiple identities and shifting ties, in which the certitudes and loyalties of the nation-state are replaced at will from a whole range of new identities on offer. In this moral emporium, few will choose to identify themselves with either nation or state and, if their attachment is in any way territorial,

it is as likely as not to derive its rationale and vigour from the face-to-face community of local neighbourhoods. This *lateral* dispersion of identity may seem both over-fanciful in the kaleidoscope of identities it can offer, and romantic in its celebration of the local in the face of the global. Yet in Britain, we are currently witnessing unprecedented confusions of national consciousness, arising from the prospect of a *vertical* displacement of old loyalties by those widely believed to be demanded by an emerging European 'super-state'. On this reckoning, the old tales of solidarity within bounded territorial (but not ethnic) communities have not been forgotten but are being re-told on a supra-national scale appropriate to the emotionally powerful appeal of a united Europe (Schlesinger, 1992). To the extent that people feel themselves to be citizens of this new Europe, they might be expected to be the weaker in their national attachments; indeed, it was just such a hope, after two devastating world wars, that underpinned the original European project. On this view, the gradual eclipse of national by European identity is both natural and welcome.

(Dowds and Young, 1996, pp. 141–2)

Those people, supranationalists, 'who are insouciant in their support for full [European] unification', for complete 'European integration' (*ibid.*, p. 154), who are attached to a European identity at the expense of any national identity – or, perhaps more to the point, of any nation-state identity[11] – and so who are committed to the European project as represented by the (institutionally defined) supranational European Union, are harbingers of supranationalism.

Charles de Gaulle (head of the provisional government of France following the August 1944 Allied liberation of what had been German-occupied Paris and later, in December 1958, elected as the first president of the Fifth Republic) was familiar with the 'doctrine of supranationalism', as he called it, and with its post-Second World War manifestation, the *European Economic Community*, as originally created by the 1957 Treaty of Rome:

It must be said that [. . .] the spirit and terms of the Treaty of Rome did not meet our country's requirements. The industrial provisions were as precise and explicit as those concerning agriculture were vague. This was evidently due to the fact that our negotiators in 1957, caught up in the dream of a supranational Europe and anxious at any price to settle for something approaching it, had not felt it their duty to insist that a French interest, no matter how crucial, should receive satisfaction at the outset. It would, therefore, be necessary either to obtain it *en route*, or to liquidate the Common Market.   (De Gaulle, 1994, p. 34)

De Gaulle unequivocally and disdainfully dismissed 'the hopes and illusions of the supranational school', of 'these champions of integration [. . .]

who wanted Europe to be a federation' (*ibid.*, p. 35). He regarded supranationalism as dangerous for France – as incompatible with French interests – but, at the same time and in any case, doomed as a serious doctrine:

> once the war was over, [. . .] for the leading school of thought in each [French] political party, national self-effacement had become an established and flaunted doctrine. [All] the old party formations professed the doctrine of 'supranationalism', in other words France's submission to a law that was not her own. Hence the support for 'Europe' seen as an edifice in which technocrats forming an 'executive' and parliamentarians assuming legislative powers – the great majority of them being foreigners – would have the authority to decide the fate of the French people [. . .]. Hence, again, the eagerness to submit the acts of our government to the approval of [an] international [organisation] in which, under a semblance of collective deliberation, the authority of the protector [i.e. of supranational institutions] reigned supreme.   (De Gaulle, 1994, p. 30)

Apart from being unacceptable to de Gaulle, supranationalism would fail in post-Second World War Europe just as it had failed previously, under 'the Roman emperors [. . .], Charlemagne, Charles V and Napoleon', not to mentioned 'Hitler' (*ibid.*, p. 31): 'not one of these federators succeeded in inducing the subject countries to surrender their individuality. On the contrary, arbitrary centralization always provoked an upsurge of violent nationalism by way of a reaction [see note 11]. It was [de Gaulle's] belief that a united Europe could not today, any more than in previous times, be a fusion of its peoples' (*ibid.*, pp. 31–2).[12] De Gaulle's alternative 'policy therefore aimed at the setting up of a concert of European states which in developing all sorts of ties between them would increase their interdependence and solidarity. From this starting point, there was every reason to believe that the process of evolution might lead to their confederation' (*ibid.*, p. 32); and it is on the basis of this starting assumption about European integration that de Gaulle proceeded to help, when president of France, 'to put the European Economic Community into effect' (*ibid.*, p. 32).

Further clarification of what de Gaulle presumably had in mind when trying to re-shape the Community in accordance with what was for him both possible and preferable is given by Klaus-Dieter Borchardt, who explains that European integration has been 'shaped by two fundamentally different approaches – the "confederalist" and the "federalist"' (Borchardt, 1995, p. 27):

> the confederalist approach means that countries agree to cooperate with each other without ceding any of their national sovereignty. The aim is not to create a new 'super State' enbracing them all but to link sovereign States in a confederation in which they retain their own national structures.
> (Borchardt, 1995, p. 27)

The confederalist approach to European integration can be contrasted with the federalist, the object of which is 'to dissolve the traditional distinctions between nation States' (*ibid.*, p. 27).[13] In a manner which implies both his sympathy with the federalist approach and his assumption that this approach has been the main driving force behind the progress of the European Union, Borchardt argues:

> The outdated notion of inviolable and indivisible national sovereignty gives way to the view that the imperfections of social and international coexistence, the specific shortcomings of the nation-State system, and the dangers of dominance by one State over others (all too familiar a phenomenon in European history) can only be overcome by individual States pooling their sovereignty under a supranational community. The result is a European federation in which the common destiny of its peoples – while still retaining their individual identities – is guided and their future assured by common (federal) authorities. The European Union is essentially a product of this federalist approach.   (Borchardt, 1995, p. 27)[14]

The European Union represents an attempt 'to bridge the gap between national autonomy and European federation in a gradual process. Rather than relinquish sovereignty overnight, the Member States [have been] asked merely to abandon the dogma of indivisibility', thereby enabling them 'to yield some sovereignty to a supranational community' by way of 'the Treaties establishing the three communities' (*ibid.*, p. 28): the Treaty establishing the European Coal and Steel Community (ECSC), signed in Paris on 18 April 1951 and entering into force on 23 July 1952 (*ibid.*, p. 9); and the Treaties establishing the European Economic Community (EEC) and the European Atomic Energy Community (Euratom) – collectively known as the Treaty of Rome (Fontaine, 1995, p. 42) – signed in Rome on 25 March 1957 and entering into force on 1 January 1958 (Borchardt, 1995, p. 10). The 'gradual process' of bridging the gap between national autonomy (or nation-state sovereignty) and European (supranational) federation has since occurred by way of 'subsequent Treaties amending or supplementing' the three founding Treaties. Thus, on 8 April 1965, a Treaty merging the executives of the three Communities was signed in Brussels, entering into force on 1 July 1967; on 22 April 1970 a Treaty which extended the budgetary powers of the European Parliament was signed in Luxembourg; in February 1986, the Single European Act was signed in Luxembourg and The Hague, entering into force on 1 July 1987 (*ibid.*, p. 13). Borchardt describes the Single European Act (SEA), as a 'very important milestone along the road' to European Union':

> Its preamble reiterated a broad objective – the creation of a European Union – which the Community and European politial cooperation are

meant to help achieve. It then laid down the detailed framework for establishing the single [internal] market by 1992 [or, more accurately, by 1 January 1993] and closer political cooperation on the environment, research and technology. Formally, this involved a series of amendments and additions to the Treaties establishing the Communities. Finally the third part of the Single Act dealt with foreign policy cooperation under EPC [European political co-operation], setting out a formal legal framework for what had until then been an informal arrangement.

(Borchardt, 1995, p. 13; see also Swann, 1992; and European Commission, *From Single Market to European Union*, April 1992)

During the period when the single internal market was being constructed, the gradual process of bridging the gap between nation-state sovereignty and European (supranational) federation proceeded further. A major step was taken by the European Council at its summit meeting in Maastricht on 9 and 10 December 1991 when it reached agreement on the Treaty on European Union. Subsequently, the Maastricht Treaty was signed on behalf of the Community's Member State governments on 7 February 1992, and eventually came into force on 1 November 1993 (Fontaine, 1995, pp. 42–6; see also O'Keefe and Twomey, 1994; and Wistrich, 1994, especially Chapter 1).

Gradually, therefore, the 'transfer to the Community of the power to legislate in a wide range of policy areas' (Borchardt, 1995, p. 28) has taken place – or perhaps more accurately, reverting to the terminology employed by Sir James Goldsmith, has been decided and directed, managed and manipulated by 'our political leaders', by 'the European political caste' (Goldsmith, 1997, p. 3; see also Amin and Tomaney, 1995; Andersen and Eliassen, 1993; Lane and Ersson, 1994, 1996; Nelsen and Stubb, 1994, especially Part 3; Richardson, 1996, especially Parts 2 and 3), beginning with the founding fathers of the Community (most notably Jean Monnet and Robert Schuman (Shaw, 1996, p. 12; Nelsen and Stubb, 1994, Chapters 2 and 4) and continuing under the stewardship of the most recent European Commission presidents, Jacques Delors (Nelsen and Stubb, 1996, Chapter 8) and Jacques Santer – in a manner which is consistent with the so-called *neo-functionalist* (political, practical) approach to and (scholarly, theoretical) account of the process of European integration (Shaw, 1996, p. 12; Nelsen and Stubb, 1994, Chapters 11–13 and 17–19; Gillespie, 1996). Neo-functionalist political leaders take a 'pragmatic position' on European integration, advocating an 'incremental and piecemeal' approach to the process, whereby power (competence and sovereignty) 'is transferred [from Member States] to a central authority which exists at a level above the nation state, and which exercises its powers [competences, sovereignty] independently of the Member States – a *supranational* body' (Shaw, 1996, p. 12). For Shaw, if 'the functionalist logic is followed to its conclusion the supranational authority will, at a certain point, merge into a federal authority as more and more [sovereign] powers [(competences)] are transferred, and as the mechanism for exercising these powers become increasingly separated from the nation state level' (*ibid.*, p. 13; see also Gillespie, 1996; Nelsen and Stubb, 1994; O'Keefe and Twomey, 1994, especially Part 2; Wistrich, 1994) – separated from Member States, having been 'persuaded in the interests of economic welfare to relinquish control over certain areas of policy' (Shaw, 1996, p. 12); having been persuaded to relinquish, in other words, more and more competence, power and sovereignty to an increasingly overarching *central authority*, or set of supranational institutions.

Despite this process, claims Borchardt, the gradual transfer of power, competence and sovereignty in a wide range of policy areas is not 'intended to cement in place a central State with rigid structures' (Borchardt, 1995, p. 28). This conclusion is highly debatable in the light of at least two considerations, the first being definitions of 'the state' according to which the term refers to 'a recognizably separate institution or set of institutions, so differentiated from the rest of society as to create identifiable public and private spheres': the 'state is sovereign, or the supreme power, within its territory, and by definition the ultimate authority for all law, i.e. binding rules supported by coercive sanctions' (Dunleavy and O'Leary, 1987, p. 2; see also Giddens, 1985; Giddens, 1993, Chapter 10; Padfield and Byrne, 1987, pp. 2–3).[15] In addition, the second consideration which renders Borchardt's claim about a shift towards a *central European state* somewhat contentious is brought to mind by Borchardt's own recognition of the 'possibility of progress towards [ever] closer integration in [various policy] areas [. . .] in the future' (Borchardt, 1995, p. 27), including especially in those areas represented by 'the second and third pillars of the European Union – the common foreign and security policy and cooperation in the fields of justice and home affairs' (*ibid.*, p. 27). The possibility of greater integration in a manner which, in effect, endorses the neo-functionalist, gradual and incremental political approach (Shaw, 1996, p. 12) is being seriously addressed and negotiated at the 1996 IGC, the purpose of which is to assess and modify the 1992 Maastricht Treaty on European Union.[16] As conveniently, if somewhat dramatically, summarised by Julie Wolf:

The inter-governmental conference will prepare the European Union (EU) for the addition of 10 or more new members. Many European politicians believe that unless changes are made in the way EU business is handled, the union will become paralysed when more countries are added [. . .]. One of the most important issues under discussion is the question of the national veto and qualified majority voting (QMV). This is at the centre of the dabate over European integration and national sovereignty.

(Wolf, 26 March 1996)

Wolf points out that prior to the IGC, 'unanimity' was required 'for decisions which relate to foreign policy, justice and home affairs, taxation, some employment laws and changes to the EU treaty' – that is, for the passage of amendments to any existing Treaty or the addition of any further Treaty (*ibid.*; see also Curtin, 1996). On the other hand, as we have previously noted, according to Wolf:

> At the moment, qualified majority voting (QMV) applies to laws covering agriculture, health and safety, foreign trade, transport and most environmental matters. It has been used to establish the single market, setting common industrial and social standards to stop member states using local regulations to keep out goods from other EU countries. Under QMV a proposal needs just 70 per cent of the total votes allocated to EU member states to become law [...]. Most member states [...] and the European Commission are in favour of extending [QMV] to cover other areas of policy. They argue that it will speed up decision-making. They also argue that in an increasingly global political environment, EU countries gain more from 'pooling their sovereignty' and [more and more] acting together than by standing [...] on their own. In other words, the rest of the world pays more attention to a strong and united [or, that is, to an increasingly *supranational*] Europe than to lone European voices.
>
> (Wolf, 26 March 1996)

Wolf reports that although 'many member states' – especially Belgium, Germany, Luxembourg and the Netherlands – 'are in favour of extending majority voting, the UK government is determined to maintain each nation's right of veto' (*ibid.*). Like Britain, Wolf claims, 'France is also reluctant to give up the national veto, but has shown more willingness to compromise' (*ibid.*).[17]

However, a year later, a somewhat different picture was painted by Larry Elliott and Mark Milner, for whom the UK government's stance on European integration and reluctance to accept expanded supranational decision-making was, in fact, shared by a number of other Member States; that Britain was merely openly expressing views and misgivings which other Member States more covertly held; and even that Britain's approach could become the most influential one:

> The UK has an umbrella which other countries are glad to huddle under [...]. [The popular image is of] Britain as the bad boy of Europe, obstructive, isolated, friendless in the councils of the Continent. But the myth of 14 countries plunging headlong into a federal superstate while only Britain holds them back is just that: a myth [...]. While many in Europe's capitals look to a federal organisation [...] Britain does not. But Britain may eventually be as successful in exporting its idea of European governance

as it has been in setting the tone for reform of labour markets [in favour of *flexibility*, rather than *continental corporatism*].

(Elliott and Milner, 8 March 1997)

Whatever the treaty outcome of the 1996 IGC, for now, 'the second and third pillars of the EU – the common foreign and security policy' (CFSP) 'and cooperation in the fields of justice and home affairs' (CJHA) – exemplify what Borchardt distinguishes as *confederalist co-operation*, and otherwise variously refers to as 'inter-State cooperation' and 'intergovernmental cooperation' (*ibid.*, p. 27). Both the CFSP and the CJHA illustrate this type of co-operation, as do an array of other organisations, including the Organisation for Economic Co-operation and Development (OECD), the Council of Europe (*ibid.*, pp. 6–7, 27), the Western European Union (WEU), NATO and the United Nations (in particular, the UN's Security Council) (*ibid.*, pp. 6–7); as well as the Organisation for Security and Co-operation in Europe (OCSE), the North Atlantic Co-operation Council (Drost, 1995, p. 440), the European Economic Area (EEA), the European Free Trade Area (EFTA), the Nordic Council (of Ministers) (*ibid.*, pp. 438–9), the Council of Baltic States (the Baltic Council) (*ibid.*, p. 38, 121), the Council of Baltic Sea States (CBSS) (*ibid.*, p. 121), the Central European Initiative (CEI) (*ibid.*, p. 86), the Visegrad Group (*ibid.*, p. 628), the Black Sea Economic Co-operation Organisation (*ibid.*, p. 56), and the Commonwealth of Independent States (CIS) (see our note 24; Deacon, 1992; Drost, 1995, pp. 104–5; Gowland *et al.*, 1995, pp. 291–2; Manning, 1992).

Writing on behalf of the European Commission in January 1995, Borchardt suggests that 'the postwar steps towards European unification offer a confusing picture' of different organisations, including the European Union, 'which itself is built on the foundations of the European Coal and Steel Community [ECSC], the European Atomic Energy Community [Euratom] and the European (Economic) Community [originally the EEC, now the EC]' (Borchardt, 1995, p. 6). Borchardt argues that the confusion is somewhat superficial. Viewed in terms of 'their underlying aims [. . .] a clear pattern begins to emerge, revealing three major groups' of organisations (*ibid.*, p. 6).[18]

The first of these three types 'consists of the transatlantic organizations that grew out of the close links forged between Western Europe and the United States of America' after the Second World War (*ibid.*, p. 6). An example here is that organisation which has evolved out of 'the first postwar European organization' founded in 1948 (*ibid.*, p. 6): that of the Organisation for European Economic Co-operation (OEEC), 'later named the Organization for Economic Cooperation and Development [OECD] when, in 1960, the United States and Canada also joined' (*ibid.*, p. 6). Since the inclusion of the USA and Canada, the OECD has expanded its membership considerably, and moreover has done so by taking in further non-European countries.

Consequently, the OECD has otherwise been described as an 'international organization of 24 industrialized countries that provides a forum for discussion and coordination of [the] economic and social policies' of its member states (Dresner, 1994, p. 362). By the end of 1996, the membership of the OECD had grown to twenty-nine with the admission of South Korea.[19]

The founding of the OEEC was quickly followed in 1949 by the creation of NATO, 'a military pact' between the USA, Canada and several European countries (Borchardt, 1995, p. 6). NATO has been otherwise described by Harry Drost (1995) as an '[i]ntergovernmental organization', founded on the basis of the North Atlantic Treaty, signed in Washington on 4 April 1949 and brought into force from 24 August 1949, as 'a military and political alliance of Western European countries, the United States and Canada [and] as a counterweight to the Soviet Union and its allies, which [subsequently] formed the Warsaw Pact in 1955' (Drost, 1995, pp. 440–1). NATO has sixteen member states, including twelve founding members: Belgium, Canada, Denmark, France, Germany, Greece, Iceland, Italy, Luxembourg, the Netherlands, Norway, Portugal, Spain, Turkey, the United Kingdom and the United States. Greece and Turkey joined in February 1952, West Germany in May 1955, and Spain in May 1982 (ibid., pp. 440–1). Germany as a whole became a member of NATO following its reunification in October 1990.[20]

The Warsaw Pact (or Warsaw Treaty Organisation) is likewise an example of an 'intergovernmental organization' (ibid., p. 633), founded as 'a regional defence alliance of the Eastern European communist countries led by the Soviet Union'; and as, in turn, a 'counterweight to the North Atlantic Treaty Organization' (ibid., p. 633). Its members, apart from the Soviet Union, were Bulgaria, Czechoslovakia, East Germany (the German Democratic Republic), Hungary, Poland and Romania (Albania had been a member before withdrawing in 1968) (ibid., p. 633). As Drost goes on to explain, in October 1990, the members 'renounced the so-called Brezhnev doctrine,[21] under which Pact members were obliged to intervene militarily in any [alliance member] where "socialism" was perceived to be under threat' (ibid., pp. 633–4). Then:

> The Pact effectively disintegrated after the collapse of communist rule in Eastern Europe in 1989. It was formally disbanded as a military alliance in February 1991 and as a political alliance in July. All Soviet and Russian troops were withdrawn from Czechoslovakia and Hungary by June 1991, from Poland by September 1993 and from [what had been] East Germany by August 1994. (Drost, 1995, p. 634)

The economic counterpart to the Warsaw Pact[22] was the Council for Mutual Economic Assistance (CMEA or COMECON), also described by Drost as a '[f]ormer intergovernmental organization' (ibid., p. 121). It was founded in 1949, 'with the aim of facilitating and coordinating economic development on orthodox economic principles' (*ibid.*, p. 121):

> Its original members were the seven communist countries of Eastern Europe: Bulgaria, Czechoslovakia, East Germany, Hungary, Poland, Romania and the Soviet Union. They were later joined by Cuba, Mongolia and Vietnam. In March 1990, in the wake of the collapse of communist rule in Eastern Europe and the new governments' declared intention to develop trade and other links with Western Europe, the members agreed to abolish multilateral cooperation and coordination of economic planning, two of COMECON's most important functions. After an attempt to remodel the organization along market-oriented lines failed, it was formally dissolved in June 1991.   (*ibid.*, p. 121)

By February 1996, in accordance with their decisions to reconstruct their economies along market-capitalist lines in conjunction with seeking closer trading and other economic links with Western Europe, all of the former East European members of COMECON[23] had either (in the case of East Germany) been absorbed into or had applied to join the principal West European economic organisation, the European Union – all, that is, except the Soviet Union. The Soviet Union itself collapsed in 1991, breaking down into its fifteen constituent republics, which as a result became known as the 'Soviet successor states' (*ibid.*, p. 567). These fifteen, now independent republics,[24] include the three Baltic countries – Estonia, Latvia and Lithuania – again, all of which had applied to join the EU by February 1996. In a similar way to the Soviet Union, on 1 January 1993, Czechoslovakia was dissolved into the Czech Republic and Slovakia, the former (i.e., the Czech Republic) becoming 'the ninth [ex-]East European country to embark on the road to membership' of the EU (European Commission, *Frontier-Free Europe*, March 1996), the others being Bulgaria, Hungary, Poland, Romania, Slovakia, and the three Baltic countries. On 10 June 1996, 'Slovenia officially applied to join the European Union', becoming thereby the tenth 'Central and East European country to sign [...] an agreement, which implies the prospect of membership in due course. Slovenia [thus became] the only ex-Yugoslav republic' to have applied for membership (European Commission, *Frontier-Free Europe*, July–August 1996 p. 3; see also Nørgaard *et al.*, 1993, Part II). At the same time, these ten central and eastern European countries were accompanying three Mediterranean applicants: Cyprus (which had applied to join on 4 July 1990), Malta (16 July 1990) and Turkey (14 April 1987) (Fontaine, 1995, pp. 44–5).

Furthermore, as the 1990s progressed, several of the same ex-COMECON countries began to signal their interest in becoming members of another western (intergovernmental) organisation, which according to Borchardt has played an important part in the postwar steps towards European unification (Borchardt, 1995, p. 6), namely the North Atlantic Treaty Organisation (NATO), the result being (as reported in January 1997) that 'Nato is expected to choose three to four new members at a summit in Madrid in July 1997, most likely led by Poland, the Czech Republic and Hungary' (Barber, 20 January 1997). In other words, as Ian Black suggested in February 1997, 'the definites are [. . .] Poland, Hungary and the Czech Republic. Slovenia is a strong possibility, Romania a weak one. The Baltic states are to be excluded' (Black, 15 February 1997).[25]

However, because NATO is an intergovernmental organisation, then its expansion to include even one additional member requires the unanimous agreement of all its current members, something it would seem is not inevitable. Each of NATO's Member States has the right to veto the expansion of the organisation, and 'Turkey has privately warned [its] allies that it will block entry to Nato by former communist countries of central and eastern Europe unless it obtains a promise of membership from the European Union' (Barber, 20 January 1997). Turkey issued this threat as a response to its frustration at being itself kept out of another organisation, the European Union: the 'EU has long viewed the idea of opening its doors to Turkey as unrealistic, citing its size, poverty, and, less publicly, its Moslem tradition and human rights record' (*ibid.*).[26]

The European Union's problem with Turkey's 'Moslem tradition' did not stay out of the public domain for much longer:

Helmut Kohl hurriedly invited Turkey's Islamist prime minister, Necmettin Erbakan, to Bonn yesterday [6 March 1997] after an eruption of Turkish anger at the German chancellor's sudden snub to their country's European Union ambitions [. . .]. At a meeting in Brussels of the European People's Party (EPP), an alliance of European Christian Democratic parties led by Mr Kohl and including six EU heads of government, several participants said that Turkey would not be allowed to join the EU, despite 34 years of negotiations and several agreements between Brussels and Ankara. Sources at the meeting said that Mr Kohl, exasperated by Turkey's threats to block the eastwards expansion of Nato unless Ankara's prospects of EU membership improved, and tired of pressure from the United States on the issue, ordered a clear signal on the issue. Wilfried Martens, the former Belgian prime minister, who is president of the EPP, said 'We are creating a European Union. This is a European project.' He made it plain that Turkey was not seen as part of Europe [. . .]. 'For 34 years we have been deceived and betrayed by the EU,' said a senior Turkish official. He added that Mr Kohl was the most influential figure trying to ensure that the EU remained a 'Christian club' and that the importance of Islam in Turkey was the main reason for excluding it. (Traynor and Nuttall, 7 March 1997)

Turkey's 'gambit risks complicating [even further] the [already] tricky process on Nato enlargement' (Barber, 20 January 1997). That is, the prospect of NATO's successful expansion eastwards was already full of uncertainties and difficulties due to the strong disapproval, opposition and, indeed, threats being expressed by Russia: 'the Kremlin insisted yesterday that its objections to the enlargement of Nato, a process which the alliance plans to launch at a summit in July, remained intact' (Thornhill, 6 January 1997). In fact, Russia became increasingly vociferous in its objections: the 'Russians are turning up the volume on their megaphone diplomacy against Nato's plan to offer membership to a number of Russia's former Warsaw Pact allies in eastern Europe' (Davidson, 5 February 1997).

The squabble between NATO and Russia over NATO's eastward expansion hung over the proceedings of one 'European' organisation which already brings together NATO members and ex-COMECON countries, including Russia, namely the Organisation for Security and Co-operation in Europe (OSCE). This forum was originally set up as the Conference on Security and Co-operation in Europe (CSCE) in 1975 under the Helsinki Final Act, which 'sought to reduce tension and build confidence between the two [Cold War] military blocs confronting each other on the continent, the North Atlantic Treaty Organization (NATO) and the Warsaw Pact' (Drost, 1995, pp. 108–9). The OSCE remains an '[i]ntergovernmental organization' (*ibid.*, p. 108), of which '[a]ll sovereign states in Europe, the successor states of the Soviet Union as well as Canada and the United States are members [...], in total 54 states' (*ibid.*, p. 109). As then reported by Ian Black in December 1996:

at today's European security summit, Western countries look likely to face trouble as Moscow grows increasingly jittery about an expanding Nato. [The] leaders of the 54-country Organisation for Security and Co-operation in Europe (OSCE) [are holding] a two-day meeting in Lisbon to finalise [...] ambitious plans for a 'security model' for the next century [...]. At the meeting today, Mr Chernomyrdin [the Russian prime minister] is expected to press for a stronger pan-European role for the OSCE, the world's widest but probably least-known security body. The United States [...] will be resisting the demands [in the hope] that by [...] enhancing co-operation between Nato, the OSCE and the European Union, Russian concerns about Nato enlargement can be assuaged.

(Black, 2 December 1996)

The United States' hopes in this regard appear to have been dashed. If anything, the concern and anger felt in Russia towards NATO grew, as reflected in one February 1997 newspaper report which carried the claim 'Moscow hints at nuclear retaliation' (Freeland, 12 February 1997):

Russia's hostility to Nato's planned eastward expansion took a new twist yesterday when the Kremlin security chief said Moscow should be ready to unleash its nuclear missiles in response to an attack by conventional forces. In a sharp break from Mikhail Gorbachev's pledge that Russia would never launch a first strike nuclear attack, Mr Ivan Rybkin, secretary of the security council, made the policy proposal in an interview published yesterday.   (*ibid.*)

After the formation of NATO, the next transatlantic organisation to be founded was the Western European Union (WEU) in 1954 (Borchardt, 1995, p. 6; see also Archer, 1990, Chapter 10; Harrison, 1995, Chapter 8; and Nørgaard *et al.*, 1993):

> which was intended to strengthen security cooperation between the countries of Europe. This widened the existing Brussels Treaty between the United Kingdom, France, Belgium, Luxembourg and the Netherlands to include the Federal Republic of Germany and Italy, and has subsequently also taken in Portugal, Spain and Greece. The WEU offers its members a platform for closer cooperation on security and defence, helping them forge a European identity in this field and so lend greater weight to the European voice in the Atlantic Alliance.   (Borchardt, 1995, p. 6)

Harry Drost concurs with Borchardt on this latter point while drawing attention to further significant features and developments: the WEU is an '[i]ntergovernmental organization' which, as we have previously noted, 'was reactivated in [October] 1984 in response to a growing desire among Western European governments to cooperate more closely on defence policy and arms procurement. In recent years the WEU's role has been redefined as a "bridge" between the European Union (EU) and the North Atlantic Treaty Organization (NATO) and [as] an "integral component" of the European integration process' (Drost, 1995, p. 636) – as, that is, an integral feature of the development of the European Union (*ibid.*, p. 636). As we have already discussed:

> The Maastricht Treaty establishing the European Union (EU), agreed in December 1991 and in force since November 1993, states that 'the objective is to build up the WEU as the defence component of the European Union' and 'to develop the WEU as a means to strengthen the European pillar of the Atlantic Alliance'.
> (Drost, 1995, p. 636; see also Harrison, 1995, pp. 170–1; and Petersen, 1993)

Drost suggests that in 'recognition of the WEU's changing role, six new countries were admitted in November 1992 as full, associate or observer members' (Drost, 1995, p. 636). As a result, the membership of the WEU reflects its overlap with NATO (see Ougaard, 1993) and its growing link with the EU. It has fifteen members: Belgium, France, Germany, Greece, Italy, Luxembourg, the Netherlands, Portugal, Spain and the United Kingdom are full members (Drost, 1995, p. 636), just as they are of the European Union. In addition, Iceland, Norway and Turkey are associate members, and Denmark and Ireland are observer members (*ibid.*, p. 636). Of course, Iceland, Norway and Turkey are members of NATO; Denmark is a member of NATO and the EU; and Ireland is a member of the EU.

Borchardt distinguishes the first group of organisations he regards as having played a part in post-Second World War 'European unification' (Borchardt, 1995, p. 6) from a second group, a principal 'characteristic feature of' which is that the organisations involved 'are designed to enable as many countries as possible to become members'. Consequently, the organisations are based on the concession 'that their activities [will] not extend beyond the scope of normal international cooperation. One such organization is the Council of Europe, founded on 5 May 1949 to foster political cooperation' (*ibid.*, pp. 6–7; see also Archer, 1990, Chapter 4; Close, 1995, especially Chapters 2 and 3):

> The Council of Europe [. . .] serves merely as an instrument of intergovernmental cooperation [. . .]. Its membership has grown from the 10 original founders to 25 (the United Kingdom, France, Belgium, the Netherlands, Luxembourg, Italy, Ireland, Denmark, Norway and Sweden, plus Greece, Turkey, [. . .] Germany, Austria, Cyprus, Switzerland, Malta, Iceland, Portugal, Spain, Liechtenstein, Finland, San Marino, Hungary and Poland). (Borchardt, 1995, p. 7)

By October 1996, the membership of the Council of Europe (CE) had swollen much further, reaching forty, following the controversial admission of Croatia (Seacombe, 20 October 1996). Borchardt claims that the contribution of the CE to 'the cause of European unity and solidarity cannot be rated highly enough' (Borchardt, 1995, p. 7):

> Under its auspices a wide range of economic, cultural, social and legal conventions have been concluded, the most significant and best known of them being the European Convention for the Protection of Human Rights and Fundamental Freedoms adopted on 4 November 1950. This not only laid down a practical minimum standard of human rights to be applied in member States but also set up a system for legal remedy, empowering the institutions established under the Convention – the European Commission for Human Rights and the European Court of Human Rights [located in Strasbourg] – to condemn infringements of human rights by the signatories. (Borchardt, 1995, pp. 6–7)

Drost likewise counts the CE as an '[i]ntergovernmental organization', founded in 1949 'to protect and strengthen pluralist democracy and human rights and to promote awareness of a European cultural identity' (Drost, 1995, p. 121). The CE is 'the oldest major institution of pan-European cooperation. Originally solely a Western European organization, it has admitted most of the former communist countries' (*ibid.*, p. 121) of central and eastern Europe during the 1990s – since, that is, the end of the Cold War. The Council, Drost claims, 'has become a key institutional link between Eastern and Western Europe' (*ibid.*, p. 121), and in particular between the former members of the Eastern bloc and the European Union:

> In May 1989 the Committee of Ministers [the Council's senior (inter-govern-mental) decision-making body] adopted a declaration on the future role of the Council which stressed closer cooperation with the European Community (EC, now the European Union, EU) and the Eastern European countries. Since then much of the Council's work has been directed towards helping the former communist countries reform their institutions and legislation. In 1990 Hungary became the first former communist country to be admitted to the Council. Others were admitted as they were deemed to have introduced multiparty political systems and free elections.
>
> (Drost, 1995, p. 123)

Drost's decision to categorise the CE alongside the WEU and NATO as *intergovernmental* is based on one of the most conceptually distinctive, empirically important and theoretically significant features of the Council, the WEU and NATO. Drost's categorisation draws attention to a basic feature of the Council of Europe which it shares with the WEU, NATO, the OSCE and the OECD (not to mention the former COMECON and Warsaw Pact), but which distinguishes the Council along with all those other organisations which belong to the intergovernmental category from the European Union; or, more precisely, from the European Community within the EU.[27]

Borchardt has this feature in mind when he elaborates on the character of the Council of Europe:

> Its statute contains no reference to any such goals as federation or union, nor does it foresee any transfer or pooling of portions of national sovereignty. Decision-making rests entirely with a Committee of Ministers and unanimity is required for all decisions on matters of substance, which means that any country can veto a decision as in the United Nations Security Council. In addition there is a Parliamentary Assembly, but its role is purely consultative and it has no legislative powers. All it can do is to put recommendations to the Committee of Ministers. However, any recommendation can be turned down by a single vote, as the Committee is not answerable to the Assembly. And even after a proposal has been adopted by the Committee of Ministers, it still has to be ratified by the

national parliaments before it can have the force of law. The Council of Europe, then, serves merely as an instrument of intergovernmental cooperation.   (Borchardt, 1995, p. 7)

The Council of Europe, the WEU, NATO *and*, as indicated by Borchardt, the United Nations (at the decision-making pinnacle of which is the Security Council) are all intergovernmental organisations, as is the OSCE, and as were COMECON and the Warsaw Pact.

Drost points out that intergovernmental co-operation is also a feature of the European Union: in 'the European Union (EU), cooperation among member states outside the "supranational" structures of the European Community (EC), the core of the organization', is of the intergovernmental type (Drost, 1995, p. 320). Drost adds that the 'Maastricht Treaty, which entered into force in November 1993, formalized intergovernmental cooperation in two "pillars", the Common Foreign and Security Policy (CFSP) and the Cooperation on Justice and Home Affairs (CJHA)' (*ibid.*, p. 320). Consequently, the EU overall qualifies as an intergovernmental organisation (*ibid.*, p. 206), the origins of which lie initially in the 1952 European Coal and Steel Community (ECSC), but subsequently and with greater (institutional) impact in the construction of 'the more comprehensive European Economic Community', created as this was by the 1957 Treaty of Rome (or the Treaties of Rome, the second Treaty being the foundation of the European Atomic Energy Community, or Euratom). Since 1957, as previously indicated, the Treaty of Rome has been amended by the Treaty Establishing a Single Council and a Single Commission of the European Communities (the Merger Treaty), signed on 8 April 1965 and brought into force on 1 July 1967 (*ibid.*, p. 206); and more recently has been subjected to 'two comprehensive revisions' (*ibid.*, p. 206). That is, the Treaty of Rome has been 'amended and supplemented by the 1986 Single European Act [signed on 17 February 1986] and the 1992 Maastricht Treaty establishing the European Union' (*ibid.*, p. 601).

The Treaty on European Union was agreed on 11 December 1991 at a summit meeting of the European Council in the Dutch city of Maastricht (*ibid.*, p. 602),[28] signed on 7 February 1992 and has been in force since 1 November 1993 (*ibid.*, p. 206):

> The Maastricht Treaty represents a comprehensive revision of the organization's founding treaties, in particular the 1957 Treaty of Rome establishing the European Economic Community (EEC) – now formally renamed the European Community [...] – and its amendments contained in the 1986 Single European Act. It establishes the European Union, composed of three 'pillars': (i) the European Communities, with the European Community at its core and including the European Coal and Steel Community (ECSC) and the European Atomic Energy Community (EAEC or EURATOM); (ii) the

Common Foreign and Security Policy (CFSP); and (iii) Cooperation on Justice and Home Affairs (CJHA). The latter two are forms of 'intergovernmental cooperation'. The incorporation of these policy spheres into the supranational EC framework was not acceptable to several member states because of the transfer of sovereignty it implied. [Despite this, however, the Treaty] expands the Community's existing responsibilities[29] and incorporates new policy areas or aspects thereof (e.g. education, culture, health, development cooperation, consumer protection, industry, research and technology, trans-European transport and telecommunications networks, environment); [...] expands Community responsibilities in social policy (not applicable in the United Kingdom); [...] lays down the structural framework and a timetable for economic and monetary union (EMU); [...] extends majority voting in the Council of Ministers to certain policy areas (e.g. health, aspects of social policy, energy, tourism); [...] increases the legislative powers of the European Parliament in certain policy areas (e.g. internal-market matters, education, health, consumer protection, environment); [...] establishes several new institutions (e.g. European Monetary Institute, Committee of the Regions) and programmes (e.g. Cohesion Fund) and restructures others (e.g. European Investment Bank); [...] defines the limits of [apart from extending] Community competence ('subsidiarity')[30]; [...] introduces the concept of EU citizenship and strengthens citizens' rights; [...] establishes a common foreign and security policy; [...] establishes a common policy on judicial affairs (covering asylum, border controls, immigration, police cooperation, etc); and [...] lays the foundation for an eventual common defence policy.   (Drost, 1995, pp. 602–3)

Even though the Maastricht Treaty comprehensively revised the Treaty of Rome (*ibid.*, p. 206), nevertheless the 'core of the European Union is still the European Economic Community, extended to include economic and monetary union'. On the other hand, Borchardt explains, the formal re-naming of the EEC is significant:

In Maastricht the [European Council] deleted the word 'Economic' in the title of the Treaty. This minor change can be taken to symbolize the intention that the EC should gradually become transformed from an economic community into a political union. It does not, however, affect the separate existence of the three Communities (ECSC, Euratom and EC), since they were in no way formally merged. (Borchardt, 1995, p. 59)

Borchardt makes the important point that '[e]conomic integration has always been the driving force behind the movement towards European unity' (*ibid.*, p. 24). But, Borchardt adds:

The Community's founding fathers believed that economic integration would inevitably lead to the political unification of Europe. While economic integration was the first practical step, it was never seen as an end in itself but merely as a stage on the road to political union [...]. The idea was taken up [...] in 1987 in the Single European Act, the preamble spelling out the will of the [European Council] 'to transform relations as a whole among their States into a European Union'. With the signing of the Treaty on European Union in Maastricht on 7 February 1992 and its entry into force on 1 November 1993 [...], that European Union became a reality. The EU Treaty marks a 'new stage' in the [...] progress towards the goal of political unity [...].   (Borchardt, 1995, pp. 25–6)[31]

Economic integration as the driving force behind, if not the final goal of, 'European unity' is well-reflected in the areas of (decision-making) responsibility, competence, power and sovereignty which the Treaty on European Union has confirmed belong to or has newly extended to the core pillar of the EU – to, that is, the European Community:

Within the EU, the EC is competent to formulate and decide policy in 17 areas: free movement of goods (an aspect of the single market); agriculture and fisheries; free movement of persons, services and capital (an aspect of the single market); transport; competition, taxation and approximation laws; economic and monetary policy; commercial policy (i.e. foreign-trade issues); social policy, education, vocational training and youth; culture; public health; consumer protection; trans-European networks (i.e. infrastructure and communications); industry; economic and social cohesion; research and technological development; environment; and development cooperation.   (Drost, 1995, p. 207)

Given this list, the Treaty on European Union would seem to vindicate the neo-functionalist (political, practical) approach to and (scholarly, theoretical) perspective on European integration. As previously mentioned, following Jo Shaw, the neo-functionalists 'have advocated [an] incremental and piecemeal approach to European integration in the spheres of both practical politics and integration theory literature' (Shaw, 1996, p. 12). The centrepiece of the neo-functionalist political approach to or theoretical perspective on European integration is a process 'termed *"spill-over"* ', which operates through 'the extension of the powers [competences] of the old European Economic Community out of the purely "economic" field into other related areas such as environmental and social policy' (*ibid.*, pp. 12–13; see also Gillespie, 1996, pp. 152–3). However, this (what we will refer to as) *lateral spillover* is complemented by a further manifestation of the same process: by, what we will distinguish as, *domain spillover*. As Shaw tells us, neo-functionalists anticipate the evolution not just of economic union, but also of '*political union* in the EU' (*ibid.*, pp. 12–13). For neo-functionalists, the spillover process means that European integration will pass 'through a number of stages [...] involving progressive transfers of power to [the Community and now to the Union] by the Member States' (*ibid.*, p. 12), the eventual outcome being full political, even federal, union (*ibid.*, p. 13 and pp. 76–9).

We subscribe to the neo-functionalist perspective on European integration, but only in so far as it can accommodate the occurrence of *domain spillover* towards political union; and, moreover, anticipate the evolution of European political union not just in sequential stages, but also in a concurrent fashion, even without lateral spillover. For us, the progressive *vertical* transfer of (decision-making) responsibility, competence, power and sovereignty from Member States to the EC's supranational institutions within the economic field inherently entails the concurrent vertical transfer of *political power*, thereby marking a further step (or stage) on the way towards *political union*.

That is, the progressive vertical transfer of competence, power and sovereignty in favour of a European political union is already well underway. It is taking place in conjunction with, due to and as an integral aspect of, the way in which the European Community, at the core of the EU, is gradually accumulating decision-making responsibility, competence, power and sovereignty *vis-à-vis* economic, not to mention (following Shaw) related, matters. The gradual transformation of the EU into a political union is already firmly established; the foundation of the EU as a political union is already in place, simply by virtue of the incremental but increasingly substantial transfer of decision-making sovereignty (in relation to economic and related matters) from the EU's Member States to the EC's supranational institutions. Whatever shifts, if any, have yet to take place in the second and third pillars of the EU (and, at least in the long term, these may be considerable), the EC at the core of the European Union is already an organisation with firmly embedded (independent) supranational institutions and decision-making procedures; and accordingly is already, categorically a supranational political union.

Guided by Anthony Giddens:

> *Politics* concerns the means whereby power is used to affect the scope and content of governmental activities. The sphere of the *political* may therefore range well beyond that of state institutions [...]. For there may be many ways in which those who are not part of the governmental apparatus seek to influence it.   (Giddens, 1993, p. 310)

Here, Giddens is inferring not only an empirical relationship but also a conceptual overlap between politics, government and 'the state'. He is somewhat more explicit about this when he tells us:

> All states, traditional and modern, share some general characteristics. A state exists where there is a political apparatus (governmental institutions,

such as a court, parliament or congress, plus civil service officials), ruling over a given *territory*, whose authority is backed by a *legal system* and by the capacity to use force to implement its policies. (Giddens, 1993, p. 309)

According to this definition, 'the state' is a collection of *political apparatuses* or *governmental institutions*. But, this gives rise to the questions of what is 'government' (a government); and what is the difference, if any, between 'government' (a government) and 'the state' (states)? For Giddens, both a *state* and a *government* are composed of a set of 'specialized political institutions or agencies of political administration' (*ibid.*, p. 309). He then adds in a way which does not obviously indicate any conceptual distinction between 'state' and 'government', that the latter term 'will be used [...] to refer to the regular enactment of policies and decisions on the part of the officials within a political apparatus. These officials include kings or emperors, their courts, elected representatives and members of the civil service. We can speak of government as a process, or of *the* government, referring to the apparatus responsible for the administrative process' (*ibid.*, p. 310).

For us, a government is a political institution, apparatus or agency which in conjunction with other (but not necessarily all other) political institutions (such as monarchs, legislatures, parliaments (elected or otherwise), executive administrative bodies – perhaps a 'civil service' – courts, police forces, 'armed forces', 'defence forces') within a society or social system constitute *a* state. A state is always more inclusive than a government, and indeed may exist without including a government (see *ibid.*, p. 309). When a state includes a government, the latter may have sharply defined (legally, perhaps constitutionally circumscribed) competences, powers and sovereignty which clearly both divide it from and relate it to that state's other constituent bodies – competences, powers and sovereignty that may, for instance, place it (the government) in a location which bridges the legislative and executive branches of the state (see Padfield and Byrne, 1987, p. 2). However, all the institutions, apparatuses or agencies which comprise a state participate to some extent in the process of governing the territory over which, following Giddens, that state has authority; or (to paraphrase Giddens) in the *process of government* (Giddens, 1993, p. 310) within this geographical (or geo-social) arena; or (our preferred phrase) in the process of *governance*, which may be otherwise expressed as *geo-political administration* or *geo-political management*.

Allan Johnson's notion of 'politics' is perhaps clearer and also closer to our own:

politics [...] is the social process through which collective power is generated, organized, distributed, and used in social systems. In most [modern] societies [or social systems], politics is organized primarily around the state [...]. Although the concept of politics is most often associated with governing institutions at international, national, regional, and community levels, [...] it can be applied to virtually any social system in which power plays a significant role.   (Johnson, 1995, pp. 205–6)

The European Union is a *social system in which the (unequal) distribution, accumulation and enjoyment of (social, economic and political) power plays a significant role.* It is a social system in which economic power and, integrally (see Harrop, 1992), political power are unevenly divided and exercised along various cross-cutting dimensions, including those which separate Member States, regions, ethnic groupings, social classes and gender categories from each other (see Bailey, 1992; Close, 1995; Hantrais, 1995; Ugur, 1995), as well as that which separates the nation-state level from the supranational level of decision-making responsibility, competence, power and sovereignty. As a supranational political union, the European Community is organised around a set of somewhat independent institutions through which the organisation can make decisions over and above – in place of and on behalf of – its Member States and their institutions, governments, citizens, and so on: decisions with regard to economic and related matters (as spelled out by Drost, 1995, p. 207; see also O'Keefe and Twomey, 1994).

While it may be stretching the definition of 'government' too far to claim that the EC itself is, or at least incorporates, a government, none the less what is evident is that the EC at the core of the EU engages in government-like activities – in, that is, the process of *governance*.

As Thomas Christiansen says about one of the EC's main institutions, the 'lack of formal powers to "govern" the Commission [has] been very challenging for successive holders of [the] office [of] Commission President', who 'has to oversee an increasingly large administration and a diverse group of Commissioners' (Christiansen, 1996, p. 87). Nevertheless, following Christiansen, the Commission as an EC/EU institution still plays a part in 'governing' *within* the Community:

In governing the process of European integration the Commission's fundamental strength is to practise, or experiment with, innovative forms of policy-making and continuous institutional reform [Snyder, 1993]. With the help of such methods, administrative growth and functional specialisation have allowed the Commission to expand its influence in an increasing number of policy sectors. Yet, at the same time, the expansion of tasks has made the maintenance of the overall coherence of its programme more difficult [...]. Consequently, in so far as the Commission has been able, on its own behalf and also on behalf of he EC/EU as a whole, to project the image of 'corporate actor' [Kenis and Schneider, 1987; Fuchs, 1995], and indeed continue functioning as a unified institution, it is important to look at the institutional arrangements which bind it together.

(Christiansen, 1996, p. 87)

To this end, Christiansen mentions the 'absence of hierarchical organisation in [...] the Commission', something which 'is habitually seen as a problem. "If everyone is in charge, no-one is in charge" sums up this critical attitude to non-hierarchical governance' (*ibid.*, p. 86).

Governance, guided by the *Concise Oxford Dictionary* (1990, p. 511), refers to 'the act or manner of governing', which in the European Community as elsewhere is not exclusively confined to government(s), defined, distinguished and identified in terms of a particular type, range and set of political institutions (or apparatuses) – a set of political institutions which, at the same time, constitutes part (but only part) of 'the state' (of states) (see Giddens, 1993, pp. 309–10).

After drawing attention to the association in modern societies or social systems between politics and the state, Allan Johnson points out that the 'state is not the same as *government* [...]. The state is a social institution [or set of social institutions], which [perform(s)] various functions [and] various tasks of governance, such as enacting legislation' (Johnson, 1995, p. 275). However, the social institutions entailed extend beyond 'government'; and the character of overall sets or systems of state institutions varies considerably. The 'parliamentary system, for example, is [just] one way of accomplishing various tasks of governance' (*ibid.*, p. 275), there being a range of different ways, of alternative systems. Having said this, as Padfield and Byrne point out, nevertheless there 'are two main types of states: (i) Federal, and (ii) Unitary' (Padfield and Byrne, 1987, p. 2): in *unitary* states, 'power is concentrated in one body and the departments of government are centralised in one institution. The United Kingdom is' such a state (*ibid.*, p. 3). In contrast:

A Federal State [sic] is a group of constituent units (States or Territories) which aims to reconcile national unity and power with the maintenance of individual State rights. Here power is divided between (i) a National Government which, in matters of common concern, e.g. defence, is supreme over the whole country [geo-social arena]; and (ii) State Governments which are supreme in those matters left to them, e.g. State schools. For citizens living under Federal authorities there are in fact two sets of laws: (i) Federal Law, and (ii) State Law. The main examples of Federal States are: the United States of America, Australia, Canada, [...] Germany and Switzerland. (Padfield and Byrne, 1987, p. 3; see also Gillespie, 1996)

Padfield and Byrne's notion of a 'federal state',[32] resting as it does on the principle of a division of power or sovereignty between a federal state, or central set of governing institutions, on the one hand, and a set of constituent (or member) 'states' (as in the United States of America; or *Bundeslander* in Germany and Austria; or *cantons* in Switzerland) and their governing – including legislative – institutions, on the other, reminds us of the so-called *principle of subsidiarity* as included in the Treaty on European Union in connection with (following Drost) defining 'the limits of Community competence' (Drost, 1995, p. 603). Drost expands:

> In the European Union (EU), [the principle of subsidiarity is] the principle that decisions should be taken at the most appropriate level of government (i.e. local, regional, national or supranational) and specifically at the lowest practicable level and as closely as possible to the citizen. (Drost, 1995, p. 580)

The issues surrounding the meaning and operation of the principle of subsidiarity have attracted a great deal of attention for a number of reasons,[33] but for present purposes what is of interest is the way in which the principle (as reflected in Drost's clarification), if anything, appears to confirm the EC as a level – as the supranational level – of 'government' within the European Union.

Essentially, the European Union's status as a political union has already been established in so far as the (set of institutions of the) European Community at the core of the Union has acquired supranational decision-making responsibility, competence, power and sovereignty, and thereby political power – and accordingly plays an independent part in internal (intra-territorial; geo-social) process of governance – *vis-à-vis* an array of economic and other (however related) policy areas. As we have already noted, guided by Drost, the framework of the EU as a political union consists of three 'pillars', each with its distinctive competences and structure. First, there is the *European Communities*, which in turn is composed of the European Community (the original EEC; the ECSC; and the EAEC or Euratom). At the same time, however, these three Communities have 'a joint institutional framework and are for all practical purposes a single unit – hence the common usage of "European Community" and "EC" to cover all three' (*ibid.*, p. 207), even though formally and constitutionally speaking they are separate 'legal entities'. Second, there is the Common Foreign and Security Policy (CFSP) pillar; and third, the Cooperation on Justice and Home Affairs (CJHA) pillar. However, Drost adds the important point about the EU overall:

> The core of the EU, the EC, is a 'supranational' organization, ie one to which the member states have transferred specified legislative and executive powers [competences] and whose decisions are binding on them and their citizens. The CFSP and CJHA are forms of intergovernmental cooperation, in which the member states retain full sovereign rights, and hence decision making unanimity. All legislation is adopted within the supranational framework of the EC. Technically there is thus no such thing as 'EU legislation', only EC legislation.   (Drost, 1995, p. 207)

Because the CFSP and CJHA pillars of the EU are intergovernmental in character – in their decision-making procedures – then, as Drost says, the EU as a whole is an 'intergovernmental organization' (*ibid.*, p. 206). None the less, at the core of the EU, the European Community (or European Communities)[34] has a different character, one which means that it cannot be categorised alongside the CFSP, the CJHA, the EU, the WEU, NATO, the OSCE, the OECD and the UN as 'intergovernmental'.

The 'European Communities (EC)' is the '[f]ormal name of the three supranational organizations at the core of the European Union (EU)' (*ibid.*, p. 193), hence Borchardt's 'third group of organizations' which have played a part in furthering post-Second World War 'European unification' (Borchardt, 1995, pp. 6–7). This group:

> comprises the European Coal and Steel Community, the European Atomic Energy Community and the European (Economic) Community. From a legal point of view the three communities continue to exist separately side by side. In terms of political reality, however, they can be treated as a single unit. Their creation can be regarded as marking the birth of the 'European Community'. The major innovation compared with other international bodies is that its members have given up part of their national sovereignty with the goal of forming a cohesive, indissoluble organizational and political unit. They have conferred on it sovereign powers of its own, independent of the Member States, which it can exercise to adopt acts that have the force of national law. The EC also forms the core of the 'European union' established on 1 November 1993 with the entry into force of the Maastricht Treaty. The European Communities, then, offer the most advanced example of European integration.
>
> (Borchardt, 1995, pp. 7–8)

The EC is the most advanced example of European integration in that it has progressed furthest along the road of political union and, moreover, of *supranational* political union. As well as being integrally, extensively and (institutionally, legally, constitutionally) deeply engaged in government-like activities – that is, in the process of governance – the EC is a supranational political union with *federal* qualities:

> Federalism has formed an important current in much thinking about European integration; although self-evidently the EU is not a federal state, nonetheless power is now in fact divided between the Union and the Member States in a manner which partially mimics a federal system. Moreover, as many writers have stressed, federalism is potentially a very broad concept capable of describing any type of governance system involving a divided power structure [. . .]. In that spirit, it can be shown that a number of important constitutional principles of the EU[35] seek to organise the exercise of political and legal authority in a way which is not wholly dissimilar to the basic framework of a federal state with a federal authority

and constitutent states. Certainly, the organisation of the relationship between EC law and national law [...] demonstrates the hallmarks of a federal system. EC (federal) law is a higher source of normative authority than national (state) law, and takes effect within the national legal systems [...] without the need for intermediate action by the Member States.

(Shaw, 1996, p. 76)

The issues of whether the EC/EU is becoming, or has already become (at least partially), a federal system and whether it should be (more of) a federal system have attracted great interest, concern and consternation, and have been responsible for a large outpouring of literature, of the scholastic, journalistic, politically committed and other kinds.[36] It does not serve our particular purpose to delve very far into the intricacies of the issues and debates in this regard, but it is of relevance to touch on certain points, including one raised by Drost:

In the European Union (EU), [*federal Europe* is] a concept associated with those who argue that the process of integration should be aimed at the creation of a closely knit union in which many [nation-state] powers are transferred to a supranational or federal level of government. In recent years it has become linked with a call for a 'Europe of the regions', in which many powers are devolved to the regional level [...]. Unlike most other intergovernmental organizations, the EU has always had a strong federal dimension in that national governments have transferred certain sovereign powers to it from the beginning, primarily in the economic field. Over the years other policy areas have been incorporated into the supra-national framework [...]. The issue came to a head in the negotiations and subsequent debate on the the Maastricht Treaty [...]. In particular, its provisions for economic and monetary union and cooperation in foreign affairs and defence are described by critics as 'centralizing' or 'federalist'. In this context the concept of 'subsidiarity', i.e. the most appropriate level of government (local, regional, national or supranational) at which decisions should be taken, has become a major focus of debate.

(Drost, 1995, pp. 222–4)

We have already mentioned how the general notion of 'federal state', as defined by Padfield and Byrne (1987, pp. 2–3) for instance, brings to mind the so-called *principle of subsidiarity* as outlined by Drost.[37] But, what Drost also draws attention to is the question (not unconnected with the issues surrounding the meaning and operation of the principle of subsidiarity) of regional and local – or, what may be more appropriately referred to as, *sub*-nation-state – decision-making responsibility, competence, power and sovereignty. At the same time, the call for a Europe of the regions, as Drost puts it, is not just inspired by the (top-down) objective of ensuring that decision-making occurs 'as closely as possible to the citizen' (Drost, 1995, p. 50; see also Elliott, 3 March 1997), or of the purported ideal of forging a *People's Europe* (see Fontaine, 1995, Chapter 10) or of a *Citizen's Europe* (Fontaine, 1993); but also, and perhaps principally, driven by the (bottom-up) pressures of nation(s) and nationalism(s), rooted as these things are in such matters as culture and ethnicity, a sense of common heritage and common destiny, a common identity and feelings of community, or an *imaginary community*[38]; and working against, as these things sometimes do, the cohesion, stability and integrity of particular nation-states (in practice, the cases of Belgium, France, Italy, Spain and the United Kingdom, all of which are within the EU, come to mind).

As inferred by Drost, the call for a Europe of the regions may be boosted by, and in turn may boost, the aims and achievements of European supra-nationalism, given that each (nationalism and supranationalism) has a tendency to undermine, respectively, particular nation-states and the nation-state in general – nation-states as a generic social form (see, for instance, Keating and Hooge, 1996). At the same time, however, while supranationalism and nationalism are mutually subversive of nation-states (including European Union Member States, perhaps some more than others), this does not mean that these movements (or, to borrow Charles de Gaulle's term, *doctrines*) are necessarily mutually supportive and unproblematic in relation to each other. Just as nation(s) and nationalism(s) can be a threat to nation-states, so they could present an increasing problem for (they could, in a sense, be increasingly transposed as a problem to) the European Union as an advancing supranational (even federal) political union – a problem, in other words, of (internal) governance.[39]

In this chapter, we have been very much guided by Borchardt's categorisation of organisations which have played a part in 'postwar steps towards European unification' (Borchardt, 1995, p. 6). But, as we have already indicated (see note 17), we recognise that Borchardt's categorisation of such organisations is not the only one. A useful examination of, what are variously referred to as, categorisations, classifications or typologies has been provided by Paul Gillespie (1996) under the heading of 'models of integration'. Gillespie focuses on placing 'the European Union within the framework of theories of integration' (Gillespie, 1996, p. 140), and favours the argument that the EU has an 'original and exemplary character'. The EU's originality 'can be seen in its institutional innovation and [in] how it differs from other models of international political association and community' (*ibid.*).

Following Ludlow (1993, p. 22), Gillespie suggests that the 'debate about the Community's future has been dominated [. . .] by the federalists and the intergovernmentalists' (Gillespie, 1996, p. 140), something inferred by Borchardt when he suggests that 'European integration has been shaped by two fundamentally different approaches – the "confederalist" [or inter-govern-mental] and the "federalist" [or supranational]' (Borchardt, 1995, p. 27). Borchardt adds, however, that the 'European Union is essentially a product of [the] federalist approach', albeit that 'the gap between national autonomy [or nation-state sovereignty] and European federation [or supranational sovereignty]' has been bridged by way of 'a gradual process' (*ibid.*, p. 28) – a process, in other words, of the kind advocated by neo-functionalists (Shaw, 1996, p. 12). Gillespie quotes with approval Stanley Hoffmann's view that ' "the EC has a more federal character than any other regional organisation that has ever existed. It is a unique experiment [. . .]" ([Hoffmann,] 1993, p. 30)' (Gillespie, 1996, pp. 146–7), 'combining federal and intergovernmental elements' (*ibid.*, p. 153), although Gillespie (following Sbragia, 1992) suggests that describing the EU as 'unique' carries the danger of *inhibiting compar-ison*, and so prefers to describe the EU as 'original' (Gillespie, 1996, p. 153), allowing for the possibility, it would seem, of similar regional organisations emerging (and even already existing) in its wake.

This aside, Gillespie mentions that hitherto 'Hoffmann has been a strong advocate of the realist/intergovernmentalist approach to international rela-tions, which emphasises "the role of national governments as the main determinants of the pace of integration" (Laffan, 1992, p. 11)' (Gillespie, 1996, p. 153). Hoffmann's perspective on the 'European integration process', whether best described as unique or original, appears to distance him from – or indicates his adoption of a modified version of – the *realist inter-govern-mentalist* approach; and appears to bring him closer to that theorist of European integration whom Gillespie seems to most admire, namely Philippe Schmitter (1991, 1992; see also Traxler and Schmitter, 1995). Gillespie describes Schmitter as 'a prominent neofunctionalist' (Gillespie, 1996, pp. 153–4), and proceeds to outline 'Schmitter's classification of regimes' (*ibid.*, p. 153), inspired as this is 'by a realisation that "our political vocabulary lacks the proper terminology" to comprehend the EU, which [Schmitter] has described as "an emergent and novel form of political domination". It will also be', argues Schmitter, ' "unique" ' (*ibid.*, pp. 154–5). The EU ' "[. . .] may resemble some existing polities: the United States [for example], and it may be described in terms that could sound familiar: federal, confederal, techno-cratic, democratic, corporatist, pluralist, and so forth, but it will be differ-ent" (Schmitter, 1991, p. 29)' (Gillespie, 1996, pp. 154–5).

For Schmitter, the EU may not be evolving into, categorically speaking, a 'supranational state' (Traxler and Schmitter, 1995, p. 196 – quoted in Gille-spie, 1996, p. 157). Gillespie tells us that what this means for Schmitter is 'the possibility that [the EU's current] variable geometry represents "[. . .] an enduring feature of the basic architecture of the Euro polity" (Traxler and Schmitter, 1995, p. 196)' (Gillespie, 1996, p. 157). Despite this, it seems to us that Gillespie still draws on familiar terms (or notions) when attempting to otherwise describe this architecture and, at the same time, to recommend a theoretical perspective: 'Although it is still only a semi-formed polity it operates at supranational, functional, intergovernmental and subnational levels, each of which tends to attract a strand of theorising from a range of disciplines. [A]ttempts are being made to combine several of the approaches in a comparative framework, which can be very helpful in considering the likely outcome of the [current, 1996–7] round of intergovernmental [IGC] negotiations' (*ibid.*, p. 153).

In a manner which is consistent with this conclusion, Gillespie argues for a 'multifaceted approach' to 'theorising on the EU', entailing a fusion of 'federalism, neofunctionalism and realism' (*ibid.*, p. 164). Essentially:

> [This] is made [. . .] necessary by the fact that the Union operates at several different levels. These include the international, analysed in particular by the realist school of international relations, at which, through IGCs and European Councils, high political questions and basic ground rules are established; the supranational, dealt with by legal and federal and neo-functional modes of analysis, in which primary legislation is the main agenda; and the intranational, analysed typically by policy studies and sociology, which has to do with the medium to low matters of governance, but ones that can be rightly salient for publics when they become visible [Weiler *et al.*, 1995, p. 26]. (Gillespie, 1996, pp. 164–5)

While we subscribe to the view that the European Union is a novel, even unique (at least for the time being), organisation, and to the argument that the Union can be most fruitfully studied, analysed and understood by employing a hitherto unknown theoretical framework (albeit one which entails fusing several previously applied perspectives), we are not convinced by Gillespie's representation of 'governance' as a 'medium to low', intra-national (or, he might have said, *intra*-nation-state) matter – although we do acknowledge that we may have misinterpreted Gillespie's representation, hindered as we are by not knowing for sure what he means by 'governance'. For us, governance refers to the process of *geo-political management*, and as such governance is universal in its province and is performed without exception – that is, inclusively – by all political institutions and at all political levels.[40]

Governance is universal and inclusive as a process, just as concomitantly governance is universal and inclusive as a *problem*. It is a problem – if in no other ways than those indicated by such conundrums as how best to engage in the process of governance; whether it is possible to engage in the process fully or even at all; and how to respond to the consequences of having engaged in, having not engaged in or having not fully engaged in the process – which confronts political institutions and systems everywhere and at every level. Governance is a problem for all political systems and, at the same time, is performed by all political institutions (including, variously, governments, legislatures, parliaments, administrative bodies, courts, police forces, and so on) – some of which specialise in governance – at all political levels: including the sub-nation-state (or local) level; the intra-nation-state (or simply the nation-state) level; the supranational (or what may warrant the label the *supra-state*) level; and the regional level (geo-political, geo-economic and geo-cultural arenas exemplified by, for instance, southern Italy, western European and the Asia-Pacific among many others).

Furthermore, at each level, the problem and process of governance is not just an internal matter: is not internally confined. In all cases, the problem and process will have an external aspect or dimension. Political institutions at the nation-state (that is, at the Member State) level within the EU, for instance, will face an internal problem of political governance and will, in handling this problem, engage in internal governance as a process. At the same time, however, this problem and this process will occur alongside and, moreover, will be affected by an external (*extra*-nation-state) problem of governance to be handled by the same institutions. For us, at any political level, an institutional system faces an internal problem of governance and an external problem of governance, each of which (while being distinctive in type or quality, difficulty or intensity, etc.) will impinge on the other; and the same institutional system will engage in a process of governance (of geo-political management) which in its details will be shaped by both of these two problems along with the relationship between them.

One crucial factor which will help make the internal problem of governance faced by any nation-state different from the external problem is that the former occurs within the territory, or geo-social arena, over which this nation-state's system of political institutions (or state) enjoys sovereignty. On the other hand, the organisational, institutional and constitutional character of the EU, in that it is a *supranational* political union, is a complicating development in this regard. Being a supranational political union, the EU's Member States have, after all, 'pooled' their sovereignty, at least to some extent. This means that there has been, simultaneously, a vertical redistribution of sovereignty upwards from the nation-state level to the supranational level, along with something of a horizontal (lateral) redistribution of sovereignty at the nation-state level. Within the EU, each Member State, as a nation-state, shares its sovereignty with all the other Member States; while in return, or in exchange, each Member State shares in (has a share or a stake in) the sovereignty of all the others – although, of course, this lateral exchange of sovereignty does not necessarily translate into an *equal* distribution between the EU's Member States of decision-making power within the EU, at whatever level. Thus, Germany is generally regarded as being the 'powerhouse' of Europe (see, for instance, Baring, 1994; Gowland *et al.*, 1995; Norman, 29 November 1996).

Mention of the redistribution of sovereignty within the EU in the context of the problem(s) and process of governance brings to mind Julie Wolf's point about how (to paraphrase) most EU Member States are in favour of 'pooling their sovereignty' more and more, because of the way the resulting unity (supranational political union) is experienced as a source of strength, and in particular of the kind of strength which each Member State by itself would not have while needing to have 'in an increasingly global political environment' (Wolf, 26 March 1996). Although Wolf's argument is somewhat vague, the gist is clear, and appears consistent *both* with the messages coming from a broad range of other writers[41] *and* with the starting point we have proposed for studying, analysing and understanding the process of European integration by way of the progress of the European Union along the road of supranational political union.

As summarised by Barrie Axford (1995), for instance:

> the institutionalist[42] reworking of the traditional model of international relations draws attention to the ways in which interdependence, or mutually accepted constraints which may arise from market failure (Keohane, 1984; Stein, 1990), can breed cooperation and perhaps a growing trust between states, sufficient to encourage the 'surrendering' or 'pooling' of key areas of sovereignty (Wendt, 1994). This is seen most obviously in the history of the European Union, but would apply presumably to many situations in which cooperative behaviour produces outcomes that are more preferred or less costly than individual, self-interested action (Stein, 1990). Thus regimes may appear not just as pragmatic responses to insecurity, but as institutional anchors in a turbulent world. The moral overtones of this line of argument are in some ways akin to idealist solutions to the problem of international anarchy.   (Axford, 1995, p. 41)

The process of European integration can only be understood by studying and analysing it in its global context – in a context characterised by the process of globalisation (see, for instance, Robertson, 1992; Woodiwiss, 1996), augmented as this has been by the end of the Cold War, and thereby the advent of the New World Order (see, for instance, Ambrose, 1993), and marked as this process has increasingly been by the proliferation of organisations which display various basic similarities to the European Union. The result is a new world order in which the problem and process of *global governance* is being increasingly assumed by, what can be collectively called (guided by Hoffmann's and Axford's terminology), regional (political) organisations or regimes; and are being increasingly addressed and handled within the relationships (the negotiations, disputes, conflicts, compromises, agreements, etc.) among these regional regimes.

For instance, Nicholas Cumming-Bruce summed up the meeting between the EU and the Association of South East Asian Nations (ASEAN) in February 1997 with the heading 'East–West dialogue enters new era':

> A sense of relief could be detected yesterday after a meeting between 15 European and seven south-east Asian foreign ministers [...]. Today the European Union will agree measures to strengthen economic relations after clashes over European concern about human rights and Asean members' hostility to any formal debate on the issues. Indonesia threatened to walk out if anyone raised the issue of the annexation of East Timor. Asean countries did not wish to debate their 'constructive engagement' with Burma [since 1989, *Myanmar*]. In the end, East Timor was informally raised – if hardly discussed – at a dinner, but it will not feature in the final communiqué. Discussion on Burma was diverted from the plenary session to a working lunch. EU and Asean ministers have been meeting regularly for 20 years, but seem only now to be acquiring any sense of how one another's community's work and the gap between them. For much of those 20 years the core of the EU relationship with Asean has been economic. Now a rapidly broadening agenda reflects a growing impetus on both sides to bridge the gap [...]. What started 30 years ago as a grouping of Indonesia, Malaysia, the Philippines, Singapore, Thailand and later Brunei, is having a diplomatic success only partially explained by its economic performance. [In 1995,] Vietnam was admitted. This year [1997] Asean seems likely to embrace Burma, Camodia and Laos [...]. [A] membership of 10 would fulfil Asean's original hope of bringing the whole of South-east Asia under a single regional umbrella and could further enhance its standing as a crossroads between China and India.
>
> (Cumming-Bruce, 14 February 1997)

ASEAN is not the only organisation which resembles the EU as a regional 'umbrella', organisation or regime. Other regional regimes, at various stages of organisational, institutional and constitutional development, include the Amazon Pact, based on a treaty signed in 1978 by Bolivia, Brazil, Colombia, Ecuador, Guyana, Peru, Surinam, and Venezuela; and the Andean Group, or Pact, established under the Treaty of Cartagena in 1969 by Bolivia, Chile Colombia, Ecuador and Peru (Venezuela joined in 1973; and Chile withdrew in 1976). In 1996, the Andean Pact was re-launched as the *Andean Community*, inspired by 'the example of the European Union' (European Commission, *Frontier-Free Europe*, April 1996, p. 3).

There is the Arab Maghreb Union (AMU), an association formed in 1989 by Algeria, Libya, Mauritania, Morocco and Tunisia to co-ordinate policies on economic, cultural, international and military matters; the Asia Pacific Economic Co-operation (APEC) forum, which was formed in 1989 as a trading bloc, and which by the time of its summit meeting in November

1996 had acquired eighteen members from around the Asia Pacific region; and the emerging Association of Caribbean States:

> Ministers from 25 Caribbean Basin countries hold a two-day meeting [this week] in Havana to continue efforts towards economic co-operation by breathing life into the Association of Caribbean States. They contend it to be one of the world's largest trade blocks [sic]. Members ranging from St. Kitts-Nevis (population 42,000) to Mexico, plan intensified co-operation in trade, transportation and tourism. The US, upset that Cuba is a founding member, has told the dependencies of Puerto Rico and the US Virgin Islands not to accept an invitation to be among the 15 'associate' members.   (*Financial Times*, 9 December 1996)

Further, there is the Caribbean Community and Common Market (CAR-ICOM), an organisation with the aim of co-ordinating economic and foreign policy among its members; the (embryonic) East Asian Economic Caucus (EAEC); the Economic Community of Central African States (CEEAC); the Economic Community of West African States (ECOWAS); the Latin American Economic System; the Latin American Integration Association; Mercosur, an international organisation formed in 1991 with the objective of establishing a South American 'common market', its members being Argentina, Brazil, Paraguay, Uruguay and (since December 1996) Bolivia (see *Financial Times*, 16 December 1996); and the North American Free Trade Agreement or Area (NAFTA), established in November 1993 by Canada, Mexico and the United States: the 'first trade pact of its kind to link two highly-industrialized countries to a developing one', creating 'a free market of 360 million people with a total GDP of US$6.45 trillion' (Dresner, 1994, p. 362). While NAFTA is relatively new, 'Latin America's first attempt to form a free trade area was the Central American Common Market (ODECA) in 1960' (Buckley, 1994, p. 18). Moving back again to the other side of the Atlantic, there is the Preferential Trade Area of Eastern and Southern Africa (PTA), an organisation established in 1981 for the purpose of enhancing economic and commercial co-operation between its Member States, to harmonise tariffs and to reduce trade barriers, the aim being to create a common market (Dresner, 1994, pp. 362–3); and shifting again to Asia, there is the South Asian Association for Regional Co-operation (SAARC), an international organisation 'formed in 1985 to foster economic cooperation between its member states, which include Bangladesh, Bhutan, India, the Maldives, Nepal, Pakistan, and Sir Lanka' (*ibid.*, p. 363; see also European Commission, 'The European Union and Asia' (*Frontier-Free Europe* [Supplement], April 1996).

Many of these regional regimes, apart from being nowhere near as advanced organisationally as the European Union, are little known beyond their own borders. None the less, their growing presence and importance as global players, individually and collectively, is well reflected most notably in their trading activities, and most significantly in their external trading relationships, such as with each other and with the European Union. Thus, between 1984 and 1994, the two-way trade between the SAARC group of countries and the EU Twelve almost doubled. In 1984, the EU Twelve's imports from the SAARC group amounted to 5 billion ECU (on 30 November 1995, 1 ECU (European Currency Unit) was equivalent to UK£0.854 and US$1.328 (*ibid.*)); but by 1994, the corresponding figure was 11 billion ECU (*ibid.*). In 1984, the EU Twelve's exports to the SAARC group was worth 7 billion ECU, but by 1994 the corresponding figure was 11 billion ECU. Equally, however, the way in which the global presence and importance of some regional regimes is growing at a faster rate than others is likewise reflected in their relative trading performance; and in particular in the relative progress in their external trading profiles. Thus, between 1984 and 1994, the two-way trade between the EU and ASEAN increased almost six-fold. In 1984, the EU's Twelve's imports from the ASEAN Seven were worth 10 billion ECU; but by 1994, the corresponding figure was 30 billion ECU. Similarly, whereas the EU Twelve's exports to the ASEAN Seven amounted to 10 billion ECU in 1984, by 1994 the figure had risen to 28 billion ECU (*ibid.*)

Returning to Europe, there are several existing, emerging, embryonic or proposed regional 'umbrella' regimes, some of which we have previously listed. The lesser known ones beyond their own boundaries include the Baltic Council, an intergovernmental organisation comprising Estonia, Latvia and Lithuania, established in May 1990 'to coordinate policy in all areas of common interest' (Drost, 1995, p. 38); and 'not to be confused with the Council of Baltic Sea States' (*ibid.*, p. 38; see also *ibid.*, p. 121). The latter has ten members: Denmark, Estonia, Finland, Germany, Latvia, Lithuania, Norway, Poland, Russia and Sweden (the European Commission being an 'observer' on behalf of the European Union – *ibid.*, p. 121). Clearly, there is overlapping membership between the Council of Baltic Sea States (CBSS), the Baltic Council and the European Union, not to mention the Nordic Council (of Ministers), the membership of which is Denmark, Finland, Iceland, Norway and Sweden (*ibid.*, pp. 438–9; see also Gowland *et al.*, 1995, pp. 291–2).

Further south – apart from the Central European Initiative (CEI – Drost, 1995, p. 86), the Visegrad Group (or Visegrad Four – *ibid.*, p. 628), and the Black Sea Economic Co-operation Organisation (*ibid.*, p. 56) – there is the recently and optimistically proposed Southeast European Co-operation Initiative (SECI) for the Balkans region:

No other region of the world, of a similar size, offers such rich choice in terms of conflicts past and future as does the Balkans. Almost all of its 12 states [Albania, Bosnia, Bulgaria, Croatia, Greece, Hungary, Macedonia, Moldova, Romania, Slovenia, Turkey and Yugoslavia (Serbia, Montenegro)] – speaking between them 14 languages – have seen war in the past 10 years or are perparing for it now. But the Americans have decided to introduce a little bit of order by inventing the Southeast European Co-operation Initiative (SECI) to bring the Balkan nations together to promote economic and ecological co-operation. This is meant to stabilise the region [...]. Although the idea was America's, Europe would finance it while the Balkan peoples would have to consent to it.

(Zercin, *The Guardian*, 5 February 1997).

Among the existing and better known European regional regimes are ones to which we have already paid quite close attention, in particular the European Free Trade Association (EFTA) and the European Economic Area (EEA), the memberships of which overlap due to, as we have noted, their respective relationships with the most prominent and advanced European (not to say global) regional regime, the EU. It serves our purpose to retrace and review certain details about EFTA and the EEA and their relationships with the EU, the lessons of which provide a springboard for exploring further aspects of supranationalism in the new world order.

Both EFTA and the EEA are intergovernmental organisations (Drost, 1995, pp. 196–8), EFTA being formed in 1960 by Austria, Denmark, Norway, Portugal, Sweden, Switzerland and the United Kingdom. In 1970, Iceland joined; but at the end of 1972, Denmark and the United Kingdom left in preparation for their admission to the European Community on 1 January 1973. Likewise, Portugal withdrew from EFTA at the end of 1985 on the way to joining the Community. On the other hand, in January 1986, Finland became a full member (having been an associate member since 1961); and in May 1991, Liechtenstein became a full member: previously Liechtenstein had been an associate memberof EFTA through its customs union with Switzerland (*ibid.*, p. 198).

For Harry Drost, EFTA was formed 'in order to remove obstacles to free trade among its members and to contribute to the liberalization and expansion of European and world trade' (*ibid.*, p. 198). However, this may be regarded as a somewhat simplistic, naive or idealised view of EFTA's objectives, especially in the light of the much more detailed and searching accounts of the origins, purposes and development of EFTA provided by Helen Wallace and her colleagues on the relationship between EFTA and the EC/EU (Wallace, 1992). Thus, according to Thomas Pedersen:

After the collapse of [...] free trade negotiations [with the European Community (see Pedersen, 1992, pp. 13–116)], the UK and six like-minded countries in Western Europe formed with the Stockholm Convention of 1960 the European Free Trade Area (EFTA), as a reaction to the EC [...].

The original idea was that the EFTA grouping would strengthen the hand of the member states in their negotiations with the EC, which were widely expected to continue. To most of its members, EFTA was clearly a second best: Austria went on hoping till the last moment for a resumption of negotiations with the EC.					(Pedersen, 1992, p. 16)

Despite the original idea behind the formation of EFTA, as Helen Wallace and Wolfgang Wessels point out, the 'EC–EFTA relationship' was and remained 'asymmetrical in terms of power, procedures, political attention and ambition' (Wallace and Wessels, 1992, pp. 2–3). Several members of EFTA clung on to their ambition to transfer from EFTA to the European Community, the much stronger and increasingly more powerful organisation, notwithstanding also (perhaps not unconnectedly) its progress along the road of supranational political union:

> The EC–EFTA relationship [has a] history rooted in the post-war debates and traumas about European reconstruction. That history remains a potent force in shaping basic attitudes, in particular in segregating the adventurers willing to pursue some form of European Union [...] from the cautious pragmatists, preferring limited functional cooperation. In the early 1970s, as a consequence of the first enlargement of the EC and the first 'defections' from EFTA, a series of free trade agreements was established between the remaining EFTA members and the EC [...]. Since then quietly, undramatically and pragmatically a number of bridges have been constructed to take account of the implications of both economic interdependence and the relative similarities of political values and affiliation [...]. Yet by the early 1980s it was becoming evident that the loose relationship was insufficient. The Luxembourg Declaration of April 1984 [see Pedersen, 1992, pp. 20–1] was the first solid evidence of a shared concern to push the EC-EFTA relationship beyond the free-trade area and *ad hoc* cooperation, involving EFTA as an organization in the process. The resulting joint commitment to create a 'European Economic Space' (EES) [...] was proof of the concerns of politicians and the shifting entrepreneurial dynamics.					(Wallace and Wessels, 1992, p. 2)

Reflecting the continuing *asymmetrical* character of the relationship between EFTA and the Community, as Drost reports, the 'call for the creation of a "European economic space" was first issued by EFTA leaders at a summit meeting in March 1989, which had been called to discuss the implications of the plans by the then European Community (EC) to establish a single internal market by the end of 1992' (Drost, 1995, p. 197). Consequently, their 'efforts led to [...] a joint affirmation by the EC and EFTA ministers on 19 December 1989 to proceed from exploratory discussions to full negotiations on the establishment of the EES' (Pedersen, 1992, pp. 2–3).

The outcome was the Agreement on the European Economic Area, signed on 5 May 1992, between the twelve-member EC/EU and EFTA (Drost, 1995, p. 196), the purpose of the European Economic Area (EEA) being to '(i) establish a single market based on the freedom of movement of goods, persons, services and capital, and (ii) foster closer cooperation in other fields such as research and development, the environment, education and social policy' (*ibid.*, p. 196). In other words, the purpose was largely to extend the Community's single internal market to embrace EFTA: to create 'the largest multi-nation single market and free-trade zone in the world' (*ibid.*, p. 196). Indeed, the plan was for the Agreement to be ratified by all the Member States of both the EC/EU and EFTA in time for the EEA to get underway at precisely the same time as the Community's single internal market on 1 January 1993. However, there was a delay 'when Swiss voters rejected the [Agreement] in a referendum in December. Several technical aspects then had to be renegotiated, [including] the future links between Liechtenstein and Switzerland (which form a customs union)' (*ibid.*, p. 197). Despite this setback, the 'EEA was established at the start of 1994, initially without the participation of Liechtenstein' (*ibid.*, p. 197; see also European Commission, *Frontier-Free Europe*, February 1994 p. 2). Following its own referendum, Liechtenstein joined the EEA on 1 May 1995 (European Commission, *Frontier-Free Europe*, May 1995, p. 3).

Following the creation of the EEA, of course, on 1 January 1995, three more countries became full members of the European Union: Austria, Finland and Sweden. As Borchardt has then put it: 'Now that Austria, Finland and Sweden have become members of the Union, a new question mark hangs over the future of the EEA Agreement, which now covers only Norway, Iceland and (from 1 May 1995) Liechtenstein' (Borchardt, 1995, p. 77). Clearly, if nothing else, the asymmetrical, uneven and unequal relationship between the EC/EU and the rump of EFTA has been hugely enlarged.

In a manner which is consistent with our – what we will refer to as – *global* perspective on the process of European integration by way of the progress of the European Union, Wallace and Wessels at the start of their early-1990s examination of the EC–EFTA relationship (Wallace and Wessels, 1992) then draw attention to the following important consideration:

The dialogue between the EC and the members of the European Free Trade Association (EFTA) started as an apparently self-contained set of discussions in Western Europe, but it is now caught in a web of the wider transformation of Europe as a whole. This makes the practical business of the EC–EFTA dialogue look comparatively straightforward. Yet it renders more strategic the choices for the EC about the new forms of partnership that may lie ahead and it forces the members of EFTA to look at their European policies in terms far broader than they have hitherto preferred. What is crystal clear is that the status quo is not a durable option for either group. It should also be recalled that three [sets] of European countries are currently in the process of reappraising their relationships with the EC: the members of EFTA; the Mediterranean 'orphans', to use [Jacques] Delors' term [see Rhein, 1996]; and the East Europeans. Beyond them, on the EC's southern borders, are the other Mediterraneans, not European, but linked by history and geography to the fortunes of the EC.[43] Further afield the partners and the competitors of the Europeans watch closely to assess the outcome of the 1992 [single internal market] experiment within the EC and the way in which it chooses to handle the realities of interdependence without compromising the central integrationist ambitions. [An adequate understanding of] the EC–EFTA relationship, [depends upon] recognizing the impossibility of separating this from the broader European and global picture.

(Wallace and Wessels, 1992, pp. 1–2)

As Borchardt has suggested, with 'the attraction of the Community boosted by the single market and the impetus towards political union gathering pace with the EU Treaty, other European countries' began to recognise that European 'integration was moving up a gear' and that it was preferable 'to play an active part in shaping the new order as [a] partner rather than [perhaps] having to adapt to firmly cemented structures at a later stage' (Borchardt, 1995, p. 20), while in the meantime being greatly affected by these structures anyway. Borchardt claims that here 'were the kind of considerations that prompted Austria, Finland, Sweden and Norway to open accession negotiations which were successfully concluded in 1994' (*ibid.*, p. 20).

However, in addition, guided by Wallace and Wessels, we can assume that considerations stemming from the broader European and global picture will have played a not inconsiderable part in affecting the decisions, negotiations, applications and conclusions which took place. Moreover, for each side, one aspect in particular of the broader European and global picture had to be taken into account in their deliberations on the Community's relationships and development, the future of the EEA, whether (in the case of the Community) to expand by embracing EFTA members, whether (in the case of the members of EFTA) to seek membership of the Community. This aspect was the post-1989 'wider transformation of Europe as a whole' and associated interest shown by central and eastern European countries in EC/EU membership. In view of the 1989 events and transformation not just of Europe, but of the whole global system, as Wallace and Wessels propose:

For the [EC/EU] the issues have become a good deal more challenging as a result of the dramatic changes in Central and Eastern Europe during 1989. The debate is no longer about the future shape of Western Europe, but about the future shape of Europe [. . .]. The [EC/EU] has acquired the role of tutelage *vis-à-vis* Central and Eastern European countries set on reform and it has to be assumed that these will apply to the [EC/EU] for [. . .] membership.   (Wallace and Wessels, 1992, p. 1)

Indeed, with the application lodged by Slovenia on 10 June 1996, ten central and eastern European countries had applied to join the Union (European Commission, *Frontier-Free Europe* July–August 1996, p. 3).

However, in its role as tutor to, or guardian over the reforms and fate of, the central and eastern Europe countries, the question arises of not just when but also if the Union will accept the applications it has received from the countries involved. As with the issue of the inclusion of EFTA countries, the Union's decisions on which central and eastern European countries to admit and when, if at all, to admit them will depend on the broader European and global picture (Wallace and Wessels, 1992, p. 2). It is far from inevitable that the former Eastern bloc countries of Europe will be allowed to join the European Union as full members within the next few years – even within the next decade – in spite of the rhetoric surrounding the 1996–7 Intergovernmental Conference.

Already, there are signs that among the central and eastern European countries there is a sense of undue delay and procrastination over their applications, and evidence that this is generating considerable frustration, as pessimistically reported by Jonathan Steele:

[In spite of] the annus mirabilis of 1989, [. . .] Central Europe is to remain a periphery. It is doomed to hang about in a permanent ante-room, while envoys from Nato and the European Union flit through the area but no one ever names the date for joining either club [. . .]. [One] idea [has been] regional integration. At Visegrad castle above the Danube, the presidents of Czechoslovakia, Poland and Hungary signed a treaty of co-operation in October 1991. Its spirit was soon sabotaged as the three governments (four, when Slovakia split off) began to compete with each other to get the best possible deal from Western Europe [. . .]. [However, with] no guarantee of early accession to the European Union or Nato, Central Europeans have started to reinvent themselves. [There is] a new interest in the regional free trade area (CEFTA) [see Rhein, 1996], which plans to remove all internal tariffs by 2000. Part of Central Europe's anger at the long wait comes from realising that the EU's leading member-states prefer the present limbo. In 1989 Poland and Hungary had a rough balance of trade with the EU. Now they import far more than they sell. Western corporations, led by the Germans, operate freely within the region. To them it makes no difference whether the region joins the EU. Meanwhile, the EU need not adjust its common agricultural policy or enlarge the structural funds which go to poorer members.   (Steele, 25 May 1996)

There is a possibility that 'the present limbo' in which ten central and eastern European countries are held in an 'ante-room' adjacent to the Union suits not only German and other west European corporations, but also the European Union, its institutions and present Member States, on both economic and political grounds. Holding the former Eastern bloc applicants in an institutional hinterland may suit the EU and its members. This is not just because of various economic (trading, investment, fiscal) considerations, but also because of certain political concerns, stemming from the current drive further and further along the road of political integration, and more to the point of supranational political union; and, connectedly, stemming from the problems and process of governance – of geo-political management in the interests of the EU and its objectives. Our assumption is that the EU has an interest in not merely internal governance, but also external governance, if for no other reason than the process of governance in which it is engaged depends upon the internal 'problem', the external 'problem' and the relationship between these two sides of the same coin. It is not too fanciful to assume that the EU is interested in, and so is motivated by the prospect of leading the process of, pan-European governance; and to anticipate that the EU may decide that this interest is best served by approaching its eastward expansion cautiously and slowly.

The EU and its Member States may decide that there are geo-politial management benefits to be gained from, following Jonathan Steele, keeping central European countries (the Visegrad Four), not to mention eastern European ones, in the periphery, instead of allowing them inside the core: fully into the Union. The considerations which may encourage the EU to adopt this kind of approach to the applicants beyond its eastern border are alluded to by Wallace and Wessels in their reference to the 'three sets of European countries which are reappraising their relationships with the EC/EU' (Wallace and Wessels, 1992, p. 2), two of which are 'the East Europeans' and 'the Mediterranean "orphans" ', the euphemism for Cyprus, Malta and Turkey. As we noted earlier, according to Lionel Barber, the 'EU has long viewed the idea of opening its doors to Turkey as unrealistic, citing' among other things 'its Moslem tradition and human rights record' (Barber, 20 January 1997). Well, the EU may decide that there is a geo-political management advantage to be had from keeping central and eastern European countries in the periphery, in that the EU is thereby better able to maintain its distance – territorially, geo-socially and symbolically (that is, by example) – from the geo-political 'problems', even threats, posed by yet other countries; by countries which the EU regards as an actual or potential source of a geo-political management 'problem' rooted in their distance, judged not just in geographical terms, but also with reference to economic, political, cultural, religious, human rights and other considerations. This theme is pursued in the next chapter.

5 A Global Perspective

The context has altered [but] not only within the Union [itself]. The international context has changed even more radically. The historic shock waves of 1989 – on the Union's very doorstep – are still reverberating. The upheavals which followed the fall of the Berlin Wall have borne fruit. At tremendous cost, the new democracies in Central and Eastern Europe have confirmed their attachment to the values that are the very basis of the Union. The Union, for its part, has committed itself to accepting these countries. (European Commission, Intergovernmental Conference 1996: Commission's Report for the Reflection Group, 1995, p. 4).

For us, European integration by way of the evolution of the European Union – that is, by way of *both* the institutional deepening *and* the geo-political expansion of the Union – entails, and so can only be understood in terms of, four interdependent developments:

(i) the progressive consolidation of the EU's supranational institutions and decision-making powers, authority and sovereignty;
(ii) the Union's increasing engagement in pan-European governance; or, that is, in pan-European geo-political management;
(iii) the EU's construction and re-construction of zones of pan-European, and even more extensive, governance which are centred on itself as the inner (core, or umbral) zone, *and* are managed and manipulated very largely in the Union's own (economic, political, security) interests;
(iv) the EU's increasing engagement in extra-EU geo-political management in a manner which is consistent with a (suitably modified) *realist* approach to the study and analysis of 'international relations', or global-system relationships, structures, processes and change.

This last development brings to mind further guiding assumptions. For us, the EU's supranational progress, geo-political expansion and gathering involvement in pan-European governance can only be understood in terms of: (a) the EU's status, roles and relationships *as a global player*; (b) the EU's circumstances within an encompassing global (economic, political, cultural) system (see Axford, 1995), and accordingly within various enveloping global conditions, processes and trends – which amount to, resorting to Brigid Laffan's terminology (1996b, p. 1; see our Chapter 3), the EU's external challenge or imperative; (c) the way in which the EU as a supranational regional organisation, or regime (SRR), is part of a global trend entailing the spread of SRRs and, connectedly, the search for 'supranational solutions' to such issues or problems as global order–disorder, global stability and global governance; and (d) the particular problems of global order–disorder, stability and governance associated with the post-Cold War new world order, or geo-political power configuration.[1] There are other potentially globally prominent, but as yet much less organisationally advanced – merely emerging, embryonic or *promissory* – SRRs, including NAFTA, APEC, ASEAN and the East Asia Economic Area (EAEA) or Caucus (EAEC).

As we have already made clear, for us, the European Union's engagement in pan-European governance is manifested in its maintenance and manipulation of the EEA – the origins of the notion 'European economic space' (see Drost, 1995, pp. 196–7) – as a zone of extra-EU political management, even though it now includes in addition to itself only Iceland, Liechtenstein and Norway. On the other hand, the EU's increasing engagement in pan-European governance, and moreover in global governance, is reflected in the presence of, in effect, further economic spaces, both European and non-European.

These *economic spaces*, simultaneously representing as they do extra-EU zones of geo-political management, are created by the EU in response to applications from non-EU organisations and countries for a degree of integration with or inclusion in – perhaps full membership of – the EU (see our Chapter 3, note 11). The resulting economic spaces are occupied by organisations and countries which are variously open (susceptible, vulnerable) to the EU's governance: geo-political management; economic, political and cultural manipulation. As zones of governance, these economic spaces are maintained by the EU in so far as they 'function' on its own behalf; they facilitate the EU's economic, political and security interests, reflecting the EU's realist approach to the global system and new world order; and they serve, in particular, the EU's (pre-membership) preparatory requirements and protectionist objectives, including those of the *political-security* and the *national-ethnic* kinds (see our Chapter 3; Mandel, 1994; Close, 1995).

In its 1993 outline of the EC's 'external relations', the European Commission (*Europe in a Changing World*, 1993) refers to the Community's 'global network of agreements', there being 'several types' of agreement (*ibid.*, p. 19). First, the Commission mentions how it had concluded free trade agreements with its 'individual EFTA neighbours', these having 'been combined and strengthened to form the European Economic Area (EEA)' (*ibid.*, p. 19; see also pp. 28–30). Second, there were ' "Europe" agreements (also called association agreements)' with central and eastern European countries, the aim in this case being 'to integrate' the economies of these countries with 'that of the Community as quickly as possible' (*ibid.*, p. 19).

As Klaus-Dieter Borchardt, puts it, association agreements 'establish special links with non-member countries extending beyond the purely trade aspect to include close economic cooperation and financial assistance' (Borchardt, 1995, p. 76); and in the particular case of *Europe agreements*, they 'are also important in preparing for the accession of new members' (*ibid.*, p. 76):

> They form a kind of preliminary stage to accession, designed to help a country that has applied for membership to bring its economy into line with the rest of the Community. [An] example is the Association Agreement [sic] with Turkey in [the early 1960s]; this [...] holds out the ultimate prospect of accession. The Union has followed the same line in relations with the countries of Central and Eastern Europe. In the 'Europe Agreements' concluded since 1989 with Poland, Hungary [and several other central and eastern European countries], the EU has in principle committed itself to the [...] goal of membership for them. Here, too, association is meant to help [these countries] fulfil the conditions for access to the EU, which they are seeking for economic and foreign policy reasons.
>
> (*ibid.*, p. 76)

By June 1996, the EU had signed ten Europe agreements:

> Slovenia officially applied to join the European Union on 10 June, on the occasion of the signature in Brussels of a Europe agreement between Ljubljana and the European Union. Slovenia thus becomes the 10th Central and East European country to sign such an agreement, which implies the prospect of membership [of the EU] in due course. Slovenia is also the only ex-Yugoslav Republic to find itself in this situation. (European Commission, 'Slovenia applies for membership', *Frontier-Free Europe*, July/August 1996, p. 3)

Slovenia's application followed the Czech Republic's in January 1996, when it too signed a Europe agreement. The other eight countries which had been granted Europe agreements by mid-1996 were Bulgaria, Estonia, Hungary, Latvia, Lithuania, Poland, Romania and Slovakia (European Commission, 'Prague seeks EU membership', *Frontier-Free Europe*, March 1996, p. 3).

The third type of *economic space* agreements which the EC had concluded with several external countries by the end of 1993 were also 'association agreements', but in this case warranted being referred to otherwise as 'customs union agreements'. Again, these agreements were 'designed to lead to [...] full membership of the Community' (European Commission, *Europe in a Changing World*, 1993, pp. 19, 34–5), and they had been concluded with Turkey, Malta and Cyprus. In the case of Turkey, this customs union agreement might have been taken to have confirmed its imminent acceptance as a full member of the Union, Turkey having formally applied for full membership in April 1987. In July 1990, Cyprus and Malta also applied for full membership. The character, purpose and impact of the customs union agreements is indicated in a report relating to Cyprus:

'We expect that the day we begin our entry negotiations, we will have bridged not less than 80% of the gap which separates us from the acquis *communautaire*', Cyprus's Minister for Foreign Affairs [...] declared on 14 May [1996], during the EU/Cyprus association council. The minister stressed that his country began to bring its laws, policies and practices into line with those of the EU at the end of 1993. For the EU's Heads of State or Government, Cyprus would be part of the next wave of adhesions to the Union, with negotiations starting after the intergovernmental conference, designed to reform the Treaty on European Union.

(European Commission, 'Cyprus prepares to join the EU', *Frontier-Free Europe*, June 1996, p. 3)

At the same time, however, the urgency which the Cyprus government has shown in seeking and preparing itself for EU membership does not necessarily mean, even if it succeeds in fully incorporating the *acquis communautaire*, that it will be finally accepted:

In its opinions issued in June 1993, the Commission said that [Cyprus and Malta] were potential candidates for membership provided the problem of the division of Cyrpus could be resolved first and on condition that Malta took important steps to modernize its current economic and financial structures.

(European Commission, *Europe in a Changing World*, 1993, p. 35)

While the Union remained 'pledged to open accession talks with Cyprus six months after the end of the Maastricht treaty review conference [...] due to finish in mid-summer' 1997 (Barber, 26 February 1997), the 'problem of the division of Cyprus' remained far from resolved:

Greece yesterday [25 February 1997] threatened to delay the European Union's planned enlargement to central and eastern Europe after the rest of the EU proposed involving the Turkish community [of the northern Cyprus] in talks on the entry of Cyprus.   (Barber, 26 February 1997)

Furthermore, Malta's accession was far from certain, but in this case due to signs of a reassessment, growing reluctance and some resistance from the Maltese side:

Alfred Sant was sworn in yesterday as Malta's first Labour prime minister for nine years after electors opted to scrap their country's application for European Union membership. Malta's outgoing prime minister [...] who submitted his country's application to join the EU six years ago, had expected to begin membership negotiations next year [1997]. His opponent campaigned successfully on a pledge to abolish value added tax and reinstate customs duties – a move that would be anathema to Brussels. Mr Sant argued that the island's expanding but fragile and specialised economy could not bear the strains of full membership.

(Hooper, 29 October 1996)

In practice, Alfred Sant turned out to be slow in meeting his promise to withdraw Malta's application for EU membership, hence a planned meeting between European Union foreign ministers and 'their 12 Mediterranean partners' due to be held in Malta in April 1997 remained in place, albeit accompanied by some trepidation on the part of the EU:

Manuel Marin, the European commissioner in charge of relations with Europe's southern flank, has warned that the political crisis in Algeria must not be allowed to compromise efforts to forge links with the Mediterranean countries in north Africa. [He] said that Algeria [...] has after all signed the Barcelona Declaration for a Euro-Mediterranean zone of shared prosperity [...]. According to Marin, concern over terrorist attacks in France linked to the Algerian crisis and fear of Islamic fundamentalism spreading in North Africa [sic] were in danger of alienating public opinion from the Euro-Med project, set up 18 months ago to forge closer links. He also cited fears of further northwards emigration to Europe, and of the drugs trade emanating from the region [...]. Marin said that the first step to a more productive relationship lay in 'confidence-building security measures'. A senior colleague of Marin confirmed that the hope was to create a 'security partnership' aimed at 'containing destabilising forces across the Mediterranean', through greater exchange of information on drug trafficking, illegal migration and money laundering.

(Rollnick, 13 March 1997)

Rollnick's reference here to the 'fear of Islamic fundamentalism' within the European Union, and its affect on the EU's external relationships, acts as a reminder of the EU's Turkey problem. This problem is rooted in part in Turkey's ethnic, cultural and religious character (not forgetting its human rights record – see, for instance, Nuttall, 29 June 1996), its population being almost totally Sunni Muslims, and its government being an 'Islamist-led coalition' under prime minister Necmettin Erbakan (Nuttall, 9 October 1996). Ian Traynor and Chris Nuttall have suggested that the Turkish government is convinced that 'the importance of Islam in Turkey [is] the main reason from excluding it' from the EU (Traynor and Nuttall, 7 March 1997).

Turkey first signed an association agreement with the EU in 1963; it applied to join the Community in 1987; and it has subsequently secured a 'preparatory' customs union agreement with the EU. However, the

'Commission, which must deliver an opinion on each application for membership before entry negotiations can begin, [has consistently taken] the view that Turkey [is] not ready for membership' (European Commission, *Europe in a Changing World*, 1993, p. 34); and, as reported by Traynor and Nuttall, in March 1997, there was 'an eruption of Turkish anger at' what appeared to be the endorsement given by Helmut Kohl, the German chancellor, to the view 'that Turkey had no chance of joining the EU'; and that, essentially, Turkey is 'not seen as part of Europe' (Traynor and Nuttall, 7 March 1997). But:

> The Turkish secular establishment fears that the Islamic Welfare Party, which heads [the] coalition government, will use the dismissal of Turkey's claims [for EU membership] to renew its call for a reorientation of the country towards the East and Muslim countries. (*ibid.*)

What this rift between the European Union and Turkey raises is the issue of, as Axford puts it, 'civilizational conflict' (Axford, 1995, p. 190, and Chapters 6 to 8):

> In Africa [and elsewhere] Islamic fundamentalism is a growing force [. . .]. For disciples of the idea of an NWO come [sic] at the 'end of History' [Fukuyama, 1991, 1992, 1995], this makes depressing reading. Instead of a world joyously taking up, or being constrained to enjoin with, the [modern, Western, supposedly increasingly globalised] liberal-democratic rule of law and ideals of economic liberalism, we stumble towards a different perhaps more treacherous future [. . .]. We have [. . .] rediscovered the concept and the fear of civilizational conflict, and, more than the postmodern politics of identity or the gun culture of ethnic banditry [see Ignatieff, 1994], this spectre is offered by some observers as the defining conflict of the post-Cold-War age (Huntington, 1993). Such at any rate is the argument of Samuel Huntington (1993) [in his account of] the civilizational challenges to the cultural hegemony of Western modernity [. . .]. Huntington argues that civilizational identities – he refers to the Western but also to the Confucian, Japanese, Islamic, Hindu, Slavic Orthodox, Latin American and possibly African – will be the principal sources of global politics in the post-Cold-War world, superseding the Western model of international politics based on the nation-state and the conflict of ideologies which informed the Cold War. (Axford, 1995, pp. 190–1)

As we have indicated, for us, 'the Western model of international politics based on the nation-state' is indeed being superseded, but by another initially western (and more precisely, European) model of *global system politics*: a global (economic, political, cultural) system in which supranationalism is a (doctrinal) driving force in favour of the spread of SSRs at the expense of the nation-state. For us, the rift between Turkey and by far the most organisationally advanced SRR, the European Union, may well be rooted in civilisational, cultural and religious – perhaps along with further, related 'ethnic' – differences and divisions, but Turkey has still been eager to join the EU; has still reacted with dismay, anger and frustration as to its treatment by and exclusion from the EU; and has still been prompted by the (exclusive and protectionist) presence and model of the EU to promote the idea of an alternative, but none the less organisationally similar, regional regime:

> This month [. . .] Necmettin Erbakan, the first Islamist prime minister of the militantly secular state which rose from the ruins of the Ottoman Empire, chose militantly Islamist Iran for his first foreign visit [. . .]. In Tehran, he hinted at broader regional ambitions, proposing a four-nation summit of Turkey, Iran, Iraq and Syria to discuss the Kurdish problem [. . .]. The disruptive potential of Turkey's new direction is great. After all, before he came to power, Mr Erbakan spoke scathingly of the European Union, and advocated Turkey's adhesion to an Islamic common market or Islamic Nato instead.   (Hirst, 31 August 1996)

It makes sense in terms of its realist approach to the global system for the EU to be troubled by 'Turkey's new direction', and for the EU to try to hold Turkey in its current economic space – its extra-EU zone of governance – instead of (assuming the EU has decided against admitting Turkey as a full member) allowing Turkey to slip its moorings and lend its weight to the construction of a competitive – even threatening – (Islamist) SRR next door. It is perhaps not surprising that, as reported by Traynor and Nuttall, 'Helmut Kohl hurriedly invited Turkey's prime minister [. . .] to Bonn [on 6 March 1997] after [the] eruption of Turkish anger at the German chancellor's sudden snub to their country's European ambitions' (Traynor and Nuttall, 7 March 1997).

Just as the EC/EU's agreements with Cyprus, Malta and Turkey can be understood in terms of its realist economic, political and security objectives, so can its agreements with and the economic spaces it has created to cover various other Mediterranean basin countries. By 1993, as reported by the European Commission (*Europe in a Changing World*, 1993) the Community had concluded 'preferential agreements' (otherwise known as 'co-operation agreements') with most of the other Mediterranean countries (*ibid.*, p. 19), including most of the Islamic ones:

> the Community is linked with almost all the Mediterranean countries by a network of separate cooperation or association agreements. Only Libya has no such links. The agreements [. . .] are part of what has been termed the Community's global Mediterranean policy [. . .]. The Maghreb countries (Algeria, Morocco, Tunisia) and the Mashreq [countries] (Egypt, Jordan, Syria and Lebanon) plus Israel are linked to the Community

through cooperation agreements covering trade, industrial cooperation and technical and financial assistance [...]. [A]ll the EC's Mediterranean agreements have certain common elements. Each provides for unlimited duty-free access for industrial products originating in the country in question. The agreements also provide for individual concessions of various sorts for their major agricultural exports, including fruit and vegetables, wines and olive oil [...]. The association agreements between the Community and the Maghreb countries are being upgraded to 'partnership' agreements, aimed at creating a full free trade area with deeper economic and social cooperation and a political dialogue [...]. To an even greater extent than in the past, the Community is the major economic power in the [Mediterranean] region. It thus has to bear a correspondingly greater share for regional economic stability and well-being. (European Commission, *Europe in a Changing World*, 1993, pp. 34–6)

But, the EU recognises that the region's 'economic stability and well-being' is intimately tied to its political stability and well-being: hence the EU's interest in political dialogue with the Mediterranean countries; in 'confidence-building security measures' (Manuel Marin, quoted in Rollnick, 13 March 1997); and in a 'security partnership' aimed at 'containing destabilising forces across the Mediterranean' (quoted in Rollnick, *ibid.*):

The Community's [...] neighbours [...] to the south in the Mediterranean basin [...] were among the first to establish special economic and trade relations with the Community. For its part, the Community has accepted from the outset that it has, *inter alia* out of enlightened self-interest, a particular responsibility for the social (and thus the political) stability of the Mediterranean region. It should therefore contribute to the region's economic and social development. This responsibility has increased following the 1990 war in the Gulf region. Moreover, the Community is aware that immigration pressures could build up from these countries if the pace of their economic development proves inadequate to the needs of their swelling populations.   (*ibid.*, p. 34)[2]

The EU's 'enlightened self-interest' *vis-à-vis* its economic, political and security objectives accounts for the EU's concern about the economic and political stability of its southern flank; and for the EU's contribution to this stability through its Mediterranean economic spaces agreements and provisions. Through these spaces, agreements and provisions – and the accompanying EU determined conditions, rules and requirements – the EU maintains in effect a set of extra-EU zones of governance around the Mediterranean region, zones which extend into northern Africa and the Middle East, and which complement those in northern, central and eastern Europe.

The purpose behind, or 'function' of, the EU's Mediterranean zones of governance is patently centred on *protection*; and moreover, protection of the political-security and the nationality-ethnic varieties (see our Chapter 3). The EU's agreements with the Maghreb countries are not intended to prepare these countries for EU membership (even though eventual Maghreb membership has not been ruled out and is a long-term possibility) (see Borchardt, 1995, pp. 77–8). Instead, they are meant to facilitate the EU's realist, self-interested engagement in the process of extra-EU geo-political management and manipulation in a region which poses, what the EU regards as, various problems, dangers and threats, including those listed by Manuel Marin in advance of the planned April 1997 foreign ministers meeting in Malta: terrorist attacks in France linked to the Algerian crisis; the spread of Islamic fundamentalism in northern Africa; northwards emigration to Europe, and especially illegal migration; the drugs trade stemming from the region; and money laundering (Rollnick, 13 March 1997) (see note 2).

At the same time, however, the EU's bilateral agreements are far from confined to Europe, northern Africa and the Middle East. For instance, the EU has extensive arrangements under the Lomé Convention with a range of African, Caribbean and Pacific (ACP) countries, arrangements which give 'privileged access to the EC market for [the ACP countries'] exports plus financial and technical assistance' (European Commission, *Europe in a Changing World*, 1990 p. 19). By the end of 1996, the Convention covered 70 ACP states, and South Africa was 'negotiating membership' (European Commission, *The European Union and the Developing World*, 1996; and European Commission, *Development: 20 questions and answers*, 1996).[3]

Also by 1993, the Community had 'a series of non-preferential commercial and economic cooperation agreements such as those with the countries of Latin America and Asia' (European Commission, *Europe in a Changing World*, 1990, p. 19). In Latin America, by 1993 the Community had 'framework cooperation agreements with Mexico, Argentina, Brazil and Uruguay. By the end of 1996, these had been extended to Chile and Paraguay (European Commission, *The European Union and the Developing World*, 1996; and European Commission, *Development: 20 questions and answers*, 1996). In 'line with its policy of supporting organizations committed to regional economic integration, the Community [had] signed a non-preferential framework agreement for commercial and economic cooperation with the countries of the Andean Pact. These are Bolivia, Columbia, Ecuador, Peru and Venezuela' (European Commission, *Europe in a Changing World*, 1993, pp. 40–1). On 10 March 1996, the Andean Pact was re-formed as the Andean Community, taking its 'inspiration from the example of the European Union' (European Commission, 'Europe inspires Andean Community', *Frontier-Free Europe*, April 1996, p. 3). Likewise, a framework agreement 'was concluded in 1985 with the signatories of the General Treaty on Central American Economic Integration (Costa Rica, Guatemala, Honduras, Nicaragua and El Salvador)'; and with Panama (European Commission, *Europe in a Changing World*, 1993, p. 41).

Moving from the Americas across the Pacific to Asia, a 'regional agreement with the member countries of the Association of South-East Asian Nations (ASEAN) was concluded in 1980, setting a framework for commercial, economic and development co-operation. A regular political dialogue also takes place between the Community and the members of ASEAN' (*ibid.*, p. 42). The Commission reported that in 1993 preparations were underway to negotiate a cooperation agreement with Vietnam, which subsequently joined ASEAN in 1995. Furthermore, non-preferential 'cooperation agreements [had] been concluded with the individual countries of the Indian sub-continent – Sri Lanka, Bangladesh, India, and Pakistan' (*ibid.*, p. 42), countries which happen to be members – along with Bhutan, the Maldives and Nepal – of the South Asian Association for Regional Co-operation (SAARC) (see European Commission, 'The European Union and Asia', *Frontier-Free Europe* [Supplement], April 1996). By the end of 1996, the European Union had signed framework co-operation agreements with Nepal and the Maldives (European Commission, *The European Union and the Developing World*, 1996). In addition, the EC had concluded non-preferential co-operation agreements with China and Mongolia (European Commission, *Europe in a Changing World*, 1993, p. 42); and by the end of 1996, the EU had signed a framework co-operation agreement with Yemen (European Commission, *The European Union and the Developing World*, 1996).

But, even in Europe, there are yet further agreements to mention. In 1993 the Commission reported: the 'collapse of the Soviet system after the failed coup in Moscow in August 1991 caused the Community to recast its relations with Russia and the other republics of the former Soviet Union. The Community is ready to negotiate so-called partnership agreements with those [ex-Soviet Union republics] who wish to do so. The partnership agreement with Russia is the most ambitious.' But also, negotiations 'for a partnership agreement took place in 1993 with the Ukraine', and negotiations were expected to take place with Belarus and Kazakhstan (European Commission, *Europe in a Changing World*, 1993, p. 32).

Of course, these partnership agreements are in addition to and distinct from the EU's 'Europe agreements',[4] which are purportedly specifically designed with EU accession in mind; or, as Klaus-Dieter Borchardt puts it, Europe agreements are 'important in preparing for the accession of new members' (Borchardt, 1995, p. 76). As we have noted, by June 1996, the EU had signed ten Europe agreements, with Bulgaria, the Czech Republic, Estonia, Hungary, Latvia, Lithuania, Poland, Romania, Slovenia and Slovakia (European Commission, 'Prague seeks EU membership', *Frontier-Free*

Europe, March 1996, p. 3; European Commission, 'Slovenia applies for membership', *Frontier-Free Europe*, July–August 1996, p. 3).

However, the conclusion of these *preparatory* agreements does not necessarily mean that in practice the countries involved will either in the near future or, indeed, in the foreseeable future accede to full membership of the Union. In the build up to and during the 1996–7 IGC there was widespread discussion of the link between the progress and result of the IGC, on the one hand, and of EU enlargement, on the other. Thus:

> For the European Union, the coming year will be dominated by two issues: the intergovernmental conference and members' progress towards the criteria for monetary union. Both are important issues – the IGC is meant to provide a much-needed overhaul of the framework and structures within which EU business is conducted [...]. [Other] crucial, related issues [include] enlargement. It could be argued that without the reform of the EU's institutions, the concept of enlargement – opening the membership door to countries in central and eastern Europe, for example – is nothing more than a chimera.   (Milner, 28 December 1996)

For us, Milner's argument brings to mind the following question: precisely what kind and degree of institutional reform is necessary to allow what proportion of central and eastern European countries to be admitted into the Union? By the middle of March 1997, John Palmer claimed:

> The prospects for the adoption of a new European Union treaty at June's Amsterdam summit have been boosted by signals that Paris, Bonn and the British Labour Party are ready to compromise. [Nevertheless, there] is still no agreement on how to redistribute the votes held by member states in the [supranational] Council of Ministers to give a bigger voice to the more populous countries. This issue is, in turn, linked to [as a report by the European Commission this week envisaged] the planned enlargement of the EU to perhaps 30 or more [nation-]states in the next 10 years.
> (Palmer, 15 March 1997)

This estimate of the extent, or at least pace, of the EU's enlargement may be over-optimistic. In November 1996, Ian Traynor identified the 'six next in line for EU membership' (Traynor, 21 November 1996) – as a result of the negotiations which 'are supposed to start within six months of the intergovernmental conference ending in Amsterdam' in the summer of 1997 – as Cyprus, the Czech Republic, Hungary, Malta, Poland and Slovenia, while at the same time suggesting that if the German government 'does not get its way in Amsterdam [...], its enthusiasm for the year 2000 union of about 20 could fade' (*ibid.*).

Following Traynor, whether, when and how far the EU expands depends on the IGC agreeing to certain internal institutional changes:

> The German word is *Hanlungsfähigkeit* – the capacity for action. This quality, Bonn insists, is the prerequisite for expansion – meaning hard core integration and no more national vetoes. Otherwise the union will be crippled and its relevance as an international power player undermined.
>
> (Traynor, 21 November 1997)

In our view, however, even if internal institutional change in favour of more integration – and, more specifically, supranational integration and decision-making – is *necessary* to permit further expansion, such change by itself would not be *sufficient* to ensure further expansion, even to the limited extent of taking in (what we will refer to as) the *favoured four* central European countries of the Czech Republic, Hungary, Poland and Slovenia – the four countries which also happen to be the strongest contenders for joining NATO: 'The Clinton administration report to Congress indicated that the Czech Republic, Hungary, Poland and perhaps Slovenia were expected to become Nato's newest members' (Barber, 12 March 1997).

The EU's further enlargement, whatever the outcome of the 1996–7 IGC *vis-à-vis* internal change, will depend upon the EU's assessment of how it can best realise its self-interested (economic, political and security) objectives within the encompassing global system, wherein lies its external conditions, challenge and imperative (cf., Laffan, 1996b, p. 1). The EU's realist approach to the global system will mean that the issue of its further enlargement will be decided with reference to the interdependent factors of: (i) any EU internal institutional changes; (ii) the EU's external circumstances, and in particular those which have implications for its economic, political and security interests; and (iii) the global system, with its distinctive new world order distribution of (economic, political and military) power and associated configuration of (to paraphrase Traynor) *international power players*. These three considerations *will* underpin the EU's engagement in the process of pan-European and global governance (and so extra-EU zones of geo-political management); and *may* mean the EU limiting its enlargement, delaying its enlargement, or both.

The EU will have a programme, or more precisely a *rolling programme*, of geo-political expansion and governance in relation to eastern Europe – to the central and eastern European countries of the former Eastern bloc or Soviet empire – hence its Europe agreements, as well as its partnership agreements with CIS members (European Commission, *Europe in a Changing World*, 1993, pp. 19, 30–4). The EU's Europe agreements can only be understood by taking into account both (i) the EU's political-security objectives and concerns (intimately linked as these are to its economic objectives and considerations), and so the EU's political interests in maintaining and manipulating extra-EU zones of governance; and (ii) the EU's global circumstances whereby, apart from anything else, the EU is finding itself increasingly confronted by, competing against and to some extent in conflict with other regional regimes with similar supranational tendencies.

Whether and when the EU expands eastwards by admitting, in the first instance it would seem, the favoured four (which overlap with, but are not identical to the Visegrad Four – see Drost, 1995, p. 628), will depend on whether the EU estimates that the geo-political benefits of this move will outweigh the geo-political costs; or, to put it another way, will outweigh the geo-politically 'functional' advantages of holding the countries involved in an extra-EU zone of governance. Whether and when the EU decides to fully embrace the favoured four, will depend on the EU's assessment of the economic, political and security advantages and disadvantages of transferring the countries involved from their extra-EU zone of governance – within which these countries, as relatively weak participants (reflecting their non-membership of the EU), are subjected to the EU's self-interested geo-political management and manipulation – into the inner-EU zone of governance.

Any decision to admit the favoured four, as well as any other central or eastern European countries, to the EU's inner zone of governance will depend on their achievements in meeting the EU's formal conditions of entry judged with reference to their economies (their economic performance; their progress in adopting market capitalism) and their conformity to the *acquis communautaire* – the two sets of conditions entailed being *formally* linked. In a report at the end of 1994, *The Economist* pointed out that before 'they can join the European Union, the countries of Eastern Europe must adopt the rules of the "acquis communautaire"' (*The Economist*, 10 December 1994, p. 40), elaborating as follows:

> At its [European Council] summit in Essen on December 9th and 10th, the European Union will announce what it calls a 'pre-accession' strategy for its East European applicants [...]. One proposal [...] is [that] by the end of next June [1995] the EU will prepare a white paper that will define the main bits of the *acquis communautaire* (the EU's body of laws and regulations) that the East Europeans must adopt to be ready for [the] single market [...]. The white paper will 'identify the relevant *acquis* [...] which will contribute to the creation of the conditions for establishing a single market'. Translation: 'We'll give you an idea of what you need to do, but we won't promise anything on our side.' (*ibid.*)

While central and eastern European countries wanting to join the European Union will be required to achieve a certain minimum level of progress in the interrelated areas of *political economy* (Harrop, 1992) and the law, these countries will not in return receive any guarantee that on achieving this minimum, they will be allowed to join the EU.

The EU may decide that continuing to hold countries in extra-EU zones of governance in central and eastern Europe is 'functionally' advantageous on political grounds, albeit ultimately with its economic objectives in mind. Extra-EU zones of governance bring politically manipulable *economic* spaces, with various trade, investment and other economic (including *protectionist*) advantages. In this respect, we can note:

> In 1989, eastern Europe had a billion dollar trade surplus with the OECD countries, mainly the EU. By last year [1993] this had been turned into a $8 billion deficit. The imbalance is harder to bear for the east because the EU is by far its biggest export market. By contrast, EU exports to Poland, Hungary, Slovakia and the Czech republic [to the Visegrad Four] comprised 2 per cent of EU exports last year. 'The widening trade and currency account deficits are widely regarded as the major obstacles to sustained economic recovery for the east Europeans,' notes Vienna's Institute for Comparative Economics, which monitors the post-communist economies. (Traynor, 19 November 1994)

Ian Traynor explains:

> In 1989 the rallying cry across half the continent was 'Back to Europe', a conviction that the collapse of the Soviet bloc, the Warsaw Pact, and the Comecon trade regime would trigger a reintegration of east and west. The painstaking work on realising this vision has chalked up some remarkable transformations. In 1989 more than half the foreign trade of the most advanced quartet in the bloc – Poland, Hungary and what are now the Czech and Slovak republics – was with the Soviet Union and its clients. Today more than half is with the EU. Nonetheless, Brussels' attitude towards the east has left the aspiring members bitter [...]. The main grumble concerns west European trade barriers to free trade. While western politicians preach the merits of the market economy to the post-communists, the EU has erected stringent non-tariff barriers in the areas of farm produce, steel, and textiles. These sectors accounted for more than half of east European exports to the EU last year. 'The main threat to eastern European exports and investment comes from actual, threatened and "latent" trade remedy action employed for purposes of managing trade to support industrial policy objectives in the EU,' the European Bank said last month [October 1994]. (Traynor, 19 November 1994)

Traynor tells us that, on the other hand, these protectionist 'trade restrictions will be dismantled or reduced over the next few years' (*ibid.*), under the provisions of the Europe agreements, for instance. None the less, towards the end of 1995, the EU's own Publications Office raised the question 'is the EU turning the screw on Eastern Europe?', answering:

Even though the Europe agreements with the countries of Central and Eastern Europe (CCEEs) are preferential agreements, meaning that the EU market was, for the CCEEs, to be opened up at a fast pace, the reality has proved different. Trade with the CCEEs accounts for a relatively small share of EU manufacturing imports. In 1993 only 4.6% of that total came from the CCEEs. On the other hand, for the CCEEs, the EU has become the largest trading partner, absorbing more than 50% of their manufacturing exports. The importance of trade with the CCEEs varies for each of the Member States. Germany plays the dominant role with 60.3% of total EU imports from and 55.8% of exports to the CCEEs [...]. The trade balance has been constantly improving in the EU's favour since the CCEEs' liberalizing progress began. In 1993, the EU ran a huge surplus in trade with the CCEEs in [various] sectors [...]. An EU surplus in manufacturing trade in 1993 of ECU 2 billion with Poland, [for instance,] was registered [...]. One of the main problems is that CCEE exports to the EU are concentrated, and specialized in sectors in which there is restricted access to EU markets.   (*Eur-op News*, 1995, p. 4)

Over the following months, signs began to appear of an economic turn-around in central and eastern Europe, albeit in some countries more than others:

Economic output in central and eastern Europe and the former Soviet Union is still lagging behind pre-1990 levels, according to the European Bank of Reconstruction and Development. But this year should see Poland become the first country where post-Communist output surpasses that recorded under the former centrally planned system, and Slovenia is expected to follow suit during 1997. According to the EBRD, the Czech Republic, Hungary and Slovakia are among those countries where recovery has brought output within hailing distance of pre-1990 levels.

(Milner, 2 April 1996).

By early 1997, the economic progress of the same five countries was attracting comparisons with the so-called 'tiger economies' of East Asia (as surveyed by, for instance, Dixon, 1991; and So and Chiu, 1995); just as it was evidently attracting an infusion of self-fulfilling trading and investment involvement from the European Union, and from individual EU Member States, such as the UK:

The British government today launches a drive to double trade with the fast-growing Czech, Hungarian, Polish, Slovakian and Slovene markets over the next two years [...]. 'Central Europe is now an economic tiger on our doorstep,' says [Ian Lang, the Trade Secretary]. Trade had grown by up to 35 per cent a year in these markets over the last two years – although from a low base. Trade with the former Soviet bloc accounted for only 2 per cent of UK imports and 2.6 per cent of exports in 1995. But trade with central Europe is increasing much faster than UK trade generally. UK exports to Poland, the largest single market with 39m people, broke the £1bn ($1.67bn) barrier last year [...]. Until now UK companies have lagged behind their European Union competitors in both trade and investment with this region of 65m consumers whose foreign trade is forecast to exceed £125bn by the end of 1998. Germany's trade with the former Soviet bloc is now bigger than its trade with the US [...]. The UK is well placed for further growth in central Europe [...]. The target countries are all 'fast track' reform economies which were quick to reorientate their trade from Comecon to western markets. All aspire to join the EU soon. Tight macro-economic policies have cut inflation to single figures in the Czech republic and Slovakia, while Poland combines high growth with declining inflation. Hungary is emerging fitter from two years of austerity accompanied by rapid privatisation and record high investment, while Slovenia's open economy is poised to gain from peace in the Balkans. Privatisation of state assets, rising foreign investment and new entrepreneurial companies have created dynamic and largely private economies eager for investment and access to foreign markets and technology.

(Robinson, 15 January 1997)

The signs of rapid economic recovery, growth and confidence in central Europe may not only inspire – and in return itself be further inspired by – enhanced trading and investment involvement from EU Member States (their governments; their companies); it may also encourage a firmer commitment from the EU overall to open post-IGC negotiations with a view to admitting as soon as possible – perhaps during 1998–9 – four or five central European countries.

But, to recall the point made by *The Economist* in December 1994, although the central and eastern European countries which aspire to EU membership are required to meet certain minimum conditions of entry, and although – guided by Anthony Robinson (15 January 1997) – four or five central European countries may well be on the way to meeting these conditions, no CCEE country has received a guarantee that it will be admitted to the EU whatever the outcome of the 1996–7 IGC with regard to, in particular, institutional and decision-making arrangements. The EU may still decide that its economic, political and security objectives will be best served by postponing further enlargement, while encouraging its eastern neighbours (a) to persevere with their economic reforms, with opening up their economies to trade and investment, with their participation in the single market (in goods, services and capital, if not labour), with embracing the *acquis communautaire*, and so on; (b) to cling to their goal of becoming full (franchised; voting) members of the EU; but (c) to accept, for the time being, their peripheral occupation of EU-manipulated economic spaces, and so of extra-EU zones of governance.

The Economist reported:

> In most [CCEE] countries new legislation must be compatible with that of the EU already. The Hungarians set up a European Affairs Scrutiny Committee in parliament [...] for just this purpose. This year [1994] they made compatibility a legal requirement, as the Poles and Czechs have already done. The outgoing Slovak prime minister, Jozef Moravcik, claims that his first thought, when a new law crossed his desk, was 'Is this compatible with the laws of the European Union?' Some have gone further: the Poles will soon [make the] changes they think their legal system needs to bring it up to EU standards [...]. The Polish anti-monopoly commission is proving surprisingly effective; its rules are similar to those that work in the EU [...]. State aids, another EU concern, are trickier. (*The Economist*, 10 December 1994, pp. 40–3)

Nevertheless, even in the *trickier* economic area of state aids, tariffs, quotas and economic protection, the EU has persisted in pursuing its cause and, moreover, has done so with notable success, due in the end to the fact that the EU is dealing with compliant, eager-to-please, keen-to-join central and eastern European countries. Of particular significance in this context is the Poland-Daewoo case, as reported by Christopher Bobinski in 1997:

> Poland has bowed to intense pressure from the European Union and agreed to tighten tariffs on car imports by Daewoo, the South Korean industrial conglomerate, which is committed to a $1.4bn investment in Poland's car manufacturing. Brussels had warned Poland that tariff incentives being extended to Daewoo would hinder Warsaw's negotiations with the EU on Polish membership. The negotiations are expected to start next year. The Polish decision [...] will come as a relief to Fiat, another big investor in Polish industry. The Italian carmaker is fighting to retain market share for sales of its locally assembled imported Punto and Bravo models – against Daewoo's Nexia and Espero cars [...]. Daewoo has been informed by the Poles of their decision and will now have to bring cars into Poland in more pieces at a greater cost. (Bobinski, 3 February 1997)

The Polish government's decision to concede to the EU's demands in the area of state aids, tariffs and economic protection as in this particular instance is important in its ramifications for Poland, the EU, the EU's Member States, and the EU's car making industry and companies; for, of course, the Korean car maker Daewoo, and Korea; for the relationships between Korea and both Poland and the EU; and for the overall global system. The Polish-Daewoo decision is highly significant in view of what it tells us about how the EU endeavours to realise and, indeed, manages to realise its objectives – economic, political, security – within the global system. The Poland-Daewoo case demonstrates how the EU can pursue and achieve its economic objectives, including its protectionist ones, by establishing, maintaining and manipulating extra-EU zones of governance – zones which, in effect, doubly advantage the EU in that they are occupied by non-member (non-voting) countries, which none the less in a compliant (or surrogate) manner act as if they were members; and so act as an external buffer on behalf of the EU: to protect the EU, not to mention its car industry.

The EU's economic spaces and external zones of governance provide economic protection; but they do more than this on behalf of the EU, its Member States, its car industry, and so on. The EU's external zones of governance provide it with a useful penumbral geo-political defensive bulwark, or supporting buttress, in relation to more distant geo-political arenas which for the EU present various political-security and national-ethnic concerns and challenges. The EU may decide to maintain a particular zone of governance because of the political-security and national-ethnic protection it brings, perhaps in view of what the EU regards as external migratory pressures and problems, for instance, especially since the collapse of the Soviet empire.

In an article published in *The Guardian* early in 1996, Hans-Dietrich Genscher, the (West) German foreign minister between 1974 and 1992, argued for promoting European integration through the continued development, and in particular the further deepening, of the European Union. He argued that the European Union is a 'zone of stability', and as such is 'crucial to the stability and security of the whole of Europe'. Genscher's portrayal of the EU clearly corresponds with our own description of it as the inner, or core, zone of pan-European governance. We propose that the conceptual coincidence is far from fatuous; that it makes sense in terms of effective governance, this being signalled by (zones of relative) 'stability'. But, Genscher goes on to argue that within the (inner) zone of European stability, 'EU citizens [...] expect progress in dealing with urgent questions of justice and home affairs policy, such as asylum policy and the fight against crime' (Genscher, 19 February 1996).

Apart from failing to refer to any supporting evidence on EU citizens' expectations, however, Genscher does not indicate what he means by 'progress' – what he takes to be distinctively *progressive* policies. But, in the light of his juxtaposition of 'asylum policy' and 'the fight against crime', we will venture to suggest that for Genscher, being *progressive* in the area of asylum policy means being similarly tough on both 'asylum seekers' and 'criminals'.

Assuming that this interpretation of Hans-Dietrich Genscher's views on asylum and asylum-seekers is well-founded, then there is an impressive body of evidence, research and writings which lends itself to the conclusion that his views: (i) are widely held within west European 'political circles' (Collinson, 1994; see below), or the west European *politial elite*; (ii) are the bedrock on which stand the EU's various policies, programmes and practices in relation to asylum and immigration; and (iii) are otherwise popular: are a common feature (as inferred by Genscher) of political communities throughout western Europe (see our Chapter 3; see also Close, 1995; Collinson, 1994; Gowland *et al.*, 1995; Handoll, 1995; Wrench and Solomos, 1993). They are the views which underpin the construction of 'Fortress Europe' in other than a narrow economic sense – in the sense, in other words, which covers *national-ethnic protectionism*.

Sarah Collinson succinctly outlines the Fortress Europe approach to the issue of migration, and furthermore does so by indicating how western Europe is in the grip of worries fanned by migratory pressures from both the east and the south:

> Since the end of the cold war, international migration has risen rapidly up the political agenda in Western Europe. A number of developments have coalesced to create a high degree of anxiety over the issue, an anxiety which is not confined to political circles, but now stretches across virtually every sector of society. The lifting of emigration restrictions in the former Eastern bloc, coupled with growing economic instability in the region, appeared to set the scene for millions of economic migrants moving from East to West in search of a better life. More recent events in the former Yugoslavia have raised the spectre of further future mass dislocations of population in Europe stemming from a resurgence in ethnic tensions and generalized political instability following in the wake of the collapse of the Soviet Empire. In addition, an increase in asylum applications and illegal immigration from outside of Europe, together with a rise in extreme anti-immigration attitudes in Western Europe, have intensified longer-standing worries about migration from the 'South', particularly from the less-developed countries of the Mediterranean-rim and sub-Saharan Africa. Suddenly it appears that Western Europe is under siege from its poorer and less stable neighbours, and that a new threat of mass population movements has come to replace the old and more distant peril of a Communist Eastern bloc. (Collinson, 1994, p. viii)

The evidence gathered during the research conducted for *Citizenship, Europe and Change* (Close, 1995) strongly supports the conclusion that a feeling of being under 'siege' has taken hold in western Europe, especially in the European Union. It is argued that, accompanying the creation (through the Maastricht Treaty) of the European Union together with the introduction of the legal status and rights of Citizenship of the Union what has emerged is an entrenched west European 'siege mentality', a *state of mind* – a sense of anxiety, fear and threat – in relation to 'outsiders', and in particular those outsiders who are actual, would-be, putative or perhaps fictive immigrants, 'economic migrants', asylum seekers, refugees and the like from both the east and the south. This siege mentality then lies behind a broad consensus on the need to protect – to shield – the European Union and its new 'supra-citizens' within the walls of a strengthened Fortress Europe. The resulting drive towards greater protection against 'outsiders', however, has had ramifications which are riddled with national, ethnic and racial overtones, entailing bias and discrimination. Moreover, these ramifications are evident not only at the outer boundaries – the external frontiers – of the EU, but also within and throughout the EU, most prominently in public places and spaces.

Within the Union, there has been something of a concerted effort to reduce and eventually eliminate all controls and checks at the borders between Member States, especially through the Schengen agreement (see Drost, 1995, p. 530), which 'was brought into operation on March 26 [1995] by a hard core of seven countries, led by France and Germany' (Conradi, 30 April 1995), but including also Belgium, Luxembourg, the Netherlands, Portugal and Spain – this Schengen Group being described by Harry Drost as an intergovernmental organisation (Drost, 1995, p. 530) within the EU. According to Peter Conradi:

> Schengen was based on a simple idea: European [Union] members who signed up would gradually eliminate border checks for those travelling between them, while jointly tightening controls around their external borders [...]. Fundamental problems [...] remain about Italy and Greece, which have signed the agreement but have not been able to introduce the kind of controls along their external borders needed to satisfy the rest. Germany, in particular, is worried that too many immigrants from the former Yugoslavia can make their way through Italy's long porous border. [A few days ago,] officials [...] gathered in Brussels [...] to review progress and welcome Austria as the 10th signatory.   (Conradi, 30 April 1995)

On March 26 1995, the Schengen agreement was, to be more precise, brought into operation for a three-month trial period, the intention being for all border controls and checks between the Schengen Seven to be fully and permanently removed from 1 July 1995 – a goal not actually achieved:

> The drive to eliminate internal border controls between a core group of European Union states was in shambles last night [the day before the end of the three-month trial period], after France declared it was keeping its controls unilaterally [...]. Britain has consistently refused to join the project to life internal checks – the Schengen agreement – arguing that it

will not produce adequate curbs on illegal immigration and criminal activities. France's decision yesterday was an implicit endorsement of the British view that the project was not yet workable. (*The Guardian*, 30 June 1995)

A year before, the French government's misgivings about the workability of the project were presaged by the soon-to-be-elected French president, Jacques Chirac:

Jacques Chirac, favourite to win next Sunday's second round of the French elections, has [warned] that he may [...] demand a revision of the agreement if it turns out not to be working. 'Schengen was aimed at easing the passage between seven European countries and strengthening our frontiers against illegal immigrants,' he said. 'We have to ask ourselves if it has succeeded or not.' (Conradi, 30 April 1995)

But, the Schengen group persevered in spite of persistent doubts, difficulties and delays. In February 1996, John Palmer reported:

Seven European Union countries defused a crisis yesterday which had threatened their plans to abolish internal border controls. An emergency meeting of justice ministers from the seven Schengen countries – France, Germany, Belgium, Holland, Luxembourg, Portugal and Spain – agreed to press the EU to improve co-operation among its member states on extradition, following a Belgian court's refusal last week to extradite two suspected Basque terrorists to Spain [...]. The [resulting row] was the latest in a series of problems frustrating attempts to sweep away frontier controls among the Schengen countries [...]. However, the seven countries have now dropped all passport checks on internal flights within the Schengen area [...]. Although Italy, Greece and the Nordic countries plan to join the Schengen agreement, Britain and Ireland insist on retaining border controls. The European Commission has warned that until the EU's internal borders are swept away, its citizens will not enjoy the full benefits of the internal market. (Palmer, 22 February 1996)

A year later, about halfway through the 1996–7 'intergovernmental conference which is negotiating a new treaty', John Palmer added:

Thirteen of the 15 EU countries now appear ready to abolish all internal frontier controls and to transfer responsibility for a common external border to the European Union. As part of the new treaty to be adopted in Amsterdam, Britain and Ireland will be given an opt-out from what is planned to be a 'common European area of freedom and security'.
(Palmer, 12 February 1997)

Britain consistently refused to drop its firm stance against participating in the scheme, in spite of the way in which the concerns behind its stance were shared by other Member States and the European Commission, and in spite of the latter's long-running efforts and tactics:

> The European Commission yesterday launched a new drive to sweep away all internal frontiers in the European Union, but Britain immediately threatened a veto. The Commission proposal is designed to achieve the border-free European Union promised ever since the introduction of the single market, and speed up progress towards the right of free movement of people inside the EU. Although all internal passport and customs checks would go, controls on people entering the EU would be strengthened [...]. Britain insists passport controls are needed to counter illegal immigration and drug smuggling. Other EU states believe stronger external border controls can check on illegal immigration [...].
>
> (*The Guardian*, 13 July 1995)

West European governments and the European Commission display a shared siege mentality in relation to 'outsiders', something which is well-reflected in a passage from a fairly recent (March 1993) European Commission publication on *Questions and Answers about the European Community*:

> The removal of internal frontiers within the Community is being matched by a corresponding strengthening of controls at the EC's external frontiers. These are aimed at preventing terrorists, drug smugglers and other criminals as well as illegal immigrants from entering the Community. In addition, spot identity checks will be possible inside the territory of the Member States. Community countries have drawn up a common list of States whose nationals will need visas to enter the Community. In addition, the conditions of granting asylum to political refugees will be tightened to make it more difficult for so-called 'economic' migrants to settle in the EC. National police forces will cooperate through a new body called Europol.
>
> (*ibid.*, p. 1)

The internal spot identity checks have necessarily, not to say ironically, meant restrictions on the free movement of people within the European Union, including on the free movement of the Citizens of the Union, even though the Treaty on European Union specifically announced: 'Every citizen of the Union shall have the right to move and reside freely within the territory of the Member States' (Article 8). The strengthening of Fortress Europe, however, works against the everyday realisation, exercise and enjoyment of this particular right, especially in the case of those *supra-citizens* who happen to be black.

There is ample evidence from France in particular that the police's 'spot identity checks' are greatly racially skewed in character (see Close, 1995, Chapter 3). In the case of Britain, one possible manifestation of the siege and Fortress Europe approach to 'outsiders' is the 1996 passage of the Asylum and Immigration Bill. This interpretation is not challenged by the fact that on 23 April 1996, the government suffered a defeat on the Bill when the House of Lords voted 143 to 124 to exempt torture victims from the new fast-track, seventeen-day appeals procedure. That is, the fast-track procedure remains firmly in place as the centre-piece of the Bill, leading to a welter of criticism from those concerned about the consequences for asylum-seekers and would-be immigrants in general, and for non-EU nationals, non-Europeans and non-whites in particular.

Fortress Europe in relation to 'outsiders' is not impenetrable. Outsiders pass regularly through the reinforced external walls in various ways: as legal immigrants, as illegal immigrants, as asylum seekers, as refugees, as temporary 'guests'; but the inward flow and the continuous (albeit somewhat undulating) external migratory pressure from the east, the south-east and the south has merely served to confirm the west European siege mentality and to strengthen yet further the EU's protective measures and zeal.

In January 1997, Albania began a slide into crisis, conflict and chaos:

> There were bright expectations six years ago when Europe's poorest country emerged from a communist regime's repression. Now those hopes are in tatters [...]. Albania's President Sali Berisha is reaping the whirlwind. After a reckless 12 months in which his ruling Democratic party [sic] staged deeply-flawed general elections to consolidate its hold on power, the country has been plunged into turmoil again by the collapse of a string of fraudulent pyramid finance schemes. Weeks of violent clashes [...] have led to the authorities losing control of several towns [...]. The turmoil raises fresh doubts about Albania's ability to achieve its long-term goals of joining Nato and the European Union. The chaos poses awkward [problems] for western countries [...].
>
> (Done and Hope, 19 February 1997)

By mid-March, newspaper headlines were dramatically declaring: 'Albania sinks deeper into anarchy' (Helena Smith, 13 March 1997); 'Albania teeters on the brink of chaos' (Martin Woollacott, 15 March 1997); 'Albania's anarchy' (*The Guardian*, 15 March 1997); 'Farce and tragedy amid the creeping chaos' (Julian Borger, 15 March 1997); 'World stands back as anarchy reigns in Albania' (Robertson and Bates, 16 March 1997); 'In the shadow of the gun: lacking the established institutions of market democracy, Albania is reverting to disorder and isolation' (Dinmore and Done, 15/16 March 1997).

The news media also reported on the resulting surge of refugees. For instance:

> Italy yesterday declared a state of emergency as panic-stricken officials sought to cope with the influx of destitute Albanians trying to flee [across

the Adriatic Sea] on a flotilla of dilapidated vessels. The emergency [...] gives Italy powers to forcibly repatriate Albanians 'deemed to be a danger to public security' while permitting genuine refugees a maximum stay of three months [...]. Ten thousand Albanians have so far fled to Italy [...]. The mayor of Brindisi [...] said the flight had assumed 'biblical proportions'.   (Helena Smith, 20 March 1997)

It was not only Italy which was being troubled by the Albanian refugee threat, so was Germany:

Alarmed at the prospect of an influx of refugees from crisis-ridden Albania, Germany is moving to seal its borders against a new wave of migrants from the Balkans and stepping up the forced repatriation of Bosnians. The interior ministers of Germany's 16 states [have decided on] the phased deportation of more than 300,000 Bosnians [...]. Many of those affected are Muslims from Serb-held parts of Bosnia, to which they cannot return [...]. As a result of the Albanian chaos, Bonn has served notice that its doors are closed in the event of a refugee emergency [...]. During the Bosnian crisis, Germany took in about 350,000 refugees [...]. According to senior German politicians, the combination of the Albanian chaos and the scheduled end next year of the Nato peacekeeping mission in Bosnia is causing Bonn to revise its enthusiasm for the Schengen accord among some EU countries, which provides for freedom of movement between the participating [nation-]states. Austria is scheduled to join the Schengen club in October. But risking a row with Vienna, the Bavarian interior minister [...] demanded this week that Austria's accession be postponed for years because its membership would put former Yugoslavia on the border with 'Schengen Europe'. [The] Chairman of the home affairs committee in the German parliament's lower house [...] said yesterday: 'All the Bosnians came here via Austria. The Albanians would come the same way. If Austria joins Schengen, that means we have no external border with Austria. It has to ensure that its southern and eastern borders hold, and that's not easy for Austria. The EU countries have no interest in porous borders.' Bonn has been leading the push for the Schengen accord to be incorporated into EU law at this summer's European summit in Amsterdam. But [the chairman of the home affairs committee] said Germany could be getting cold feet and may prefer a delay. Since the beginning of the year, Germany has doubled its patrols on its eastern borders with Poland and the Czech Republic to try to minimise illegal entry. While EU leaders again agonise over how to respond to the crisis unfolding in their Balkan backyard, there appears to be agreement on strengthening 'Fortress Europe'.   (Traynor, 20 March 1997)

Or as Ronald Payne somewhat more colourfully summarised:

Nothing ruffles the feathers of our comfortable European nest more than angry mobs seething in our backyard. We have troubles enough as European Union economies tough it out in search of the coupons required to ensure a dream holiday of a lifetime for 15 member states to a united prosperous currency. Suddenly we need to answer the tie-breaker question: what to do about Albania? (Payne, 20 March 1997)

Ian Traynor tells us the answer, or at least the one offered by EU leaders: it is strengthen Fortress Europe (Traynor, 20 March 1997).

Following Collinson (1994), the immediate result of the end of the Cold War and the collapse of the Soviet empire, with its destabilising and destructive impact on the former Eastern bloc, was a push–pull effect fuelling 'mass population movements' from eastern Europe into western Europe, thereby greatly heightening the migratory pressures on the EU. Subsequently, however, the Union has successfully constructed around itself protective zones of governance – of geo-political management – which stretch eastwards well into the former Eastern bloc. These zones are occupied by countries which during 1989–91 were suddenly and swiftly jettisoned from the (albeit not always actually relished) embrace and relative certitudes of the Soviet empire and socialist system into the mire of the inherent uncertainties of the new world order, market-capitalist-dominated global system; and which, cast adrift, were suddenly vulnerable and susceptible, wide open to the appeal, influence and manipulation of the EU.

The appeal and influence of the EU has, if anything, grown markedly since the 1989–91 revolution, if only because of the intervening admission of three more Member States. As reported by John Palmer on the eve of the EU's last enlargement:

From midnight tonight, the European Union will become the world's richest supra-national commercial and political grouping, with the accession of Austria, Finland and Sweden. The 15-strong EU will have a population of more than 370 million, and a land mass stretching from the Mediterranean to the Arctic, including for the first time a land frontier with Russia [...]. The EU's land mass will expand by one-third, its population by 6.2 per cent and its total economic output by 7 per cent [...]. All three newcomers are wealthy countries and [...] will not only reinforce the EU's global industrial power but bring substantial revenues to its budget. (Palmer, 31 December 1994)

The EU's eastern external zones of geo-political management have been constructed around and upon the availability of a set of European countries which are eager to become attached to or to join, to become integrated with or full members of, the EU; and which are willing to sign agreements and eager to meet conditions that have been more or less dictated by the EU.

These agreements and conditions have been largely decided by the EU in accordance with its realist, self-interested pursuit of its economic, political and security objectives which befits a major player within the prevailing post-Cold War global system.

The extra-EU zone of geo-political management, manipulation and (relative) stability occupied by the favoured four currently provides a 'functionally' advantageous buffer against any migratory pressures from its still somewhat less stable, more remote (more easterly and south-easterly) zones of governance. This is in addition to the way the same zone provides an EU-managed extension to the EU's single market (in goods, services and capital, if not labour), with the enabling contribution this brings to the EU's attempts to realise its economic, political and security objectives. The current benefits afforded by this particular zone of governance *vis-à-vis* the EU's various objectives will be taken into account during the process whereby the EU decides whether or not there are any realist, self-interested advantages in admitting the favoured four as full members.

The EU's decisions on whether and when to admit central and eastern European countries as full members will depend to a considerable extent on the Union being satisfied that it will, nevertheless, retain adequate extra-EU zones of geo-political management, manipulation and protection. The EU's decision on when to admit even the favoured four will hinge on it being confident that its remaining bilateral agreements and economic spaces – such as those entailing the EEA, its remaining Europe agreements, its partnership agreements, its co-operation agreements and its customs union agreements – are sufficient substitutes as adjacent extra-EU zones of governance, given its economic, political and security objectives.

What could help the EU to admit the favoured four during 1998–9 is the way in which the EU would still enjoy agreements, economic spaces and zones of governance which not only spread further, even much further, east than the Czech Republic, Hungary, Poland and Slovenia, but also appear to be getting firmer and deeper, as reflected in the following *Guardian* report:

> The European Union and Russia finalise a trade pact today while Nato opens landmark talks on a 'special relationship', signalling the West's willingness to move on following Moscow's crackdown in Chechenia. The Russian foreign minister, Andrei Kozyrev, will meet his 15 EU counterparts and attend a ceremony for an accord which will give Moscow some badly needed trade concessions. The pact, a stop-gap measure while a broader EU-Russia co-operation agreement awaits ratification, was put on ice after Moscow's harsh military campaign in Chechenia. The West's criticisms of human rights abuses and Nato's plans to expand its membership to former communist central and eastern Europe created a chill in relations, prompting warnings that a 'cold peace' was replacing the 'cold

war'. Now the EU says Moscow has made enough concessions, essentially by opening peace talks with Chechen leaders, to meet the terms of human rights clauses contained in all accords signed by the Union and third parties. (*The Guardian*, 17 July 1995)

The trade implications of the pact were subsequently acknowledged by *The European*:

Russia signed a key trade pact with the EU on 17 July [1995], ushering in a new era of co-operation between the two giants and ending months of hiatus caused by the fighting in breakaway Chechnya. 'The joint interests of the European Union and Russia lie in ever closer co-operation,' said the Spanish Foreign Minister [...] for the EU's presidency. The pact links the EU, the world's largest trading bloc of nearly 350 million people, with the Russian Federation whose 150 million people occupy the world's largest [nation-]state sprawling from the Baltic to the Pacific.

(*The European*, 21 July 1995, p. 7)

However, the implications of this EU–Russia agreement are by no means limited to trade matters. The implications include the possibility that the EU was able to influence Russia's strategy in response to Chechnya's lurch for independence; and that, more specifically, the EU was able to persuade Russia to halt its military campaign and associated 'human rights abuses'. What makes the Russian compliance all the more remarkable is Russia's continuing insistence that the Chechen Republic remain an integral part of the Federation: 'an indication of the underlying tension between Russia and the Chechen government [came when] Mr Gennady Selezniev, the Communist speaker of the Russian parliament, insisted "Chechnya was, is and will remain part of the Russian Federation"' (Freeland and Thornhill, 29 January 1997).

The EU's 'carrot' and Russia's reward for being prepared to alter its tactics with regard to its internal Chechnya problem was a trade pact and the ratification of a co-operation agreement. Russia willingly – keenly, if not desperately – became burrowed more deeply and firmly into one of the EU's economic spaces and external zones of governance, within which Russia thereby became to some extent formally managed and manipulated by the EU in its realist, self-interested manner; in pursuit of its own, self-centred economic, political and security objectives. The EU's sense of influence, security and protection within the global system will have been bolstered; and the chances of the Czech Republic, Hungary, Poland and Slovenia (perhaps of Slovakia) being admitted into the Union before the end of the century may have been boosted.

As *The Guardian* points out human rights clauses are 'contained in all accords signed by the Union and third parties' (*The Guardian*, 17 July 1995).

Indeed, the EU expects not only all its Member States, but also any European country with which it has a trade agreement and with which, therefore, it shares an economic space to qualify for membership of the Council of Europe, described by Harry Drost as an intergovernmental organisation which was founded in 1949 'to protect and strengthen pluralist democracy and human rights and promote awareness of a European cultural identity' (Drost, 1995, p. 121). Drost adds:

> The Council has adopted over 145 conventions and other agreements covering human rights, health, social welfare, education, culture, media issues, legal issues and other areas. The most important conventions [include] the European Convention for the Protection of Human Rights and Fundamental Freedoms (European Convention on Human Rights) [...]. Two key bodies attached to the Council are the European Commission of Human Rights and the European Court of Human Rights, which examine and adjudicate cases brought under the European Convention on Human Rights [...]. In May 1989 the Committee of Ministers [the Council's senior decision-making body] adopted a declaration on the future role of the Council which stressed closer cooperation with the European Community (EC, now the European Union, EU) and the Eastern European countries [...]. In November 1990 Hungary became the first former communist country to be admitted to the Council.   (Drost, 1995, pp. 122–3)

Czechoslovakia joined the Council of Europe in 1991, Poland in November 1991, Bulgaria in May 1992, Estonia, Lithuania and Slovenia in May 1993, the Czech Republic and Slovakia (following Czechoslovakia's January 1993 split) in June 1993, and Romania in November 1993 (*ibid.*, p. 122). Subsequently most of the other former Eastern bloc countries, including Russia, joined. By the end of 1996 the membership of the Council of Europe had risen to forty, although somewhat controversially with the entry of Croatia. As reported by John Palmer in October 1996, the European Union had been critical of Croatia's human rights record and persistent abuses:

> The European Union has told Croatia it cannot expect privileged economic trading links unless there are improvements in its record of democracy and human rights. A senior Croatian government delegation sent to Brussels this week to plead for closer relations has been told that Zagreb must first fully co-operate with the international war crimes tribunal in the Hague, cease interfering with the independent media and recognise the rights of its political opposition. However, Croatia's diplomatic campaign to improve its relations with western Europe may be given further momentum today, if the 39-member Council of Europe admits it as a member.
> (Palmer, 16 October 1996)

Croatia was indeed successful in its application to be accepted into the Council of Europe: 'The admission of Croatia to the Western European club [(the CE)] as its fortieth member was agreed last week. But it confers a cloak of respectability on the country – very much the victor in the Balkan War – which many believe it does not deserve' (Seacombe, 20 October 1996). Mark Seacombe elaborates by telling us that even though 'Croatia is now subject to the jurisdiction of the European Court of Human Rights', back 'in The Hague, they are worried that Croatia has ignored an international warrant for the arrest of an indicted war criminal, Dario Kordic, now living openly in the capital, Zagreb' (*ibid.*). Accordingly, human rights activists in Croatia 'will not be reassured to learn [that their] country has been admitted to the Council of Europe, whose main aim is to protect human rights. [They know that] the pledges of President Franjo Tudjman's Ministers to the Council, ante-room to the European Union, are worthless' (*ibid.*).

Seacombe's representation of the Council of Europe as an 'ante-room' to the European Union – as a 'small room leading into the main chamber' – is empirically well-founded and analytically useful. It is consistent with the idea that the CE qualifies as a zone of EU pan-European governance which is similar, if not identical, to the EU's more formal external zones of geo-political management based on its trade agreements and economic space. The Council of Europe's ante-room role in relation to the EU seems to have been confirmed and consolidated by the CE's Committee of Ministers' May 1989 declaration on closer co-operation with both the Eastern European countries and the EC (Drost, 1995, pp. 122–3). Certainly, the EC/EU has not just regarded membership of the CE as a prerequisite for EC/EU membership, but furthermore indicated that it regards the process of admission to the CE as a matter over which it should exercise control with its own interests and objectives in mind. In this context, John Palmer's May 1996 report on the EU's approach to Croatia's bid for CE membership is intriguing:

European Union governments are considering an unprecedented last-minute move to block Croatian membership of the Council of Europe in protest at President Franjo Tudjman's crackdown on the independent media and his refusal to recognise elections for Zagreb city council. Only last month the parliamentary assembly of the [then] 37-country Council of Europe voted to admit Croatia, in spite of protests by civil liberties groups, and its entry had been considered a formality. EU foreign ministers will consider whether to veto it when they meet in Brussels on Monday [13 May]. There is growing anger in EU capitals at the way President Tudjman and his Croat government have violated promises made to the council to uphold press freedom and the rights of democratically elected local authorities [...]. Because of its dissatisfaction with the Croatian government's role in the wider Bosnia peace process, the EU earlier this year suspended all negotiations for closer economic and trading ties.

(Palmer, 11 May 1996)

The EU had suspended negotiations for closer economic and trading ties – for privileged economic trading links – because of Croatia's record of democracy and human rights (Palmer, 16 October 1996); and had considered blocking Croatia's admission to the Council of Europe on the same grounds – something the EU could do by exercising its collective weight in the Committee of Ministers. However, the EU then proceeded to act in a manner which may be seen as inconsistent, and even hypocritical. The EU could have been consistent by preventing Croatia from becoming a member of the CE in view of Croatia's record of democracy and human rights, but the EU was not. On the other hand, it can be argued that allowing Croatia into the CE was consistent with the EU's own economic, political and security interests and objectives; that the EU was demonstrating that its own interests and objectives take precedence over other considerations, including those to do with human rights; that the EU was, nevertheless, still defending human rights and democracy in Croatia in that it had withdrawn from negotiations on a trade agreement; and that, despite the absence of a trade agreement, Croatia had entered what was, in effect, an extra-EU zone of geo-political management.

Most, if not all, of the Council of Europe's members that are not EU Member States are queuing to join the EU. This *both* largely helps to account for the eagerness of these countries to join the Council of Europe *and*, relatedly, means that these countries are vulnerable to the exigencies of the EU's pan-European governance, conducted as this is within the new world order global system. The commitment of the governments of these countries to the process of joining the EU makes them keen to fully comply with the terms and conditions being decided and demanded (essentially dictated) by the EU for the admission of new members. At the same time, these terms and conditions are heavily contingent upon the EU's need to compete within the NWO global system, with its distinctive distribution of (economic, political and military) power and associated configuration of power players.

A possible lesson of Croatia's admission to the Council of Europe in the face of what the EU regarded as Croatia's doubtful human rights record is the prospect that – while it could suit the EU to manage and manipulate non-members by making tough human rights demands as a condition for admitting new Member States – it could suit the EU to accept further countries in spite of their miscreant human rights activities. It could be acceptable to the EU to accept as full members certain countries which are evidently indulging in dubious human rights activities because of the priority the Union gives to its economic, political and security objectives and strategies – strategies which are being increasingly compromised by growing competition from other regional regimes: other embryonic supranational regional regimes.

The CE–Croatia case raises the issue of the extent to which the EU's governance, including its external governance, and expansion (by means of both its acceptance of new full Member States and its engagement in pan-European governance through the construction and re-construction of zones of geo-political management) can be understood in terms of its global circumstances. For us, these circumstances are ones in which SRRs are set to play an increasingly prominent part in the pattern of global governance, the distribution and exercise of global power, and the global configuration of power players. That is, as far as we can see, there is a global trend underway which entails the spread of SRRs – a trend spurred by exigencies rooted in the competitive interplay, struggle and, to some extent, conflict among current or budding SRRs; and otherwise fuelled by the various concurrent events, processes and trends associated with the continuing process of globalisation.

Any decision by the EU to allow the favoured four central European countries into the inner zone of pan-European governance will depend on the EU's global circumstances and concerns, challenge and imperative – as manifested in, for instance, the threat to the EU's car industry from Korean and other East Asian car companies. Accordingly, the decision will depend to some extent on the character and development of the geo-politically distant social formations of Korea, of other places in East Asia and of East Asia as a whole. In turn, however, the decision will depend on (as well as having, dialectically, an effect on) the character and development of the encompassing NWO global (economic, political and cultural) system, one feature of which is the spread of regional regimes guided by the doctrine of supranationalism. That is, an evolving feature of the NWO global system is that of a preponderance of competing, somewhat conflicting and mutually influential SRRs, heralded by the creation of the European Community. East Asia is just one region with an organisation which shows signs of following the EU along the supranational road – it has, that is, the Association of South East Asian Nations (ASEAN). While Korea is not a member of ASEAN, it has been invited to be a founder member of another regional regime – the East Asian Economic Caucus (EAEC). But this aside, Korea already belongs, along with seventeen other countries, to the Asia Pacific Economic Co-operation forum (APEC), a regional regime which overlaps with another, that of the North American Free Trade Agreement (NAFTA).

Any decision by the EU to admit the favoured four central European countries as full Member States will depend in part on the evolution and character of other SRRs as global players in the NWO. It will depend on the competition from and threat posed by such organisations – no matter how geo-politically remote they happen to be – *vis-à-vis* the EU's economic, political and security interests and objectives. Essentially, that is, the EU's approach to the issues of its future geo-political enlargement, its further institutional deepening, will depend on the competition posed by other global players – including other regional regimes and SRRs – by virtue of *their* particular social characteristics.

In this regard, it is pertinent to refer again to the 1994 *Economist* report on 'Eastern Europe and the EU':

> Two areas where the East Europeans face particular difficulties adopting EU legislation are the social chapter and the environment. Technically, the social chapter is not part of the *acquis*. So the easterners could, like the British, opt out. They don't want to. But their nascent private business can ill afford the complexities and costs of much West European labour legislation.   (*The Economist*, 10 December 1994, p. 43)

What this suggestion reminds us of are the factors which appear to have led the Norwegian people to decide not to join the European Union (see our Chapters 3 and 4). But, in addition, the suggestion raises the possibility (remote or otherwise) that, due to the social character of its global system competitors, especially the most successful ones, there will come a time when the EU as a whole can ill afford the complexities and costs of much west European labour legislation, as *The Economist* puts it. We can imagine the EU in global circumstances which lead it to ease up on, or even to regressively back-track on, its social programmes, policies and practices – those designed to promote human rights and citizenship rights – perhaps to the point of seeming to vindicate the UK government's stance against the proposed Maastricht Social Chapter and subsequent supranational social legislation.

A global perspective on European integration of the kind we are advocating would appear to be widely endorsed, including among scholars (see, for instance, Dent, 1997) and journalists, *inter alia*. For example, reporting on the build up to the November 1996 European Court of Justice judgement in the dispute between the European Commission and the UK government over the Working Hours Directive, Hugo Young explains that at 'one level, this is a technical dispute about the nature of EU law: is it legal for the Commission to impose the 48-hour-week directive under the heading of health and safety, thus evading the exemption Britain thought [it] had secured from such horrors [sic] by opting out of the social chapter provisions at Maastricht?' Young adds: 'At the bottom of the judgement is an argument about the nature of work, the role of regulation, the effect of global competition, the very future of European societies' (Young, 12 November 1996).

For us, the 'global competition' facing the EU is increasingly from other regional regimes which are similarly evolving as supranational regional regimes (under the *doctrine of supranationalism*; and in a manner which is consistent with the neo-functionalist practical approach to and theoretical interpretation of SRRs), and doing so to a large extent precisely because of – in response to – the exigencies (the *external* challenge and imperative) presented by this competition. In other words, the European Union is increasingly caught up in a dialectical, mutually reinforcing, spiralling relationship with other regional regimes in favour of supranational solutions to global system characteristics and developments, challenges and problems – to, for instance and crucially, the challenge and problem of participating in the process of NWO global governance, the incentive being to realise self-interested economic, political and security objectives.

The EU remains the most organisationally advanced supranational regional regime, a position within the global system which the Union's Member States and supranational institutions are likely to try to preserve given its recognised *realist* advantages. Certainly the European Commission is clear on the matter, as reflected in various Commission reports, proposals and machinations marking the build-up to the EU's 1996–7 IGC. Thus, in its publication on 'A Europe for Citizens', the Commission argued that 'it is essential for the EU "to respond more effectively to its internal needs and have a stronger presence in international affairs"', and accordingly for 'the Maastricht treaty [sic] review conference [...] to extend majority voting, to curb the use of the national veto and to allow countries which wish to integrate faster to do so' (Palmer, 26 February 1996).

Although Europe currently has the most organisationally advanced regional regime within the global system, the Asia Pacific region is well on the way to constructing its own, rival regimes, including ASEAN, NAFTA, APEC and an East Asian Economic Area (EAEA). ASEAN is the Asia Pacific region's most organisationally advanced regional regime, while the East Asian Economic Area is little more than a proposal, although it has otherwise been formally labelled the East Asian Economic Caucus (EAEC), a title which has acquired widespread currency, as indicated by Tamio Nakamura (1995), a leading researcher in the Faculty of Law at Tokyo's Seikei University:

the EAEC [...] was proposed by Malaysian Prime Minister Mahathir Mohamad in December 1990. Because this caucus aims to group only East Asian members, the United States [...] criticised it as an attempt to create an East Asian trading bloc. Even among ASEAN members, Indonesia did not give support to the idea at first. Meanwhile, the European community's [sic] 1992 internal market project proceeded successfully, and North American countries concluded NAFTA (the North American Free Trade Agreement) in 1993. In January 1993 President Clinton took office in the United States and he suggested that APEC should be more formalised and expanded to include political and economic cooperation in the Pacific region. In reaction to these economic developments and political proposals, all ASEAN member states came to support the EAEC plan in July 1993, and in October the same year, they decided to invite Japan, South Korea, Hong Kong and Taiwan to become founding members of the EAEC. Japan, as the middleman between the US and ASEAN, is yet to make its position clear on the EAEC.   (Nakamura, 1995, p. 10)

The implication here is that the EAEC proposal and prospect represents a tactical response to what is seen as the challenge presented by other – alternative, competing – regimes within the global system and within the Asia Pacific region, including primarily by the US-led development of APEC (the Asia Pacific Economic Co-operation forum). United States President Bill Clinton, perhaps reinvigorated by his November 1996 re-election and perhaps spurred on by the evident advances being made by European Union (by way of its single internal market programme, for instance), not to mention the presence and promise of regional regimes confined to the western side of the Pacific Ocean, showed signs of digging his heels in during the preparations for APEC's November 1996 summit, as reported by Martin Walker:

Bill Clinton is planning to bounce [hustle; coerce] the European Union on his free trade agenda again. Playing the Asian card [has] worked so well [in the past], he cannot resist the temptation to play it once more. Three years ago, when United States and European trade negotiators were deadlocked on the last lap of the Uruguay Round of the Gatt world trade pact, Clinton convened the first Pacific Rim summit, in Seattle in November 1993. Dubbed the Asia-Pacific Economic Conference (Apec) [sic], it was designed to exclude the Europeans [who] grew very nervous. If the Gatt round failed, the US was content to arrange its own trading strategy with the Pacific Rim, the fastest growing economies on the planet. 'We had no choice but to reach a settlement,' commented a top European negotiator. 'The Americans had an alternative and we didn't.' [Conveniently,] the fourth Apec summit [is soon to be held] at the old US naval base of Subic Bay in the Philippines [...]. [The] first Apec summit agreed to explore whether the Pacific Rim countries could 'achieve free and open trade and investment in the region'. The second, at Bodor, Indonesia, agreed they could, and formalised a plan for the industrialised Apec members to achieve free trade among themselves by 2010, with the less industrialised countries following suit by 2020. The third [summit meeting], at Osaka [in 1995], laid down the procedure to achieve this, with each country expected to produce an individual action plan, and co-ordinate this with a comprehensive action plan [...]. [An] awesome potential is being built, whose implications range far beyond trade. This is a forum where Taiwan and China sit together, where countries such as Chile and

Peru are being steered into membership [...]. The US [will, therefore, be] at the heart of what will be one of the central [organisations] of the next century [...]. [At] the Subic Bay conference [the] idea is to secure an Apec consensus and then move to the World Trade Organisation's first minis- terial meeting in Singapore, and bounce the Europeans into agreement, as was done with the Uruguay Round. Important voices [including that of Fred Bergsten, Chairman of APEC's Eminent Persons Group] hope to get the WTO to follow the Apec commitment to achieve global free trade for all developed nations by 2010, and for all others by 2020 [...]. Fred Bergsten [wants to] '[...] install Apec definitively as a permanent bulwark of regional co-operation and a decisive force for world prosperity and stability,' [and, moreover, assumes APEC will] 'assert leadership of the global trading system.'   (Walker, 17 November 1996)

Walker gives the impression that the United States has been intent on *throwing down the gauntlet* to the European Union, and doing so with the support of a cohort, or coterie, of Asia Pacific basin countries, acting together in an increasingly cohesive, unified and organised manner – a manner which could resemble the EU's own approach to realising its objectives within the prevailing global system.

For the time being, however – organisationally, institutionally and constitu- tionally – while APEC may be more advanced than EAEC, it is far less advanced than the EU and quite a lot less advanced than its main Asia Pacific rival, ASEAN. A broad range of commentators, journalists, scholars and politicians have implicitly or explicitly portrayed ASEAN as the next-most advanced regional regime within the global system, and even as the successor-in-waiting to the EU as eventually the most advanced, this development being in line with ASEAN's persistently impressive economic achievements (see, for instance, *The Euro Japanese Journal*, August–November 1995; and April–July, 1996). There is a widely held view supported by a growing body of evidence that ASEAN will become, in a similar way to the EU, institutionally deeper and regionally more encompassing, perhaps to the point of embracing as Mem- ber States all the countries of South-east Asia, including Myanmar (which already has observer status, and which has been promised full membership during 1997), Cambodia and Laos; Australia and New Zealand; and even Japan – although by then, ASEAN may have been re-constructed under EAEC (see Dobbs-Higginson, 1994; So and Chiu, 1995; and Wilkinson, 1991). Any progress of this kind could then be interpreted as reflecting the growing rivalry, struggle and to some extent conflict among the various evolving – existing or embryonic; prospective or proposed – supranational regional regimes and other major global players, such as the People's Repub- lic of China, not to mention Russia. Indeed, 1996 saw major strides in the progress of new world order co-operation between China and Russia:

Russia yesterday signed a wide range of agreements on the transfer of nuclear and military technology to China, hoping to use Beijing as a counterweight to Nato expansion [...]. In comments clearly directed at Washington, a presidential spokesman [...] said [that President Boris Yeltsin and the Chinese prime minister, Li Peng] had agreed that the future political map of the world should be a 'Bi-polar one which is not divided' into leaders and those who are being led' [...]. As an indication of the two countries' determination to forge closer links, it was announced that the Russian prime minister [...] would meet [his Chinese counterpart] twice a year [...]. The two sides also set themselves a target of raising annual trade turnover to as much as £6.2 billion next year [1997]. The sale of Russian military and nuclear hardware will be at the forefront of the new Sino-Russian relationship [...]. Both countries regard themselves as victims of the transition to a market economy and, starved of state orders and funds for conversion, are desparate to find new markets.

(Hearst, 28 December 1996)

But also in Asia, to the south of China, is located a highly successful player in the NWO's global spread of market capitalism, namely ASEAN. The Association of South East Asian Nations' economic achievements are, in turn, reflected in its growing political presence and influence on the world stage, as demonstrated in the way it played host to and, indeed, steered the course of, the March 1996 EU–Asian summit in Bangkok. There is clear evidence that ASEAN largely dictated the summit's agenda and 'closing statement', ensuring the marginalisation or neglect of ' "controversial and irrelevant" topics' (Field, 1996), especially those to do with 'human rights abuses and proposals for minimum global labour standards' (Palmer, 1 March 1996). Thus, if for no other reason than the fact that 'Asia is one of the world's few regions where military spending budgets continue to grow in the post-Cold War era [...with] Britain's share of the arms trade there [being] worth an estimated £520 million', then 'all questions of human rights [were] sidestepped as European leaders [chased] lucrative trade deals, including arms sales worth billions of pounds' (Field, 1996).

In 1995, total EU–ASEAN trade amounted to £62.2 billion (or US\$99.5 billion), but both sides were agreed that this 'lagged behind its potential', as perhaps indicated by the fact that in 1995 'Asean–US trade was nearly US\$110bn' (Kynge and Buckley, 12 February 1997).

Among the human rights questions deliberately, and supinely on the part of the EU, sidestepped were those relating to Myanmar (or Burma) and East Timor, questions which none the less did not evaporate, as reported by Kynge and Buckley in February 1997:

Foreign ministers from the European Union and Asia will this week engage in a testing diplomatic encounter: to add substance to the vague optimism of a new dawn in relations between the two regions. But such hopes appear imperilled by disputes over human rights in Burma and East Timor. The increasingly assertive nations of Asia have made it clear Europe cannot hope to deepen economic ties with the world's fastest growing region unless it becomes less confrontational about human rights. The issue could make or break the talks in Singapore [on 13 February 1997] between the 15 EU countries and the seven members of the South East Asian Nations (Asean), and on [15 February] between the EU and Asean, plus China, Japan and South Korea. The weekend meeting will be the first foreign ministers' meeting between the countries which took part in last year's inaugural Asia-Europe summit in Bangkok. Singapore officials said Asean had informed EU officials that if the Europeans raised the issue of Indonesia's occupation of East Timor, the 'whole [EU–Asean] relationship would be seriously affected' [...]. Even more sensitive for the EU is Burma, expected to join Asean later this year. EU ministers have expressed concern over human rights abuses there, and have suspended Burma's tariff privileges [see European Parliament, *EP News*, March 1997, p. 4]. The concern in Brussels is that Burma's entry into Asean could strain ties with the whole grouping [...]. One EU diplomat said Burma's accession to Asean [...] could be interpreted as endorsement of [Burma's government's] attempts to suppress Ms Aung San Suu Kyi's democracy movement. (Kynge and Buckley, 12 February 1997)

Encouraged by 'Asean officials' to concentrate on 'boosting trade and promoting investment'; and agreeing on an EU–ASEAN 'Action Plan' – with the aim of scrapping non-tariff barriers, the promotion of investment and the setting up of European Business Information Centres in ASEAN countries (*ibid.*) – again at the behest of ASEAN, the sensitive (and, for ASEAN, the internal) issues of human rights, democracy and so on were sidestepped. Here, we can recall (see our Chapter 3) how Nicholas Cumming-Bruce reported that the 13 February 1997 meeting between the fifteen EU and seven ASEAN foreign ministers ended with an EU–ASEAN agreement on 'measures to strengthen economic relations'; and with an all-round 'sense of relief' that the 'European concern about human rights' and ASEAN's 'hostility to any formal debate on [such] issues' had not resulted in an acrimonious and failed encounter. The topic of East Timor had been only informally raised, had hardly been discussed, and would 'not feature in the final communiqué'; and the discussion of the EU's problem with human rights and democracy in Myanmar had been 'diverted [...] to a working lunch':

> Asean leaders, stressing that there are no political criteria for membership, such as exist for the EU, [partly] rationalise Burma's admission as a necessary step to checking the influence and leverage of Asia's emerging

superpower, China. But Asean's particular achievement of the past 10 years has been to make it the interface between West and East and a political and economic community through which to engage China. Asean's foreign ministers' conference [now the ASEAN Regional Forum] is a meeting point where 'dialogue partners' such as the US, Canada, and Australia hobnob with China, Japan and South Korea. Two years ago it created the Asean regional forum (ARF) [also attended by the European Union] to try to fill a regional vacuum on security issues [...]. Asean's free trade area [AFTA – see El-Agraa, 1995], if slow to emerge, now gives its members added weight in the Asia-Pacific economic co-operation forum [sic], which is aiming at free trade in the next 25 years in an area that already accounts for half the world's production.

(Cumming-Bruce, 14 February 1997)

While the outcome of the 1996 and 1997 EU–ASEAN summits may have been unfortunate for the people of East Timor and of Burma, and in particular for Suu Kyi, it may turn out to be especially regrettable for women rather than men more generally, recalling how the controversial topics (Field, 1996) which were marginalised in the 1996 summit's agenda and 'closing statement' included that of establishing 'minimum global labour standards' (Palmer, 1 March 1996). Thus:

Left out of Asia's economic success story, women from poorer parts of the region have become the world's fastest growing pool of cheap and often abused migrant labour, according to the International Labour Office [...]. About 1.5 million women, mostly from the Philippines, Indonesia, Sri Lanka and Thailand, now work abroad, mostly as maids, nurses and 'entertainers', a euphemism for a booming sex industry. Whereas women accounted for only 15 per cent of the Asian migrant workforce in the 1970s, they now equal or outnumber male migrant workers [...]. Domestic service and entertainment are rarely covered by labour laws or social security, leaving many female migrants defenceless against abuse [...].

(Higgins, 6 February 1996)

The EU has shied away from pressing ahead with its original demand that accompanying any EU–ASEAN economic agreement should be a *labour standards* agreement, understanding or common approach. The result is that in ASEAN countries as well as in East Asia more generally, the social and legal rights, apart from the remuneration, enjoyed by labour are far less developed than those across western Europe; and are negligible compared with those enshrined in the EC/EU's Social Charter, the basis for the proposed Social Chapter of the Treaty on European Union – a proposal which was not carried due to British opposition, the Social Chapter being relegated to the Treaty's Social Protocol (see Barnard, 1996; Burrows and

Mair, 1996; Hantrais, 1995; Hervey and O'Keefe, 1996). The question raised by the EU's approach to human rights, democracy and labour standards in ASEAN and East Asia is that of 'how does the 1996–7 EU–ASEAN summits and overall relationship bode for western Europe's social rights, laws and policies given the EU's *realist* approach to the competition it faces within the NWO global system?'

For us, the answer lies to a large extent in the distinctive (local) social character of the SRRs which are emerging within the Asia Pacific region, and perhaps especially within the East Asia (or Pacific Asia) sector of this region. The answer lies largely in, for example, the evolution of and prospects for ASEAN, with its *local* approach to human, citizenship and labour rights; and, following Cumming-Bruce, with its added weight in the Asia Pacific Economic Co-operation forum, and much further beyond. Hence, the debate now underway about the possibility of Europe 'emulating' the 'Asian Tigers' by, for instance, adopting the East Asian social model (see Hutton, 28 October 1995; Macwhirter, 29 October 1995; Tang, 1995a). Perhaps the rise of ASEAN as a weighty alternative SRR global player, helps account for the following report: '[s]ocial protection spending in the European Union has fallen [...] to 28.6 per cent of gross domestic product, according to the latest figures from Eurostat' (*Financial Times*, 5 April 1997), although of course we acknowledge the as yet tentative character of any explanatory link.

6 Globalisation and Supranationalism

Many European citizens feel that their national culture is threatened by moves towards economic and political unification. Some cultural communities in Europe, however, welcome this trend since their particular identities have not always been respected by nation-states. We are exhorted to preserve the variety of cultures in Europe, whilst at the same time urged to recognize commonalities, collaborate, integrate and unify for the common good. Is this a paradox? Can we preserve our identification with local, regional and national cultures whilst still embracing European integration?

(Shelley and Winck, 1995)

This extract from Shelley and Winck's contribution to a quartet of books on *What is Europe?* draws attention to some of the main practical (everyday), political (policy) and sociological (theoretical) issues concerning the patterns, ramifications and implications of late-twentieth-century European cultures.[1]

These issues include how the drive towards European social, or structural (economic, political), integration may be inhibited, if not finally prevented,[2] by the presence of European *cultural diversity*[3]; and how, perhaps (as intimated by Shelley and Winck) paradoxically, the same process of integration is helping to weaken the nation-state and thereby, if anything, encourage and enhance cultural (ethnic, national) diversity, as well as – to recall the discussion in our Introduction – social, or systemic, *disorderliness* (see Axford, 1995, p. 7).

A trend towards greater cultural diversity, or at least towards the appearance – even assertive display – of such diversity, is clearly reflected in the proceedings of the International Press Institute's world congress of March 1997 on the theme 'The European Union – a federation of nations and regions':

As the debate about European Union rages,[4] a vociferous minority representing the regions in Europe is taking a stand. Politicians from some of the 300 regions maintain that only further integration would give them the opportunity to further develop their cultural and historical identity as well as their economic interests independently of the country [i.e., nation-state] to which they belong [...]. Nelly Maes from the Flemish Nationalist Party (Volksunie) and MEP Allan Macartney, deputy leader of the Scottish National party, both demanded recognition for their region's right to self-determination in Europe [...]. Catalan leader Jordi Pujol said that

[...] Catalonia's identity is as a nation within a Spanish and European framework. Luc van den Brande, president of the Assembly of European Regions, outlined the four levels of authority in Europe: the Union, member states, the regions and the cities.   (Smith, 27 March 1997)

An apposite way of expressing what is taking place is to suggest that Europe is travelling in somewhat *contradictory* directions, being simultaneously *en route* towards both greater *unity* and greater (displays of) *diversity*. These contradictory trends may well foster growing tensions, clashes and conflicts both (i) between the *cultural* (ethnic, national) level, on the one hand, and the *structural* (economic, political) level, on the other; and (ii) among the various distinct, occasionally highly divergent, *cultural communities* and *cultural agendas*.[5] An empirically evident and experiential (subjectively experienced) symptom of such contradictory trends would be the social, or systemic, disorderliness and 'the disordered feel of the contemporary world' (Axford, 1995, p. 12).

Having said this, however, one of the most striking features of Shelley and Winck's particular study of *Aspects of European Cultural Diversity* is the way in which its scope and perspective stands in contrast to that of another of the *What is Europe?* quartet of books. As Kevin Wilson says in his General Preface to the *What is Europe?* series, Shelley and Winck's objective is to 'consider aspects of European cultural diversity through investigations into language, education, mass-media and everyday culture' (Wilson, 1995, p. 7). Accordingly, Shelley and Winck's approach to the cultural dimension of European patterns, processes and trends can be distinguished from Bernard Waites', whose *objective* in *Europe and the Wider World* (Waites, 1995) is to 'locate Europe as a political and economic entity in a context of global change' (Wilson, 1995, p. 8).

Our perspective on the process of European regional integration – and, for that matter, on regional integration wherever it occurs within the global system – is guided by (what we take to be) the axiom that it is empirically, analytically and theoretically beneficial to merge the two objectives identified by Kevin Wilson. Aspects of European cultural diversity and their, perhaps somewhat contradictory, relationship with the process of European structural (economic, political) integration towards greater European unity are, for us, most profitably investigated by locating Europe *as a political and economic entity in a context of global change* – a context (i) within which cultural (ethnic, national) diversity, on the one hand, and structural (economic and political) integration, on the other, are embroiled in *dialectical relationships* in several global regions; and also (ii) within which structural integration between global regions is dialectically interrelated.

While we cannot claim that this merging of objectives amounts to anything as grand as a paradigm shift, we can claim that it represents something of a *perspective shift* away from the kind of approach adopted by, for instance, Staffan Zetterholm who (in the Introduction to his *National Cultures and European Integration*) informs us:

> Many observers interested in the dynamics and future of the European Community single out one aspect of Western Europe, namely its cultural diversity, as sufficient reason for a pessimistic assessment of the future of EC integration [...]. There are [...] many different positions regarding culture as a factor influencing political and economic integration in Europe [...]. In many of the most influential integration theories [...] the focus is now upon how institutional and policy changes lead to changes in the actions and interactions of the actors in the system.
>
> (Zetterholm, 1994b, pp. 1–2)

In our view, 'the system' Zetterholm is referring to, in that it is confined to Europe, can be adequately understood only by viewing it within a much greater compass; within a far more enveloping economic, political and cultural framework or system. For us, the kind of inter-dependent cultural and structural[6] developments addressed by Zetterholm, as well as by (if only by implication) Shelley and Winck *inter alia*, are – with analytical, interpretative and theoretical objectives in mind – best approached in the broadest possible way, by examining *Europe within the wider world* or, that is, Europe within the global system (Axford, 1995).

The global perspective on European cultures has been signalled in a range of relevant writings, but often little more than just signalled. This shortcoming is underscored by the way, on the other hand, the global perspective has been widely and productively employed in the study of other areas and dimensions of European social life, including those that have focused on economic, political and military matters. For instance, in Bernard Waites' *Europe and the Wider World* (1995), a whole section is devoted to 'Europe in the global economy', while poignantly 'culture' as a distinct dimension of social life attracts little attention.[7] Yet other texts, including ones of great merit, while adopting a global perspective appear none the less myopic when it comes to culture. Thus, Jonathan Story's *The New Europe: politics, government and economy since 1945* (1993) has sections and chapters on 'Europe in the Cold War', 'Changes in world politics', 'Europe and America in the 1990s', 'Japan and Europe in global perspective', and 'Europe and the changing global agenda', but includes neither a chapter nor an index listing on *culture*.

There is a growing and, in some ways, impressive body of literature on European cultures, but one which is impoverished by the absence of a firm commitment to a global perspective; and accordingly by a failure to keep abreast with the methods, debates and insights to be found in both other areas of European studies (see Scott, 1992; Woods *et al.*, 1993) and in that broad field of scholarship which we can cautiously label *cultural studies* (see Lash and Friedman, 1992b, p. 3).[8] Various contributors to cultural studies, having established that Europe is the birthplace of much that constitutes the 'Western cultural account' (Meyer *et al.*, 1987, p. 29; Axford, 1995, p. 2), have also tended to portray this account (i) as having once been dominant within the global system; (ii) but as having recently entered a phase of decline relative to and, if only in part, due to its relationships with other, alternative accounts (see, for instance, Friedman, 1992; Giddens, 1991, pp. 51–2; Smart, 1993).

A central, distinguishing and defining thread running through the *western* cultural account would appear to be 'Western individualism' (Friedman, 1992, pp. 355–6; cf., Meštrović, 1994, pp. 66–7), one notable account of the European origins of individualism being that offered by Lawrence Stone in *Family, Sex and Marriage in England, 1500–1800* (1977), according to which:

> during the late seventeenth and early eighteenth [centuries, both] social life in general and family life in particular were characterised by an increase not only in affection, but also by what Stone terms 'individualism'. By this he means 'two rather distinct things: a growing introspection and interest in the individual personality and, secondly, a demand for personal autonomy and a corresponding respect for the individual's right to privacy, to self expression and to the free exercise of his (or her) will within limits set by the need for social cohesion' (Stone, 1977, pp. 223–4) [see Dunleavy and O'Leary, 1987, Chapter 1]. Puritanism had laid the foundation of individualism by stressing the conscience of the individual above the authority of the church, and the importance of personal morality and private devotion as opposed to ritual conformity and public worship.
>
> (Harris, 1983, pp. 146–7)

Stone's account raises several connected issues, queries and problems, including that of the meaning or meanings of 'individualism', given that, as demonstrated by Steven Lukes (1973), 'there are many [...] senses of the term' (Harris, 1983, p. 147). Second, there is the problem of historically pinpointing the genesis of individualism with any confidence. Alan Macfarlane (1978), for instance, argues that individualism 'predates the sixteenth century changes and shapes them all' (quoted in Harris, 1983, p. 114; see also Close, 1995, Chapters 4 and 5).

Macfarlane's argument brings to mind a third issue: that of *theorising* individualism. Thus, Stone's theoretical interpretation closely resembles Max Weber's, as discussed by Derek Sayer in *Capitalism and Modernity: an excursus on Marx and Weber* (1991). Sayer summarises by telling us that, 'the core of Weber's argument [...] lies in the case he makes for a specific subjectivity being engendered by the Reformation. This is a new kind of individuality, one that is uniquely fitted to the norms of "sober bourgeois capitalism"' (*ibid.*, p. 119); or, for Weber, 'Protestantism's greatest contribution to capitalism – and the modern world more generally – lay in its breeding of the modern subject' (*ibid.*, p. 129; see Weber, 1974). But, the problem with Weber's account of individualism is that Weber may have misread the *causal* relation – or, more specifically, the direction of this relation – linking Protestantism, capitalism and individualism. An alternative way of theorising individualism is to propose that, conversely, capitalism bred individualism, and thereby fed Protestantism (cf. Macpherson, 1962; Tawney; 1938). At the same time, however, the subsequent success but variety of capitalism(s) covering the west and the spread of market capitalism well beyond the confines of the west complicate considerably the issue of theorising individualism.

Whatever the history, origins and sources of western individualism, for many writers, the western cultural account – or what has been otherwise referred to as the *western cultural configuration* and *western modernity* (Smart, 1993) – when viewed in terms of a global perspective (Friedman, 1992, p. 355) during the last few years of the twentieth century (i) can be contrasted with other, more *collectivist cultural strategies* (Friedman, 1992, pp. 355–62); (ii) is in *decline* (*ibid.*, pp. 355, 360); and (iii) is being *challenged* – to some extent successfully, even to the point of being superseded – by alternative cultures, civilisations and modernities (see our Introduction; see also Friedman, 1992, pp. 356–7; Meštrović, 1994; Smart, 1993, pp. 149–52).

Jonathan Friedman argues:

> In those areas of the East characterized by rapid economic growth there are new forms of modernism. These have to be seen in relation to the declining dominance of the West in order to understand their particularistic cultural character and the universalistic evolutionism that they embody. On the one hand they have emphasized the moral core of the Confucian order [...] elevated to a set of generalized social principles. This has been linked to the notion that the NIC (Newly Industrializing Countries) lands, for example, have some special culture that is conducive to development, and even superior to Western individualism. There have, on the other hand, been numerous discussions of the relation between Confucian developmentalism and Western models [...]. It might be argued that the problem with Western modernity is that its individualism tends to erode the moral values that render the entire project of modernity a genuine possibility. Such a view would dovetail with [Daniel] Bell's analysis of the dialectical contradictions of modernity that generate, all by themselves, the postmodern dissipation that has taken form in the West [see Bell, 1976]. In the Eastern model [of modernity] with its weaker, if clearly present, individual, entirely oriented to the project of the group, such disintegration ought not to be possible [...]. In this sense, it might be

said that neo-Confucianism appears as a cultural movement, and is a cultural movement from the point of view of the declining hegemon, but in the same sense that Renaissance Europe was a cultural movement with respect to the declining centres of the East. [Neo-Confucianist ideology] belongs to the family of modernist cosmologies. The primary difference for us Westeners is that, while stressing all the properties of the rationalist development orientation, it does so without invoking the individualism typical of the Occident. (Friedman, 1992, pp. 356–7)

For Friedman a concomitant development to 'the decline of Western [cultural] hegemony' is that '[m]odernity moves east, leaving postmodernity in its wake' (*ibid.*, p. 360). We will avoid getting too distracted here by probing the depths of the notions and nuances and exploring the details of the pros and cons of (never mind the possible semantic and analytical distinctions between (see Smart, 1992, 1993; Giddens, 1991, pp. 45–61) *postmodernity* and *post-modernism*.[9]

It is sufficient for our purposes to do little more than (i) refer back to our Introduction; and (ii) note that the phrase 'postmodern dissipation' (Friedman, 1992, p. 356) means 'intemperate, dissolute, or debauched living', entailing 'frivolous amusement' and 'wasteful expenditure', and threatening, as inferred by Friedman, 'disintegration' (*Concise Oxford Dictionary*, 1990, p. 339; cf. Meštrović, 1994, p. 1). This view of western postmodernity can, however, be contrasted with what Friedman refers to as 'more optimistic renderings' (Lash and Friedman, 1992b, p. 7), including Doug Kellner's 'positive and politically progressive' representation of *the construction of postmodern identities* (*ibid.*, p. 7) in the same volume (Kellner, 1992):

Kellner observes that identity formation is displaced from the sphere of production to the sphere of consumption and leisure in the transition [from Western modernity to postmodernity]. But he sees such identity formation as a chance for [...] greater intensity of reflexivity [see Axford, 1995, pp. 11–23; Craib, 1992a, pp. 100–2; Giddens, 1991, pp. 36–54]. Modernism called for reflexivity in the sense of balancing a plurality of role demands. Postmodernism is on the other hand much more aware of identity choice. Individuals can consciously experiment with identities. They can make identity choices entailing far greater [identity] risk than under modernism [...]. Postmodern innovation of identity can, Kellner realizes, be akin to game-playing. (Lash and Friedman, 1992, p. 7)

While Kellner distinguishes between *modernism* and *postmodernism* around the part played in each by 'reflexivity', for others the common presence of reflexivity lends support to 'the notion that postmodernism is in important respects continuous with modernism', as opposed to the conclusion that there has been 'a radical rupture between the two' (Smart, 1993,

p. 17). Here we can recall, for instance, the contribution of Ulrich Beck (1992a, 1992b; Beck *et al.*, 1994; see our Chapter 1), through his (in our view) valuable notion of 'risk society'. But as well as Beck, Anthony Giddens adopts this approach in *The Consequences of Modernity* (1991), where he explains:

> There is a fundamental sense in which reflexivity is a defining character-istic of all human action. All human beings routinely 'keep in touch' with the grounds of what they do as an integral element of doing it. I have called this elsewhere the 'reflexive monitoring of action,' [...]. [But, with] the advent of modernity, reflexivity takes on a [particular] character. It is introduced into the very basis of system reproduction, such that thought and action are constantly refracted back upon one another. The routinisa-tion of daily life has no intrinsic connections with the past at all [...]. The reflexivity of modern social life consists in the fact that social practices are constantly examined and reformed in the light of incoming information about those very practices, thus constitutively altering their character [...]. [O]nly in the era of modernity is the revision of convention radicalised to apply (in principle) to all aspects of human life [...]. What is characteristic of modernity is [...] the presumption of wholesale reflexivity – which of course includes reflection on the nature of reflection itself [...]. At this point we can connect the discussion of reflexivity with the debates about post-modernity.   (Giddens, 1991, pp. 36–45)

Essentially, Giddens rejects the 'discontinuist interpretation' (*ibid.*, p. 52) of history which distinguishes *modernity* from *postmodernity*: 'far reaching transitions have occurred. Yet referring to these as a post-modernity is a mistake which hampers an understanding of their nature and implications' (*ibid.*, p. 51). Giddens asserts: 'We have not moved beyond modernity but are living precisely through a phase of its radicalisation' (*ibid.*, p. 51), judged in terms of the part played by reflexivity. For Giddens, 'radicalised modernity' is that phase of modernity in which 'the self is more than a product of discourse, because of its self-reflexive, self-constituting tendencies' (Craib, 1992a, p. 101); and which, accordingly, is characterised by 'a dialectic of powerless and power, loss and appropriation' (*ibid.*, p. 101).

Giddens summarises:

> I have sought to develop an interpretation of the current era which challenges the usual views of the emergence of post-modernity. As ordi-narily understood, conceptions of post-modernity [...] involve a number of distinct strands. I compare [and contrast] this conception of post-modernity (PM) with my alternative position, which I shall call radicalised modernity (RM) [...]. (Giddens, 1991, p. 149; see Giddens' table on p. 150)

Ian Craib otherwise interprets Giddens' approach as follows:

While reflexivity defines all human activity, it takes on a specific meaning in the modern world [...]. In the modern world [...] routinisation has no intrinsic connection to the past and social practices are constantly examined in the light of new information. Nothing is fixed simply because it is there, and new information is constantly reconstituting practices [...]. It is part of the reflexivity of modernity that the increasing progress of science involves the increasing questioning of science, a relativising of knowledge, and the realisation that there are no guarantees to knowledge. This [...] is not a new social form, a new type of society, but a logical outcome of modernity. The realisation that there are no absolute foundations to knowledge amounts to 'modernity coming to understand itself' [...]. As the remnants of traditional society and thought are cleared, modernity becomes radicalised. (Craib, 1992a, pp. 100–1)

Although, Giddens argues, we 'have not moved beyond modernity but are living through a phase of its radicalisation' (1991, p. 51), he none the less refers, by way of an explanation, to the 'gradual decline of European or Western global hegemony, the other side of which is the increasing expansion of modern institutions worldwide' (*ibid.*, p. 51). That is:

The declining grip of the West over the rest of the world is not a result of the diminishing impact of the institutions which first arose there but, on the contrary, a result of their gobal spread. The economic, political and military power which gave the West its primacy, and which was founded upon the conjunction of the [...] institutional dimensions of modernity [capitalism, industrialism, the nation-state (see Giddens' Chapter II)], no longer distinctly differentiates the Western countries from others elsewhere. We can interpret this process as one of *globalisation* [...].

(*ibid.*, pp. 51–2)

Therefore, Giddens concurs with Friedman in so far as he rejects the globalisation of *postmodernity* (and *postmodernism*); but he opposes Friedman in that he proposes the successful globalisation of Western modernity, including in its *current radicalised phase* (Giddens, 1991, p. 149). For Friedman, we can recall, 'In those areas of the East characterized by rapid economic growth there are new forms of modernism', forms which being rooted in the Confucian order, Confucianism, and 'Confucian developmentalism' are not centred on western 'individualism,' the source of 'the problem with Western modernity' and (following Daniel Bell, 1976) of 'the postmodern dissipation that has taken form in the West'. The 'Eastern model' of modernity shields the east from the postmodern disintegration which is apparent in the west, largely by virtue of its *weaker individual*, in that neo-Confucianist ideology does not invoke the 'individualism typical of the Occident' (Friedman, 1992, pp. 356–7). Friedman claims that, in the east, 'Asian modernism displays

most of the basic characteristics of the Western model, the main difference
lying in the role of the individual as an instrument of the group rather than
as an autonomous agent' (*ibid.*, pp. 360–1).

Friedman's view of the distinction and disjunction (if not 'radical rupture'
(Smart, 1993, p. 17)) between modernity and postmodernity and of the
associated separation between the west (or the Occident) and the east (or
the Orient) distances him from Giddens' view of the globalisation of western
institutions, which for Giddens has persisted into the 'current phase of
radicalised modernity' (Giddens, 1991, p. 149), with its 'thoroughgoing,
constitutive reflexivity' (*ibid.*, p. 52), or its self-reflexivity (Craib, 1992a, p.
101) of, it would seem, obsessive and excessive proportions (Bell, 1976;
Friedman, 1992, pp. 355–63). Friedman's view, therefore, overlaps with
while differing in at least one crucial respect from Barrie Smart's – whose
view, in turn, provides a bridge between Friedman's and Giddens'.

Barrie Smart argues that postmodernism 'may be described as a cultural
configuration that is broadly continuous with modernism, that is not significantly different' (Smart, 1993, p. 16). However, this is not to say that the
terms 'postmodernism' and 'postmodernity' (*ibid.*, p. 23) are redundant
(*ibid.*, p. 16), are to be discarded as superfluous. That is, the 'idea of postmodernity indicates a modification or change in the way(s) in which we
experience and relate to modern thought, modern conditions and modern
forms of life, in short to modernity' (*ibid.*, p. 39). It is in outlining this
'modification or change' that Smart's account comes to resemble Friedman's:

discussion of the idea of postmodernity arises in the light (and shadow) of
modernity and needs to be explored in relation to its complex and uneven
consequences. In an age in which the world has been pictured as a 'single
place', as a whole, reference has been made to both a pervasive process of
'Europeanisation' and subsequently to what is frequently represented as an
even more extensive global process of 'Americanisation'. And it is here in
the context of a range of complex cultural exchanges and inter-relation-
ships between Europe and America that different aspects of the postmodern configuration receive their initial articulation [. . .]. The depth of
contemporary interest in the idea of postmodernity arises in substantial
part from the fact that the universal significance once accorded to goals
and values articulated in 'Euro-American' master narratives and equated
with modern Western civilisation no longer seem persuasive. The very idea
of modernity as a project associated with the West is in question [. . .]. For
example, Western modernity (and its institutional dimensions, developmental directions, and social consequences) has been challenged by the
resurgence of Islam. Indeed, it might be argued that Islam has become the
main counter-force to modern Western civilisation [. . .]. To what extent

the regeneration of Islam and its corollary, the turn away from Western modernity, contributes to what has been termed the condition of postmodernity awaits further clarification [Ahmed, 1992; Gellner, 1992; Meštrović, 1994; see our Introduction]. The configuration of Western modernity has been placed in question and challenged in a second, somewhat different manner by increasing evidence that the economic and cultural momentum has swung away from Europe and America towards the Pacific rim and the modernising societies of the East. [T]he growing prominence of Japan and the possibility that its successful modernisation and increasing economic hegemony[10] have been achieved without cultural Westernisation [means that the] idea of a [lone] universal project of [Western] modernity becomes difficult to sustain [...The] 'specific – and highly dynamic – constellation of economic, political and cultural determinants sets the Japanese road to modernity apart and relativises all parallels with earlier or more frequent patterns' [Arnasen, 1987/88, p. 59]. The rapid achievement of an economically modern form of life through the promotion of capitalism and perpetuation of paternalistic authoritarianism in other societies in South-East Asia, notably the 'Four Tigers' of Hong Kong, Singapore, South Korea and Taiwan, lends further weight to the argument that modernity is multi-dimensional and multi-directional. It is in this context of a recognition of the [...] realisation that there are other increasingly powerful non-Western civilisations exercising a globally extensive and growing influence over economic, cultural and political life, that a notion of *post*modernity has been invoked. A notion that suggests not the passing of modernity, not the end of history [...] but a different way of relating to modern conditions and their consequences, to present circumstances and future prospects.   (Smart, 1993, pp. 150–2)

Smart might have been more specific and detailed about how western modernity differs from its non-western counterparts and challengers, as exemplified by Islam and as otherwise found in, for instance, Japan and, what Smart refers to as, South-East Asia. We are left to assume that what Smart has in mind is something similar to Friedman's claim that 'the main difference between Western modernism and Asian modernism lies in the role of the individual and of individualism' (Friedman, 1992, pp. 35–62; cf., Meštrović, 1994, especially Chapter 3). As we can then recall from our Introduction, central to the concept of (western) modernity, following Anthony Giddens (1993) is the 'idea of reflexivity, or "self-monitoring"' (Axford, 1995, p. 11); the possibility being that 'the notionally "postmodern" [merely] represents a [...] further intensification of contingency with even greater scope for individual reflexivity', the result being 'the disordered feel of the contemporary [western] world' (Axford, 1995, p. 12). Accordingly, the 'notionally postmodern' – whether following Giddens it is more appropriately called 'radicalised modernity' (Giddens, 1991, p. 149) or following Beck it merely qualifies as *'second* modernity' (Axford, 1995, p. 16), or 'risk society' (Beck, 1992a, 1992b; Beck *et al.*, 1994) – is characterised by an 'excess of contingency' (Axford, 1995, p. 15), of individual reflexivity (self-monitoring), and so of individualism (see Axford, 1995, pp. 19–20; Fukuyama, 1995; Mongardini, 1992).

A rapidly swelling number of writers are examining the details of the contrast, and to some extent the 'clash' (see Axford, 1995, Chapters 6 and 7), between western cultures and modernity, on the one hand, and non-western cultures and modernity (or modernities), on the other. Furthermore, they are referring to, and sometimes emphasising, items and issues relating to the *role of the individual* and of *individualism.* For some, for instance, there is evidence that the models of individual and human rights which are professed and purveyed by the west are being increasingly and successfully challenged by alternative models from 'the east'. Thus, according to James Tang:

> Human rights concerns have come to the forefront of the international stage in the post-Cold War world. As the United States trumpeted ideological victory in the aftermath of the Cold War, East Asian states mounted a challenge to Western beliefs on human rights. In the Asia-Pacific region, the different human rights positions of East Asian states and the West have generated tensions with far-reaching regional and global implications. This book addresses the post-Cold War East Asian challenge to the contemporary 'Western' understanding of human rights and its implications for regional and international relations.
>
> (Tang, 1995b, p. 1)

The East Asia challenge to which Tang refers was apparent at the World Conference on Human Rights held in Vienna in June 1993, not to mention at the United Nations' (fourth) world Women's Conference held in Beijing in 1995. In the build-up to the Vienna conference, an Asian regional preparatory meeting was held, the result being the Bangkok Declaration, 'signed by over forty Asian governments' (*ibid.*, pp. 1–2), and challenging the west's view of the universal applicability of its version of human rights. The Declaration asserts:

> universality should be considered 'in the context of a dynamic and evolving process of international norm-setting, bearing in mind the significance of national and regional particularities and various historical, cultural and religious backgrounds'.   (Tang, 1995b, p. 2)

In Tang's view, the post-Cold War 'confrontation between East Asia and the West over human rights [...] has to be understood in the context of the spectacular economic development of the Asia-Pacific region' (*ibid.*, p. 2). That is, Tang tells us:

> The emergence of the Pacific region as a focal point of global activities has led to intense discussions about whether a fundamental shift in world politics has taken place, marking the beginning of a new epoch. The growing importance of the Asia-Pacific region has prompted suggestions that [...] East Asian states will provide a Pacific paradigm of the future. [S]ome East Asian states seem to have drawn the conclusion that their political systems and economic policies are better than the Western [...] models, and they can offer 'an alternative vision of the values needed for a better world'.
>
> (Tang, 1995b, p. 2, and see note 10)

The spectacular economic development of the Asia Pacific region has meant shifts in the distributions of both economic and political power within the global system; can be seen as reflecting and reinforcing, and as endorsing or vindicating, an East Asia-led *Pacific* paradigm *vis-à-vis both* economic and political policies and practices *and* 'social' models and human rights programmes. The East Asian challenge is not just economic; concurrently and concomitantly, it has political, 'social' and human rights dimensions. It follows that East Asia's economic and political development and its alternative 'social' and human rights models have far-reaching regional and global implications, especially within the post-Cold War new world order. While the west's cultural account and individualism – and even its notional postmodernism or 'radicalised modernity' (Giddens, 1991, p. 14) – may have gained footholds in East Asia, these *globalised* themes have, none the less, been variously mediated and modified, resisted and localised, and selectively absorbed and re-worked into a distinctively East Asian alternative cultural account and modernism.

The East Asian cultural account is then being presented and asserted not just as different from, but also as 'better' than the western alternative, given the prevailing character and circumstances, the conditions and contingencies, and the (other) challenges and imperatives of the NWO. East Asian modernity is being increasingly paraded as preferable and advantageous in comparison with the western version, especially since the latter's radicalised metamorphosis with its excesses of contingency, reflexivity, self-monitoring and individualism – with its 'narcissism' (Friedman, 1992). There is a possibility that the relative economic and political success of East Asia and the rest of the Asia Pacific region in combination with (i) the west's radicalised individualism, and (ii) the west's (like the east's) broadly realist approach to global system imperatives, challenges and problems, will translate into growing 'cultural' pressures in favour of a major modification – or a transformation – of the west's cultural account, individualism, 'social' model and human rights programmes. Of considerable importance to the everyday lives of people in the west, there is a possibility that these pressures will be in a *regressive* direction when judged in terms of the west's own cultural traditions.

Signs of regressive pressures on Europe, and in particular on Britain, can be read into a report by Will Hutton towards the end of 1995 under the heading: 'Tory fantasy of far eastern promise: should Britain become an Asian tiger economy?' (Hutton, 28 October 1995). Hutton writes about the growing number of Conservative Members of Parliament and other Conservative policy-makers attracted to the idea of 'reinventing Britain as an Asian style success story'; who look to the 'extraordinary growth rates of the "Asian tiger" economies' and argue that 'Britain must follow their example' (*ibid.*). Hutton suggests that this 'requires, as a minimum, a semi-detached relationship with over-regulated Europe'; but also, it invites a thoroughgoing social and cultural overhaul, a prospect which Hutton finds misguided and unacceptable:

> the foundations of growth [in East Asia] – suppressing demands for decent living standards and working conditions from newly-industrial workforces, often through banning trade unions and military intervention – are neither sustainable nor tolerable. Ralph Dahrendorf stresses this: success has been delivered by a social authoritarianism that is anathema to Western liberal democracies. Yet to a Conservative Party increasingly attracted to social authoritarianism, this is a positive merit.
>
> (Hutton, 28 October 1995)

Hutton is convinced about 'the foredoomed attempt to emulate the Asians' in the area of economic matters, simply because of what he sees as the answer to the 'larger question of values. Social authoritarianism and purposeful neglect of the living conditions of the majority have no parallel in British cultural and political traditions' (*ibid.*). Hutton tells us that Britain 'stood as the first custodian of universal human rights, threw over repression as a means of social and political regulation, and curbed the excesses of capitalism. There is no political or cultural validation for the Conservative path' (*ibid.*).

Whether the East Asian paradigm is acceptable or applicable in Britain, Europe and the west, it would seem that none the less there are pressures on the west to adopt it, and those in the west who are seriously tempted by the prospect of re-working the western paradigm to some extent in accordance with it.

At this point, it is pertinent and profitable to return to the thoughts of Francis Fukuyama, and in particular to ones presented since his *The End of History and the Last Man*.[11] We can recall that in *The End of History* (1992), Fukuyama argues that:

the collapse of communism meant that liberal democracy had proved superior to all its competitors. Everyone had not gotten there yet, but everyone strove for a democratic political system and a market economy. This meant the end of history, in the sense of seaching for the best system. It also meant [...] the end of large-scale war.   (Ambrose, 1993, p. 374)

In his later book on *Trust* (1995), however, Fukuyama shifts his ground somewhat by recognising that 'free markets, competition and hard work are *not* the sole precursors for prosperity. There is another key ingredient – trust. Without this quality, capitalist economies [cannot] go far' (Hutton, 20 October 1995). But, for Fukuyama, trust cannot simply 'be invented'; instead, it is something which 'is embedded in [...] social institutions and culture', in 'what Fukuyama dubs "social capital"' (*ibid.*). Fukuyama suggests that societies vary in their stock of *social capital* – one country which 'is good at generating trust [being] Japan' (*ibid.*). For Fukuyama, that is:

The Japanese institution of lifetime employment and family firms are symbols of [...] trust relations, and have been the means through which Japan has raised productivity and investment levels to extraordinary heights – and enabled its companies to grow. Workers are loyal to their companies, reciprocating the commitment to life-time employment; and the networks are sources of long-term finance and captive markets.

(Hutton, 20 October 1995)

As reported by Will Hutton, Fukuyama's 'account of the way different cultures and social capital have developed [...] always [returns] to family structure and [what is referred to as] "density of associations"'. In this context Fukuyama compares Japanese culture and social capital with their Chinese counterparts: the Chinese have 'always regarded the inclusive family as [a] moral imperative; the Japanese [have] had a looser idea, with adoption [being] much more acceptable than in China'. The Chinese 'have always put kinship first, resisting outsiders', the result being that the Chinese 'are culturally plagued by distrust' (*ibid.*), to their relative disadvantage within global market-capitalism.

The queries and doubts about the details of Fukuyama's Japan–China comparison and analysis aside (cf. Akira Iriye's *China and Japan in the Global Setting*, 1992, for instance), Fukuyama's point that in this comparison there are lessons for the west – the United States and Europe – is germane and of value for present purposes. The overall message of Fukuyama's comparative treatment of trust and social capital is that there is an East Asia paradigm (exemplified most notably by the case of Japan) which presents a genuine alternative and serious challenge to the west, where it is not so much the traditional family system which helps weaken trust (as illustrated by the case of China), but the breakdown of 'the family' *per se* (cf.

Close, 1985, 1989, 1992a), this breakdown being indicative of the drive towards *excessive individualism*.

As mentioned by Hutton, Fukuyama's

> aim is to warn the US, especially the American right, not to put as much faith in economic individualism, free markets and their apologists. American individualism, says Fukuyama, was always leavened by strong loyalties to kin, community and club which generated strong social capital – but as those have broken down, so trust relations [have] evaporated. The US has not only been under-investing in human and physical capital for decades; it has been allowing its once strong social capital to run down, too. Litigiousness [resorting to lawsuits] is growing hugely because individuals are no longer bound by trust relations; the parasitic US lawyer is but the most obvious example of the way distrust becomes an economic tax. US industry is suffering from lack of trust, so that it cannot make the same productivity gains as Japanese capitalism – and is suffering from short-termist, exploitative asset-stripping and the hollowing-out of its basic infrastructure.   (Hutton, 20 October 1995)

Hutton explains:

> This is the heart of Fukuyama's theory, and [...] it is both important and full of insight. Here is a leading luminary of the American right demonstrating that excessive individualism and the prosecution of self-interest along the lines of Friedmanite economics is paradoxically an economic dead-end. Trust reduces the cost of doing business; distrust operates as a tax on all forms of economic activity.   (*ibid.*)

Following Fukuyama, the west with its excessive individualism – or, guided by Giddens, its *radical individualism* – is depleted of 'trust' and, consequently, of (culturally based) 'social capital'[12] on which it can draw in its competition with and in meeting the challenge of, most forcefully, East Asia, the economic (and political) surge of which is facilitated by its alternative (East Asian) economic, political, 'social' and human rights paradigm, as displayed most prominently and deployed most successfully by Japan.

If so, however, because trust and so *bottom-up* social capital cannot simply 'be invented', then the west, in our view, has turned to what amounts to an alternative – remedial or countervailing – top-down (imposed) *invention*. The west, and more specifically Europe, has invented the SRR. SRRs, as exemplified and trailed by the EU, may be initially and basically trading blocs and so largely economic-oriented, but they also have political, 'social' and human rights dimensions. The EU represents a co-operative attempt to respond to and deal with the (external) problems, challenges and imperatives confronting its Member States, individually and jointly, within the encompassing NWO global system, and accordingly an attempt to effectively engage in *global governance*, to manage global disorder(liness) in favour of greater order(liness). The problems involved are exacerbated by the internal (governance) problem rooted in the west's excessive, or radical, individualism and associated lack of (following Fukuyama) trust and social capital – as manifested in the west's *notionally postmodern* internal disorder(liness).

The EU represents a *top-down* attempt to compensate for the west's excessive individualism and lack of trust and social capital given its (its Member States') realist approach to the global system – global system conditions and contingencies, challenges and imperatives. In addition, however, the EU may see itself (may be seen by its Member State governments and its supranational institutions) as – to paraphrase the wording at the end of our Introduction – the best available (albeit recognisably partial and somewhat contradictory) solution to the governance problem of internal disorderliness. If 'the disorderliness of modern [western] conditions [. . .] and a growing sense of personal anxiety' lend appeal to 'invitations to bury individuality in the collective idyll and embrace communitarianism' (Axford, 1995, p. 13), then this disorderliness may be manageable to some extent – perhaps sufficiently for the purpose at hand – by the top-down invitation to embrace and be embraced by the appeal and advantages of the collective and communitarian, or that is the co-operative, solution represented by the EU as an SRR. This prospect – this line of thinking – appears to lie behind the considerable effort and other resources being expended by and through the European Commission, for instance, to enhance a sense of identification with, belonging to, support for and *trust in* the EU among the people of Europe around such publicity notions as 'a people's Europe' (Fontaine, 1995, Chapter 7), for example.[13]

But here, further possibilities crop up. If the East Asian challenge to the west is rooted in a stock of (culturally based) social capital and trust on which it can draw, then the possibility arises of the same feature providing a firm foundation on which to build SRRs, and indeed a firmer foundation than that provided by the radical individualism and 'postmodern' disorderliness of the west.

As with market capitalism in the past, so with supranational regional regimes in the future. The birthplace of SRRs is Europe, but there are signs that supranationalism as a *doctrine* and SRRs as organisations and *co-operative solutions* to NWO global system problems, challenges and imperatives have begun to spread their wings, and are preparing to roost in various other parts of the world, not least in East Asia. ASEAN is firmly established as an expanding regional trading bloc in East Asia (or, that is, in the Pacific Asia sector of the Asia-Pacific region as a whole) and as an increasingly powerful regional and global player. Furthermore, it is evident that ASEAN's areas of competence are becoming more inclusive, and that its institutions are becoming more elaborate, linked to the progress of the

ASEAN Free Trade Area (AFTA) as well as the ASEAN Regional Forum (ARF) on security issues, for example. These steps may represent the seeds from which will grow an East Asian SRR, and moreover a supranational regional regime which is far more geo-politically extensive than ASEAN's current South-East Asia confinement.

Already, ASEAN has taken the initiative in establishing an East Asian Economic Caucus, having most significantly invited Japan to be a founding member.[14] If Japan agrees, then this could mark the start of the (long-term) development of a hugely powerful SSR, which while being similar in some ways to the EU, may well differ greatly from the EU. Its Member States, with their largely realist approach to NWO global system conditions, contingencies and imperatives, could steadily tread the road towards deeper supranational institutions in a manner which is more or less consistent with *neo-functionalist spillover* (see Shaw, 1996, Chapters 1 and 2). At the same time, the course plotted by any East Asian SSR would be mediated by 'culture', as indeed has been and remains very much the case with the evolution of the EU. It could be that East Asian cultural (linked to political) diversity, clashes and conflicts will inhibit supranational progress. On the other hand, it could be that, especially in conjunction with the region's mainly realist and economy-oriented approach to the global system, East Asia's culturally based social capital will facilitate this progress. The outcome (as with market capitalism) could be the construction of a distinctive (localised) type of SRR, but with global advantages over the western type as exemplified by the EU – the construction of an East Asian type of SRR which the EU could come under pressure to emulate. The post-Cold War, NWO global system could become dominated by a set of global players (super-powers), some if not all of which would be of a new breed of hegemon, one which is not congruent with particular nation-states, but which is based on the accumulation of several nation-states under the umbrella of a set of interlocking supranational institutions – in other words, a supranational regional regime. Global system patterns, processes and developments could become largely determined by the progress of such regimes and the relationships among them, as well as between them and other major global players.

As reported by Helen Milner:

A number of scholars have been predicting the demise of the GATT [General Agreement on Tariffs and Trade, and now the World Trade Organisation (WTO)]. The problem in their eyes is that the world is disintegrating into three hostile trade blocs: North America led by the United States, Asia led by Japan, and the European Community (EC) led by Germany. The rise of these blocs reflects the decline of American hegemony and the creation of a more multipolar international system. A multipolar world may create the conditions that foster the development of such economic blocs around each polar power. In this environment, it is feared that these blocs will become exclusive, promoting trade within each area and discriminating against trade with outsiders [...]. In part, the GATT's problems today reflect the development of [trading, economic] blocs. The European Community is battling with the United States, joined by Canada, over the issue of agricultural trade. Part of the US response to this battle and to the creation of a larger European space after 1992 has been to push ahead with its own trading bloc to match the European Community. It agreed on a Free Trade Area (FTA) with Canada in 1988 and has recently concluded a tripartite accord involving Mexico and Canada for a large North American FTA (NAFTA). Concerned with being left behind by these two blocs, Asian countries have started discussing an Asian FTA. These political developments could threaten the core principles of GATT: liberalisation on a multilateral basis. They could entail the rise of exclusive, regional trading blocs, each dominated by a single country. Increased conflict among the blocs could also result.

(Milner, 1994, pp. 108–9)

Milner notes that of 'the regions, Asia seems to be the least developed as a bloc' (*ibid.*, p. 111). It is indisputable that 'Asia' in the sense meant by Milner (i.e., 'Japan and the rest of Asia, including India, China, South-East Asia, and North-East Asia') does not form a *trading bloc* in the way that the EC/EU or NAFTA does. But what about ASEAN and SAARC, never mind the proposed EAEC? Milner mentions none of these (see the European Commission's 'The European Union and Asia', April 1996). The closest Milner gets to recognising a trading bloc which takes in any Asian country is in her concluding remarks:

If regionalism in Asia and North America is viewed as a political response to the European Community, then it seems that a more effective policy would be a Pacific trade area [...]. But the erection of exclusive economic blocs, particularly in Asia and North America, could have very significant costs for all the states involved; it might lower their rates of growth and their sense of security. The costs of such attempts to reorient trade should be examined carefully before choosing such a course of action.

(Milner, 1994, p. 124)

By 'Pacific trade area' it is not clear that Milner is alluding to the Asia Pacific Economic Co-operation forum (APEC), but this regional regime presumably qualifies for what she has in mind. Also, it is not clear why Milner arrives at what appears to be a highly pessimistic prognosis of the development and effects of American and Asian trading blocs. There may be grounds for a cautionary assessment – for assuming that there will be conflicts and disruption (disorderliness) within, throughout and at all levels of the global system – but it seems to us that the construction of several regional economic-cum-political regimes, even mutually hostile ones, will not necessarily lend itself to anything approaching *world disintegration*, at least any more than a global system built upon nation-states. It could be that, if anything, the major building blocks of the global system will increasingly include (geopolitically) expanding and (institutionally) deepening regional (economic, political) regimes – that the most prominent and powerful NWO building blocks will increasingly include, and indeed will themselves be dominated by, supranational regional regimes. It seems to us that SRRs could become the principal repositories of economic, political and even military power within the NWO global system, and therefore the main players in the process of managing disorderliness in favour of orderliness – in the process of global governance. At the same time, SRRs could come to accept – given their basically realist approach to global system problems, challenges and imperatives, relationships, processes and developments – the monitoring, even regulation, of their activities by global (political) regimes, such as the WTO. We will proceed to examine these issues in depth in our follow-up book, provisionally called *The Legacy of Supranationalism*.[15]

Notes

PREFACE

1. For indicative definitions of 'supranationalism' and 'new world order', see *The Cambridge International Dictionary of English* (1995), p. 952 and p. 1466. For more guidance on the notion of 'supranational', see Drost, 1995, p. 582; Shaw, 1996, pp. 12–15.
2. See for instance, the European Commission's paper on 'A Europe for Citizens', according to which 'it is essential for the EU "to respond more effectively to its internal needs and have a stronger presence in international affairs"', and so for 'the Maastricht treaty [sic] review conference [...] to extend majority voting, to curb the use of the national veto and to allow countries which wish to integrate faster to do so' (Palmer, 26 February 1996).
3. On ASEAN, see Dixon, 1991; Dobbs-Higginson, 1994; *The Euro Japanese Journal*, 1995; So and Chiu, 1995; and Wilkinson, 1991. See also Close and Ohki-Close, 1996/7.
4. Recently, doubts have been raised about the 'continuing economic upsurge' of Pacific Asia: 'The Asia economic "miracle", spearheaded by the tiger economies of the Pacific Rim, has stalled and sent world trade growth into a slump, according to figures released yesterday by the World Trade Organisation' (Thomas, 11 April 1997). Thomas adds: 'After a decade of spectacular growth – which was the envy of European nations – the countries of South-east Asia have been hit by a slowing world economy and a strong dollar, putting the region at the bottom of the global export table' (*ibid.*).
5. See Hutton, 28 October 1985; Macwhirter, 29 October 1995; Tang, 1995.
6. A strong thread linking the CEC and SNWO projects is the issue of the way (a) the relationship between policy, law, citizenship and gender within the EU is (b) manifested in the differential use and experience of 'space', both public and private. Some recent work by, for instance, Louise Ackers (1995) touches on this question by examining the implications of European Community law for labour mobility mediated by gender. For us, Ackers' work and preliminary results are consistent with a more inclusive range of information and ideas which suggests that within the EU there are strong forces operating in favour of programmes, policies and laws whereby the use of (or consumption of and through) public and private 'space' – such as by way of labour mobility among other forms of migration – by *Citizens of the Union* remains highly gender-skewed, to the considerable disadvantage (and relative social exclusion) of women. The evidence emerging from the SNWO enquiry appears to endorse this conclusion (see Close, 1996). See also Massey, 1994; Trench *et al.*, 1992.

INTRODUCTION

1. Barrie Axford (1995) refers to the 'problem of world order, or the lack of it', and mentions how, faced with this problem some 'institutionalists [...] have chosen to [see] hegemonic power [...] as a source of stability and, *contra* realism, as a vehicle for the promotion of cooperation in the form of interna-

tional regimes. The position of the United States as a global hegemon has prompted much of this debate, along with the consequences for international cooperation which follows from its putative decline as a "manager" of the world order (Giplin, 1987) or as a relatively benign facilitator of interstate cooperative behaviour (Keohane, 1984)' (Axford, 1995, pp. 41–2). We will return to this possibility.

2. Francis Fukuyama's (1989; 1992) 'The End of History' thesis has otherwise been summarised as follows: 'the collapse of communism meant that liberal democracy had proved superior to all its competitors. Everyone had not gotten there yet, but everyone strove for a democratic political system and a market economy. This meant the end of history, in the sense of searching for the best system. It also meant the end of [...] large scale war' (Ambrose, 1993, p. 374).

3. Stephen Ambrose tells us that by the time of the '1990–91 crisis with Iraq' (Ambrose, 1993, p. 372), the 'Cold War was over, no one threatened the security of the United States [...]. All the great "isms" of the twentieth century against which the United States had fought – colonialism, fascism, Communism – had been defeated'; except, Ambrose adds, 'for Communism in Cuba, China and Southeast Asia' (*ibid.*, p. 374). Stjepan Meštrović (1994) similarly mentions that 'the "collapse of communism" was not complete, because communism continues to rule China, Cuba, North Korea and other nations of the world' (*ibid.*, p. 1). But, in so far as 'communist' nation-states have survived the end of the Cold War, they have hardly done so as a bloc, as a coalition. This is evident in the following newspaper report: 'China has withdrawn an oil exploration vessel that prompted a row with Vietnam when it started drilling in part of the South China Sea between the two communist neighbours [...]. The Association of South-east Asian Nations (Asean) has offered verbal support for Vietnam, its newest member. Its concern stems from fears that China will make similar moves on the Spratly Islands, also believed to contain oil and gas. These are further south and are claimed by Beijing and most Asean nations' (Grant, 1997). In our view, the Association of South East Asian Nations (ASEAN) is currently the next most advanced (organisationally and institutionally speaking) supranational regional regime (SRR) after the European Union.

4. In support of his view of NWO disorder(liness), Axford refers to Jonathan Friedman's 'Order and disorder in global systems: a sketch' (1993). But see also, Jonathan Friedman, 'Narcissism, roots and postmodernity: the constitution of selfhood in the global crisis', in Scott Lash and Jonathan Friedman (1994a).

5. On international regimes, see Alec Stone, 'What is a supranational constitution?' (1994).

6. On supranational constitution-building, see Alec Stone, 'What is a supranational constitution?' (1994).

7. While, on the one hand, Meštrović suggests that 'it is nearly impossible to settle on a consistent definition of "postmodernism" [Rosenau, 1992]' (Meštrović, 1994, p. 1); on the other hand, he tells us: (i) that there is a 'widespread understanding of postmodernism as rebellion against the grand narratives of the Enlightenment [Gellner, 1992; Lyotard, 1984; Rosenau, 1992]'; and (ii) that 'postmodernism [is] itself a confluence of apocalyptic themes found in the previous *fin de siècle*' (Meštrović, 1994, p. 1) and the fun-culture uncovered by David Riesman in his *Lonely Crowd* (*ibid.*, p. 1). For Meštrović, in other words, 'postmodernism' distils down to 'a fun version of the apocalypse' (*ibid.*, p. 1). It is pertinent to mention at this point that for Meštrović himself, Islam is 'a distinct form of postmodernism or antimodernism' (*ibid.*, p. 1), and recommends Akbar Ahmed (1992) for assuming the same. Meštrović also agrees 'with

Ahmed (1992) that the East–West dichotomy is cultural, not geographical, so that Australia, for example, is often considered to be part of the West. Furthermore, Islamic nations are considered Eastern even though they span much of the globe from North Africa to Indonesia. But even as a cultural dichotomy, the East–West distinction is problematic' (Meštrović, 1994, p. 61).

8. For other attempts to clarify, apply and assess the related notions of 'postmodernism' and 'postmodernity', see Axford, 1995, pp. 14–28, and Chapters 6 and 8; Giddens, 1990 (1991); Harvey, 1989; Hollinger, 1994; Lash and Friedman, 1992a; Sarup, 1993; Smart, 1992; Smart, 1993.

9. Here, Axford seems to be employing 'order' in the sense implied in the phrase 'new world order', and so in the sense of arrangement, configuration or pattern.

10. See Stjepan Meštrović's discussion of 'Zygmunt Bauman's (1992) elaboration of the theme that the collapse of communism is a symptom of postmodernity defined as rebellion against Enlightenment narratives' (Meštrović, 1994, p. 17).

11. Meštrović attributes the notion of New World Order to which he is referring to President George Bush of the United States (see Meštrović, 1994, pp. 34–5), while also mentioning 'H. G. Well's New World Order [which] was going to be a socialist society of the entire world that would promote compassion and justice in opposition to the evils that were attributed to capitalism. President Bush's use of the phrase, New World Order, reversed Wells's high regard for socialism – in that it posited the victory of capitalism and democracy – but it kept the moral temper of the original formulation' (*ibid.*, p. 153).

1. THE NEW WORLD ORDER AND SUPRANATIONALISM

1. The Ukraine was a constituent republic of the Union of Soviet Socialist Republics (USSR), or Soviet Union, between 1922 (when the USSR was established) and 1991. Towards the end of 1991, the Ukraine announced its provisional independence from the USSR. A referendum held on 1 December 1991 resulted in a large majority of voters wanting independence. The Ukranian declaration of independence was accompanied by similar declarations from several of the other fourteen republics, signalling 'the dissolution of the USSR, a process formally recognized by the Congress of People's Deputies voting itself out of existence on 5 September 1991' (Upsall, 1991b, pp. 677–9).

'Joseph Stalin' was the adopted name of Joseph Vissarionovich Djugashvili ('stalin' being the Russian for 'steel'). In 1922, he became the General Secretary of the Communist Party of the Soviet Union, and by 1928 'emerged as absolute ruler after ousting Trotsky' (*ibid.*, p. 677). He is notorious for being responsible for a series of purges during the 1930s when all opposition to his policies and rule was ruthlessly eliminated (see Hosking, 1985, Chapters 7 and 8; see also Hosking, 1996).

2. See Immanuel Wallerstein's *The Modern World System* (1974). For a brief assessment of Wallerstein's perspective, see Anthony Giddens, 1991a, pp. 65–9.

3. See Barrie Axford's *The Global System: economics, politics and culture* (1995).

4. Charles Tilly otherwise considers 'a revolution to be a forcible transfer of power over a state in the course of which two distinct blocs of contenders make incompatible claims to control the state, and some significant portion of the population subject to the state's jurisdication acquiesces in the claims of each bloc' (Tilly, 1993, p. 8).

5. This is not to suggest that the transformation involved ceased at the end of 1991. It is only to suggest that during 1989 to 1991 a fundamental and especially *intense* alteration in the character of the global system occurred. What was initiated in 1989 was firmly and probably irreversibly established by 1991, if not finally completed by that time. Certainly, the history of revolutions (depending, of course, on how the term 'revolution' is defined) is littered with examples which may be seen to have taken several years to complete. Tilly refers to France's revolution 'between 1789 and 1799 [and] Russia's between 1917 and 1921' (Tilly, 1993, p. 4). See also Orlando Figes' *A People's Tragedy: The Russian Revolution 1891–1924* (1996).

6. It is by no means just Barrie Axford (1995) who attributes the origins of the phrase 'new world order' to United States President George Bush. Stephen Ambrose, for instance, mentions how 'President Bush called the crisis that began when Iraq invaded Kuwait in August 1990 the "defining moment" in setting a new foreign policy for a "new world order"' (Ambrose, 1993, p. 377). See also Axford, 1995, p. 180; Kenichi Ohmae, 1995, p. 7; Christopher Coker, 1992. However, we have spotted that the phrase and notion were presaged quite a few years before 1990, by Charles de Gaulle in his *Memoirs of Hope* (1971), extracts of which are reprinted in Brent Nelsen and Alexander Stubb's *The European Union* (1994, pp. 25–41). De Gaulle refers to 'setting up a new order to replace the Cold war' (Neslen and Stubb, 1994, p. 27). Much earlier still, the prime minister of Japan between 1937 and 1939, Prince Konoye, came up with a similar phrase, although this was in a very different context and with a very different sense (see Richard Storry, 1995, pp. 235–54). In the autumn of 1938, 'Konoye issued a declaration that Japan's "immutable policy" was the establishment of a New Order in East Asia – meaning a political, economic and cultural union of Japan, Manchukuo, and China' (*ibid.*, p. 249). Konoye's declaration was consistent with the 'philosophy of ultra-nationalism' which had taken hold in Japan at the time (Megarry, 1995, pp. 232–3), as well as with 'the threat of Japanese hegemony in East Asia, which the Japanese came to describe as the Greater East Asia Co-Prosperity Sphere' (Reischauer and Jansen, 1995, p. 101). Finally at this juncture, it is poignant to note how the French Revolution, given that it began precisely 200 years before the global transformation marking the conclusion of the Cold War, has been described as 'the forcible abolition of the *Ancien Régime* "old order of things" (feudalism and absolute monarchy) 1789–99' (Upsall, 1991b, p. 690). Similarly, the 1989–92 *global revolution* entailed the abolition of the 'old world order' and the advent of the 'new world order'.

7. On the idea that bipolarity as a global institution 'provided a context or frame of reference for most independent states', see Axford, 1995, pp. 180–1; Koslowski and Kratochwil, 1994; and Wendt, 1994.

8. Hugh Miall (1993) singles out Hedley Bull (1977) as having 'made the classic statement of the realist position' on international order (Miall, 1993, p. 19). Bull 'argued that an international order should be seen as "a pattern of activity that sustains the elementary or primary goals of the society of states, or international society". These goals [include] the preservation of the system of states itself [and] the preservation of the independence and sovereignty of individual states' (*ibid.*, pp. 19–20). In other words, '[f]rom a realist perspective, the basic institution of the international system is the sovereign state [. . .]. Between states, order is [. . .] fragile, given the absence of a supreme authority and the unwillingness of some states to accommodate the interests of others. Nevertheless, international order can exist to some degree, in so far as states observe common

norms and act in such a way as to preserve themselves individually and collectively' (*ibid.*, p. 19). For Barrie Axford, the Cold War bipolar global system temporarily sidelined the realist perspective on international order. Whereas before the Cold War there was 'an international system which had been structured by the realist strategies of nation-states in shifting and unstable alliances', this 'was transformed into' a 'moment of global stability' (Axford, 1995, p. 4) by the Cold War. Against this, however, writers such as Andrew Moravcsik (1991; 1994) insist that the process of European integration throughout the Cold War and subsequently is best studied, analysed and understood in terms of a realist perspective. That is, Moravcsik and other realists, 'who assume that nation-states operating in an anarchic (or near-anarchic) world are still the most important actors, [have] reacted to the emphasis [placed by other writers] on supranational institutions and processes with their own explanation of recent events in Europe' (Nelsen and Stubb, 1994, p. 211). Accordingly, Moravcsik contradicts such writers as Wayne Sandholt and John Zysman (1989; 1994) who focus on the part played by 'supranational institutions' in the process of European integration, including in the '1992 process' (Nelsen and Stubb, 1994, p. 189) through which the European Community's (and now Union's) single internal market was established. For Sandholtz and Zysman, 'first [of all,] changes in the international structure – specifically the decline of the United States and the rise of Japan – "triggered the 1992 process." They then couple this idea with neofunctionalist and domestic politics notions to explain the timing and specific nature of the new integration process. [For instance, from] neofunctionalism, they draw the importance of supranational institutions [...]. The focus for Sandholt and Zysman is primarily, although not exclusively, on the actors working in the realm above the member states. For this reason, other scholars have often labelled their view supranationalist' (Nelsen and Stubb, 1994, pp. 189–90). Our perspective on the process of European integration is similarly *supranationalist*. Our (theoretical) perspective on the global system, and in particular on the global new world order, draws strongly on the realist perspective, while being tempered and modified in accordance with our recognition of the increasingly 'major role' (*ibid.*, p. 211) being played within the global system and NWO by supranational organisations or regimes, institutions and constitutions.

9. See Gorbachev, 1996; and Bernstein and Politi, 1996. Reviews of these two books in *The Guardian* (3 October 1996) are prefaced with the questions: 'Why did the Soviet Union collapse? Because Pope John Paul II saw things the American way, or because Gorbachev lost control of his great experiment?' Michael Walsh begins his review of the book about Pope John Paul II by reporting that, according to the authors, 'John Paul II is credited with helping bring about the downfall of Communism in eastern Europe.'

10. During 1996, the headline-grabbing events were those in Chechenya (or Chechenia). See, for instance, James Meek (25 August 1986); Jonathan Eyal (26 August 1996). However, the Caucasus region is not the only one in which there have been movements towards, if not full independence, at least greater autonomy. Roman Rollnick has reported 'a growing desire for greater regional autonomy [in] the Primorski Krai region in which Vladivostok lies' (3 October 1996, p. 5).

11. See Misha Glenny's *The Rebirth of History: Eastern Europe in the Age of Democracy* (1990).

12. Lane and Ersson (1996) give supporting references to Sachs, 1993; Åslund, 1995; and Gowan, 1995.

13. The label 'eastern Europe' is a left-over from the Cold War era. It covers and conflates the more traditional distinction between 'central' and 'eastern' Europe, where the former conventionally includes what are known as the Visegrad Four (see Drost, 1995, p. 628) – the Czech Republic, Hungary, Poland and the Slovak Republic – as well as the three Baltic states: Estonia, Latvia and Lithuania. As far as possible, when discussing the post-Cold War era, we will operate with the distinction between western, central and eastern Europe. However, especially given that some writers, such as Lane and Ersson (1996) persist in using the more inclusive 'east Europe' and 'eastern Europe', as opposed to 'west Europe' and 'western Europe', sometimes it will be necessary or appropriate for us to revert to these labels.

14. Similarly, as reported by Laura Zelenko, 'Polish shares are poised to rise much further this year than other eastern European equities' (3 October 1996).

15. As reported by Phil Reeves (18 September 1996): 'Two years after the last Russian soldiers left its soil, Estonia was the first post-Soviet nation to begin to be weaned from Washington's foreign aid, US diplomats [have] said. The days of dependency [are] drawing to a close. Estonia [does] not need it; it [is] an "economic miracle", a shining example of the free market triumphing over stifling central planning [...]. What's the secret? Geography and size help, but so does Estonia's agressive de-nationalisation. Preliminary moves are even being made to sell off the railways and energy industries. For the Estonians, such policies amount to installing another buffer against the east.'

16. Accordingly, Rob Urban and Jill Hamburg have reported how 'Bulgaria, low on cash and facing foreign debt payments of $250 million, is going to sell stakes in state-owned companies after years of political bickering and bureaucratic delay. Oliver Decamps, head of the European Bank for Reconstruction and Development's team in Bulgaria, says the sales will involve 18 companies during the next few months [...]. The government hopes to raise $1 billion from the sale of the chemicals, metals and refining companies, shipyards and hotels' (Urban and Hamburg, 3 October 1996).

17. Lane and Ersson refer to several writers who have attempted to incorporate the convergence thesis into 'macro social theory': Kerr, 1983; Sztompka, 1993; Chirot, 1994; Langlois *et al.*, 1994. They also refer to 'a couple of good overviews of the various scholarly contributions': Bennett, 1991; Coughlin, 1992; Kalberg, 1993. See the account by Davis and Scase (1985) of the convergence thesis as applied to the then east–west divide and confrontation, according to which the thesis's 'claims seem absurd' (Davis and Scase, 1985, p. 5). For a Marxist-influenced perspective, see the world-system theory of Immanuel Wallerstein, 1974; 1979; 1983; 1984; 1989; 1991b; and 1994. On 'modernisation' in general, see Anthony Giddens, 1991b. For a 'modernisation' account of the 'post-communist social transformation' by a sociologist from a former east European country, see Pavel Machonin's 'Post-communist social transformation and modernization', 1996. Machonin argues that the 'state socialist social structure was not able to stimulate further progress of modernization. The lag in modernization still remains the crucial problem of the post-communist societies. The success or failure in modernization will be the decisive criterion for the evaluation of the results of the post-communist social transformation' (1996, p. 5). Machonin regards 'the present processes in the post-communist' societies as undergoing 'convergence with [the] basic developmental trajectories' of the 'advanced European countries' (*ibid.*, pp. 8–9). See also Przeworski's *Democracy and the Market: Political and Economic Reforms in Eastern Europe and Latin America* (1991).

18. Lane and Ersson's enquiry also warrants the description 'thin' when judged in terms of its geo-political scope: 'We have included 31 countries in our analysis of convergence, drawing the line between inside Europe and outside Europe along the borders to Russia, Belo-Russia [Byelorussia], the Ukraine and Turkey' (Lane and Ersson, 1996, p. xi). As Lane and Ersson put it, their 'analysis of European politics [covers only] the major states from the Atlantic Ocean to the borders of the former Soviet Union' (*ibid.*, p. 2).

19. By the middle of 1996, the European Union had signed association agreements with another four 'eastern states': 'Slovenia officially applied to join the European Union on 10 June [1996], on the occasion of the signature in Brussels of a European [association] agreement between Ljubljana and the European Union. Slovenia thus [became] the 10th Central and East European country to sign such an agreement, which implies the prospect of membership in due course. Slovenia is the only ex-Yugoslav Republic to [have found] itself in this situation' (European Commission, 'Slovenia applies for membership', 1996). The other 'former east European' countries which had applied to join and had association agreements with the EU by June 1996 were 'Hungary, Poland, Slovakia, Romania, Bulgaria [and] the three Baltic States – Estonia, Latvia and Lithuania' (European Commission, 'Prague seeks EU membership, March 1996). At the same time, three other European countries had applied for membership and had acquired association agreements: 'Turkey, Cyprus and Malta have Association Agreements with the Union, aimed at the gradual creation of a customs union. All three have formally applied for Union membership (Turkey in 1987, Cyprus and Malta in 1990)' (Fontaine, 1995, p. 35).

20. The 1996 European Union's 1996–7 intergovernmental conference (IGC), or 'so-called Maastricht 2 [negotiations] formally open[ed] in Turin' on 29 March 1996, marking the start of a 'year of deliberations [...] about a range of European issues – common foreign and security policy, common justice and home affairs policy, EU institutional reform and accountability – which [...] will inevitably impact on domestic and international politics for years to come. The IGC will have to decide about big questions, like the structure of western European defence [...]. But it will also take decisions about smaller matters – like the adoption of a uniform proportional representation system for European Parliament elections [...]. The principal problem for this IGC, and perhaps for all European Union negotiations always, is to find a workable and popular EU-wide compromise between necessary European cooperation and necessary national decision-making. [I]t is clear that the powers of a strengthened union must be subject to legal scrutiny, parliamentary accountability and popular consent' (*The Guardian*, 29 March 1996). In practice, the IGC has progressed far from smoothly. In October 1996, according to John Palmer, 'European Union heads of government begin an eight-hour closed summit in Dublin [on 5 October] to try to break the deadlock in negotiations for a new treaty on closer union. Frustrated at the protracted talks, most EU leaders are determined to conclude a successor to the 1991 Maastricht treaty by next summer – even if this means that more ambitious moves to a federal-style political union are left to yet another constitutional reform treaty by the end of the decade [...]. Most of the 15 heads of government accept the urgent need for more effective and democratic structures, to allow the EU to accept new members from central Europe and the Mediterranean. [...] Germany, France and virtually all other countries will insist on Britain accepting more majority voting and a greater role for the European Parliament in less contentious fields, such as social, environmental, transport and other policies' (Palmer, 5 October 1996). See also note 25.

21. See *Roget's Thesaurus of English Words and Phrases* (1987, p. 342; p. 368); and *New Webster's Dictionary and Thesaurus* (1991, p. 171). See also Robert Monks and Nell Minow's *Watching the Watchers: Corporate Governance for the 21st Century* (1996), reviewed by Martin Dickinson (15 July 1996); cf. Neville Bain and David Band's, *Winning Ways Through Corporate Governance* (1996), reviewed by Ben Laurence (13 October 1996).

22. The argument that Europe as a whole is converging towards a 'post-industrial society' conforms with Lane and Ersson's suggestion that there are 'many striking similarities between the societies in Europe, whether they are located in the [...] West or East, because the tertiary sector [of the economy] is increasing everywhere' (Lane and Ersson, 1996, p. 197).

23. In effect, this was one of the main arguments used by the Norwegian government, and in particular by the Norwegian prime minister, Gro Harlem Brundtland, when trying to persuade the Norwegian electorate to vote in favour of joining the European Union in the November 1994 referendum on the issue. As it turned out, the electorate were not impressed: 52 per cent of those voting chose not to join. The argument has also been recognised by the Swiss government in its 'search for a new bilateral relationship' with the EU which 'began after the Swiss voted in December 1992 not to join the European Economic Area (EEA), under which some non-EU countries gain access to the benefits of the single market. Because 60 per cent of Swiss exports go to the EU and Switzerland remains the EU's second most important export market, it [has been] vital to find some new arrangement' (Barber, 15 July 1996). However, the 'EU, irritated at being snubbed in the EEA referendum, [has been] determined to drive a hard bargain. In return for upgraded access to the single market, the Swiss would have to offer concessions on two sensitive issues: freedom of movement of people and increased land transit rights [...]. A Swiss official admits that the negotiations have again exposed a cultural gap between the Swiss and their European neighbours. But Switzerland needs a deal more than the EU, which probably explains why the Commission and the member states are taking their time – and making the Swiss sweat a little more than they are used to' (*ibid.*).

24. See also Cheles *et al.*, 1996.

25. Here, Lane and Ersson are arguing that the EU is becoming more institutionally 'supranational', something favoured by what John Palmer identifies as the 'integrationist' intentions and impetus behind the 1996–7 Intergovernmental Conference which is negotiating a successor treaty to the Treaty on European Union (the Maastricht Treaty) of 1992. Following the 'special one-day EU summit meeting in Dublin' (see note 20), Palmer tells us that the United Kingdom's prime minister, John Major, 'was left in little doubt that [his] fellow leaders [were] determined to sign the new treaty at the end of the Dutch EU Presidency [in the] summer' of 1997 (Palmer, 6 October 1996). Palmer expands: 'Maastricht One [...] involves only a modest degree of sovereignty sharing by EU member states. But a combination of monetary union in 1999 and Maastricht Two next year will mean important moves towards a supranational community. There will be more majority voting in the Council of Ministers in such areas as social and environmental policy, as well as parallel increases in the role of the European Parliament. The distribution of votes between large and small countries will also be changed to favour the large countries. The Commission will get very few new powers but it will become more involved in some aspects of justice and home affairs – when the EU is given direct responsibility for immigration, visas and asylum policy. National governments will remain in

charge of foreign security and defence policy – as well as the fight against international crime. But the new treaty will commit them to act more effectively together. Meanwhile the advent of monetary union in 1999 would oblige common decision-making over an increasing area of macro-economic policy – including "eco" taxes and targets for growth and employment' (*ibid.*). Palmer regards 'the planned new "Maastricht Two" treaty on European Union' as one of 'three separate trains all bound for European Union and all due to depart before the end of the decade' (*ibid.*), the second of these trains being the 'monetary union project'. Palmer asserts that 'the 1999 single currency express now seems certain to depart on time – in January 1999. The signs are that a large majority of the 15 EU member countries will qualify for the move to a single currency. Apart from Germany, France, the Benelux countries, Austria and Ireland, the Nordic countries, Spain and possibly Italy could yet join the EMU "first wave". That would leave Greece and possibly Portugal behind, together with the UK, should it choose not to join' (*ibid.*). The 'third train' is that which is 'scheduled to take the EU much further down the road to a federal-style political union.' Speaking just before 'the special one-day EU summit' on 5 October 1996, Germany's 'Chancellor [Helmut] Kohl called for a "Maastricht Three" treaty. While he accepted that it might not be possible for the EU to agree on all the institutional and political changes needed to enable the EU to operate in future with perhaps 30 member states, Kohl and other integrationists plan to tackle some of the unfinished business of Maastricht Two with a Maastricht Three. "Any problems which we cannot resolve will have to be dealt with in a Maastricht Three," he said [...]. At least 15 countries want to join the EU in the next 10 or 15 years and the first half dozen – the Czech Republic, Cyprus, Hungary, Malta, Poland and Slovenia – expect to begin entry negotiations at the end of next year [1997]. The German government has earmarked another review of the EU's constitution and decision-making system to be linked with the final stages of the first enlargement negotiations, towards the end of 1999. "The process of European integration is [...] a continuing process [...]," said a senior German official [on 5 October 1996]. "To be able to respond to the enormous responsibilities that go with a community of 20 or 30 members means there must be major changes in the European Union. Some of them will not come with the new treaty next year. But they will have to come soon after" ' (*ibid.*). Here, the integrationist impetus behind the 1996–7 IGC negotiations, the anticipated 1997 'Maastricht Two' treaty and any subsequent (1999) 'Maastricht Three' treaty is captured by Palmer's interpretation of these events as being about 'moves towards a supranational community', whereby the EU will be taken 'much further down the road to a federal-style political union'. It is about the distribution of 'sovereignty' within the 'decision-making system', and more specifically about the division of decision-making powers between the Member State level and the EU level. The more there is a re-distribution of decision-making power towards the EU level, the more the EU will be a 'supranational community'. For us, the EU is already a 'supranational community' (organisation or regime), while not being – at least not yet – a *federal union* in the full sense (as exemplified by the United States, Canada, Australia, Switzerland, Germany and, since 1993, Belgium). The integrationists within the EU (such as Helmut Kohl) perhaps conveniently – in that it suits their supranationalist, perhaps federationalist, intentions – argue that any expansion of the EU to between 20 and 30 Member States requires an overhaul of the decision-making system in favour of greater 'majority voting' in the Council of Ministers, and perhaps more decision-making power for the European Parliament; and thereby a re-allocation of sovereignty to the EU's supranational institutions away from Member State level institutions.

26. According to the European Commission, 'the European Parliament [...] has seen its own democratic legitimacy reinforced through the introduction in 1979 of the direct election by voters throughout the EC of its 518 Members [...]. In 1975, the Parliament acquired the right of co-decision alongside the Council of Ministers over the Community's annual budget [...]. The first real extension of the Parliament's legislative power came in 1987 with the Single European Act (SEA). This gave Parliament [...] the right [...] to propose amendments [to draft legislation concerning the single internal market]. But the final decisions still lie with the Council of Ministers. Under the SEA, Parliament acquired the right to veto treaties signed by the Community concerning the accession of non-member countries. A further step in democratic control [was] taken under the 1992 Maastricht Treaty [which] extends the Parliament's right of co-decision to all legislation concerning the single market and to other areas like the free movement of workers, research and development policy, the environment, health, education, consumer protection and so on. In these areas, Parliament [has] the power to veto draft EC legislation it does not approve of' (European Commission, *Strengthening Democracy in the EC*, 1993, pp. 7–8). The Maastricht Treaty also resulted in an increase in the number of Parliamentary seats to 626: 'Germany has 99 seats, France, Italy and the United Kingdom 87 seats each, Spain 64, the Netherlands 31, Belgium, Greece and Portugal 25 each, Sweden 22, Austria 21, Denmark and Finland 16 each, Ireland 15 and Luxembourg 6' (Fontaine, 1995, p. 10).

2. EUROPEAN SUPRANATIONALISM AND THE GLOBAL SYSTEM

1. For some, the EU's lack of accountability at the Member State level is accompanied and exacerbated by insufficient supranational 'transparency' and 'openness'. According to Jacob Söderman the European Ombudsman, 'Glasnost became a fashionable term in the 1980s. Everyone in the West supported greater glasnost in the Soviet Union, but few people claimed to know exactly what it was supposed to be. More recently, we have heard a lot about transparency in the European Union. Everyone knows that transparency is a good thing and that we should have more of it. But what does it mean? One meaning is that citizens should be able to understand official documents, especially legislation. Unfortunately, many of the Union texts are quite unreadable' (Söderman, 28 January 1997).

2. 'Case 7/71, *Commission* v. *France*, [1971] ECR 1003' (Bovis, 1996, p. 22, footnote 1).

3. 'See the Maastricht Treaty on European Union and the Protocol that allows the United Kingdom to opt out of the Social Charter' (Bovis, 1996, p. 22, footnote 2).

4. See also Stephen Weatherill, 1996.

5. See John Palmer (6 October 1996), who refers to Chancellor Helmut Kohl of Germany as an 'integrationist'; and Victor Smart (10 October 1996), according to whom 'the only leader whose sense of purpose has not been sapped [by the 1996–7 IGC deliberations] is Germany's Chancellor Helmut Kohl, whose view

of a federal Europe remains indomitable', even though 'his loose talk of the need to stage a Maastricht III, long before Maastricht II has been agreed is startling.' See also, Ernest Wistrich's *The United States of Europe* (1994), which (according to the book's cover) 'points the way to a federation, meaningful to its citizens, which will integrate the whole of Europe and play a significant role in world affairs'; and Nelsen and Stubb, 1994.

6. See Weatherill, 1996, p. 234, footnote 3: 'Weatherill and Beaumont [1995], Chapter 12. In Case 6/64 *Costa v. ENEL* [1964] ECR 585 the Court declared memorably that "The transfer by the States from their domestic legal system to the Community legal system of the rights and obligations arising under the [EEC] Treaty carries with it a permanent limitation of their sovereign rights, against which a subsequent unilateral act incompatible with the concept of the Community cannot prevail [...]"' (Weatherill, 1996, p. 234). Referring to the same case, Klaus-Dieter Borchardt says: the 'Court's answer was unequivocal. "By contrast with ordinary international treaties, the EEC Treaty has created its own legal system which, on entry into force of the Treaty, became an integral part of the legal systems of the Member States and which their courts are bound to apply. By creating a Community of unlimited duration, having its own institutions, its own legal capacity [...] and, more particularly, real powers [...], the Member States have limited their sovereign rights, albeit within limited fields, and have thus created a body of law which binds both their nationals and themselves"' (Borchardt, 1994, p. 56). On the 'supremacy of Community law', see Josephine Shaw's *European Community Law* (1993, pp. 151, 164–6, 175, 232); and her *Law of the European Union* (1996). As reported by Shaw, 'the supremacy of Community law [was] a concept well entrenched in the Community legal order before the UK [for instance] accepted the [founding] Treaties' (Shaw, 1993, p. 175). It follows that this concept is 'part of the *acquis communautaire* (general policy framework) which [has] to be accepted as non-negotiable by any new members' (Williams, 1991, p. 44), including the UK.

7. 'Weatherill and Beaumont [1995], Chapter 11. The Court explained in Case 26/ 26 *Van Gend en Loos* [1963] ECR 1 that "The objective of the EEC Treaty, which is to establish a common market, the functioning of which is of direct concern to interested parties in the Community, implies that this Treaty is more than an agreement which merely creates mutual obligations between the contracting states [...]. [T]he Community constitutes a new legal order of international law for the benefit of which the states have limited their sovereign rights, albeit within limited fields, and the subjects of which comprise not only Member States but also their nationals. Independently of the legislation of the Member States, Community law therefore not only imposes obligations on individuals but is also intended to confer on them rights which become part of their legal heritage"' (Weatherill, 1996, p. 234, footnote 4). See note 6.

8. See note 7. See also, Borchardt, 1994, pp. 33–4 on 'the Community is a legal order'; and pp. 55–62 on 'the position of Community law in relation to the legal order as a whole'.

9. See note 6.

10. According to Colin Padfield and Tony Byrne, a 'constitution may [...] be defined as "the system or body of fundamental principles according to which a nation, state, or body politic is constituted and governed"' (Padfield and Byrne, 1987, p. 1). Similarly, for Alec Stone: 'a constitution denotes a body of *metanorms, rules that specify how legal norms are produced, applied, and interpreted*. Metanorms are thus not only higher-order but prior, organic norms – they *constitute* a polity [...]. Thus, mentanorms fix the *rules of the game*, as a

means of investing lower-order norms with authority (legitimacy)' (Stone, 1994, p. 444). Stone argues that 'the EU regime has been "constitutionalized"' (*ibid.*, p. 448); that the process of 'European integration' can be viewed as 'a dynamic process of supranational constitution-building that [so far has] culminated in the Treaty of European Union (1992)' (*ibid.*, pp. 467–8), and so a supranational 'higher law' (*ibid.*, p. 446) constitutional regime (*ibid.*, p. 273). As Klaus-Dieter Borchardt then points out: 'there are provisions scattered throughout the [EU] treaty texts whose content is intended to protect Community citizens and which are very similar to certain of the Member States' guarantees of fundamental rights. This is especially the case as far as the numerous prohibitions on discrimination are concerned [...]. The Community rules that establish the four fundamental freedoms of the Community [of, that is, the movement of goods, capital, services and people] can be regarded as *constituting* a Community fundamental right to freedom of movement' (Borchardt, 1994, p. 14 – our emphasis). Borchardt adds that 'the cases decided by the Court of Justice have given the Community an extensive body of quasi-constitutional law' (*ibid.*, p. 17); and that in the course of carrying out its functions, the Court of Justice 'acts as a constitutional court' (*ibid.*, p. 27). On the other hand, according to Josephine Shaw: the 'constitutive treaties themselves contain little indication of the precise nature of the relationship between Community law and national law [...]. With the exception of [a few treaty] provisions, the principles of a unique supranational order [as represented by the European Community/Union] have evolved entirely judicially' (Shaw, 1993, p. 151). See also Josephine Shaw's discussion of the European Community and the issue of 'fundamental rights' (*ibid.*, pp. 105–9), where she argues that the 'emergence of a specific category of general principles termed "fundamental rights" is [evolving] and is attributable to the need on the part of the Court of Justice to assert the supremacy of the Community legal order, even in the face of national constitutions, such as that of the Federal Republic of Germany, which enshrine the protection of fundamental human rights' (*ibid.*, p. 105; p. 165). Borchardt expands on this by mentioning that 'the national courts of Germany and Italy initially refused to accept the primacy of Community law over national constitutional law, in particular regarding the guaranteed protection of fundamental rights. They abandoned their objections only after the protection of fundamental rights in the Community legal order had reached a standard that corresponded in essence to that of their national constitutions. Since then the primacy of Community law even over national constitutional law has been generally recognized' (Borchardt, 1994, pp. 61–2).

11. See Nelsen and Stubb, 1994, Chapter 3.
12. The European Union's Working Time Directive requires all Member States to implement a maximum 48-hour week; rest breaks after six consecutive hours; a minimum daily rest period of 11 consecutive hours; at least one day off a week; no more than eight hours a shift on average for night work; a minimum of three weeks paid holiday a year, rising to four weeks in 1999 (Atkinson, 8 September 1996). At the same time, however, 'the scope of the directive is severely limited thanks to a wide range of exemptions, some of them negotiated by the British Government. Entire industries are excluded: air, rail, road, sea, inland waterway and lake transport, sea fishing, other work at sea and doctors in training. Certain types of workers can also be exempted where "the duration of the working time is not measured and/or predetermined, or can be determined by the workers themselves" – in other words, bosses and professionals. The directive also allows for employees to work longer than 48 hours if they want to. If

and when it comes into force in November [1996], any member state can delay implementation of the provision on the 48-hour week until 2003' (*ibid.*).

13. Interestingly, within the United Kingdom, the 'Health and Safety Act 1974 already imposes wide-ranging obligations on employers to take reasonable care of their employees' health. [For instance, an] over-stressful working environment, including working excessive hours, is already classified as a health hazard in the same way as potentially dangerous substances or machinery' (Moorman, 19 October 1996).

14. The 'EC Advocate General Philippe Leger who, in his judgement [of] March [1996], stated quite firmly that regulating working hours, rest breaks and paid holidays fell unequivocally into the field of health and safety' (Jane Moorman, 19 October 1996). As the European Commission explains: the 'Court of Justice comprises 15 judges assisted by nine advocates general' (European Commission, *The Institutions of the European Union*, May 1995, p. 10).

15. 'Even the dramatic non-cooperation of the French "empty chair" policy in 1965 (which led to the so-called "Luxembourg compromise") on majority voting does not appear to have been accompanied by extensive French breaches of existing Community law' (Daintith, 1995b, p. 3, footnote 4). See Brent Nelsen and Alexander Stubb (1994), especially Chapter 5 on 'A concert of European states', reprinted from Charles de Gaulle, *Memoirs of Hope: Renewal and endeavour* (1971). As Nelsen and Stubb explain: 'De Gaulle [...] criticized the supranational vision of Europe [...]. He argued [that] states [should] not give up their rights as sovereign entities to a European "superstate". De Gaulle's unwillingness to concede France's right to control its vital affairs led to the 1965 crisis in the Communities and eventually the Luxembourg compromise that, in practice, gave every member state the right to veto Community decisions. In effect, the Six were forced to accept de Gaulle's vision of an intergovernmental Europe' (Nelsen and Stubb, 1994, p. 25). Subsequently, however, the Community shifted its vision and direction as far as Community decision-making and, in particular, the availability of the veto are concerned, most notably by way of the provisions of the Single European Act (SEA), which came into force in 1987, and of the Maastricht Treaty on European Union, which after being signed in February 1992 finally came into force on 1 November 1993. Thus, the 'major innovation' of the SEA 'was to extend to practically all of [the] required legislation' for the creation of a 'single internal market [...] a system of qualified majority voting in the Council of Ministers' (Wistrich, 1994, p. 4). Similarly, in the case of the Maastricht Treaty while 'unanimity was still retained in the formulation of new policies in some of the [Community] competences, legislation implementing the policies would largely be enacted by qualified majority voting in the Council of Ministers' (*ibid.*, p. 8).

16. On the topic of the development of social policy and law within the European Union, see for instance: Andersen and Eliassen, 1993; Burrows and Mair, 1996; Hantrais, 1995; and Ugur, 1995.

17. On the network of European Community and Union institutions, see European Commission, *The Institutions of the European Union*, 1995; European Commission, *Questions and Answers about the European Union*, 1994; Borchardt, 1994; Borchardt, 1995; Fontaine, 1995; and Emile Noël, 1993. As summarised by Borchardt, the 'primary role of the Community institutions is to put practical legislation in place to flesh out the framework for integration marked out by the Member States. The main actors in the legislative process are the Council of the European Union, the European Commission, the European Parliament and two consultative committees – the Economic and Social Committee and the Com-

mittee of the Regions [. . .]. The task of ensuring that these institutions observe
the law in their work rests with the Court of Justice of the European Communities. The European Court of Auditors keeps watch to ensure the legality and
regularity of Community revenue and expenditure and to monitor sound budget management' (Borchardt, 1995, p. 30). A point of clarification over the
nomenclature being used here is worth noting: that concerning 'the renaming of
some of the EC institutions following the creation of the European Union'
(*ibid.*, p. 59) through the coming into force of the Treaty on European Union on
1 November 1993. That is, on '8 November 1993 the Council of the European
Communities adopted the title "Council of the European Union". The "Commission of the European Communities" became the "European Commission".
And the "Court of Auditors" renamed itself the "European Court of Auditors"
on 17 January 1994' (*ibid.*, p. 59). With this point in mind, we can then note
how Pascal Fontaine tells us: 'What sets the European Union apart from more
traditional international organizations is its unique institutional structure. In
accepting the Treaties of Paris [1951], Rome [1957] and Maastricht [1992],
Member States relinquish a measure of sovereignty to independent institutions
[. . .]. The Council of the European Union is the main decision-making institution', being 'made up of Ministers from the 15 Member States with responsibility for the policy area under discussion [. . .]. Most decisions are taken by
[the] qualified majority' voting procedure (Fontaine, 1995, p. 9). Fontaine also
lists the European Parliament (*ibid.*, pp. 10–11), the Commission (*ibid.*, pp. 11–
12), the Court of Justice (*ibid.*, pp. 12–13), the Court of Auditors (*ibid.*, p. 13),
the Economic and Social Committee (*ibid.*, p. 13), and the Committee of the
Regions (*ibid.*, p. 13). In addition, Fontaine includes the 'European Council'
under the institutions of the Union (*ibid.*, pp. 9–10), which, as he explains,
'evolved from the practice, started in 1974, of organizing regular meettings of
Heads of Government of the Community (the Head of State in the case of
France). The arrangement was formalized by the Single European Act in 1987'
(*ibid.*, p. 9). See also Borchardt, who points out that the 'EU Treaty confirmed
[the European Council's] role, which is to provide the Union with the necessary
impetus for its development and to define general political guidelines' (1995, p.
30). Accounts of EC/EU institutions sometimes include also the European
Investment Bank (see, for instance, the European Commission's, *The Institutions of the European Union*, 1995, p. 14). A highly pertinent issue to the theme
of *Supranationalism in the New World Order* arising here stems from, on the one
hand, the Commission's suggestion that the 'Union is managed by these institutions' (*ibid.*, p. 3) and, on the other hand, Klaus-Dieter Borchardt's question:
'Since the Community exercises functions normally reserved for States, does it
have a government [. . .]?' (Borchardt, 1995, p. 17). Whatever the answer to the
question of whether the EC/EU can be said to have a 'government', for us the
EC/EU (its institutions) *can* be said to engage in 'governance', which (to revert
to the Commission's terminology) can be otherwise regarded as a form of
'management' (i.e. of geo-political management).

18.   As summarised by the European Commission (*The Institutions of the European
Union*, 1995): 'The Court can find that a Member State has failed to fulfil an
obligation under the Treaties. If the Member State does not comply with the
judgement, the Court may impose a lump-sum or penalty payment on it' (*ibid.*,
p. 10). See also Francis Snyder, who refers to, for instance, the 'financial
sanctions [which can] be imposed by the Court of Justice in an action for failure
to comply with a previous judgement of the Court of Justice' (Snyder, 1995, p.
57). Snyder singles out in this context 'Articles 169, 171 of the EC Treaty, as

amended by the Maastricht Treaty' (*ibid.*, p. 57, note 29). According to Article 171, 'If the Court of Justice finds that a Member State has failed to fulfil an obligation under this Treaty, the State shall be required to take the necessary measures to comply with the judgement of the Court of Justice [...]. If the Court of Justice finds that the Member State concerned has not complied with its judgement it may impose a lump-sum or penalty payment on it' (*The Treaty on European Union*, 1992, Article 171).

19. See Klaus-Dieter Borchardt, 1994, especially pp. 32–43.
20. See note 17.

3. THE SUPRANATIONAL REGIONAL REGIME AND GOVERNANCE

1. Or, as Stephen Ambrose has summarised: on 'August 21, [Boris] Yeltsin told the Russian Parliament that he was issuing decrees establishing Russia's economic sovereignty, taking control of Soviet agencies, and abolishing the Communist party [sic]. Before the year was out, Gorbachev had resigned and the leaders of Russia, Belarus, and the Ukraine declared "the USSR as a subject of international law and geopolitical reality is ceasing its existence." It was a declaration of independence of the republics from the union; it was also a declaration of the independence by the people of the old union from communism [...]. [US President George] Bush recognized and established relations with the new republics on December 25, 1991. In so far as the republics were pledged to create a democratic, market-oriented state, it was a wonderful Christmas present for them and the world' (Ambrose, 1993, p. 373). More succinctly: 'On 25 December 1991 the USSR came to an end after many constituent republics declared independence in the aftermath of the failed hard-line putsch in August [1991]' (Almond *et al.*, 1994, p. 191).

2. Those who assume that 'the world today is largely organised as nation-states' (Johnson, 1995, p. 188) are referred to as 'realists': from 'a realist perspective, the basic institution of the international system is the sovereign state. The 180-odd states are the constituent legal personalities of international society' (Miall, 1993, p. 19; see also, Nelsen and Stubb, 1994, Part 3). Our approach, with its emphasis on *supranational constitutional regimes* or *supranational regional regimes*, which are emerging at the expense of nation-states, can be labelled 'post-realist'.

3. On the somewhat controversial notion of 'geo-politics', see Goodall, 1987, pp. 190–1.

4. Drost's description of EFTA as an intergovernmental organisation is consistent with the fact that 'EFTA's governing body is the Council, which meets regularly at ministerial or ambassadorial level. Its decisions are binding [but] must be unanimous' (Drost, 1995, p. 198).

5. The exceptional case of Norway is examined later.

6. See also, Jo Shaw, 1996, pp. 33–4.

7. In this document, the European Commission reports on its response to a request from the European Council that 'the Community institutions review the operation of the Treaty on European Union' (*Commission Report for the Reflection Group: Intergovernmental Conference 1996*, 1995, p. 3). See in particular Section II (External Policies) B on the 'common foreign and security policy', in which the issues of (i) the 'connection between the pillars'; and (ii)

the 'Western European Union' are addressed. See also, Nikolaj Petersen, 1993; Thomas Pedersen, 1993.

8. On the conflicts in Bosnia and the Balkans, which sealed the break up of Yugoslavia, as well conflicts elsewhere in Eastern Europe, see Glenny, 1993; Jeffries, 1993; Meštrović, 1994; Sellers, 1996; Swain and Swain, 1993.

9. The *acquis communautaire* has been described as follows: 'In the European Community (EC) and now the European Union (EU), the body of existing laws, regulations etc. It comprises all the decisions of the Council of Ministers and the Commission under the Treaty of Rome and its amendments and all relevant case law of the Court of Justice. Countries joining the EU are expected to accept the *acquis communautaire* [...] and to amend national legislation to accord with it' (Drost, 1995, pp. 1–2). The phrase *acquis communautaire* can be translated as 'Community patrimony' (*ibid.*, p. 1), meaning *Community heritage* or *Community endowment*. For further discussion of the *acquis communautaire*, see Shaw, 1996, pp. 98–100.

10. For more detail about the relationships between the European Community, EFTA and the EEA, see Wallace, 1992; Harrison, 1995, especially Chapter 8; and Shaw, 1996, pp. 33–5 and pp. 94–5.

11. We have in mind here specifically extra-EU organisations and countries when applying for 'integration' or 'inclusion', and in response the EU maintaining a 'European economic space' in relation to such organisations and countries, for preparatory and protectionist purposes. The European Commission in its 1993 outline of the European Community's 'external relations' (European Commission, *Europe in a Changing World*, 1993) refers to the Community's 'global network of agreements', there being 'several types' of agreement (*ibid.*, p. 19). Thus, the 'Community has concluded customs union agreements with Turkey, Malta and Cyprus'; '[f]ree trade agreements [with its] individual EFTA neighbours', these having 'been combined and strengthened to form the European Economic Area, (EEA); and '"Europe" agreements (also called association agreements) with Central and Eastern European countries' (*ibid.*, p. 19). The aim of the Europe Agreements is to integrate [the] economies [of the countries involved] with that of the Community as quickly as possible' (*ibid.*, p. 19). There are also 'preferential agreements with [most] Mediterranean countries' (*ibid.*, p. 19) – in this case, by the end of 1996 the EU had 'signed cooperation or association agreements with [...] Maghreb countries (Algeria, Morocco, Tunisia), Mashrek countries (Egypt, Jordan, Lebanon, Syria)' and Israel (apart from those with Cyprus, Malta and Turkey) (European Commission, *The European Union and the Developing World*, 1996; and European Commission, *Development: 20 questions and answers*, 1996). There are the arrangements under 'the Lomé Convention with ACP [African, Caribbean and Pacific] States', these 'agreements [giving] privileged access to the EC market for [the ACP countries'] exports plus financial and technical assistance' (European Commission, *Europe in a Changing World*, 1993, p. 19). By the end of 1996, the Convention covered 70 ACP states, and South Africa was 'negotiating membership' (European Commission, *Lomé Revised*, 1996). The 'Community also has a series of non-preferential commercial and economic cooperation agreements such as those with the countries of Latin America and Asia' (European Commission, *Europe in a Changing World*, 1993, p. 19). In Latin America, the Commission reported in 1993 that it had 'framework cooperation agreements with Mexico, Argentina, Brazil and Uruguay. By the end of 1996, these had been extended to Chile and Paraguay (European Commission, *Development: 20 questions and answers*, 1996). In 'line with its policy of supporting organizations committed to regional

economic integration, the Community [has] signed a non-preferential frame-work agreement for commercial and economic cooperation with the countries of the Andean Pact. These are Bolivia, Columbia, Ecuador, Peru and Vene-zuela' (European Commission, 1993, *Europe in a Changing World*, pp. 40–1). On 10 March 1996, the Andean Pact was re-formed as the Andean Community, taking its 'inspiration from the example of the European Union' (European Commission, 'Europe inspires Andean community', *Frontier-Free Europe*, April 1996, p. 3). Likewise, a framework agreement 'was concluded in 1985 with the signatories of the General Treaty on Central American Economic Integration (Costa Rica, Guatemala, Honduras, Nicaragua and El Salvador)'; and with Panama (European Commission, *Europe in a Changing World*, 1993, p. 41). Turning to Asia, a 'regional agreement with the member countries of the Association of South-East Asian Nations (ASEAN) was concluded in 1980, setting a framework for commercial, economic and development cooperation. A regular political dialogue also takes place between the Community and the members of ASEAN' (*ibid.*, p. 42). The Commission reported that in 1993 'preparations were underway to negotiate a cooperation agreement with Viet-nam', which subsequently joined ASEAN in 1995. Furthermore, non-preferen-tial 'cooperation agreements have been concluded with the individual countries of the Indian sub-continent – Sri Lanka, Bangladesh, India, and Pakistan' (*ibid.*, p. 42), countries which happen to be members – along with Bhutan, the Maldives and Nepal – of the South Asian Association for Regional Co-opera-tion (SAARC) (see European Commission, 'The European Union and Asia', *Frontier-Free Europe* (Supplement), April 1996). By the end of 1996, the Eur-opean Union had signed framework co-operation agreements with Nepal and the Maldives (European Commission, *Development: 20 questions and answers*, 1996). In addition, the EC had concluded non-preferential co-operation agree-ments with China and Mongolia (European Commission, *Europpe in a changing World,* 1993 p. 42); and by the end of 1996, the EU had signed a framework co-operation agreement with Yemen (European Commission, *Development: 20 questions and answers*, 1996). These various and numerous agreements aside, there is the matter of the EU's links with 'its major industrialized partners outside Europe, particularly the United States and Japan' (European Commis-sion, *Europe in a Changing World*, 1993, p. 24). In the case of the USA: in 'the wake of changes in East–West relations resulting from the return to democracy in Central and Eastern Europe and the unification of Germany, the USA and the Community put their bilateral relations on a new footing in November 1990 with the adoption of a Declaration on EC–US Relations', which 'set out [a] framework for bilateral consultations [...] at five levels' (*ibid.*, p. 25). The Commission has pointed out that in 1993 the 'Community's ties with Japan [had] not [...] developed to the extent of the Atlantic relationship' (*ibid.*, p. 26); an assessment which remains valid. Finally here, apart from the EU's 'Europe agreements' with, by June 1996, ten central and eastern European countries (European Commission, 'Slovenia applies for membership', *Frontier-Free Europe*, July–August 1996, p. 3), in 1993 the Commission reported: 'The collapse of the Soviet system after the failed coup in Moscow in August 1991 caused the Community to recast its relations with Russia and the other republics of the former Soviet Union. The Community is ready to negotiate so-called partnership agreements with those [ex-Soviet Union republics] who wish to do so. The partnership agreement with Russia is the most ambitious [...]. [But also, negotiations] for a partnership agreement took place in 1993 with the Ukraine', and negotiations were expected to take place with Belarus and Kazakhstan (European Commission, *Europe in a Changing World* 1993, p. 32).

12.	Which the Union has already done and seems likely to do again, as reported by the European Commission: 'The historic shock waves of 1989 – on the Union's very doorstep – are still reverberating. The upheavals which followed the fall of the Berlin Wall have born fruit. At tremendous cost, the new democracies of Central and Eastern Europe have confirmed their attachment to the values that are the very basis of the Union. The Union, for its part, has committed itself to accepting these countries' ('Commission Report for the Reflection Group: Intergovernmental Conference', 1995, p. 4). Accordingly, the 'intergovernmental conference (IGC)', which got underway in Turin on 29 March 1996 for the purpose of reviewing the 1992 Maastricht Treaty, and with a revised treaty (or Maastricht 2) as the goal, will 'prepare the European Union (EU) for the addition of 10 or more new members', mostly from central and eastern Europe (Wolf, 26 March 1996). For us, however, it is not only the IGC which is preparing the way for this expansion. Other preparatory mechanisms are already in place, ones whereby the European Union is engaged in governance – geo-political management – beyond its own territorial jurisdiction, as represented by the operation of the European Economic Area (EEA).

13.	In an article published in *The Guardian* (19 February 1996), Hans-Dietrich Genscher, the (West) German foreign minister between 1974 and 1992, argued forcefully in favour of promoting European integration through the further development and deepening of the European Union, asserting that the EU is a 'zone of stability' which is 'crucial to the stability and security of the whole of Europe'. Our view overlaps with Genscher's, in that for us the EU represents an inner-zone (or core) of EU supranational governance, or geo-political management, beyond which there are further, extra-EU zones of such management. For us, in so far as the EU is a 'zone of stability', it is an inner-zone, the *stability* of which can be understood in terms of the EU's supranational engagement in geo-political management both within its own frontiers and beyond. The EU's geo-political management in zones beyond its own frontiers ensures the maintenance of a bulwark in defence of itself as an inner-zone of (if only relative) geo-political stability.

14.	We are aware that we are using the term 'order' in two different senses here. We are also aware that the two senses of the term 'order' are not adequately distinguished – are conflated – within much sociological and other theoretically oriented analyses of global systems, patterns, processes and trends. The distinction and relationship between 'order' in each sense within the post-Cold War global system need to be addressed and clarified.

15.	The *Concise Oxford Dictionary of Current English* (1990, p. 511) defines 'government' as 'a body of persons governing a State'. Similarly, for Patrick Dunleavy and Brendan O'Leary (1987): 'Government is the process of making rules, controlling, guiding and regulating. More loosely, especially in Western Europe, government is synonymous with the elected ministers who are formally in charge of departments. [. . . A] modern state is a very special type of government' (*ibid.*, pp. 1–2). See also Nugent, 1991, especially Chapter 14.

16.	See Shaw, 1996, pp. 42–4.

17.	There is evidence that the Norwegians' anxieties about these particular matters were well founded, as reflected in Norman Warner's discussion of 'spending policies in an era when monetary union is supposed to bring [EU] countries closer together' (Warner, 30 October 1996): 'Welfare austerity has hit Europe. That was the key message from a recent meeting in Barcelona of social services experts from 15 European countries, all struggling to balance the needs of disadvantaged groups with scarcity of resources [...]. In Germany and France [for instance] political leaderships relentlessly trying to meet the Maastricht criteria for European Monetary Union are slashing social security and social welfare programmes', the result being a widespread 'sense of European welfare crisis'. In contrast, outside the Union, the Norwegian economy continued to flourish: 'Norway's bureau of statistics yesterday raised its forecast for economic growth, emphasising the strong upswing the oil-fueled nation is already enjoying. It said it expected gross national product to grow by 4.8 per cent this year [1996], against its earler 4.3 per cent, and by 3 per cent in 1997 against previous expectations of 2.3 per cent [...]. These forecasts remained below those of the finance ministry, however, which is expecting 5.4 per cent this year and 3.1 per cent next' (Carnegy, 6 December 1996; see also Ryle, 1996).

18. Also in this regard, as David Harrison suggests, the 'innovations in institutional terms which the EEA [have] introduced might yet have some future bearing elsewhere – for example in relations with post-communist eastern Europe' (Harrison, 1995, p. 164).

19. Norway is a member of the Nordic Council, or Nordic Council of Ministers, an intergovernmental organisation which acts as 'the executive arm of what is formally called Nordic Cooperation' (Drost, 1995, p. 438). The Nordic Council 'was set up in 1971 on the basis of the 1962 Helsinki Convention, which formalized the already extensive cooperation among the five Nordic countries': Denmark, Finland, Iceland, Norway and Sweden (*ibid.*, p. 438).

4. THE SUPRA-STATE, GOVERNANCE AND GLOBAL PROCESSES

1. There was far from universal confidence in the planned launch date for the European single currency: 'German business leaders expressed doubts last weekend over whether the European single currency would start on its January 1999 target date, and held out the prospect of market turmoil if Italy were among the first members. Mr Ulrich Cartellieri, a Deutsche Bank board member, noted that there were only 400 working days until the target date and said "only a tiny fraction" of businesses had begun technical preparations. "Even fewer have considered the strategy implications"' (Jackson, 3 February 1997). On the question of the possibility and implications of Italy being among the first to join the euro, *The Guardian* claims: 'In his heart, Chancellor Kohl has always known that he could not afford to let Italy into the first wave of monetary union. What he has not known is quite how to break the news to Rome' (*The Guardian*, 5 February 1997)

2. As reported in *The Guardian*: 'The Japanese car giant Toyota threw a timebomb into the European single currency debate yesterday by issuing a threat to Britain that failure to join could see its multi-million pound investment switched to the Continent' (MacAskill and Hetherington, 30 January 1997). At the same time, it was not only Toyota, or more specifically Toyota's president, Hiroshi Okuda, who expressed concern over the prospect of the UK not joining the European single currency. As reported by Anthony Barnett and Mark Atkinson, '[l]eading British businessmen this weekend supported Toyota's president by warning that jobs and future investment will drain from the UK if it stays outside the single European currency' (Barnett and

Atkinson, 2 February 1997). Moreover, in a similar vein, a letter to the *Financial Times* from Jonathan Price, an 'investment banker working with Japanese and other Asian companies' claimed: 'It is [very much] membership of the European Union that makes the UK the location of first preference' for investment. Jonathan Price adds: 'the UK has been successful in attracting investment from Japan and Korea and will attract more in the future from the Asean [the Association of South East Asian Nations] countries if, but only if, it remains a full member of the EU', which means 'joining something as critical as Emu' (Price, 5 February 1997).

3.   A 'state of the parties opinion poll' carried out between 31 January and 2 February 1997, and reported in *The Guardian* on 5 February 1997, 'showed Labour's [...] lead over the Conservatives at 16 per cent', with Labour scoring 48 per cent and the Conservatives scoring 32 per cent of those expressing their 'voting intention'. The Liberal Democrats registered 15 per cent and 'others' 4 per cent. An opinion poll carried out in November 1996 resulted in 47 per cent for Labour, 34 per cent for the Conservatives, 15 per cent for the Liberal Democrats and 4 per cent for 'others' (Kettle, 5 February 1997). The 'others' include the Referendum Party, the UK Independence Party (which achieved 'some 1,300 votes in the Staffordshire South-East by election' in April 1996 [*The Guardian*, 7 February 1997]), the Socialist Labour Party (led by miners' leader Arthur Scargill), the Green Party (which won '14.9 per cent of the vote in the 1989 European elections, pushing the Liberal Democrats into fourth place' [*The Guardian*, 7 February 1997]), the Legalise Cannabis party, and the Pro-Life (anti-abortion) Alliance (*The Guardian*, 7 February 1997; and Smithers, 7 February 1997). There is some overlap between the views of the members of the Referendum Party and the UK Independence Party, on the one hand, and sections of the main ('traditional') UK political parties and especially the Conservative Party, on the other. See, for instance, the article by 'Conservative Eurosceptic MP Bill Cash' in *The European* (6 February 1997), where Cash 'argues that the euro is the slippery slope to the loss of sovereignty' and that '[o]ur historic role in Europe is to prevent a superstate' (*ibid.*).

4.   Various estimates of the number of candidates that would be fielded by the UK Independence Party in the General Election were published in the newspapers during the election campaign. According to *The Guardian*, the Party 'claims it will field around 600 general election candidates' (*ibid.*, 7 February 1997).

5.   Dowds and Young refer the reader of the *British Social Attitudes* survey report to Appendix 1 'for the construction of the libertarian-authoritarian scale' (Dowds and Young, 1996, p. 155).

6.   In 1995, 14 per cent of respondents in 'mainland Britain' and 7 per cent of respondents in Northern Ireland thought that the UK should leave the European Union. The corresponding figures that emerged during the 1994 survey were 11 per cent and 6 per cent respectively (Dowds and Young, 1996, p. 150).

7.   In 1995, 29 per cent of respondents in 'mainland Britain' and 39 per cent of respondents in Northern Ireland thought that the UK's 'relationship with the European Union ... should be closer'. The corresponding figures that emerged during the 1994 survey were 37 per cent and 45 per cent respectively (Dowds and Young, 1996, p. 150).

8.   In 1995, 32 per cent of respondents in 'mainland Britain' and 45 per cent of respondents in Northern Ireland thought that the UK 'should do all it can to ... unite fully with the European Union'. The corresponding figures that emerged during the 1994 survey were 40 per cent and 48 per cent respectively (Dowds and Young, 1996, p. 150). Also in 1995, 60 per cent of respondents in

'mainland Britain' and 41 per cent of respondents in Northern Ireland thought that the UK 'should do all that it can to...protect its independence from the European Union'. The corresponding figures that emerged during the 1994 survey were 53 per cent and 41 per cent respectively (*ibid.*, p. 150).

9. Edmund Burke (1729–97) was an 'Irish statesman and philosopher' (Magnusson, 1990, p. 231).

10. For further evidence from across Europe on people's views, attitudes and identities *vis-à-vis* European integration and the European Union, see the results of the 'Eurobarometer opinion surveys ("standard Eurobarometer surveys") [which] have been conducted on behalf of the Directorate-General for Information [...] of the European Commission each Spring and Autumn since 1973' (European Commission, *Trends*, 1995, p. ii).

11. Dowds and Young tell us that their 'findings must be understood in the light of [the] distinction between *nation* and *state*. These separate words have commonly been used as interchangeable abbreviations for a much more specific entity – the *nation-state*. The hyphenated term was coined specifically to describe the case of a territorial-political unit (the state) whose borders coincided with the territorial distribution of a national group (the nation). Such nation-states are less common than is often imagined (Connor, 1978). And Britain is not among them' (Dowds and Young, 1996, p. 153). We also recognise distinctions between 'nation', 'state' and 'nation-state', but along the more conventional lines from which Dowds and Young distance themselves. We regard *nation-states* as geopolitical entities (on the somewhat controversial notion of 'geo-politics', see Goodall, 1987, pp. 190–1); as geographically, or territorally, bounded but politically constructed, shaped and sustained social formations; as constructed by, through and around 'states': 'As defined by Max Weber, the state is the social institution [or set of social institutions] that holds a monopoly over the use of force. In this sense, the state is defined by its authority to generate and apply collective power. As with all [sets of] social institutions, the state is organized around a set of social functions, including maintaining law, order, and stability, resolving various kinds of disputes through the legal system, providing common defense, and looking out for the welfare of the population in ways that are beyond the means of the individual [...]. From a conflict perspective, however, the state also operates in the interest of various dominant groups, such as economic classes' (Johnson, 1995, p. 275; see also Giddens, 1993, Chapter 10, and Dunleavy and O'Leary, 1987, pp. 1–4). In effect, as Dunleavy and O'Leary put it, the 'state is sovereign, or the supreme power, within its territory' (Dunleavy and O'Leary, 1987, p. 2). In practice, the geopolitical territorial boundaries *defended* by *the state*, do not necessarily coincide in a neat and tidy way with what may be defined, distinguished and discerned as 'nations' (see Gellner 1983, especially Chapter 1). In practice, the relationship between *nation-states* and *nations* is complex, and connectedly is characterised by tensions, conflicts and flux. The character of the relationship between nation-states and nations is then prominent in accounting for the everyday (often coercive) activities of states aimed at defending (perhaps extending) their 'national' (geo-political) boundaries; as well as at, connectedly, maintaining social order, stability and cohesion within these boundaries. But, in addition, the same factors very much help account for the way nation-state boundaries sometimes change, break down, disappear, and so on. In this regard we can note Charles de Gaulle's assertion (in the context of a rejection of European supranationalism) that, in Europe, 'arbitrary centralization [has] always provoked an upsure of violent nationalism by way of a reaction' (de

Gaulle, 1994, p. 32). See Gellner, 1983 and 1994; especially Gellner, 1983, Chapter 1.

12.   De Gaulle asks 'What depths of illusion or prejudice would have to be plumbed in order to believe that European nations forged through long centuries [. . .], each with its own geography, history, language, traditions and institutions, could cease to be themselves and form a single entity? What a perfunctory view is reflected in the parallel [which is] often naively drawn between what Europe ought to do and what the United States have done, when the latter was created from nothing in a completely new territory by successive waves of uprooted colonists?' (de Gaulle, 1994, pp. 39–40; see also Gillespie, 1996, especially pp. 144–8). De Gaulle asserts: 'The truth is that [each *state*] of Europe [. . .] has its own genius, history and language, its own sorrows, glories and ambitions [. . .]. [Therefore], while recognizing [. . .] the technical value of certain more or less extranational or supranational organisms, [. . .] they [cannot] be politically effective' (de Gaulle, 1994, p. 41).

13.   See, for instance, Pistone, 1990, and 1994 Chapter 10. See also Wistrich, 1994; Gillespie, 1996.

14.   Apart from 'the notion of inviolable and indivisible national sovereignty' being contravened the idea that by 'pooling their sovereignty under a supranational community' the 'specific shortcomings of the nation-State system [. . .] can [. . .] be overcome' (Borchardt, 1995, p. 27), the same notion comes up against the view that by 'pooling their sovereignty' nation-states actually *gain* 'sovereignty'. Thus, the 'Irish ambassador in London, Ted Barringon, told the *Observer*' that the ' "[Irish] experience of membership [of the European Union] is that it enhances our sovereignty in a real sense, if you define sovereignty as a capacity to define your own destiny, by being able to take decisions on huge issues, which affect the economic welfare of the continent" ' (Kemp, 2 February 1997). For us, however, Barrington appears to be confusing, or conflating, (i) 'sovereignty' defined in terms of the enjoyment and exercise of 'political authority' (Held, 1992b) within a particular territorial space (Axford, 1995, pp. 136–40), or geo-political area; of the authority to engage in independent, *internal* decision-making activities, procedures and processes; and (ii) the ability of a nation-state and other global players to exercise *external* influence, power and control within the global system (*ibid.*). A global player's (such as Ireland's or the European Union's) internal sovereignty and its external influence are conceptually and empirically distinct, albeit also empirically and theoretically interdependent.

15.   As reported by Emma Tucker, 'European Union members that defy rulings by the European Court of Justice would be heavily fined under proposals before the European Commission today. The new system would produce penalties steep enough to force member states to comply with European law. The gravity of the violation and the wealth of the offending state would be included in the fine calculations [. . .]. The penalty system would be the first time member states would face financial penalties for failing to abide by European rules. The Maastricht treaty granted the Commission the right to take states to court for disobeying EU law and to specify the level of fines. However, the Commission has had to proceed cautiously because of the sensitivity of member states. Britain, though assiduous in implementing the European Court's judgements, is particularly anxious about extending its powers. Other governments are also worried about the imposition of cash fines. The first countries to be targeted under the new system would be Italy, over the failure of the Campania region to produce plans for waste disposal, and Germany, for infringements of legislation

on birds and ground and surface water. Many infringements relate to environmental legislation, but single market legislation is another blackspot. For example, Greece could face a penalty for not recognising certain higher education qualifications from other member states [...]. The Commission would recommend the level of the fines according to [a particular] formula, but the European Court would make the final decision on imposing penalties [...]' (Tucker, 6 January 1997); see also Bates, 9 January 1997; and European Commission, *Frontier-Free Europe*, July–August 1996, p. 2). As the European Commission itself puts it: 'In order to sanction those Member States that do not implement the rulings of the European Court of Justice, the European Commission will ask the same Court to impose periodic penalty payments, while the infringement continues. As for the infringements that would attract the severest penalties, the Commission has put at the top of its list violations of the principle of non-discrimination between EU citizens, along with attacks on the EU's four freedoms: the free movement of people, goods, services and capital [...]. This [...] is how the Commission intends to implement Article 171 of the EC Treaty, as modified by the Maastricht Treaty, according to its decision on 5 June [1996]' (European Commission, *Frontier-Free Europe*, July–August 1996, p. 2). To this end, in February 1997, the 'Commission promised to keep open the possibility of taking legal action against France in the European Court until it was "convinced that in practice ski instructors from other member states can become established in France without facing excessive obstacles"' (Buckley, 8 February 1997).

16. Harry Drost explains that, within the European Union, the intergovernmental conference (IGC) is 'a conference of the member states convened to debate and decide on amendments to the basic treaties of the Union or to draft new ones. An IGC can be convened with the support of a majority of member states, but its conclusions must be agreed unanimously and ratified by all. The two most recent IGCs, on economic and monetary union and political union, were held concurrently in 1990–1 and resulted in the Maastricht Treaty establishing the EU' (Drost, 1995, p. 320). Following the establishment of the EU, with the coming into force of the (Maastricht) Treaty on European Union on 1 November 1993, a subsequent IGC was formally opened in Turin (under the Italian presidency of the European Community) on 29 March 1996, with the intention of negotiating and agreeing 'the so-called Maastricht 2' (*The Guardian*, 29 March 1996): 'The principal problem for this IGC, and perhaps for all European Union negotiations always, is to find a workable and popular EU-wide compromise between necessary European cooperation and necessary national decision-making. The weakness of Maastricht was that the EU over-reached itself and lost popular legitimacy [...]. [European integration] has to be a compromise. [A]ny approach which pretends that European cooperation is optional is as dishonest as one which claims the same about national sovereignty.' See also European Commission, Intergovernmental Conference 1990: Commission report for the Reflection Group, 1995; Shaw, 1996, especially Chapters 2 and 4; and Curtin, 1996. The European Commission in its pre-IGC report and recommendations tells us that the '1996 Intergovernmental conference will be a key encounter for Europe and its future [...]. Two factors make [the IGC] particularly important. First, the Union's internal context has changed' in a manner which suggests that the Maastricht 'Treaty's objective of a Community closer to the citizen' should be regarded 'as an overriding principle which guides its actions' (European Commission, Intergovernmental Conference 1996, Commission report for the Reflection Group, 1995, p. 3). But

also, the 'context has altered not only within the Union. The international context has changed even more radically. The historic shock waves of 1989 – on the Union's very doorstep – are still reverberating. The upheavals which followed the fall of the Berlin Wall have borne fruit. At tremendous cost, the new democracies in Central and Eastern Europe have confirmed their attachment to the values that are at the very basis of the Union. The Union, for its part, has committed itself to accepting these countries' (European Commission, Intergovernmental Conference 1996, Commission report for the Reflection Group, 1995, p. 4). However, it is generally agreed within the European Union that any 'future enlargement' by taking in the applicant governments of central and eastern Europe, as well as of the Mediterranean (Cyprus, Malta, Turkey), depends on and so can only take place following the successful conclusion of the IGC leading to a final agreement on 'Maastrict 2' (*The Guardian*, 29 March 1996). On 10 June 1996, 'Slovenia officially applied to join the European Union [...]. Slovenia thus [became] the 10th Central and East European country [to apply for] membership' (European Commission, *Frontier-Free Europe*, July–August 1996, p. 3). A few days before the opening of the 1996 IGC, a 'powerful coalition of governments – led by Chancellor Helmut Kohl and President Jacques Chirac – [warned] John Major [...] not to derail plans for closer European unity or risk being excluded from the final agreement [...]. [T]hey fear that a protracted delay in the timetable for the new treaty could damage plans to enlarge the EU' (Palmer, 26 March 1996).

17. As reported by David Wighton in February 1997: the 'European Commission is pushing ahead with plans to extend majority voting to immigration and civil justice matters in the face of fierce opposition from the UK. Mrs Anita Gradin, commissioner for justice and home affairs, told a London press conference she was "quite optimistic" that EU member states could reach agreement at the Amsterdam summit in June. She said Denmark appeared to be softening but "flexibility" might be necessary so the UK could remain outside' (Wighton, 11 February 1997).

18. We recognise that Borchardt's categorisation of organisations which have played a part in 'the postwar steps towards European unification' (Borchardt, 1995, p. 6) is not the only one. A valuable examination of, what are variously referred to as, categorisations, classifications or typologies has been provided by, for instance, Paul Gillespie under the heading of 'models of integration' (Gillespie, 1996). Gillespie focuses on placing 'the European Union within the framework of theories of integration' (*ibid.*, p. 140), and favours the argument that the EU has an 'original and exemplary character'. The EU's originality 'can be seen in its institutional innovation and [in] how it differs from other models of international political association and community' (*ibid.*, p. 140). Thus, when Gillespie summarises what he refers to as, following Philippe Schmitter (1991, 1992; and Traxler and Schmitter, 1995), 'the basic architecture of the Euro-polity', he tells us: 'Although it is still only a semi-formed polity it operates at supranational, functional, intergovernmental and subnational levels, each of which tends to attract a strand of theorising from a range of disciplines. [A]ttempts are being made to combine several of the approaches in a comparative framework, which can be very helpful in considering the likely outcome of the [current, 1996–7] round of intergovernmental [IGC] negotiations' (Gillespie, 1996, p. 153). In a manner which conforms with this assessment, Gillespie argues for a 'multifacted approach' to 'theorising on the EU', entailing a fusion of 'federalism, neofunctionalism and realism' (*ibid.*, p. 164). Essentially, this 'is made [...] necessary by the fact that the Union operates at several different

levels. These include the international, analysed in particular by the realist school of international relations, at which, through IGCs and European Councils, high political questions and basic ground rules are established; the supranational, dealt with by legal and federal and neofunctional modes of analysis, in which primary legislation is the main agenda; and the intranational, analysed typically by policy studies and sociology, which has to do with the medium to low matters of governance, but ones that can be rightly salient for publics when they become visible (Weiler *et al.*, 1995, p. 26)' (Gillespie, 1996, pp. 164–5). While we have reservations about Gillespie's account and approach, we concur with the gist of most of his points and proposals; and, for us, it is consistent with and befits Gillespie's conceptual and theoretical approach to the study, analysis and understanding of the process of European integration through the European Union to use for orienting purposes Borchardt's somewhat simplistic categorisation of the organisations he claims have played a part in this process. Later, we return to Gillespie's account.

19. On the OEEC and OECD, see Archer, 1990, Chapters 1–3; and Harrison, 1995.
20. See Archer, 1990, especially Chapter 9.
21. Leonid Brezhnev (1906–82) was the General Secretary of the Communist Party of the Soviet Union (CPSU) from October 1964, taking over from Nikita Krushchev; and 'in May 1977 [he] gained the additional title of state president [. . .]. The Brezhnev era saw the Soviet Union establish itself as a military and political superpower, extending its influence in Africa and Asia' (Magnusson, 1990, p. 205). On the Brezhnev doctrine, see Swain and Swain, 1993, especially Chapters 6–8.
22. For more on the Warsaw Pact, its details, development and demise, see Swain and Swain, 1993.
23. For more clarification of COMECON, see Swain and Swain, 1993, Chapters 5–8.
24. While with the collapse of the Eastern bloc, or Soviet empire, all fifteen former republics of the Soviet Union gained their independence, twelve – all but the three Baltic republics – formed the so-called Commonwealth of Independent States (CIS), described by Drost as an '[i]ntergovernmental organization' formed in December 1991. The CIS's purpose was 'to promote coordination of policies in the fields of trade [and] security', among other matters (Drost, 1995, pp. 104–5). Miranda Anichkina, writing in 1995 'on the rebuilding of national pride after rejection by the West', reported: 'Everybody is slowly realising that we need to reconstruct not the Soviet Union but a common market, at least along the lines of the European Union. Many traders throughout the CIS have already affected this integration. The politicians lag behind' (Anichkina, 26 May 1995) – see our Chapter 5. For more detail on the CIS, see Deacon, 1992, especially the chapter by Nick Manning on 'Social policy in the Soviet Union and its successors' (Deacon, 1992, Chapter 2). Intriguingly, it would seem that Belorussia (Byelorussia, Belarus), or more specifically its president, Alexander Lukashenko, wants to to go further along the path of integration than is represented by the CIS or the EU. He 'wants to forge a union with Russia and maintain a military link', a wish which is consistent with the fact that the 'Belarus president is the only leader of post-Soviet eastern and central Europe with the temerity to resist privatisation. He re-nationalised most banks, has prevented shops being sold off to their managers, and insists that the state and collective farms [. . .] continue to supply them' (Steele, 4 December 1996). See also Ignatieff, 9 March 1997.

25. For more on NATO see Archer, 1990, Chapter 9; and Harrison, 1995, especially Chapters 8 and 9.

26. As reported on 7 February 1997: 'The Nato secretary-general, Javier Solana, ended a 24-hour visit to Turkey last night saying he was still hopeful he could prevent Ankara using its veto to stop Nato enlargement [. . .]. Mr Solana said he had listened and taken good note of the concerns and potential frustration of Turkey not being a full member of the European Union. He held talks with the foreign minister, Tansu Ciller, who had threatened in Rome last week to block Nato expansion if the European Union did not include Turkey in its list of potential members' (Walker and Hearst, 7 February 1997).

27. For some, the attempt to separate the EU, or even the EC, from the 'intergovernmental category' is misguided: see Gillespie, 1996; and Nelsen and Stubb, 1994, Part 3.

28. The European Council is an '[i]nstitution of the European Union (EU)', being 'the name given to the biannual summit of meetings of the [EU] member states' heads of government' and Head of State in the case of France (Drost, 1995, p. 195), in the presence also of the Member States' foreign ministers, the president and vice-president of the European Commission and the president of the European Parliament (*ibid.*, p. 195). These 'meetings are intended broadly to (i) give direction to and stimulate the EU's activities and (ii) provide a means of solving intractable policy problems at the highest level. Decisions are normally but not invariably taken by unanimity; they are subsequently worked out in detail and made official by the Council of Ministers', the 'EU's main legislative body' (*ibid.*, p. 195). The 'current format' for the European Council 'was formalized in the Single European Act adopted in 1986' (*ibid.*, p. 195). The 'EU Treaty confirmed its role [. . .]. Under the arrangements laid down in the EU Treaty for a common foreign and security policy, the European Council also has the task of coordinating the Member States' foreign policies and adopting positions on world political issues' (Borchardt, 1995, p. 30). Apart from the European Council, Borchardt summarises the *community institutions* as follows: the 'primary role of the Community institutions is to put practical legislation in place to flesh out the framework for integration marked out by the Member States. The main actors in the legislative process are the Council of the European Union [formerly the Council of Ministers], the European Commission, the European Parliament and two consultative committees – the Economic and Social Committee and the Committee of the regions [. . .]. The task of ensuring that these institutions observe the law in their work rests with the Court of Justice of the European Communities. The European Court of Auditors keeps watch to ensure the legality and regularity of Community revenue and expenditure and to monitor sound budget management' (Borchardt, 1995, p. 30). Following the creation of the European Union, 'some of the EC institutions' were renamed: on '8 November 1993 the Council of the European Communities adopted the title "Council of the European Union". The "Commission of the European Communities" became the "European Commission". And the Court of Auditors renamed itself the "European Court of Auditors" on 17 January 1994' (*ibid.*, p. 59).

29. Or *competence*, or *constitutional powers*. See Jo Shaw's *Law of the European Union* (1996), especially Chapter 3.

30. See Drost, 1995, p. 604; and Shaw, 1996, especially Chapter 3, and in particular pp. 82–6.

31. See also Borchardt, 1995, Chapter 4. This 'progressive' approach to and perspective on European integration brings to mind 'the so-called *neo-functionalists*

who have advocated [an] incremental and piecemeal approach to European integration in the spheres of both practical politics and integration theory literature' (Shaw, 1996, p. 12). Neo-functionalists assume and/or prescribe a 'process [...] termed *"spill-over"*' (*ibid.*, p. 12), a process which apart from anything else entails 'the extension of the powers [competences] of the old European Economic Community out of the purely "economic" field into other [...] areas', leading in an incremental or piecemeal fashion to '*political union*' (*ibid.*, pp. 12–13). We refer to the particular kind of (lateral) spillover from the economic sphere into the political sphere (or vice versa, for that matter) as 'domain spillover'.

32.   Also on the notions 'federal state', 'federal', 'federalism' with particular reference to Europe and the European Union, see Amin and Tomaney, 1995; Dinan, 1994; Drost, 1995, pp. 223–4; Gillespie, 1996; Laffan, 1992; Lodge, 1993; Miall, 1993; Nelsen and Stubb, 1994; Shaw, 1996, Chapter 3, especially pp. 76–9; Weigall and Stirk, 1992; Wilson and van der Dussen, 1995; Wistrich, 1994.

33.   Also on the principle of subsidiarity, see Emilou, 1994; Shaw, 1996, Chapter 3; Spicker, 1991; Steiner, 1994; Wistrich, 1994, pp. 10–15.

34.   Drost: 'After the merger of their institutions in 1967, the singular "European Community" gained wide currency to denote either the European Communities as a whole or the EEC, but far the most important of the three' (Drost, 1995, p. 193). That is, the label 'European Community' gained wide currency following the amendment of the 1957 Treaty of Rome through 'the Treaty Establishing a Single Council and a Single Commission of the European Communities (Merger Treaty), signed on 8 April 1965 and in force from 1 July 1967' (*ibid.*, p. 206).

35.   On the issue of the EC/EU as a *constitutional* regime, see Alec Stone's 'What is a supranational constitution?' (1994), for whom 'a constitution denotes a body of *metanorms, rules that specify how legal norms are to be produced, applied, and interpreted*. Metanorms are thus not only higher-order but prior, organic norms – they *constitute* a polity. Metanorms enhance the legitimacy of legal norms (and therefore social legitimacy)' (Stone, 1994, p. 444). For Stone, the EU is a 'supranational constitutional regime' (*ibid.*, pp. 470–4). For us, however, strictly speaking, it is only the EC within the EU which is a supranational constitutional regime (SCR). The other two pillars of the Union and the Union overall are not, strictly speaking, supranational organisations or regimes, only intergovernmental ones. It is not that the other two pillars and the EU overall are not *constitutional regimes*, only that they are not (unlike the EC) *supranational*. See also Jo Shaw on 'the constitutional framework of the European Union' (Shaw, 1996, Chapter 3), where she points out that '[c]onstitutional principles form the foundation for both the institutional and substantive law of the European Union' (*ibid.*, p. 62).

36.   For references to reading on European federation and federalism, see note 32.

37.   On the issues surrounding the meaning and operation of the principle of subsidiarity, see note 33.

38.   See Delamont, 1995; Gellner, 1983, 1987, 1994; Goddard *et al.*, 1994; Laffan, 1992, 1996a, 1996b; Macdonald, 1993; Meštrović, 1994; Shelley and Winck, 1993.

39.   See Axford on various aspects and dimensions of governance in the modern global system (Axford, 1995), including the issue of 'global governance' (p. 31; see also Chapter 7); that of 'forms of international governance (Strang, 1991)' (*ibid.*, p. 136); that of the United States as 'a "manager" of the world order (Gilpin, 1987)' (*ibid.*, pp. 41–2); and that of '*international* management [in] the "borderless world" (Ohmae, 1990)' (*ibid.*, p. 7; see also Ohmae, 1995).

40.   The term 'governance' seems to be increasingly, not to say generously, used in a
       wide range of disciplines and a variety of discourses. However, often the mean-
       ing of the term is left implicit, and frequently ambiguous or otherwise unclear.
       For instance, a discussion by Nira Wickramasinghe headed 'From human rights
       to good governance' comes no closer to indicating what the author means by
       'governance', never mind 'good governance', than: 'In the New World Order,
       the United States goals for South Asia are quite clearly dominated by a concern
       for good governance. They are: "to continue to support and promote security in
       the region through decreasing tensions between the states; second, to discourage
       a race towards the acquisition of weapons of mass destruction; third, to pro-
       mote and strengthen democratic institutions through economic development,
       encouraging privatization and assisting the buildup of democratic structures;
       and, finally, to seek support for a successful winding up of the issues raised by
       the Gulf War." (Leftwich, 1993)' (Wickramasinghe, 1996, p. 317). In a similar
       vein, see Paul Ekins, 1992.
41.   There is a fast growing body of literature on the European Union within 'the
       wider world' or 'the global system'. See, for instance, Barrie Axford, 1995;
       European Commission, *Europe in a Changing World*, 1993; European
       Commission, *The European Union and World Trade*, 1995; *European Foreign
       Affairs Review* (the first issue of which was published in July 1996); Fontaine,
       1995, Chapter 9; Nørgaard *et al.*, 1993; Hill, 1996; Peterson, 1996; and Waites,
       1995.
42.   On the institutionalist model of international relations (Axford, 1995, p. 41), see
       Dessler, 1989; Giddens, 1990; Gusterson, 1993; Hix, 1994; Kegley and Witt-
       kopf, 1993; Keohane, 1984; Keohane and Nye, 1988; Koslowski and Kratoch-
       wil, 1994; Krasner, 1988; Stein, 1990; March and Olsen, 1984; Wendt, 1994;
       Young, 1986.
43.   See the European Commission's *The European Community and Mediterranean
       Countries* (1991); see also Eberhard Rhein, 1996, pp. 79–86.

5.   A GLOBAL PERSPECTIVE

1.   Jonathan Green has attempted to clarify the notion of the new world order in
       the following way: 'The theory, posited by US President George Bush, that in
       the wake of the thawing of the Cold War in late 1989, and the decline of the
       Soviet Union as a superpower comparable to the US, a "new world order" of
       peace, stability and international co-operation might be created to ensure a
       better future for all. Consciously or otherwise, Bush's usage unfortunately
       echoed the last proponent of a new order, Adolf Hitler' (Green, 17 November
       1996, p. 34). For us, as by now must be clear, this is a somewhat crude and
       unduly cynical representation of the notion, at least as it is otherwise meant and
       used. A more thorough and sympathetic exposition is to be found in Stephen
       Ambrose's *Rise to Globalism* (1993).
2.   As Rollnick reports, while 'the Barcelona Declaration [was] for a Euro-Medi-
       terranean zone of shared prosperity', the associated *economic space* was no-
       where near 'shared' in the sense of 'equal': 'According to the Union's statistical
       bureau Eurostat, the Ecu 4.7 billion ($5.3bn) earmarked for the Mediterranean
       over the 1995–99 period is less than half the Ecu 12.1bn trade surplus it enjoyed
       with the region in 1993, and just over half the Ecu 9.3bn surplus of 1994.
       [Manuel] Marin disclosed that in addition to these allocations, the European

Investment Bank will make Ecu 2.3bn available "in the form of advantageous loans" to the Mediterranean over the next three years. But [...] the region, [apart from this,] draws just under four per cent of private European investment, compared with 30 per cent to Latin America and 60 per cent to Asia' (Rollnick, 13 March 1997). Such economic details perhaps suggest that the EU will not be successful in creating the kind of 'security partnership' (*ibid.*) the EU has been looking for as protection against the problems and threats North Africa has been posing. See also Eberhard Rhein, 1996.

3. On the Lomé Convention and other mechanisms through which the EU relates to ACP and so-called developing countries, see: European Commission, *The Caribbean and the European Union*, 1994; European Commission, *EC Food Aid and Food Aid Security Programme*, 1996; European Commission, *EU–ACP Cooperation in 1995: What Form of Structural Adjustment?*, 1994; European Commission, *Financial Cooperation Under the Lomé Conventions: Review of the Aid at the End of 1995*, 1996; European Commission, *Industrial and Economic Co-operation between the European Union and Developing Countries*, 1995; European Commission, *Info Finance 1995: The European Development Fund*, 1996; European Commission, *Southern Africa and the European Union*, 1994; European Commission, *Trade Relations between the European Union and the Developing Countries*, 1995. Specifically on the evolving co-operation between the EU and South Africa, see European Commission, *Southern Africa and the European Union*, 1994, pp. 48–51.

4. In addition to the EU's bilateral relations on which we are focusing here, there are others with what the European Commission has referred to as the EU's 'industrialized partners': the 'Community's links are most developed with its major industrialized partners outside Europe, particularly the United States and Japan [...]. [Thus, in] the wake of changes in East-West relations resulting from the return to democracy in Central and Eastern Europe and the unification of Germany, the USA and the Community put their bilateral relations on a new footing in November 1990 with the adoption of a Declaration of EC-US Relations. [However, the] Community's ties with Japan have not yet developed to the extent of the Atlantic relationship' (European Commission, *Europe in a Changing World*, 1993 pp. 24–7). See also Peter Coffey's *The EC and the United States* (1993); and the *Euro Japanese Journal*, published several times each year through the Anglo-Japanese Economic Institute. See Paul Close and Emiko Ohki-Close, 1996, pp. 8–11.

6. GLOBALISATION AND SUPRANATIONALISM

1. Consistent with the connotations of the title of Shelley and Winck's *Aspects of European Cultural Diversity*, we will refer to 'European cultures'. There may be something of a single, inclusive 'European culture', distinguishable from non-European cultures, which is then useful in drawing some *conventional* boundary around Europe. However, the elements which make up such a unifying and delineating 'European culture' remain uncertain, somewhat obscure and certainly controversial. For us, an appropriate analogy is 'a European mosaic of cultures' (see Gowland *et al.*, 1995), while a contender for the best simile is indicated by Masakazuku Yamazaki's description of 'Asia [as] a salad bowl – a mixture of cultures – rather than a melting pot – an integration of cultures' (quoted in Susumu Maejima, 12 October 1995).

2. John Fletcher (1995) is one writer who is convinced that in the long term European integration is *unstoppable* by *culture*.
3. What we are reminded of here is both Masakazuku Yamazaki's description of 'Asia [as] a salad bowl – a mixture of cultures – rather than a melting pot – an integration of cultures' (quoted in Susumu Maejima, 12 October 1995); and of Endymion Wilkinson's claim that '[i]n spite of the trend towards regional economic cooperation in other parts of the world, it is unlikely that a tightly organized trading bloc will emerge in the Asia Pacific region in the near future. The region is to large; its political systems, economies and cultures too hetrogeneous' (Wilkinson, 1991, p. 27).
4. In the same edition of *The European* (27 March 1997) as Sandra Smith's article, are several pieces on the politically contentious and highly charged issue of the future direction, speed and eventual reach of European integration through the progress of the European Union: Victor Smart and Paola Buonadonna, 'Dutch in race against clock to save treaty'; Nigel Dudley, 'Rifkind berates Labour on drift to superstate'; Ian Mather, 'New moves on defence shake Nato'; Paola Buonadonna, 'Forty years on, a birthday for thousands'; Marcello Burattini, 'From early dreams to shaky adulthood . . . the heady days of the old European Economic Community'; *The European*, 'New life for EU begins at 40'; Malcolm Rifkind, 'Do we really need "more Europe"?'
5. On contradictions, see Daniel Bell's *The Cultural Contradictions of Capitalism* (1976); as well as Close, 1992, 1995.
6. Our working definition of 'culture' is informed by the anthropological tradition of conceptually–analytically distinguishing between 'culture' and '(social) structure', which in turn – according to a firmly established sociological tradition – are empirically bridged by 'agency'. Shelley and Winck's interest in European economic and political unification or integration is about developments at the *level of social structure*, even though these developments are intimately tied to what is taking place at the *cultural level*. The latter may be otherwise referred to as the *ideational level* of social systems (loosely interpreted), processes and change. Therefore, our working definition of 'culture' is that the term refers to, quite simply, sets of shared ideas. A similar approach is inferred by Margaret Archer in her *Culture and Agency* (1989). Archer lists among 'the principal ideational elements', the following: 'knowledge, belief, norms, language, mythology' (*ibid.*, p. 4). The third book in the *What is Europe?* series (that on *European Democratic Culture*, edited by Alain-Marc Rieu and Gerard Duprat, 1995) alludes to, but somewhat fudges, this ideational approach to the notion of culture: 'By "culture" we mean precisely an organized ensemble of attitudes, values, patterns of individual or group behaviour, forms of knowledge and discourse' (*ibid.*, p. 10). This caveat aside, given the ideational notion, the remaining book in the *What is Europe?* series (that on *The History of the Idea of Europe*, edited by Kevin Wilson and Jan van der Dussen, 1995), it follows about the history of an element or dimension of European cultures; and, moreover, of an increasingly salient element or dimension, that of the idea of an integrated and unified Europe (economically, politically, and even culturally), contrary to the current diversity of shared ideas on the matter. It then makes sense that Wilson and van der Dussen 'set out to explore the history of the idea of Europe within a welter of political, social and cultural processess, and, in so doing, inevitably raise questions that cross the boundaries of history, culture and politics' (*ibid.*, p. 10).
7. As reflected in the book's Index listing: 'culture, American influences 120, 123, 135–41' (Waites, 1995, p. 220).

8. For a taste of cultural studies, see Robert Bocock and Kenneth Thompson (eds), *Social and Cultural Forms of Modernity*, 1992; Simon During (ed.), *The Cultural Studies Reader*, 1993; Ken Gelder and Sarah Thornton (eds), *The Subcultures Reader*, 1997; Stuart Hall and Bram Gieben (eds), *Formations of Modernity*, 1992; Stuart Hall *et al.* (eds), *Modernity and its Futures*, 1992; Graeme Turner, *British Cultural Studies*, 1992.

9. On postmodern conditions, postmodernity and postmodernism, see for instance: Bauman, 1992, 1988a, 1988b, 1990a, 1990b, 1991a, 1991b; Boyne and Rattansi, 1990; Callinicos, 1989; Giddens, 1990; Hollinger, 1994; Lash and Friedman, 1992a; Smart, 1992, 1993.

   On the distinction between *postmodernity* and *postmodernism*, Anthony Giddens tells us that *postmodernism*, 'if it means anything, is best kept to refer to styles or movements within literature', for example, distinguished by their '*aesthetic reflection* upon the nature of modernity' (Giddens, 1991, p. 45).

10. See also Tommy Koh's article in the *International Herald Tribune*, 11 December 1993, p. 6.

11. We are referring specifically to Fukuyama's *Trust: The Social Virtues and the Creation of Prosperity* (1995). Fukuyama is now a researcher with the Rand Corporation, a Washington-based 'think tank', but during the 1990s he worked as a member of the Policy Planning Staff of the US Department of State, specialising in Middle Eastern and European political-military affairs. His book *The End of History and the Last Man* (1992) has been translated from English into more than twenty languages. This book established Fukuyama's reputation as one of the most forceful right-wing apologists for western capitalism, liberal democracy and individualism, and for the west's Cold War 'victory'. We are aware of the widespread criticism which Fukuyama's *End of History* thesis has drawn, not least on the grounds of its ethnocentric bias, its simplistic (even naive) approach to the post-Cold War NWO, and Fukuyama's apparent lack of appreciation or awareness of other major writers of relevance and worth. See the various reference to Fukuyama in, for instance, Ambrose, 1993; Axford, 1995; Meštrović, 1994; Smart, 1992, 1993; Waters, 1995. In a brief article at the beginning of 1995, John Gray examines the significance of 'the fall of the Berlin Wall in October 1989, and the collapse of the Soviet Union which came about as the result of the coup against Gorbachev in August 1991', and questions the 'common belief that [this] collapse represented "the triumph of the Western idea" – in the words of the American neo-conservative writer Francis Fukuyama' (1992), words which symbolise 'the callow triumphalism of the New Right'. Gray argues that the 1989–91 events, rather than 'embodying a decisive victory for Western values, [...] signified the beginning of the end of the West's intellectual and political hegemony in the world' (Gray, 20 January 1995). We have touched on this argument (and so, it would seem, criticism of Fukuyama) at various points, and we will be pursue it further in our follow-up book. Our discussion here of Fukuyama's 1995 book on *Trust* draws on the critique presented by Will Hutton (20 October 1995).

12. It would be useful to compare and relate Fukuyama's notion of 'social capital' with Pierre Bourdieu's notion of 'cultural capital' (see Bourdieu, 1973; and Bourdieu and Passeron, 1977; see also Paul Close's 'State care, control and contradictions', in Close, 1992a). For Bourdieu, 'the dominant culture [is] "cultural capital" because, via the educational system, it can be translated into wealth and power' (Haralambos, 1985, p. 215).

13. See also from the European Commission: *A Citizen's Europe* (1993); *A Human Face for Europe* (1990); *A People's Europe* (1992).

14. We wish to emphasise the conceptual, analytical and empirical distinction between 'supranationalism' and 'supranational regional regime', on the one hand, and 'ultranationalism' and the pre-Second World War, Japanese-inspired East Asia Co-prosperity Sphere, on the other (see, for instance, Maruyama, 1995; Radek, 1995; So and Chiu, 1995; and Storry, 1995). The term 'supranationalism' causes problems on translation into Japanese, and in discussions about the possibility of an East Asian supranational regional regime because of the semantic similarity (and occasional confusion) in Japanese between the terms 'supranationalism' and 'ultranationalism', and because of the history of Japanese ultranationalism in East Asia, its concrete manifestations and its emotional connotations. However, 'supranationalism' and 'ultranationalism' are, in a sense, oppositional notions. As Harry Drost puts it: a 'supranational' organisation is one where 'the member states transfer specified legislative powers to it and its decisions are binding on them and their citizens' (Drost, 1995, p. 582). Or, as Jo Shaw tells us: the 'idea behind neo-functionalism is that sovereign [nation-] states may be persuaded in the interests of economic welfare to relinquish control over certain areas of policy where it can be [shown] that benefits are likely to flow from a common approach to problem solving. Power is transferred to a central authority which exists at a level above the nation state [sic], and which exercises its powers independently of the Member States – a *supranational* body' (Shaw, 1996, p. 12). Therefore, as the *Concise Oxford Dictionary of Current English* (1990) indicates, 'supranational' implies 'transcending national limits' (*ibid.*, p. 1226). As a prefix 'supra-' means above, beyond or transcending; where as an adverb in Latin '*supra*' means 'above' (*ibid.*, p. 1226). Hence, 'supreme' meaning 'highest in authority or rank'; and 'Supreme Court' meaning 'the highest judicial court' (*ibid.*, p. 1226). In the case of the European Community, the central pillar within the overall European Union, the European Court of Justice operates to some extent as a Supreme Court above the EU's Member States and their courts. As we have noted, Charles de Gaulle was opposed to 'the doctrine of "supranationalism"' because it would entail 'France's submission to a law that was not her own' (de Gaulle, 1994, p. 30). *Supranationalism* is a 'doctrine' which urges nation-states to transfer their sovereignty (sovereign powers, authority, independence) to a supranational set of institutions (perhaps, and probably, including a court) which stands over and above themselves, their institutions and citizens. Accordingly, Dowds and Young (1996) categorise those who, in the 1995 *British Social Attitudes* survey (1996), show the least 'national sentiment' (and related traits) as 'supra-nationalists' (Dowds and Young, 1996, p. 148). Supra-nationalists 'have little sense of national identity' (*ibid.*, p. 149), and so as far as feelings and expressions of 'nationalism' (*ibid.*, p. 143) are concerned stand at the opposite end of the spectrum from what Dowds and Young categorise as (given the British context) 'John Bulls' (*ibid.*, p. 149). Supranationalism is a doctrine or movement which stands opposed to *nationalism*, never mind *ultranationalism*. The prefix 'ultra-' infers 'extreme' (*Concise Oxford Dictionary of Current English*, 1990, p. 1324), so that an 'ultraist' is 'the holder of extreme positions in politics, religion, etc.' (*ibid.*, p. 1324). Thus, *ultranationalists* are *extreme nationalists*, and would presumably be extremely hostile to supranationalism, supranationalists, supranational institutions, supranational regional regimes; and in Europe, would presumably be extremely hostile to the European Community/Union, the European Court of Justice, and the EC's other supranational institutions. Guided by *Sanseido's Daily Concise English-Japanese Dictionary* (1990), 'supra-' as a prefix when translated into Japanese

becomes 'ue', 'cho' or 'mae' (*ibid.*, p. 564); and 'supranational' becomes 'cho-kokka no' (*ibid.*, p. 564). By imputation, 'supranationalism' becomes 'chokokka shugi'. However, 'ultranationalism' when translated into Japanese becomes 'cho kokusui shugi' (*ibid.*, p. 605). Interestingly, 'supreme' translates as 'shikou no', 'saijo no', 'kyukyoku no' or 'saigo no'; and 'Supreme Court' becomes 'Saikou Saibansho'. Given this, we suggest that it should be possible to coin terms or phrases in Japanese for 'supranational', 'supranationalism' and 'supranational regional regime' which draw on and are semantically consistent with the Japanese for 'supreme' and for 'Supreme Court', and which thereby avoids any confusion with the Japanese for 'ultranationalism' (with its historical, cultural and emotive connotations). It should be possible for linguists to come up with a suitable and helpful set of terms or phrases.

15. There is fast-growing body of writings on the topics of trading blocs and regional (economic, political) regimes, including within the Americas, the Asia Pacific region and the East Asia (or Pacific Asia) sector of the Asia Pacific region. See, for instance: Buckley, 1993, on the Asia Pacific region; Buckley, 1994, on the Americas; Couffignal, 1994, on the Americas; Dobbs-Higginson, 1994, on East Asia; Dixon, 1991, on South-East Asia; *The Economist*, 12 November 1994, on the Asia Pacific region; *The Economist*, 10 December 1994, on the Americas; So and Chiu, 1995, on East Asia; Wilkinson, 1991, on Japan, East Asia and the Asia Pacific. There are also some writings on the gobal spread of and relationships among trading blocs and (prospectively supranational) regional regimes. See Emilou and O'Keefe's *The European Union and World Trade Law*, 1996; and Helen Milner, 1994. See also Zaki Laidi's *Power and Purpose After the Cold War*, 1994; and Tamio Nakamura's 'Does the European Union model work for Asia?', 1995.

Bibliography

Abu-Lughod, Janet, 1989, *Before European Hegemony: the world system AD 1250–1350*, New York: Oxford University Press

Abu-Lughod, Janet, 1991, 'Writing against culture', in R. Fox (ed.), *Recapturing Anthropology*, Santa Fe, New Mexico: School of America Research Press

Ackers, Louise, 1995, 'Women, citizenship and European Community law: the gender implications of the free movement provisions', *Journal of Social Welfare and Family Law*, 17, 4

Agnew, John, 1994, 'The territorial trap: the geographical assumptions of international relations theory', *Review of International Political Economy*, 1, 1

Ahmed, Akbar, 1992, *Postmodernism and Islam: predicament and promise*, London: Routledge

Alexander, Jeffrey and Steven Seidman (eds), 1990, *Culture and Society: Contemporary debates*, Cambridge: Cambridge University Press

Almond, Mark, Jeremy Black, Felipe Fernandez-Armesto, Rosamond McKitterick and Chris Scarre, 1994, *Atlas of European History*, London: Times Books

Ambrose, Stephen, 1993, *Rise to Globalism: American foreign policy since 1938*, Harmondsworth: Penguin, seventh edition

Amin, Ash and John Tomaney (eds), 1995, *Behind the Myth of European Union: prospects for cohesion*, London: Routledge

Amin, Samir, 1996, 'The challenge of globalization', *Review of International Political Economy*, 3

Anderson, Benedict, 1983, *Imagined Communities: reflections on the origin and spread of nationalism*, London: Verso

Andersen, Svein and Kjell Eliassen (eds), 1993, *Making Policy in Europe: the Europeanification of national policy-making*, London: Sage

Anichinka, Miranda, 1995, 'Russia revives the corpse of the Soviet Union', *The European*, 26 May

Archer, Clive, 1990, *Organising Western Europe*, London: Edward Arnold

Archer, Clive, and Fiona Butler, 1992, *The European Community: structure and process*, London: Pinter

Archer, Margaret, 1989, *Culture and Agency: the place of culture in social theory*, Cambridge: Cambridge University Press

Arnason, J., 1987/88, 'The modern constellation and the Japanese enigma – Part II', *Thesis Eleven*, 18/19

Åslund, A., 1995, *How Russia Became a Market Economy*, Washington, DC: Brookings

Atkinson, Mark, 1996, 'Fewer hours? Bah, humbug. The UK is on the warpath with Europe again', *The Observer*, 8 September

Atkinson, Mark, 1997, '48-hour week "will not endanger jobs"', *The Observer*, 5 January

Axford, Barrie, 1995, *The Global System: economics, politics and culture*, Cambridge: Polity Press

Bailey, Joe (ed.), 1992, *Social Europe*, London: Longman

Bain, Neville and David Band, 1996, *Winning Ways Through Corporate Governance*, London: Macmillan

Barbé, Esther, 1996, 'Spain: the uses of foreign policy cooperation', in Christopher Hill (ed.), *The Actors in Europe's Foreign Policy*, London: Routledge

Barber, Lionel, 1996a, 'European Union leaves Swiss to swing in the wind', *Financial Times*, 15 July

Barber, Lionel, 1996b, 'EU and Nato discover togetherness', *Financial Times*, 9 December

Barber, Lionel, 1997a 'Turkey in Nato enlargement threat', *Financial Times*, 20 January

Barber, Lionel, 1997b, 'EU proposals on Cyprus spark Greek threat', *Financial Times*, 26 February

Barber, Tony, 1997, 'Nato growth to cost £20bn', *The Independent*, 12 March

Baring, Arnulf (ed.), 1994, *Germany's New Position in Europe: problems and perspectives*, Oxford: Berg

Barnard, Catherine, 1996, *EC Employment Law*, Chichester: John Wiley

Barnett, Anthony and Mark Atkinson, 1997, 'British businesses back Toyota boss's investment warning', *The Guardian*, 2 February

Barro, R., 1991, 'Economic growth in a cross section of countries', *Quarterly Journal of Economics*, 106, May

Barro, R. and X. Sala-i-Martin, 1992, 'Convergence', *Journal of Political Economy*, 100

Bates, Stephen, 1997a, 'Fines recommended for EU states defying court', *The Guardian*, 9 January

Bates, Stephen, 1997b, 'Row scuppers deal on Cuban trade', *The Guardian*, 19 February

Bauman, Zygmunt, 1988a, 'Is there a postmodern sociology?', *Theory, Culture and Society*, 5

Bauman, Zygmunt, 1988b, 'Sociology and postmodernity', *Sociological Review*, 36, 4

Bauman, Zygmunt, 1990a, 'Modernity and ambivalence', in M. Featherstone (ed.), *Global Culture*, London: Sage

Bauman, Zygmunt, 1990b, 'Sociological responses to postmodernity', *Thesis Eleven*, 23

Bauman, Zygmunt, 1991a, *Modernity and Ambivalence*, Cambridge: Polity

Bauman, Zygmunt, 1991b, 'A sociological theory of postmodernity', *Thesis Eleven*, 29

Bauman, Zygmunt, 1992, *Intimations of Postmodernity*, London: Routledge

Beazley, Mitchell, 1992, *The New Europe*, London: Mitchell Beazley International

Beck, Ulrich, 1992a, *Risk Society: towards a new modernity*, London: Sage

Beck, Ulrich, 1992b, 'From industrial society to risk society', *Theory, Culture and Society*, 9

Beck, Ulrich, Anthony Giddens and Scott Lash, 1994, *Reflexive Modernization*, Cambridge, Polity Press

Bell, Daniel, 1976, *The Cultural Contradictions of Capitalism*, New York: Basic Books

Bellamy, Christopher, 1996, 'Nato to issue Eastern bloc invitations', *The Independent*, 11 December

Bennett, C., 1991, 'What is policy convergence and what causes it?', *British Journal of Political Science*, 21

Bernstein, Carl and Marco Politi, 1996, *His Holiness: John Paul II and the Hidden History of our Time*, New York: Doubleday

Bevins, Anthony and Sarah Helm, 1996, 'Major goes into battle on Brussels "dictatorship"', *The Independent*, 13 November

Billington, Rosamund, Sheelagh Strawbridge, Lenore Greensides and Annette Fitzsimmons, 1990, *Culture and Society*, London: Macmillan

Black, Ian, 2 December 1996, 'Moscow warns it may seek new military allies', *The Guardian*

Black, Ian, 15 February 1997, 'Hard bargaining is still to come', *The Guardian*

Black, Ian, 4 March, 1997, 'Bullish Rikfind warns EU to curb ambition', *The Guardian*

Bobinski, Christopher, 1997, 'Poland tightens up on Daewoo under EU pressure', *Financial Times*, 3 February

Bocock, Robert, and Kenneth Thompson (eds), 1992, *Social and Cultural Forms of Modernity*, Cambridge: Polity Press

Borchardt, Klaus-Dieter, 1994, *The ABC of Community Law*, Luxembourg: Office for Official Publications of the European Communities, fourth edition

Borchardt, Klaus-Dieter, 1995, *European Integration: the origins and growth of the European Union*, Luxembourg: Office for Official Publications of the European Communities, fourth edition

Borger, Julian, 1997, 'Farce and tragedy amid the creeping chaos', *The Guardian*, 15 March

Bourdieu, P., 1973, 'Cultural reproduction and social reproduction', in R. Brown (ed.), *Knowledge, Education and Cultural Change*, London: Tavistock

Bourdieu, P. and J. Passeron, 1977, *Reproduction in Education, Society and Culture*, London: Sage

Bovis, Chris, 1996, 'Regulating the public markets within the European Union', in Andrew Caiger and Demetrius Floudas (eds), *1996 Onwards: lowering the barriers further*, Chichester: John Wiley

Bowles, Paul and Brian Maclean, 1996, 'Understanding trade bloc formation: the case of the ASEAN Free Trade Area', *Review of International Political Economy*, 3

Boyne, R. and A. Rattansi (eds), 1990, *Postmodernism and Society*, London: Macmillan

British Social Attitudes Survey: the 13th report (edited by Roger Jowell *et al.*), Aldershot: Dartmouth Publishing

Brummer, Alex, 1996, 'Capitalist Russia set for growth', 1996, *The Guardian*, 28 September

Buchan, David, 1997, 'Franco-German pact stresses reform of Nato', *Financial Times*, 27 January

Buckley, Neil, 1997, 'Brussels clears piste for Britons', *Financial Times*, 8 February 1997

Buckley, Roger, 1985, *Japan Today*, Cambridge: Cambridge University Press

Buckley, Roger, 1993, *The Pacific Rim: powerhouse of the 21st century*, Cheltenham: European Schoolbooks

Buckley, Roger, 1994, *NAFTA and GATT: the impact of free trade*, Cheltenham: European Schoolbooks

Bull, Hedley, 1977, *The Anarchical Society: a study of order in world politics*, London: Macmillan

Buonadonna, Paola, 1996, 'Don't leave us behind say regions', *The European*, 3 October

Buonadonna, Paola, 1997, 'Forty years on, a birthday for thousands', *The European*, 27 March

Burattini, Marcello, 1997, 'From early dreams to shaky adulthood... the heady days of the old European Economic Community', *The European*, 27 March

Burrows, Noreen and Jane Mair, 1996, *European Social Law*, Chichester: John Wiley

Caiger, Andrew and Demetrius Floudas (eds), 1996, *1996 Onwards: lowering the barriers further*, Chichester: John Wiley

Callinicos, A., 1989, *Against Postmodernism: a Marxist critique*, Cambridge: Polity

The Cambridge International Dictionary of English, 1995, Cambridge: Cambridge University Press

Carnegy, Hugh, 1996, 'Growth forecasts raised', *Financial Times*, 6 December

Cash, Bill, 1997, 'Our historic role in Europe is to prevent a superstate', *The European*, 6 February

Castoriades, C., 1987, *The Imaginary Institution of Society*, Cambridge: Cambridge University Press

Chalmers, Damian, 1996, 'Legal base and external relations of the European Community', in Nicholas Emilou and David O'Keefe (eds), *The European Union and World Trade: after the GATT Uruguay Round*, Chichester: John Wiley

Cheles, Luciano, Ronnie Ferguson and Michalina Vaughan (eds), 1996, *The Far Right in Western and Eastern Europe*, London: Longman, second edition

Chirot, D., 1994, *How Societies Change*, Thousand Oaks, CA: Pine Forge Press

Christiansen, Thomas, 1996, 'A maturing democracy? The role of the Commission in the policy process', in Jeremy Richardson (ed.), *European Union: power and policy-making*, London: Routledge

Clark, Bruce and Chrystia Freeland, 1997, 'A diplomatic mountain', *Financial Times*, 22 February

Close, Paul, 1985, 'Family form and economic production', in Paul Close and Rosemary Collins (eds), *Family and Economy in Modern Society*, London: Macmillan

Close, Paul, (ed.), 1989, *Family Divisions and Inequalities*, London: Macmillan

Close, Paul (ed.), 1992a, *The State and Caring*, London: Macmillan

Close, Paul, 1992b, 'State care, control and contradictions', in Paul Close (ed.), *The State and Caring*, London: Macmillan

Close, Paul, 1995, *Citizenship, Europe and Change*, London: Macmillan

Close, Paul, 1996, 'The European Union and "space"', *Journal of Social Welfare and Family Law*, 18, 4

Close, Paul, and Emiko Ohki-Close, 1996/7, 'European, East Asian and Japanese relations: globalisation and supranationalism', *Euro Japanese Journal*, 3, 3, December

Coffey, Peter, 1993, *The EC and the United States*, London: Pinter

Cohen, Percy, 1968, *Modern Social Theory*, London: Heinemann

Coker, Christopher, 1992, 'Britain in the New World Order', *International Affairs*, 68, 3, July

Collinson, Sarah, 1994, *Europe and International Migration*, London: Pinter, revised edition

Concise Oxford Dictionary of Current English, 1990, Oxford: Oxford University Press, eighth edition

Connor, W., 1978, 'A nation is a nation, is a state, is an ethnic group, is a ...', *Ethnic and Racial Studies*, 1, 4

Conradi, Peter, 1995, 'Europe's borders refuse to go away', *Sunday Times*, 30 April

Couffignal, Georges, 1994, 'The inter-American system after the Cold War', in Zaki Laidi (ed.), *Power and Purpose After the Cold War*, Oxford: Berg

Coughlin, R., 1992, 'Convergence theories', in E. Borgatta and M. Borgatta (eds), *Encyclopedia of Sociology*, Volume 1, New York: Macmillan

Craib, Ian, 1992a, *Anthony Giddens*, London: Routledge

Craib, Ian, 1992b, *Modern Social Theory: from Parsons to Habermas*, Hemel Hempstead: Harvester Wheatsheaf, second edition

Cumming-Bruce, Nicholas, 1997, 'East–West dialogue enters new era', *The Guardian*, 14 February

Curtin, Deirdre, 1996, 'The debate on IGC priorities for 1996', in Brigid Laffan (ed.), *Constitution-building in the European Union*, Dublin: Institute of European Affairs

Daintith, Terence (ed.), 1995a, *Implementing EC Law in the United Kingdom: structures for indirect rule*, Chichester: John Wiley

Daintith, Terence, 1995b, 'Introduction', in Terence Daintith (ed.), *Implementing EC Law in the United Kingdom: structures for indirect rule*, Chichester: John Wiley

Davidson, Ian, 1997, 'Frontier diplomacy', *Financial Times*, 5 February

Davies, Norman, 1996, *Europe: a history*, Oxford: Oxford University Press

Davis, Howard and Richard Scase, 1985, *Western Capitalism and State Socialism*, Oxford: Blackwell

Deacon, Bob (ed.), 1992, *The New Eastern Europe*, London: Sage

de Gaulle, Charles, 1971 (trans. Terence Kilmartin), *Memoirs of Hope: renewal and endeavour*, New York: Simon and Schuster

de Gaulle, Charles, 1994, 'A concert of European states', in Brent Nelsen and Alexander Stubb (eds), *The European Union*, London: Macmillan

de Jonquières, Guy, 1997, 'US dodges Brussels onslaught', *Financial Times*, 21 February

de Jonquières, Guy, and Nancy Dunne, 1997, 'US leaves door ajar in row with EU over Cuba trade', *Financial Times*, 21 February

Delamont, Sara, 1995, *Appetites and Identities: an introduction to the social anthropology of Western Europe*, London: Routledge

den Boer, Monica, 1994, 'Europe and the art of international police co-operation', in David O'Keefe and Patrick Twomey (eds), *Legal Issues of the Maastricht Treaty*, London: Wiley Chancery

Dent, Christopher, 1997, *The European Economy: the global context*, London: Routledge

Denza, Eileen, 1996, 'The Community as a member of international organizations', in Nicholas Emilou and David O'Keefe (eds), *The European Union and World Trade: after the GATT Uruguay Round*, Chichester: John Wiley

Dessler, David, 1989, 'What's at stake in the agent–structure debate?', *International Organisation*, 43, 3

Dickinson, Martin, 1996, 'Solutions to a global problem', *Financial Times*, 15 July

Dinan, Desond, 1994, *Ever Closer Union? An Introduction to the European Community*, London: Macmillan

Dinmore, Guy and Kevin Done, 1997, 'In the shadow of the gun', *Financial Times*, 15/16 March

Dixon, Chris, 1991, *South East Asia in the World Economy*, Cambridge: Cambridge University Press

Dobbs-Higginson, Michael, 1994, *Asia Pacific: its role in the new world disorder*, London: Heinemann

Done, Kevin and Kerin Hope, 1997, 'Progress shown to have a thin veneer', *Financial Times*, 19 February

Dowds, Lizanne and Ken Young, 1996, 'National identity', in Roger Jowell *et al.*, *British Social Attitudes: the 13th report*, Aldershot: Dartmouth Publishing

Dresner, Denise (ed.), 1994, *The Hutchinson Factfinder*, London: QPD, second edition

Drost, Harry, 1995, *What's What and Who's Who in Europe?*, London: Cassell

Dudley, Nigel, 1997, 'Rifkind berates Labour on drift to superstate', *The European*, 27 March

Dunleavy, Patrick and Brendan O'Leary, 1987, *Theories of the State: the politics of liberal democracy*, London: Macmillan

During, Simon (ed.), 1993, *The Cultural Studies Reader*, London: Routledge

Dyer, Geof, 1996, 'Mercosur nations drive ahead through some tricky terrain', *Financial Times*, 28 December

The Economist, 12 November 1994, 'APEC: the opening up of Asia'

The Economist, 10 December 1994, 'Eastern Europe and the EU: laying down the law'

The Economist, 10 December 1994, 'Happy ever NAFTA?'

Ekins, Paul, 1992, *A New World Order: grassroots movements for global change*, London: Routledge

El-Agraa, Ali, 1995, 'APEC: American challenge, European response', *Euro Japanese Journal*, 2, 2, August

Elles, Diana, 1996, 'The role of the EU institutions in external trade policy', in Nicholas Emilou and David O'Keefe (eds), *The European Union and World Trade: after the GATT Uruguay Round*, Chichester: John Wiley

Elliott, Larry, 18 May 1993, 'Maastricht; Europe's future in the balance', *The Guardian*

Elliott, Larry, 3 March 1997, 'The wall came tumbling down', *The Guardian*

Elliott, Larry, and Mark Milner, 8 March 1997, 'They're talking our language', *The Guardian*

Emilou, Nicholas, 1994, 'Subsidiarity: panacea or fig leaf?', in David O'Keefe and Patrick Twomey (eds), *Legal Issues of the Maastricht Treaty*, London: Wiley Chancery

Emilou, Nicholas, 1996, 'The allocation of competence between the EC and its Member States in the sphere of external relations', in Nicholas Emilou and David O'Keefe (eds), *The European Union and World Trade: after the GATT Uruguay Round*, Chichester: John Wiley

Emilou, Nicholas and David O'Keefe (eds), 1996, *The European Union and World Trade Law: after the GATT Uruguay Round*, Chichester: John Wiley

The Euro Japanese Journal, 1995, 2, 2, August

The Euro Japanese Journal, 1996, 3, 1, April

The European, 21 July 1995, 'Agenda – update on the Union – Russia', p. 7

The European, 27 March 1997, 'New life for EU begins at 40'

European Commission, 'An 11% rise in internal trade', *Frontier-Free Europe*, Luxembourg: Office for Official Publications of the European Communities, September 1995

European Commission, *The Caribbean and the European Union*, Luxembourg: Office for Official Publications of the European Communities, 1994

European Commission, *A Citizen's Europe*, Luxembourg: Office for Official Publications of the European Communities, 1993

European Commission, 'Commission Report for the Reflection Group: Intergovernmental Conference 1996', Luxembourg: Office for Official Publications of the European Communities, 1995

European Commission, 'Criteria for future sanctions', *Frontier-Free Europe*, July 1996

European Commission, 'Cyprus Prepares to join the EU', *Frontier-Free Europe*, June 1996

European Commission, *Development: 20 questions and answers*, Luxembourg: Office for Official Publications of the European Communities, 1996

European Commission, *EC Food Aid and Food Aid Security Programme*, Luxembourg: Office for Official Publications of the European Communities, 1996

European Commission, 'An economic area for 18 countries', *Frontier-Free Europe*, February 1994

European Commission, *Eurobarometer (public opinion in the European Union) Trends 1974–1994*, Luxembourg: Office for Official Publications of the European Communities, 1995

European Commission, *Europe in a Changing World: the external relations of the European Community*, Luxembourg: Office for Official Publications of the European Communities, 1993

European Commission, *Europe in a Changing World*, Luxembourg: Office for Official Publications of the European Communities, 1995

European Commission, 'Europe inspires Andean community', *Frontier-Free Europe*, April 1996

European Commission, *The European Community and Mediterranean Countries*, Luxembourg: Office for Official Publications of the European Communities, 1991

European Commission, 'The European Union and Asia', *Frontier-Free Europe* (Supplement), Luxembourg: Office for Official Publications of the European Communities, April 1996

European Commission, *The European Union and the Developing World*, Luxembourg: Office for Official Publications of the European Communities, 1996

European Commission, *The European Union and World Trade*, Luxembourg: Office for Official Publications of the European Communities, 1993

European Commission, *The European Union and World Trade*, Luxembourg: Office for Official Publications of the European Communities, 1995

European Commission, *EU-ACP Cooperation in 1995: what form of structural adjustment?*, Luxembourg: Office for Official Publications of the European Communities, 1994

European Commission, *Financial Cooperation Under the Lomé Conventions: review of the aid at the end of 1995*, Luxembourg: Office for Official Publications of the European Communities, 1996

European Commission, *From Single Market to European Union*, Luxembourg: Office for Official Publications of the European Communities, 1992

European Commission, *A Human Face for Europe*, Luxembourg: Office for Official Publications of the European Communities, 1990

European Commission, *Industrial and Economic Co-operation between the European Union and Developing Countries*, Luxembourg: Office for Official Publications of the European Communities, 1995

European Commission, *Info Finance 1995: the European Development Fund*, Luxembourg: Office for Official Publications of the European Communities, 1996

European Commission, *The Institutions of the European Union*, Luxembourg: Office for Official Publications of the European Communities, May 1995

European Commission, *Intergovernmental Conference 1996: Commission report for the Reflection Group*, Luxembourg: Office for Official Publications of the European Communities, 1995

European Commission, 'The internal market in practice: still some way to go', *Frontier-Free Europe*, June 1996

European Commission, 'Liechtenstein says "yes" to the EEA', *Frontier-Free Europe*, May 1995

European Commission, *Lomé Revised*, Luxembourg: Office for Official Publications of the European Communities, 1996

European Commission, *A People's Europe*, Luxembourg: Office for Official Publications of the European Communities, 1992

European Commission, 'Prague seeks EU membership', *Frontier-Free Europe*, March 1996

European Commission, *Questions and Answers about the European Community*, Luxembourg: Office for Official Publications of the European Communities, March 1993

European Commission, *Questions and Answers about the European Union*, Luxembourg: Office for Official Publications of the European Communities, April 1993

European Commission, *The Single Market*, Luxembourg: Office for Official Publications of the European Communities, 1995

European Commission, 'Slovenia applies for membership', *Frontier-Free Europe*, July 1996

European Commission, *Southern Africa and the European Union*, Luxembourg: Office for Official Publications of the European Communities, 1994

European Commission, *Strengthening Democracy in the EC*, Luxembourg: Office for Official Publications of the European Communities, 1993

European Commission, *Trade Relations between the European Union and the Developing Countries*, Luxembourg: Office for Official Publications of the European Communities, 1995

European Foreign Affairs Review, London: Kluwer International (first published in July 1996)

European Parliament, 1997, 'Forced labour in Burma prompts withdrawal of trade privileges', *EP News*, March

Eur-op News (Information from the European Communities' Publications Office), 1995, 'Is the EU turning the screw on Eastern Europe?', 4, 3, Autumn

Eurostat, *Facts Through Figures: a statistical portrait of the EEA*, Luxembourg: Office for Official Publications of the European Communities, 1994

Eyal, Jonathan, 1996, 'The war they can't win', *The Guardian*, 26 August

Fernández-Armesto, Felipe, 1994, *The Peoples of Europe*, London: Times Books

Field, C., 1996, 'Major in race to trade with tyrants', *The Observer*, 25 February

Figes, Orlando, 1996, *A People's Tragedy: the Russian Revolution 1891–1924*, New York: Jonathan Cape

Financial Times, 9 December 1996, 'Caribbean co-operation'

Financial Times, 16 December 1996, 'Bolivia and Mercosur'

Financial Times, 5 April 1997, 'Welfare spending falls in EU'

Fletcher, John, 1995, *The European Community: culture and society*, London: Intellect Books

Fletcher, Pascal, 1996, 'Havana's assault on US sanctions law', *Financial Times*, 27 December

Fletcher, Pascal, 1997, 'Cuba crime crackdown', *Financial Times*, 5 April

Fontaine, Pascal, 1993, *A Citizen's Europe*, Luxembourg: Office for Official Publications of the European Communities

Fontaine, Pascal, 1995, *Europe in Ten Lessons*, Luxembourg: Office for Official Publications of the European Communities

Foucault, Michel, 1978 (trans. R. Hurley), *The History of Sexuality. Volume One: an introduction*, New York: Pantheon

Foucault, Michel, 1980, *Power/Knowledge: selected interviews and other writings 1972–1977*, New York: Pantheon

Foucault, Michel, 1988 (ed. Lawrence Kritzman), *Politics, Philosophy, Culture: interviews and other writings 1977–1984*, London: Routledge

Foucault, Michel, 1993, 'Space, power, knowledge', in Simon During (ed.), *The Cultural Studies Reader*, London: Routledge

Frankland, Mark, 1994, 'Why Norway will defy Beast of Brussels', *The Observer*, 27 November

Freeland, Chrystia, 1997, 'Moscow hints at nuclear retaliation', *Financial Times*, 12 February

Freeland, Chrystia and John Thornhill, 1997, 'Army chief set for Chechen poll win', *Financial Times*, 29 January

Friedman, Jonathan, 1992, 'Narcissism, roots and postmodernity; the constitution of selfhood in the global crisis', in Scott Lash and Jonathan Friedman (eds), *Modernity and Identity*, Oxford: Blackwell

Friedman, Jonathan, 1993, 'Order and disorder in global systems: a sketch', *Social Research*, 60, 2

Friedman, Jonathan, 1994, *Cultural Identity and Global Processes*, London: Sage

Fuchs, G., 1995, 'The European Commission as a corporate actor?', in C. Rhodes and S. Mazey (eds), *The State of the European Union*, Boulder, Co: Lynne Rienner

Fukuyama, Francis, 1989, 'The end of history?', *The National Interest*, Summer

Fukuyama, Francis, 1991, 'Liberal democracy as a global phenomenon', *Politial Science and Politics*, December

Fukuyama, Francis, 1992, *The End of History and the Last Man*, London: Hamish Hamilton; New York: Free Press

Fukuyama, Francis, 1995, *Trust: the social virtues and the creation of prosperity*, London: Hamish Hamilton

Galbraith, J., 1967, *The New Industrial State*, Harmondsworth: Penguin

Gelder, Ken and Sarah Thornton (eds), 1997, *The Subcultures Reader*, London: Routledge

Gellner, Ernest, 1983, *Nations and Nationalism*, Oxford: Blackwell

Gellner, Ernest, 1987, *Culture, Identity and Politics*, Cambridge: Cambridge University Press

Gellner, Ernest, 1992, *Postmodernism, Reason and Religion*, London: Routledge

Gellner, Ernest, 1994, *Encounters with Nationalism*, Oxford: Blackwell

Genscher, Hans-Dietrich, 19 February 1996, 'Britain in Europe', *The Guardian*

Giddens, Anthony, 1985, *The Nation-State and Violence: volume two of a contemporary critique of historical materialism*, Cambridge: Polity

Giddens, Anthony, 1986, *The Constitution of Society: outline of the theory of structuration*, Cambridge: Polity (originally 1984)

Giddens, Anthony, 1990, *The Consequences of Modernity*, Cambridge: Polity

Giddens, Anthony, 1991a, *The Consequences of Modernity*, Cambridge: Polity paperback edition

Giddens, Anthony, 1991b, *Modernity and Self-Identity*, Cambridge: Polity

Giddens, Anthony, 1991c, *The Nation-State and Violence: volume two of a contemporary critique of historical materialism*, New York: Simon and Schuster, third edition

Giddens, Anthony, 1993a, *New Rules of Sociological Method*, Cambridge: Polity, second edition

Giddens, Anthony, 1993b, *Sociology*, Cambridge: Polity, second edition

Gillespie, Paul, 1996, 'Models of integration', in Brigid Laffan (ed.), *Constitution-Building in the European Union*, Dublin: Institute of European Affairs

Gilpin, Robert, 1987, *The Political Economy of International Relations*, Princeton, NJ: Princeton University Press

Glenny, Misha, 1990, *The Rebirth of History: Eastern Europe in the age of democracy*, London: Penguin

Glenny, Misha, 1993, *The Rebirth of History: eastern Europe in the age of democracy*, London: Penguin, second edition

Goddard, Victoria, 1994, Josep Llobera and Chris Shore (eds), 1994, *The Anthropology of Europe: identities and boundaries in conflict*, Oxford: Berg

Goldsmith, James, 1997, 'We are being led blindfold into a federal superstate', *News From the Referendum Party*, February

Goodall, Brian, 1987, *Dictionary of Human Geography*, London: Penguin

Gorbachev, Mikhail, 1996, *Memoirs*, New York: Doubleday

Gow, David, Rebecca Smithers and Denis Staunton, 1997, 'Kohl faces court threat over EMU', *The Guardian*, 24 February

Gowan, P., 1995, 'Neo-liberal theory and practice for Eastern Europe', *New Left Review*, 213

Gowland, David, Basil O'Neill and Alex Reid (eds), 1995, *The European Mosaic: contemporary politics, economics and culture*, London: Longman

Grant, Jeremy, 1997, 'China rig leaves disputed zone', *Financial Times*, 5 April

Gray, John, 1995, 'Cold sun rises at the end of the cold war', *The Guardian*, 20 January

Green, J., 1996, 'New world order', in *The Observer Encyclopedia of Our Times*, Volume One, *The Observer*, 17 November

Grun, Bernard, 1991, *The Timetables of History*, third edition, New York: Simon and Schuster

The Guardian, 30 June 1995, 'French reticence throws EU deal to open borders into confusion'

The Guardian, 13 July 1995, 'Britain threatens to veto EU open borders'

The Guardian, 17 July 1995, 'Russia wins trade accord'

The Guardian (editorial 29 March 1996), 'Give and take in the EU: compromise is not a bad word: it's the answer'

The Guardian, 7 September 1996, 'Josef who?'

The Guardian (editorial 5 February 1997), 'Letting Italy down gently'

The Guardian, 7 February 1997, 'Single-minded campaigners on fringes of politics aim to disrupt mainstream parties'

The Guardian, 15 March 1997, 'Albania's anarchy'

Gusterson, Hugh, 1993, 'Realism and the international order after the Cold War', *Social Research*, 60, 2

Hall, Stuart and Bram Gieben (eds), 1992, *Formations of Modernity*, Cambridge: Polity

Hall, Stuart, David Held and Tony McGrew (eds), 1992, *Modernity and its Futures*, Cambridge: Polity

Hallingan, Liam, 1997, 'Visions of a "monster" rouse the Independence party', *Financial Times*, 3 February

Hamilton, Adrian, 1994, 'Pushing east is our only hope', *The Observer*, 2 December

Hancock, M. Donald, 1993, *Politics in Western Europe*, London: Macmillan

Handoll, John, 1995, *Free Movement of Persons in the EU*, Chichester: John Wiley

Hantrais, Linda, 1995, *Social Policy in the European Union*, London: Macmillan

Haralambos, Michael, 1985, *Sociology: themes and perspectives*, Slough: UTP

Harris, Chris, 1983, *The Family and Industrial Society*, London: Allen and Unwin

Harrison, David, 1995, *The Organisation of Europe*, London: Routledge

Harrop, Jeffrey, 1992, *The Political Economy of Integration in the European Community*, Aldershot: Edward Elgar, second edition

Harvey, David, 1989, *The Conditions of Postmodernity: an inquiry into the conditions of cultural change*, Oxford: Blackwell

Hattersley, Roy, 1997, 'Euro visionaries', *The Guardian*, 25 March

Hearst, David, 1996, 'Moscow hails trade pact with China', *The Guardian*, 28 December

Hedetoft, Ulf, 1994, 'The state of sovereignty in Europe: political concept or cultural self-image', in Staffan Zetterholm (ed.), *National Cultures and European Integration*, Oxford: Berg

Held, David, 1992a, 'Democracy: from city-states to cosmopolitan order?', *Political Studies*, 42, special issue

Held, David, 1992b, 'The development of the modern state', in Stuart Hall and Bram Gieben (eds), *Formations of Modernity*, Cambridge: Polity

Held, David and John Thompson, 1991, *Social Theory of Modern Societies: Anthony Giddens and his critics*, Cambridge: Cambridge University Press

Henley, Jon, 1996, 'Brundtland seeks new pastures', *The Guardian*, 24 October

Hervey, Tamara and David O'Keefe (eds), 1996, *Sex Equality Law and the European Union*, Chichester: John Wiley

Heurlin, Bertel, 1996, 'Denmark: a new activisim in foreign and security policy', in Christopher Hill (ed.), *The Actors in Europe's Foreign Policy*, London: Routledge

Higgins, A., 1996, 'Asian women form "fastest growing pool of cheap labour"', *The Guardian*, 6 February

Hill, Christopher, (ed.), 1996, *The Actors in Europe's Foreign Policy*, London: Routledge

Hirst, David, 1996, 'Turkey beats path to Arab world', *The Guardian*, 31 August

Hix, Simon, 1994, 'The study of the European Community: the challenge to comparative approaches', *West European Politics*, 17, 1

Hobsbawm, Eric, 1990, *Nations and Nationalism since 1780*, Cambridge: Cambridge University Press

Hoffmann, Stanley, 1993, 'Goodbye to a united Europe?', *New York Review of Books*, 27 May

Hollinger, Robert, 1994, *Postmodernism and the Social Sciences*, London: Sage

Holsti, K., 1991, *Peace and War: armed conflicts and the international order*, Cambridge: Cambridge University Press

Hooper, John, 1996, 'Malta turns its back on Europe', *The Guardian*, 29 October

Hosking, Geoffrey, 1985, *A History of the Soviet Union*, London: Fontana

Hosking, Geoffrey, 1996, *Russia: people and empire, 1552–1917*, London: Harper Collins

Huntington, Samuel, 1993, 'The clash of civilizations', *Foreign Affairs*, 72, 3

Hu, Yao-Su, 1992, 'Global or stateless corporations are national firms with international operations', *California Management Review*, 34, 2

The Hutchinson Softback Encyclopedia, 1991, Oxford: Helicon Publishing

Hutton, Will, 20 October 1995, 'How to shore up the social capital', *The Guardian*

Hutton, Will, 28 October 1995, 'Tory fantasy of far eastern promise: should Britain become an Asian tiger economy?', *The Guardian*

Ignatieff, Michael, 1993, *Blood and Belonging: journeys into the new nationalism*, London: Chatto and Windus

Ignatieff, Michael, 1994, *Blood and Belonging*, London: BBC Publications

Ignatieff, Michael, 1997, 'The Russians took ages to throw off their chains. But some already want them back again', *The Observer*, 9 March

Iriye, Akira, 1992, *China and Japan in the Global Setting*, Cambridge, Mass.: Harvard University Press

Jackson, Tony, 1997, 'German business leaders doubt 1999 start date', *Financial Times*, 3 February

Jacques, Martin, 1996, 'Could anyone here direct me to Europe?', *The Observer*, 13 October

James, A., 1986, *Sovereign Statehood: the basis of international society*, London: Allen and Unwin

Jeffries, Ian, 1993, *Social Economies and the Transition to the Market*, London: Routledge

Joffe, J., 1993, 'The new Europe: yesterday's ghosts', *Foreign Affairs*, 72, 1

Johnson, Allan, 1995, *The Blackwell Dictionary of Sociology*, Oxford: Blackwell

Joll, James, 1990, *Europe Since 1870*, London: Penguin, fourth edition

Jowell, Roger, John Curtice, Alison Park, Lindsay Brook and Katarina Thomson (eds), 1996, *British Social Attitudes: the 13th report*, Aldershot: Dartmouth Publishing

Jowitt, Ken, 1992, *New World Disorder: the Leninist distinction*, Berkeley, CA: University of California Press

Kalberg, S., 1993, 'Convergence thesis', in J. Kreiger (ed.), *The Oxford Companion to Politics*, New York: Oxford University Press

Kampfner, John, 1997, 'Major takes confrontational line on EU', *Financial Times*, 5 February

Keating, Michael and Liesbet Hooge, 1996, 'By-passing the nation-state? Regions and the EU policy process', in Jeremy Richardson (ed.), *European Union: power and policy-making*, London: Routledge

Keatinge, Patrick, 1996, 'Ireland and common security: stretching the limits of commitment?', in Christopher Hill (ed.), *The Actors in Europe's Foreign Policy*, London: Routledge

Kegley, C. and E. Wittkopf, 1993, *World Politics: trend and transformation*, New York: St Martin's Press

Kellner, Doug, 1992, 'Popular culture and the construction of postmodern identities', in Scott Lash and Jonathan Friedman (eds), *Modernity and Identity*, Oxford: Blackwell

Kemp, Arnold, 1997, 'Which country is enjoying a European economic boom, Germany or Ireland?', *The Observer*, 2 February

Kenis, P. and V. Schneider, 1987, 'The EC as an international corporate actor', *European Journal of Political Research*, 15, 4

Kennedy, P. 1992, *Preparing for the Twenty-first Century*, New York: Random House

Keohane, Robert, 1984, *After Hegemony: cooperation and discord in the world political economy*, Princeton, NJ: Princeton University Press

Keohane, Robert and Joseph Nye, 1988, 'Complex interdependence, transnational relations and realism: alternative perspectives on world politics', in C. Kegley and E. Wittkopf (eds), *The Global Agenda*, New York: Random House, second edition

Kerr, C., 1983, *The Future of Industrial Societies: convergence or continuing diversity?*, Cambridge, Mass.: Harvard University Press

Kerr, C., J. Dunlop, F. Harbison and C. Myers, 1960, *Industrialism and Industrial Man*, Cambridge, Mass.: Harvard University Press

Kettle, Martin, 1997, 'Point placing gives Labour narrower lead over Tories', *The Guardian*, 5 February

Koh, Tommy, 1993, 'The 10 values that undergird East Asian strength and success', *International Herald Tribune*, 11 December

Koslowski, R. and F. Kratochwil, 1994, 'Understanding change in international politics: the Soviet Empire's demise and the international system', *International Organisation*, 48, 2

Krasner, Stephen, 1988, 'Sovereignty: an institutional perspective', *Comparative Political Studies*, 21, Spring

Krenzler, Horst and Astrid Schomaker, 1996, 'A new trans-Atlantic agenda', *European Foreign Affairs Review*, 1, 1, July

Kynge, James and Neol Buckley, 1997, 'EU and Asean face a testing encounter', *Financial Times*, 12 February

Laffan, Brigid, 1992, *Integration and Cooperation in Europe*, London: Routledge

Laffan, Brigid (ed.), 1996a, *Constitution-Building in the European Union*, Dublin: Institute of European Affairs

Laffan, Brigid, 1996b, 'Introduction', in Brigid Laffan (ed.), *Constitution-Building in the European Union*, Dublin: Institute of European Affairs

Laidi, Zaki (ed.), 1994, *Power and Purpose After the Cold War*, Oxford: Berg

Lane, Jan-Erik and Svante Ersson, 1994, *Politics and Society in Western Europe*, London: Sage, third edition

Lane, Jan-Erik and Svante Ersson, 1996, *European Politics*, London: Sage

Langlois, S., T. Caplan, H. Mendzas and W. Glatzer, 1994, *Convergence or Divergence: recent social trends in industrial societies*, Frankfurt: Campus Verlag

Lash, Scott, 1993, 'Reflexive modernization: the aesthetic dimension', *Theory, Culture and Society*, 10, 1

Lash, Scott, and Jonathan Friedman (eds), 1992a, *Modernity and Identity*, Oxford: Blackwell

Lash, Scott, and Jonathan Friedman, 1992b, 'Introduction: subjectivity and modernity's Other', in Scott Lash and Jonathan Friedman (eds), *Modernity and Identity*, Oxford: Blackwell

Laurance, Ben, 1996, 'Close relationships of the shareholder kind', *The Observer*, 13 October

Leftwich, Adrian, 1993, 'Governance, democracy and development in the Third World', *Third World Quarterly*, 14, 3

Levi, Lucio (ed.), 1990, *Altiero Spinelli and Federalism in Europe and the World*, Rome: Franco Angeli

Lipset, S., 1960, *Political Man*, London: Heinemann

Lodge, Juliet (ed.), 1993, *The European Community and the Challenge of the Future*, London: Pinter, second edition

Ludlow, Peter, 1993, *Beyond Maastricht*, Brussels: CEPS

Lukacs, J., 1992, *The End of the Twentieth Century and the End of the Modern Age*, New York: Ticknor and Fields

Lukes, Steven, 1973, *Individualism*, Oxford: Blackwell

Lyotard, J., 1984, *The Postmodern Condition*, Minneapolis: University of Minnesota Press

MacAskill, Ewen and Peter Hetherington, 1997, 'Toyota's EMU threat to Britain', *The Guardian*, 30 January

MacClancy, Jeremy, 1993, 'At play with identity in the Basque arena', in Sharon Macdonald (ed.), *Inside European Identities*, Oxford: Berg

Macdonald, Sharon, (ed.), 1993, *Inside European Identities*, Oxford: Berg

Macfarlane, Alan, 1978, *The Origins of English Individualism*, Oxford: Blackwell

Machonin, Pavel, 1996, 'Post-communist social transformation and modernization', *Slovak Sociological Review*, 1, Spring

Macpherson, C., 1962, *The Political Theory of Possessive Individualism*, Oxford: Oxford University Press

Macwhirter, I., 1995, 'Tory lions deluded by the Asian tigers', *The Observer*, 29 October

McGrew, Anthony, 1992, 'A global society?', in S. Hall, D. Held and A. McGrew (eds), *Modernity and its Futures*, Milton Keynes: Open University

McKie, David, 1996, 'Nationalism', *The Guardian*, 21 November

McSmith, Andy, 1996, 'TEC report debunks Major's job claims', *The Observer*, 17 November

Maejima, Susumu, 1995, 'Panel deabtes the notion of cohesive cultures in richly diverse community', *Asahi Evening News* (Japan), 12 October

Magnusson, Magnus (ed.), 1990, *Chambers Biographical Dictionary*, Edinburgh: Chambers, fifth edition

Mandel, Ruth, 1994, '"Fortress Europe" and the foreigners within: Germany's Turks', in Victoria Goddard, Josep Llobera and Chris Shore (eds), *The Anthropology of Europe*, Oxford: Berg

Mann, Michael, 1997, 'Has globalization ended the rise and rise of the nation state?', *Review of International Political Economy*, 4

Manning, C., 1962, *The Nature of International Society*, London: Bell

Manning, Nick, 1992, 'Social policy in the Soviet Union and its successors', in Bod Deacon (ed.), *The New Eastern Europe*, London: Sage

March, James and Johan Olsen, 1984, 'The new institutionalism', *American Political Science Review*, 78, September

Marquand, D., 1994, 'Prospects for a federal Europe', *New Left Review*, 203

Maruyama, Masao, 1995, 'Theory and psychology of ultra-nationalism', in Tim Megarry (ed.), *The Making of Modern Japan*, Dartford: Greenwich University Press

Massey, Doreen, 1991, 'A global sense of place', *Marxism Today*, June

Massey, Doreen, 1994, *Space, Place and Gender*, Oxford: Polity Press

Mather, Ian, 1997, 'New moves on defence shake Nato', *The European*, 27 March

Meek, James, 1986, 'Russia's two armies fight each other for supremacy', *The Observer*, 25 August

Meek, James, 1997, 'Georgian rebels hold out against the world', *The Observer*, 2 March

Megarry, Tim (ed.), 1995, *The Making of Modern Japan*, Dartford: Greenwich University Press

Meštrović, Stjepan, 1994, *The Balkanization of the West: the confluence of postmodernism and postcommunism*, London: Routledge

Meyer, John, Francesco Ramirez and John Boli, 1987, 'Ontology and rationalization in the Western cultural account', in George Thomas, John Meyer, Francesco Ramirez and John Boli (eds), *Institutional Structure: constituting state, society and the individual*, Beverly Hills, CA: Sage

Miall, Hugh, 1993, *Shaping the New Europe*, London: Pinter

Milne, Seamus, 1996, 'Four million get extra holiday rights', *The Guardian*, 13 November

Milner, Helen, 1994, 'The evolution of the international trade regime: a three-bloc trading system?', in Zaki Laidi (ed.), *Power and Purpose After the Cold War*, Oxford: Berg

Milner, Mark, 2 April 1996, 'Eastern bloc is recovering, says European bank', *The Guardian*

Milner, Mark, 28 December 1996, 'Enlargement will pose big questions for Europe', *The Guardian*

Milner, Mark, 5 March 1997, 'Power shared is power enhanced', *The Guardian*

Mongardini, C., 1992, 'The ideology of postmodernity', *Theory, Culture and Society*, 9

Monks, Robert and Nell Minow, 1996, *Watching the Watchers: corporate governance for the 21st century*, Oxford: Blackwell

Moorman, Jane, 1996, 'Europe set to call time on the hours we work', *The Guardian*, 19 October

Moravcsik, Andrew, 1991, 'Negotiating the Single European Act: national interests and conventional statecraft in the European Community', *International Organization*, 45, 1

Moravcsik, Andrew, 1994, 'Negotiating the Single European Act: national interests and conventional statecraft in the European Community', in Brent Nelsen and Alexander Stubb (eds), *The European Union*, London: Macmillan

Morishima, Michio, 1984, *Why Has Japan Succeeded?: Western technology and the Japanese ethos*, Cambridge: Cambridge University Press

Nakamura, Tamio, 1995, 'Does the European Union model work for Asia?', *Seikei Hogaku* (*The Journal of Legal, Political and Social Sciences*, Seikei University, Tokyo), 41, March

Nelsen, Brent and Alexander Stubb (eds), 1994, *The European Union: readings on the theory and practice of European integration*, London: Macmillan

News From the Referendum Party, February 1997

New Webster's Dictionary and Thesaurus, 1991, New York: Book Essentials

Noël, Emile, 1993, *Working Together – The Institutions of the European Community*, Luxembourg: Office for Official Publications of the European Communities

Nørgaard, Ole, Thomas Pedersen and Nikolaj Petersen (eds), 1993, *The European Community in World Politics*, London: Pinter

Norman, Peter, 1996, 'Lights flicker in the powerhouse: the German economy's slow growth', *Financial Times*, 29 November

Nugent, Neill, 1991, *The Government and Politics of the European Community*, London: Macmillan, second edition

Nuttall, Chris, 29 June 1996, 'Amnesty team in Turkey to highlight latest rights abuses', *The Guardian*

Nuttall, Chris, 9 October 1996, 'Foreign "fiasco" hits Turkish PM', *The Guardian*

Nuttall, Chris, 6 March 1997, 'Turkish PM "gives in to military pressure"', *The Guardian*

O'Brien, Oonagh, 1993, 'Good to be French? Conflicts of identity in north Catalonia', in Sharon Macdonald (ed.), *Inside European Identities*, Oxford: Berg

Offe, Claus, 1991, 'Capitalism by democratic design? Facing the triple transition in East Central Europe', *Social Research*, 58, 4

Ohmae, Kenichi, 1990, *Borderless World: power and strategy in the interlinked economy*, London: New York: Harper Collins

Ohmae, Kenichi, 1995, *The End of the Nation State*, London: Harper Collins

O'Keefe, David, and Patrick Twomey (eds), 1994, *Legal Issues of the Maastricht Treaty*, London: Wiley Chancery

Ougaard, Morten, 1993, 'Dealing with the Community: the Bush Administration's response to western European integration', in Ole Nørgaard, Thomas Pedersen and Nikolaj Petersen (eds), *The European Community in World Politics*, London: Pinter

Padfield, Colin and Tony Byrne, 1987, *British Constitution*, Oxford: Heinemann, seventh edition

Paepke, C., 1992, *The Evolution of Progress*, New York: Random House

Palmer, John, 9 December 1994, 'Advent of the east will force internal change', *The Guardian*

Palmer, John, 31 December 1994, 'EU tops global wealth league', *The Guardian*

Palmer, John, 22 February 1996, 'EU seven defuse extradition row', *The Guardian*

Palmer, John, 26 February 1996, 'EU blueprint likely to fan the flames of disunion', *The Guardian*

Palmer, John, 1 March 1996, 'Tension threatens EU-Asian summit', *The Guardian*

Palmer, John, 26 March 1996, 'EU warns Britain not to block unity', *The Guardian*

Palmer, John, 11 May 1996, 'EU moves to shut door on Croatia', *The Guardian*

Palmer, John, 5 October 1996, 'EU leaders seek to tackle Maastricht Two deadlock', *The Guardian*

Palmer, John, 6 October 1996, 'Kohl fuels the fire for a single currency: Maastricht Two appears to be steaming ahead', *The Observer*

Palmer, John, 16 October 1996, 'Croatia gets EU warning on human rights', *The Guardian*

Palmer, John, 14 January 1997, 'West offers new security pact to Moscow to soothe its fears', *The Guardian*

Palmer, John, 12 February 1997, 'EU gives way on border controls opt-out for Britain to win Blair backing for new treaty', *The Guardian*

Palmer, John, 27 February 1997, 'EU's wrangling holds up treaty', *The Guardian*

Palmer, John, 15 March 1997, 'Hopes rise for agreement on new EU treaty', *The Guardian*

Palmer, John, 4 April 1997, 'Community converges on the road to Amsterdam', *The Guardian*

Palmer, John, and Michael White, 1997, 'Major's onslaught on social chapter', *The Guardian*, 5 February

Parker, George, and Robert Peston, 1997, 'Labour would join "stable" Emu', *Financial Times*, 3 February

Payne, Ronald, 1997, 'Albanian rebellion ruffles feathers in cosy Union nest', *The European*, 20 March

Pedersen, Thomas, 1992, 'EC-EFTA relations: an historical outline', in Helen Wallace (ed.), *The Wider Western Europe: Reshaping the EC/EFTA Relationship*, London: Pinter

Pedersen, Thomas, 1993, 'The common foreign and security policy and the challenge of enlargement', in Ole Nørgaard, Thomas Pedersen and Nikolaj Petersen (eds), *The European Community in World Politics*, London: Pinter

Perry, K., 1976, *Modern European History*, Butterworth-Heinemann

Petersen, Nikolaj, 1993, 'The European Union and foreign and security policy', in Ole Nørgaard, Thomas Pedersen and Nikolaj Petersen (eds), *The European Community in World Politics*, London: Pinter

Peterson, John, 1996, *Europe and America: the prospects for partnership*, London: Routledge

Pistone, Sergio, 1990, 'Altiero Spinelli and the strategy for the United States of Europe', in Lucio Levi (ed.), *Altiero Spinelli and Federalism in Europe and the World*, Rome: Franco Angeli

Pistone, Sergio, 1994, 'Altiero Spinelli and the strategy for the United States of Europe', in B. Neslen and A. Stubb (eds), *The European Union: readings on the theory and practice of European integration*, London: Macmillan

Porter, Michael, 1990, *The Competitive Advantage of Nations*, London: Macmillan

Price, Jonathan, 1997, 'Asean investment in UK will be dependent on its joining Emu', *Financial Times*, 5 February

Przeworski, A., 1991, *Democracy and the Market: political and economic reforms in Eastern Europe and Latin America*, Cambridge: Cambridge University Press

Radek, Karl, 1995, 'Japanese and international fascisim', in Tim Megarry (ed.), *The Making of Modern Japan*, Dartford: Greenwich University Press

Rees, G. Wyn, 1993, *International Politics in Europe*, London: Routledge

Reeves, Phil, 1996, 'Estonia comes of age to capitalism', *The Independent*, 18 September

Regelsberger, Elfriede and Wolfgang Wessels, 1996, 'The CFSP institutions and procedures: a third way for the second pillar', *European Foreign Affairs Review*, 1, 1, July

Reischauer, Edwin and Marius Jansen, 1995, *The Japanese Today: change and continuity*, Cambridge, Mass.: Harvard University Press

Rhein, Eberhard, 1996, 'Europe and the Mediterranean: a newly emerging geopolitical area?', *European Foreign Affairs*, 1, 1 (first issue)

Richardson, Jeremy (ed.), 1996, *European Union: power and policy-making*, London: Routledge

Riesman, David, 1977, *The Lonely Crowd*, New Haven, CT: Yale University Press (originally 1950)

Rieu, Alain-Marc and Gerard Duprat (eds), 1995, *European Democratic Culture*, Milton Keynes, revised edition

Rifkind, Malcolm, 1997, 'Do we really need "more Europe"?', *The European*, 27 March

Robertson, Joanna and Stephen Bates, 1997, 'Death toll mounts as Berisha totters: World stands back as anarchy reigns in Albania amid rumours of President's resignation', *The Observer*, 16 March

Robertson, Roland, 1992, *Globalization: social theory and global culture*, London: Sage

Robinson, Anthony, 1997, 'Britain eyes eastern promise', *Financial Times*, 15 January

Roget's Thesaurus of English Words and Phrases, 1987, Harmondsworth: Penguin

Rollnick, Roman, 1996, 'Strike threat chills Russia', *The European*, 3 October

Rollnick, Roman, 1997, 'Algeria "must not taint friendships across the Med"', *The European*, 13 March

Room, Adrian, 1992, *Brewer's Dictionary of Names: people and places and things*, Oxford: Helicon

Room, Graham (ed.), 1991, *Towards a European Welfare State?*, Bristol: SAUS

Rosenau, P., 1992, *Post-Modernism and the Social Sciences*, Princeton, NJ: Princeton University Press

Ryle, Sarah, 1996, 'Why Maastricht super model said "No"', *The Guardian*, Spring

Sachs, J., 1993, *Poland's Jump to the Market Economy*, Cambridge: Mass.: MIT Press

Sandholtz, Wayne and John Zysman, 1989, 'Recasting the European bargain', *World Politics*, 41, 1

Sandholtz, Wayne and John Zysman, 1994, 'Recasting the European bargain', in Brent Nelsen and Alexander Stubb (eds), *The European Union: readings on the theory and practice of European integration*, London: Macmillan

Sanseido's Daily Concise English-Japanese Dictionary, 1990, Tokyo: Sanseido, fifth edition

Sarup, Madan, 1993, *Post-Structuralism and Postmodernism*, Hemel Hempstead: Harvester Wheatsheaf, second edition

Sayer, Derek, 1991, *Capitalism and Modernity: an excursus on Marx and Weber*, London: Routledge

Sbragia, Alberta (ed.), 1992, *Euro-Politics*, Washington, DC: The Brookings Institute

Schlesinger, P., 1992, 'Europeanness: a new cultural battlefield', *Innovation*, 5, 1

Schmitter, Philippe, 1991, 'The European Community as an emergent and novel form of political domination', University of Madrid: Estudio/Working Paper, September

Schmitter, Philippe, 1992, 'Interests, powers and functions: emergent properties and unintended consequences in the European polity', unpublished draft paper, Stanford University

Scott, A., 1992, *European Studies*, London: Pitman

Scott, John, 1995, *Sociological Theory: contemporary debates*, Aldershot: Edward Elgar

Seacombe, Mark, 1996, 'Bullyboy Croat regime swaggers through the door at the European club', *The Observer*, 20 October

Sellers, Mortimer (ed.), 1996, *The New World Order: sovereignty, human rights and the self-determination of peoples*, Oxford: Berg

Shaw, Josephine, 1993, *European Community Law*, London: Macmillan

Shaw, Jo, 1996, *Law of the European Union*, London: Macmillan

Shea, Jamie, 1993, 'Security: the future', in Juliet Lodge (ed.), *The European Community and the Challenge of the Future*, London: Pinter, second edition

Shelley, Monica and Margaret Winck (eds), 1993, *Aspects of European Cultural Diversity*, London: Routledge

Shelley, Monica and Margaret Winck (eds), 1995, *Aspects of European Cultural Diversity*, Milton Keynes: Open University, revised edtion

Short, David, 1997, 'European unity unpopular with the young', *The European*, 6 February

Sklair, Leslie, 1991, *The Sociology of the Global System*, Baltimore: Johns Hopkins University Press

Smart, Barrie, 1992, *Modern Conditions, Postmodern Controversies*, London: Routledge

Smart, Barrie, 1993, *Postmodernity*, London: Routledge

Smart, Victor, 1996, 'Has EMU grounded Europe's flight to a political union?', *The European*, 10 October

Smart, Victor and Paola Buonadonna, 1997, 'Dutch in race against clock to save treaty', *The European*, 27 March

Smith, Helena, 13 March 1997, 'Albania sinks deeper into anarchy', *The Guardian*

Smith, Helena, 20 March 1997, 'Italy declares emergency', *The Guardian*

Smith, Sandra, 1997, 'Europe's 300 stateless "nations" demand an independent voice', *The European*, 27 March

Smithers, Emma, 1997, 'Anti-abortion group joins election fight', *The Guardian*, 7 February

Snyder, Francis, 1993, 'The effectiveness of European Community law', *The Modern Law Review*, 56, 1

Snyder, Francis, 1995, 'The effectiveness of European Community law: institutions, processes, tools and techniques', in Terence Daintith (ed.), *Implementing EC Law in the United Kingdom: structures for indirect rule*, Chichester: John Wiley

So, Alvin and Stephen Chiu, 1995, *East Asia and the World Economy*, London: Sage

Söderman, Jacob, 1996, 'The Union needs a dose of glasnost', *The European*, 17 October

Southey, Caroline, 1997, 'Britain hailed on social policy', *Financial Times*, 28 January

Spicker, Paul, 1991, 'The principle of subsidiarity and the social policy of the European Community', *Journal of European Social Policy*, 1, 1

Stark, David, 1992, 'From system identity to organisational diversity: analysing social change in Eastern Europe', *Contemporary Sociology*, 21, 3

Steele, Jonathan, 25 May 1996, 'Doomed to live with the Marx brothers', *The Guardian*

Steele, Jonathan, 4 December 1996, 'The bear's cub stirs next door', *The Guardian*

Stein, Aurthr, 1990, *Why Nations Cooperate*, Ithaca: Cornell University Press

Steiner, Josephine, 1994, 'Subsidiarity under the Maastricht Treaty', in David O'Keefe and Patrick Twomey (eds), *Legal Issues of the Maastricht Treaty*, London: Wiley Chancery

Stone, Alec, 1994, 'What is a supranational constitution?', *The Review of Politics*, 56, 3, Summer

Stone, Lawrence, 1977, *Family, Sex and Marriage in England, 1500–1800*, London: Weidenfeld and Nicolson

Stone, Norman, 1996, 'Under Eastern eyes', *The Guardian*, 17 October

Story, Jonathan (ed.), 1993, *The New Europe: politics, government and economy since 1945*, Oxford: Blackwell

Storry, Richard, 1995, 'The dark valley', in Tim Megarry (ed.), *The Making of Modern Japan*, Dartford: Greenwich University Press

Strang, David, 1991, 'European political expansion: realist and institutional accounts', *International Organisation*, 45, 2

Strayer, J., 1970, *On the Medieval Origins of the Modern State*, Princeton, NJ: Princeton University Press

Swain, Geoffrey and Nigel Swain, 1993, *Eastern Europe Since 1945*, London: Macmillan

Swann, Dennis (ed.), 1992, *The Single European Market and Beyond: a study of the wider implications of the Single European Act*, London: Routledge

Sztompka, P., 1993, *The Sociology of Social Change*, Oxford: Blackwell

Tang, James (ed.), 1995a, *Human Rights and International Relations in the Asia Pacific*, London: Pinter

Tang, James, 1995b, 'Human rights in the Asia-Pacific region: competing perspectives, international discord, and the way ahead', in James Tang (ed.), *Human Rights and International Relations in the Asia Pacific*, London: Pinter

Tark, David, 1992, 'From system identity to organisational diversity: analysing social change in Eastern Europe', *Contemporary Sociology*, 21, 3

Tawney, R. H., 1938, *Religion and the Rise of Capitalism*, Harmondsworth: Pelican

Taylor, Robert, 1996, 'Employers may be sued over working hours', *Financial Times*, 23 November

Therborn, Goran, 1995, *European Modernity and Beyond: the trajectory of European societies*, London: Sage

Thomas, Richard, 1997, 'World trade slumps as tired Tigers lag behind', *The Guardian*, 11 April

Thompson, John, 1994, 'Ideology and modern culture', in *The Polity Reader in Social Theory*, Cambridge: Polity

Thornhill, John, 1997, 'Kohl acts to end rift with Russia over Nato expansion', *Financial Times*, 6 January

Tilly, Charles, 1993, *European Revolutions, 1492–1992*, Oxford: Blackwell

Toth, A., 1994, 'A legal analysis of subsidiarity', in David O'Keefe and Patrick Twomey (eds), *Legal Issues of the Maastricht Treaty*, London: Wiley Chancery

Traxler, Franz and Philippe Schmitter, 1995, 'The emerging Euro-polity and organised interests', *European Journal of International Relations*, 1, 2, June

Traynor, Ian, 19 November 1994, 'When the east's dreams evaporate', *The Guardian*

Traynor, Ian, 21 November 1996, 'Leading on Europe's fast track', *The Guardian*

Traynor, Ian, 4 March 1997, 'Bonn and Paris vow to get rid of veto', *The Guardian*

Traynor, Ian, 20 March 1997, 'Germany claims "our boat is full"', *The Guardian*

Traynor, Ian and Chris Nuttall, 1997, 'Kohl tries to cool row with Ankara', *The Guardian*, 7 March

The Treaty on European Union, 'Protocol on social policy', 1992

Trench, S. *et al.*, 1992, 'Safer cities for women', *Town Planning Review*, 63, 3

Tsakaloyannis, Panos, 1996, 'Greece: the limits of convergence', in Christopher Hill (ed.), *The Actors in Europe's Foreign Policy*, London: Routledge

Tucker, Emma, 1997, 'EU states could face fines for defying Euro-court', *Financial Times*, 8 January

Turner, Graeme, 1992, *British Cultural Studies: an introduction*, London: Routledge, originally published in 1990

Ugur, Mehmet (ed.), 1995, *Policy Issues in the European Union: a reader in the political economy of European integration*, Dartford: Greenwich University Press

Upsall, Michael (ed.), 1991a, *Hutchinson Encyclopedic Dictionary*, London: Random Century

Upsall Michael (ed.), 1991b, *Hutchinson Gallup Info 92*, London: Random Century

Urban, Rob and Jill Hamburg, 1996, 'Bulgaria to sell state jewels', *The European*, 3 October

Urwin, Derek, 1992, *The Community of Europe: a history of European integration since 1945*, London: Longman, fifth impression

van den Broek, Hans, 1996, 'Why Europe needs a common foreign and security policy', *European Foreign Affairs Review*, 1, 1, July

Wagner, Harrison, 1993, 'What is bipolarity?', *International Organization*, 47, 1

Waites, Bernard (ed.), 1995, *Europe and the Wider World*, Milton Keynes: Open University, revised edition

Walker, Martin, 1994, 'Americas to establish largest free trade bloc', *The Guardian*, 12 December

Walker, Martin, 1996, 'Clinton plots his new world order', *The Observer*, 17 November

Walker, Martin, 1997, 'Expanded EU backed by Portillo', *The Guardian*, 4 March

Walker, Martin and David Hearst, 1997, 'Turkey pressed to drop its veto', *The Guardian*, 7 February

Wallace, Helen (ed.), 1992, *The Wider Western Europe: reshaping the EC/EFTA relationship*, London: Pinter

Wallace, Helen and Wolfgang Wessels, 1992, 'Introduction', in Helen Wallace (ed.), *The Wider Western Europe: reshaping the EC/EFTA relationship*, London: Pinter

Wallerstein, Immanuel, 1974, *The Modern World System*, New York: Academic Press

Wallerstein, Immanuel, 1979, *The Capitalist World Economy*, Cambridge: Cambridge University Press

Wallerstein, Immanuel, 1983, *Historical Capitalism*, London: Verso

Wallerstein, Immanuel, 1984, *The Politics of the World Economy*, Cambridge: Cambridge University Press

Wallerstein, Immanuel, 1989, 'The capitalist world-economy: middle-run prospects', *Alternatives*, 14, 3

Wallerstein, Immanuel, 1991a, 'Culture as the ideological battleground of the modern world-system', in Immanuel Wallerstein (ed.), *Geopolitics and Geoculture*, Cambridge: Cambridge University Press

Wallerstein, Immanuel, 1991b, *Geopolitics and Geoculture*, Cambridge: Cambridge University Press

Wallerstein, Immanuel, 1991c, 'The lessons of the 1980s', in Immanuel Wallerstein (ed.), *Geopolitics and Geoculture*, Cambridge: Cambridge University Press

Wallerstein, Immanuel, 1994, 'The agonies of liberalism: what hope progress?', *New Left Review*, 204

Walsh, Michael, 1996, 'Yank in the Vatican', *The Guardian*, 3 October

Warner, Norman, 1996, 'A sad song for Europe', *The Guardian*, 30 October

Waters, Malcolm, 1995, *Globalization*, London: Routledge

Weatherill, Stephen, 1995, *Law and Integration in the European Union*, Oxford: Oxford University Press

Weatherill, Stephen, 1996, 'Beyond "EC law rights, national remedies"', in Andrew Caiger and Demetrius Floudas (eds), *1996 Onwards: lowering the barriers further*, Chichester: John Wiley

Weatherill, Stephen and B. Beaumont, 1995, *EC Law*, Harmondsworth: Penguin, second edition

Weber, Max, 1958, 'Politics as a vocation', in H. Gerth and C. Wright Mills (eds and trans), *From Max Weber: essays in sociology*, Oxford: Oxford University Press

Weber, Max, 1974, *The Protestant Ethic and the Spirit of Capitalism*, London: Allen and Unwin

Weber Max, 1978, *Economy and Society*, Berkeley: University of California Press (originally published in 1921)

Weigall, David and Peter Stirk (eds), 1992, *The Origins and Development of the European Community*, London: Leicester University Press

Weiler, J., 1981, 'The Community system: the dual character of supranationalism', *Yearbook of European Law*

Weiler, J., R. Ulich, R. Haltern, and Franz Mayer, 1995, 'European democracy and its critique', *West European Politics*, 18, 3 (special issue), July

Wendt, Alexander, 1992, 'Anarchy is what states make of it: social construction of power politics', *International Organisation*, 46, 2

Wendt, Alexander, 1994, 'Collective identity formation and the international state', *American Political Science Review*, 88, 2

White, Michael, 1997, 'Major reopens war over EU', *The Guardian*, 4 February

White, Michael, Larry Elliott and John Palmer, 1996, 'Tories move to scupper EU 48-hour week law', *The Guardian*, 13 November

Wickramasinghe, Nira, 1996, 'From human rights to good governance: the aid regime in the 1990s', in Mortimer Sellars (ed.), *The New World Order: sovereignty, human rights and the self-determination of peoples*, Oxford: Berg

Wighton, David, 1997, 'Majority voting plans go ahead', *Financial Times*, 11 February

Wilkinson, Endymion, 1991, *Japan Versus the West: image and reality*, London: Penguin, revised edition

Williams, Allan, 1991, *The European Community*, Oxford: Blackwell

Wilson, Kevin, 1995, General Preface to *What is Europe?*, in Monica Shelley and Margaret Winck (eds), *Aspects of European Cultural Diversity*, London: Routledge, revised edition

Wilson, Kevin and Jan van der Dussen (eds), 1995, *The History of the Idea of Europe*, Milton Keynes: Open University, revised edition

Wistrich, Ernest, 1994, *The United States of Europe*, London: Routledge

Witherick, Michael and Michael Carr, 1993, *The Changing Face of Japan*, London: Hodder and Stoughton

Wolf, Julie, 1996, 'The roads to Europe's future', *The Guardian*, 26 March

Woodiwiss, Anthony, 1996, 'Searching for signs of globalisation', *Sociology* (Journal of the British Sociological Association), 30, 4, November

Woods, Tony, Liz Bird and Maria Williams, 1993, *European Studies*, London: Hodder and Stoughton

Woollacott, Martin, 1997, 'Albania teeters on the brink of chaos', *The Guardian*, 15 March

Wrench, John and John Solomos (eds), 1993, *Racism and Migration in Western Europe*, Oxford: Berg

Young, Oran, 1986, 'International regimes: towards a new theory of institutions', *World Politics*, 39, October

Young, Hugo, 1996, 'Get real about job creation in Europe', *The Guardian*, 12 November

Young, Hugo, 1997, 'At last, an issue that makes all the difference', *The Guardian*, 4 February

Zelenko, Laura, 1996, 'Warsaw leads eastern pack', *The European*, 3 October

Zercin, Ali, 1997, 'Balkans in new bind', *The Guardian*, 5 February

Zetterholm, Staffan (ed.), 1994a, *National Cultures and European Integration: exploratory essays on cultural diversity and common policies*, Oxford: Berg

Zetterholm, Staffan, 1994b, 'Introduction: cultural diversity and common policies', in Staffan Zetterholm (ed.), *National Cultures and European Integration*, Oxford: Berg

Index